Contents

v

Contributors

Richard M. Bird, University of Toronto, Canada

Geoffrey Brennan, Australian National University, Australia

Giorgio Brosio, Università di Torino, Italy

Roger D. Congleton, George Mason University, United States

Francesco Forte, Università di Roma "La Sapienza," Italy

Gianluigi Galeotti, Università di Roma "La Sapienza," Italy

Alan Hamlin, University of Southampton, United Kingdom

Russell Hardin, New York University, United States

Robert Howse, University of Toronto, Canada

Jean-Dominique Lafay, Université de Paris I Panthéon-Sorbonne, France

Dennis C. Mueller, Universität Wien, Austria

Pierre Salmon, Université de Bourgogne, France

Anthony Scott, University of British Columbia, Canada

Michael Trebilcock, University of Toronto, Canada

Viktor Vanberg, Universität Freiburg, Germany

Stanley L. Winer, Carleton University, Canada

Ronald Wintrobe, University of Western Ontario, Canada

Robert Young, University of Western Ontario, Canada

Introduction

Gianluigi Galeotti, Pierre Salmon, and Ronald Wintrobe

Albert Breton's energy, enthusiasm, and curiosity have not abated. Both for his work and for the influence that he has exerted and still exerts on many in North America, Europe, and elsewhere, Albert clearly deserves, in our opinion and the opinion of the other contributors, to be offered this volume as a testimony of admiration and friendship. Yet, for those who interact with him on a continuous basis (as, for example, the three of us have been doing over the last fifteen years in the setting of the Villa Colombella Group), to associate his name and person with the notion or idea of a Festschrift seems somewhat odd, if not incongruous. With someone whose activity is so intense and so clearly future-oriented, who has so much work forthcoming or in progress, there does not seem to be any room or time for celebration. Nevertheless, we felt it was an appropriate gesture to make, and we believe that the papers that have been contributed to this volume by Albert's friends in the scholarly community amply justify our faith in this project. Of course, it is often true that from the reader's point of view, the fact that a book is a Festschrift remains a relatively minor element, quite inconspicuous in the process of its consumption. However, this does not mean that it is an unimportant or irrelevant element in the process of design and implementation that editors and authors, rather than readers, are concerned with. In the present case, the fact that the book is dedicated to Albert Breton has been essential.

While we cannot hope to survey Albert Breton's work in any detail in this introduction, we do feel it is important to provide a few brief remarks on the choice of the title, and on the chapters that follow. As the title of the book indicates, we believe that much, although certainly not all, of Albert Breton's work on political behavior can be thought of as revolving around the two central themes of "competition" and the way it is embedded in institutional settings, which we refer to as "structure."

1

In Breton's view, competition is pervasive in politics, and is not limited to the electoral competition typically analyzed in public-choice literature. It takes place between public institutions. Therefore, one of the main advantages of the federalist system of government is that it forces governments to compete with each other for the support of citizens. Such competition takes place within governments and among the different branches of government. Thus various "centers of power," including non-elected centers such as the judiciary, are held to compete for the support or the consent of citizens. Finally, competition takes place within and between bureaucracies, and it takes place between private and public institutions.

However, as in the standard analysis of the effects of competition in the private sector, competition in politics does not necessarily produce efficiency. Its effects depend on the environment or the structure in which that competition takes place. In private markets, this means the property rights or laws governing contracts or exchange. In politics, it means the structure of government institutions. Some examples may be useful to illustrate this point. Thus, it matters for the effectiveness of competition whether the government is structured as a federation, confederation, or a unitary state. Within the government, one important condition is whether there is a solid bridge between taxes and expenditures – what Breton (1996) refers to as the "Wicksell connection" – so that economic agents take into account the tax consequences of spending decisions. Some institutions (e.g., the U.S. Senate) also serve to stabilize competition among subnational governments. Finally, within a bureaucracy (private or public), efficiency is primarily determined by the distribution of trust, which is in turn related to the bureaucracy's formal structure.

One implication of this approach is that the public and private sectors are seen as always in competition with each other, as opposed to the standard dichotomy that considers the public sector as a response to the "failures" of the private sector. In the standard approach, for example, the public sector is often seen as producing public goods or regulating externalities. In Breton's approach, as elaborated in his presidential address to the Canadian Economics Association (Breton 1989), whether the proportion of a public good produced by government grows at the expense of the private sector depends on such things as the differential growth in the government's capacity to acquire information, to control free-riding, and to reduce deadweight costs.

Another implication is that policies such as income redistribution have to be assessed in the light of this competition, and not simply as a coercive imposition by a majority electorate, as in standard theory. It is not by chance that income redistribution has historically been conducted not only by governments, but also by extended families or kinship networks, by church-sponsored religious bodies, by humanitarian organizations, and even by business firms.

While it is not our purpose here to offer any judgments regarding the areas in which Albert's contribution has been the largest, we would like to note three problem areas that obviously have been central to his work over the years, and that are amply discussed in the chapters of this volume. These are the problems of nationalism, bureaucracy, and federalism. It may therefore be useful to say a few words about Breton's work on these topics here.

In his paper "The Economics of Nationalism" (1964), Breton showed that it was possible to use economic theory to analyze nationalism. The basic idea was that the middle class promoted nationalist ideas and supported nationalistic rhetoric out of its own self-interest: that of obtaining and keeping middle-class jobs. Thus nationalistic activity was essentially redistributional. In this sense, Breton's analysis was a precursor of the theory of rent seeking developed later by Tullock (1967) and Krueger (1974). Recently, some of these ideas have been developed further in the volume edited by Breton with the other members of the Villa Colombella Group, *Nationalism and Rationality* (1995).

Breton's work on bureaucracy focuses on trust and competition within the firm or bureau (Breton and Wintrobe 1982; see also Breton and Wintrobe 1986, Wintrobe and Breton 1986). Breton and Wintrobe emphasized the importance of competition within firms and government bureaucracies. Their analysis of its effects vitiated monopoly-based analyses of the public sector (such as that of Niskanen 1968) and anticipated the Milgrom-Roberts (1988) theory of influence costs in the private sector. The importance of trust arises from the limits on formal contracting within organizations: contracts are typically too costly to specify in detail, and too difficult to enforce. The special aspect of the Breton-Wintrobe model is its emphasis on the distribution of trust. Some forms of trust reduce productivity within the bureau or firm (e.g., "horizontal" alliances among subordinates, which permit collusion among subordinates against their superiors). Other forms ("vertical" trust between superiors and subordinates) increase it. So firm or bureaucratic productivity depends on the distribution of trust within the firm and not merely its level. The concept of trust developed by Breton and Wintrobe is closely related to James Coleman's (1990) concept of "social capital." It depicts a relationship (sometimes called a "network") between two or more persons, essentially describing the degree of confidence one has that the other party will not cheat him or her in an exchange. In this concept, trust is like a capital good in the sense that it can be invested in, and that it makes future exchanges possible. This concept of trust is very different from that used by Fukuyama (1995), Knack and Keefer (1997), and others, where "trust" essentially refers to the generalized willingness to engage in exchange with a stranger. Some societies (Italy, Japan) might rank high in the Breton-Wintrobe or Coleman concept of trust, but low in the Fukuyama concept.

Perhaps the subject which has most engaged Albert over the years is federalism. In the course of time, Breton's views on federalism, or more generally on multitiered government, have evolved from a relatively strict adherence to the welfare-maximization paradigm dominant in public finance economics to a position that, because it is based on positive rather than normative analysis and centered on competition rather than on design, is in many respects its exact opposite. Four dates signal the main stages of that evolution. In 1965, Breton proposed a solution to the problem of the assignment of powers to levels of government that was based on the minimization of interjurisdictional spillovers combined with a system of centrally designed grants. This solution is very similar to the one developed by Olson (1969) and Oates (1972). In his joint work with Anthony Scott (1978), the approach to interjurisdictional spillovers was developed in terms of transaction costs, along Coaseian lines, rather than based on Pigovian grants as was the case before. Breton's theory of competitive federalism is explicitly formulated for the first time in his "Supplementary Report" (Breton 1985), but the vertical competition side of that theory is elaborated in subsequent work. Finally, in his recent book (1996), the competitive processes occurring among governments, among centers of power within governments, and between the public and the private sectors are shown to establish a close (at the limit, perfect) connection, at the level of individual citizens, between tax prices and the valuation of the goods and services provided. This is the connection that Wicksell adopted as a benchmark for assessing the efficiency of public spending and taxation. What allows Breton to model the connection as reachable under conditions that depart from the unanimity condition assumed by Wicksell is the idea that governments are competitive rather than monolithic.

The foregoing brief sketch is not meant as a survey of Albert Breton's work, but as an introduction to some of his ideas that have inspired the contributions to this volume. The chapters that follow relate to Breton's work in different ways. Some adopt his general interpretation of the relation between competition and structure in government and try to apply it in various settings, or to complete and develop it in one way or another. Other chapters adopt a more critical line. As Albert would be the first to recognize, stimulating a fruitful discussion is an achievement that deserves much gratitude. Still other chapters deal more or less with the same problems as those Breton has addressed but in a different way. We believe that the volume as a whole advances our understanding of many of the problems that Albert has worked on. A brief summary of the topics and the chapters in the volume follows.

The chapters in Part I explore issues of trust and information, and their application to the analysis of bureaucracy. Russell Hardin explores some of the conceptual complexities of trust relationships. He makes an important distinction between two kinds of trust: the first, which he calls encapsulated interest, is basically the same as the Breton and Wintrobe concept, and refers to the confidence a specific individual places in another individual. The second, generalized trustworthiness, lies behind some of the recent work by Fukuyama and others. Hardin explores some of the ways in which government can promote trust in this latter sense, at the same time cautioning that more trustworthiness in a society is not necessarily beneficial. He also suggests that the rational accumulation of trust as encapsulated interest in effect rules out the possibility of widespread trust, and shows that while perfect trust may be impossible, there is no logical limit on perfect distrust. However, Hardin takes issue with the methodology of a number of recent studies that show trust to be in decline in the U.S. and places little faith in this hypothesis. His paper also takes up some other issues in the workings of trust, the relationship between cooperation and trust, the putative role of trust in the social structure, and what he calls parasitic abuses of trust.

Wintrobe looks at the phenomenon of downsizing, which has been so prevalent in North America in the 1980s and 1990s. The standard explanations of this phenomenon are that downsizing is the result of improved technological progress or increased trade with underdeveloped countries and is somehow "necessary" in order to improve productivity and competitiveness. Wintrobe rejects these explanations on various grounds, notably the fact that there is no evidence of productivity improvement associated with downsizing. He explains downsizing by considering the firm as a bureaucracy, one in which relationships are based on trust. Such changes as globalization, technological change, and deregulation make trust relationships within the firm more dispensable. Downsizing is then explained as a way of either *breaching* trust once it has become no longer profitable, and transferring it to shareholders, or simply *repudiating* it as a way of freeing the manager from constraints on his own compensation and that of other executives. In the absence of trust, firms substitute more intensive monitoring rather than trust to control their employees. Wintrobe shows that on either the repudiation or the breach of trust hypothesis, the fall in the incomes of low-wage Americans over the last twenty years or so, the notable increase in executive compensation over the same period, and the increase in the proportion of supervisory personnel are all directly related and not separate phenomena, as they are considered in standard theories.

The last chapter in this section, by Jean-Dominique Lafay, looks at the choice between self-decision-making by politicians and delegation to the bureaucracy. If the political superior makes the decision himself, then the bureaucracy is fundamentally a producer of information; if the decision is delegated, the bureaucracy has to be considered an agent, and thus the corresponding agency problems arise. Lafay presents a simple framework to formalize this choice. In particular, one problem with delegation that he focuses on is that, under that option, politicians are forced to reveal information to the bureaucracy – information on their preferences, and on the constraints facing them. For the politician, this revelation implies important technical, strategic, and political costs. These costs have been ignored in the literature on this topic. Lafay also suggests that the choice made by politicians is not necessarily socially optimal. They may be induced both to underdelegate and to underinvest in information, that is, to decide themselves, albeit without the necessary information.

The two chapters of Part II consider the possibility of collusive behavior within competition. Giorgio Brosio's chapter explains why, despite the pervasive presence of trade unions and modern mass parties, politics in Italy remains strongly clientelistic in vast areas of the country even today. In the south, in the 1994 elections, there was a shift of votes from the Christian Democratic Party to Forza Italia. According to most commentators, clientelistic politics made the shift possible, in the sense that local notables in the south saw Berlusconi's party as the new holder of power at the national level and channeled the votes of their clientele toward it. Brosio develops a model in which there are two possible ways of providing a public service, collective and individualist (i.e, the public provision of a private good or service). The central point is that the individualist mode creates an opportunity for setting up a clientele, because it allows politicians to build personal ties with voters. With private goods, the level of service can be varied: some voters may get quicker service or better maintenance than others, for example. This provides politicians with an opportunity to vary the level of service according to the degree of political support. Brosio shows that the private solution becomes more attractive to politicians the greater the availability of external sources or grants (external grants from the national government, Mafia money, etc.). So the persistence of clientelistic politics is explained as a consequence of both transfers to the south and the persistence of illegal activities there.

Gianluigi Galeotti explores the role of political competition in molding the evolution of constitutions, defined as the set of formal and informal rules that superintend the working of the supply side of political life. His chapter discusses the stability of past and contemporary constitutional settings, and shows how supply is constrained by the need to remain legitimate for the purpose of preserving people's acquiescence. Building on Machiavelli's remark that political conflicts are the seed of liberty, Galeotti argues that the need to coordinate leaders' actions led to the internalization of dissent (fundamental freedoms) and to the regulation of competition (division of powers). The analysis is then applied, first to the underpinnings of modern democratic constitutions, with citizens' rights as a benchmark that constrains the working of political competition, and second to extra-constitutional adjustments, which are conditional on the unanimous consent of all the formal and informal centers of political power. In such instances, it is on the competitiveness of the system itself that one should rely to prevent collusion.

Part III is devoted to decentralization and federalism. It includes five papers that are fairly closely related in one way or another to Breton's theory of competitive federalism. In the first paper, Richard Bird attempts to reconcile the view that fiscal decentralization can be analyzed profitably within a principal-agent framework (a view he has subscribed to in previous work) with the view that it cannot (Breton's position). Part of the problem, he stresses, stems from the extreme variety of federal arrangements, broadly defined, and from the confusion surrounding the notion of decentralization. With regard to real federations, this leads him to contrast two approaches, fiscal federalism and federal finance. Under the former, the central government is assumed to maximize welfare and to design the whole system. Inasmuch as these assumptions can be sustained, adopting, in spite of its limitations, the principal-agent approach seems fruitful or at least promising. In the federal finance setting, by contrast, the system evolves as a consequence of bargaining, so to speak "between principals" (somewhat as in international relations), and the most adequate theoretical framework could well be game theory. The chapter shows that neither approach is without serious weaknesses and problems. In this context, Bird considers Breton's approach, especially its focus on competition among governments and the information of citizens, to be particularly interesting. In his conclusion, however, Bird shows greater confidence in the applicability of Breton's analysis to the governments of the future than to those of the present.

The next chapter is by Stanley Winer. As Winer notes at the beginning of his chapter, Albert Breton is one of the few economists who has discussed the assignment of fiscal powers across jurisdictions in positive rather than normative or prescriptive terms. The paper adopts this perspective and concentrates on the reassignment of the powers. The claim that the phenomenon is essential is supported by the detailed analysis of two cases. In Australia, the constitution of 1901 was meant to protect decentralized government, but the intentions of the framers have been completely subverted by the evolution that has followed, and the formal constitutional framework is now largely irrelevant to an understanding of how fiscal responsibilities are actually distributed. In Canada, the main story is one of oscillation between reassignments of the power to tax in favor of the provinces and reassignments benefiting the federal government, the written constitution again being no obstacle to the changes. The recent and puzzling episode of provinces giving up voluntarily some of their powers in the area of retail sales is another, particularly revealing, illustration of the general argument. It is an important, and even fascinating, insight of this chapter that federalism might well be first of all a mechanism for the continuous reassignment of policy instruments.

As does Winer's, Anthony Scott's chapter offers a positive analysis of assignment or reassignment of powers. It studies intergovernmental competition over powers in the context of one policy area, the environment, and (mainly) one country, Canada. In that country, as in most others, environmental policies are pursued at all levels, but the level that is dominant varies in the course of time or across particular issues. One reason for this flexibility is that constitutions are mute about powers over the environment and thus governments necessarily stretch or adapt the powers that are mentioned. The main reason, however, lies in the nature of the intergovernmental competition itself. Its main characteristic, Scott stresses, is that it takes place within a short-run framework. Awareness of this is really what allows the derivation of the various factors explaining the competitive advantage at a given time that a government, or level of government, has or does not have in dealing with the environment. These factors pertain both to demand (by interest groups as well as by citizens) and to conditions of supply. The chapter also spells out some factual objections – phenomena such as governments' seeking to get rid of powers, or the endogeneity of citizens' preferences – to the theory of competitive government in its simplest form and considers how the theory should be interpreted and extended to accommodate these as well as other features of what Scott labels "competition through collusion."

Francesco Forte's chapter is concerned with another policy domain. The theories of fiscal and of competitive federalism are employed to study the question of how the powers to regulate and finance art and cultural goods should be assigned. Currently, in most European countries, the assignment is in favor of the central level of government. Forte claims that the powers should be assigned to lower levels instead. This claim relies on several arguments spelled out in the chapter. Some arguments are positive, based, for instance, on the assignment implications of policies that cost little in budgetary terms although they have a large impact on society, or stressing the general benefits of competition and emulation among governments. Others take the form of a detailed criticism of the arguments given in favor of centralization, in particular those inspired by the conventional theory of fiscal federalism. A major part of the discussion concerns the reasons why art and cultural goods must be regulated and subsidized in the first place. In addition or as an alternative to the three usual reasons – externalities, merit goods, and future generations – Forte proposes one based on the importance of fixed costs. The case for decentralization also gets some support, his conclusion stresses, from the observed negative aspects of the Italian experience of centralization.

The last chapter in this section is Salmon's, which is concerned with vertical competition (competition between governments situated at different levels) in systems specified as unitary rather than federal and structured around three or four levels rather than the two often implicitly assumed. Salmon argues that these characteristics may offer a partial solution to what is perhaps the major problem raised by vertical competition – how winners in a vertical contest can be protected against retaliation by the losers when the latter can, because they are not constitutionally entrenched, change the rules. In federations, the problem typically arises in the context of the relationship between the intermediate (provincial or state) level and the local level. In unitary systems, the relationship affected is the one between the central government and the intermediate level, whereas the competitive relationship between the intermediate and the local levels may find some protection as an effect of the central government's playing the role of monitor. As is illustrated by the decentralization experience in France, a lively vertical competition "at the bottom," between several subcentral tiers of government, may ensue.

The three chapters of Part IV deal with ethnicity and nationalism, and in particular with the question of whether political constitutions should be structured along ethnic lines. Brennan and Hamlin's and Congleton's chapters propose theoretical frameworks to address this issue. Young's chapter deals, in the context of a detailed analysis of the Quebec referendum on separation from Canada, with nationalist rhetoric and the empirical relevance of economic versus ideological factors in stimulating nationalist sentiments.

Geoffrey Brennan and Alan Hamlin suggest that standard approaches to the economics of federalism have little relevance to the actual efficiency of federalist-type arrangements. The example they have in mind in particular is the European Union. They ground their theory in an interpretation of political participation, along the lines of Brennan and Lomasky (1993), as "expressive" rather than "instrumental." Within the expressive account of politics, voting is essentially a consumption activity – something done for its own sake, by virtue of its direct expressive benefits. One such direct expressive benefit involves the voters' "identification" with the national interest. Brennan and Hamlin argue that the cost of expressing nationalist sentiments to a voter declines as the probability of a voter's determining the outcome of an election declines. Consequently, as the numbers included in the polity increase, the problem of collective irrationality also increases. On the other hand, increasing the size of political jurisdictions presumably reduces the loyalty each member feels toward any other member within the jurisdiction. On the basis of considerations like these, Brennan and Hamlin derive the optimal war-minimizing jurisdictional size. Using this line of approach, they suggest that federalism may be beneficial in reducing conflict (the likelihood of war) because it intrinsically divides political loyalties. On the other hand, they do not generally find it desirable to design the federal structure along "tribal" boundaries.

Roger Congleton's paper takes a rent-seeking approach to the problem of political nationalism. The chief problem is to structure the optimal constitution in order to minimize rent-seeking losses. According to Congleton, political competition in a unified multinational state tends to take forms that are unproductive. Thus institutional arrangements that reduce overall political competition may actually increase welfare. In contrast to Brennan and Hamlin's chapter, Congleton finds that investments in political conflict (rent seeking) are minimized by sorting ethnic groups into homogeneous local jurisdictions. The reason is that variations in local public and private services, and favoritism, encourage persons to migrate between communities. Migration yields generally more homogeneous communities that reduce potential favoritism and implies a smaller number of ethnic groups competing within each for preferential treatment.

Robert Young's chapter tells the story of the recent (1995) referendum on Quebec separation. He develops the logic of the campaign and tries to explain the shift toward the separation option as the campaign unfolded. He suggests, on the basis of an analysis of polling data, that the reason that support for separation increased over the course of the campaign was that confidence increased that a Quebec-Canada economic partnership was a viable post-referendum outcome. He argues that the separatists were more clever than the federalists in structuring the discourse of the campaign on the important issue of the economic consequences of a Yes (pro-separation) vote. They were also relatively successful on other dimensions such as national identification, the constitution, and democracy. And he suggests that the democracy issue was crucial, even though subterranean in political discourse, and that it was because the federalist side could not present a firm position on this dimension that they almost lost the contest.

Finally, in Part V, the issue of the relationship between governments and the working of markets is addressed, under a perspective of free trade in particular. Although the three papers endorse the objective of free trade, at the international or interstate (interprovincial) level, they also develop arguments that qualify, mainly for the sake of political autonomy, the priority typically given to that objective. The question studied by Dennis Mueller is whether public subsidies to private firms should be a source of concern under a free trade and competitive markets perspective. Mueller thinks not. He shows, for instance, that if members of a community are immobile, which they may have perfectly legitimate reasons to be, taxes on community residents to subsidize externally held capital may be optimal. More generally, he shows that there is no reason to expect competition for capital across communities to result in a misallocation of resources. With regard to the harm that subsidies could cause other firms, the only cause for concern from the perspective of consumers or citizens is the possibility of a subsidized firm becoming a monopoly. This is most unlikely in practice, because publicly subsidized firms are, as he puts it, "typically tottering on the brink of bankruptcy." Public subsidies to firms by subcentral authorities are common in the United States. As a rule, they should not be disallowed in the context of the Europe Union, Mueller argues.

In the next chapter, Viktor Vanberg uses a constitutional economics perspective to examine some of the basic issues underlying the question of how to respond to globalization. In the presence of powerful constraining forces and interactions, shaping an economic constitution can be considered an attempt to create an evolutionary niche. However, the constitutional preferences of citizens must be subjected to a viability test. In an international setting, economic constitutions have an effect on the competitiveness of domestic producers and the capacity of the country to retain or attract mobile factors. As a consequence, globalization – defined here as a decrease in the cost of international activities – increases the competitive pressure on economic constitutions. Globalization does not preclude, though, the possibility that members of a jurisdiction may voluntarily agree to limit their access to extrajurisdictional opportunities in exchange for some protection against extra-jurisdictional competition. For that reason and others, economic constitutions can reflect a rational preference for protectionism. The question is how to ensure that constitutional provisions of that kind do not merely reflect special interests. Vanberg does not attempt to answer this question formally, but he discusses various possibilities, including that of citizens expressing their constitutional preferences by moving across jurisdictions.

In the last chapter of the volume, Michael Trebilcok and Robert Howse acknowledge that domestic regulations are currently perceived by many proponents of free trade as a particularly costly kind of non-tariff barrier to trade, requiring new international disciplines. As a consequence, generalized policy harmonization is receiving widespread support. The authors do not endorse that prescription, however. They develop various arguments to justify their reluctance. They do not consider the experience of harmonization in Europe to be exportable to other settings, they are wary of excessive reliance on judiciary fiat or unilateral sanctions, and they stress the complexity of the welfare calculations involved. What is perhaps their major objection, however, is explicitly inspired by Albert Breton's theory of intergovernmental competition. This theory leads them to express the fear that, with excessive harmonization, the objective of a complete removal of constraints on competition in international goods and services markets could well be achieved at the cost of the monopolization or cartelization of government policy making. To avoid such an outcome, they advocate rules that, while preventing the most open forms of trade distortion, safeguard to a sufficient degree the autonomy of national policy makers.

References

Brennan, Geoffrey, and Loren Lomasky, *Democracy and Decision: The Pure Theory of Electoral Preference.* Cambridge and New York: Cambridge University Press, 1993.

Breton, Albert, "The Economics of Nationalism," *Journal of Political Economy*, vol. 72, no. 4, August 1964, 376–86.

"A Theory of Government Grants," *Canadian Journal of Economics and Political Science*, vol. 31, no. 2, May 1965, 175–87.

"Supplementary Report," in *Report of the* [Macdonald] *Royal Commission on the Economic Union and Development Prospects for Canada* (Ottawa: Supply and Services, 1985); reprinted as "Towards a Theory of Competitive Federalism," *European Journal of Political Economy*, vol. 3 (1987), nos. 1–2 (special issue: Villa Colombella Papers on Federalism), 263–329.

"The Growth of Competitive Governments," *Canadian Journal of Economics*, vol. 22 (1989), 717–50.

Competitive Governments: An Economic Theory of Politics and Public Finance. Cambridge and New York: Cambridge University Press, 1996.

Gianluigi Galeotti, Pierre Salmon, and Ronald Wintrobe (eds.), *Nationalism and Rationality*. Cambridge and New York: Cambridge University Press, 1995.

and Anthony Scott, *The Economic Constitution of Federal States*. Toronto: University of Toronto Press, 1978.

and Ronald Wintrobe, *The Logic of Bureaucratic Conduct*. Cambridge and New York: Cambridge University Press, 1982.

and Ronald Wintrobe, "The Bureaucracy of Murder Revisited," *Journal of Political Economy*, vol. 94, no. 5, October 1986, 905–26.

Coleman, James, *Foundations of Social Theory*. Cambridge, Mass: The Belknap Press of Harvard University Press, 1990.

Fukuyama, Francis, *Trust: The Social Virtues and the Creation of Prosperity*. London: Hamish Hamilton, 1995.

Knack, Stephen, and Philip Keefer, "Does Social Capital Have An Economic Payoff? A Cross Country Investigation," *Quarterly Journal of Economics*, vol. 112 (1997), 1251–88.

Krueger, Anne O., "The Political Economy of the Rent-Seeking Society," *American Economic Review*, vol. 64, no. 3, June 1974, 291–303.

Milgrom, Paul A., and John Roberts, "Employment Contracts, Influence Activities, and Efficient Organization Design," *Journal of Political Economy*, vol. 96 (1988), 42–60.

Niskanen, William A., "The Peculiar Economics of Bureaucracy," *American Economic Review, Papers and Proceedings*, vol. 58 (1968), no. 2, 293–305.

Oates, Wallace E., *Fiscal Federalism*, New York: Harcourt Brace Jovanovich, 1972.

Olson, Mancur, Jr., "The Principle of Fiscal Equivalence," *American Economic Review*, vol. 59, no. 2, May 1969, 479–87.

Tullock, Gordon, "The Welfare Costs of Tariffs, Monopolies and Theft," *Western Economic Journal*, vol. 5, no. 2, June 1967, 224–32.

Wintrobe, Ronald, and Albert Breton, "Organizational Structure and Productivity," *American Economic Review*, vol. 76, no. 3, June 1986, 530–8.

PART I

Trust, information, and bureaucracy

CHAPTER 1

Trust and society

Russell Hardin

There is a substantial literature that is essentially about conceptual, explanatory, and normative issues in trust between individuals (see further Hardin 1991b, 1999b). There is also a more recent, growing literature about trust in government and, by analogy, in larger institutions generally.[1] There is still a large array of relationships in which trust might be important that lie somewhere between these two. If I have to deal with some organization with which I am not very familiar or with you, whom I do not really know, on some matter of great importance, I may be able to rely not on trust but on backing by institutions. Very commonly, of course, we have government to back our relationships with other individuals and with various organizations and institutions. For example, we have the law of contracts for major exchanges, to protect us in our ordinary dealings, and at least to reduce the likelihood of massive endgame losses. Within this protective setting, we can take the smaller risks of giving others limited power over our well-being, as we do daily.

Hence, we are relatively secure at two quite distinct levels of social interaction. At one level, we have institutions to back our relationships regarding big issues in which the risks of loss justify, for example, the expense of using contracts and having recourse to legal devices. At another level, usually of one-on-one interactions, we have ongoing rela-

I thank the Center for Advanced Study in the Behavioral Sciences, Stanford, the National Science Foundation (grant number SBR-9022192), the Guggenheim Foundation, New York University, and the Russell Sage Foundation for support of this research. I also thank numerous commentators for their reactions to its arguments. I especially wish to thank the participants in the Russell Sage New York University conference Behavioral Evidence on Trust, 15–16 November 1997.
[1] I address this issue from the point of view of conceptual and epistemological considerations, respectively, in Hardin 1998a and 1999a.

tionships that give our partners incentive to live up to, indeed to define, our trust.

What is left over? Two large categories. First, there are interactions (1) that pose risks of losses too small to justify invoking institutional devices (2) with people who are not involved closely or frequently enough with us for us to have grounded trust in them. Such interactions are likely to be common in our lives and, while not always trivial, are typically of less importance than are our interactions with closer associates or those the law does oversee. Because they are of modest scope, they typically pose only slight burdens for those who have to fulfill our cooperative expectations. And even when there is no general expectation of iterated interaction with someone, there may be significant reputational effects that give strong incentives for fulfillment.

Second, there are many kinds of interaction that government is, for various reasons, incapable of backing strongly enough to make them work. Perhaps most obviously, there have been and still are economic interactions that go beyond government's capacity in cases when government is weak because it is nascent or in transition. And for many relationships, including those closely governed by the law of contracts, there are limits to how precisely or how well government enforcement can make them work.

It is commonly supposed that widespread trust is, loosely speaking, a public or collective good, especially in political life but also more generally in society and in the economy (Fukuyama 1995, Luhmann 1980, and Putnam 1993). This supposition cannot be generally correct. Rather, *generalized trustworthiness* would be collectively beneficial and, then, correctly acting on the trustworthiness of others would be beneficial not only to the truster of the moment but also more generally to the society (Hardin 1996). One way to say that trust is a collective good is to say that it produces positive externalities. This is clearly not true of trust in the context of generally malign relationships, such as in Stalin's Soviet Union. One who trusted there could thereby bring harm to many others. The character of the external effects of trust therefore depends on broader background conditions of trustworthiness.

Let us turn to the role of trust in society more broadly, that is to say, outside of the government and its relations with citizens but beyond individual-to-individual trust. Even if there are no grounds for trusting a government in the strong sense of trust as encapsulated interest (as discussed later), it is plausible that government can help to secure trustworthiness in many contexts, thereby making trust the conditionally beneficial thing that many authors too readily and unconditionally assume it to be. Additionally, other institutions and even spontaneous forms of relationships can help to secure trustworthiness. Consider four background considerations that make for greater trustworthiness and thereby enable sensible trust.

First, we will benefit if the state and other institutions can block the worst that others might do to us if we mistakenly trust them when they are untrustworthy. One of the most important functions of many institutions is to help individuals be trustworthy. This is often all that the law of contracts does. Suppose you have a contractual obligation to me, say to build a building to my specifications at a certain price. If you default, I can typically gain only modest redress. I cannot get you to live up to your contracted obligation, which might require you to lose substantially because, say, you miscalculated your costs. Instead of specific performance from you, I get only a default payment, and I might be worse off at that point than if I had never dealt with you at all. But at least contract enforcement will typically limit my losses. At an even more basic level, we expect the law to do for us what Thomas Hobbes ([1642] 1983, 1651) supposed to be the purpose of government: to protect us against the depredations of others.

Second, we often benefit from having a reliable state and trustworthy (or fair) institutions to engender greater cooperation. Government can provide infrastructures and information systems that enable us to be more confident in our dealings with others even when we are not sure they are sufficiently trustworthy. These institutions might be organized in ways that entail less cost than if the institutions did their work only by means of sanctions and constraints (see further Hardin 1998b).

Third, we need a reasonable capacity to detect trustworthiness or its absence. As James Coleman (1990: 180–185) argues, this is one of the roles of many institutions. An institution that has dealt with me might inform others of my trustworthiness. Intermediaries in trust can help two parties connect when they do not know enough about each other to connect on their own. These intermediaries may be better connected to some kinds of people than to others, giving the former great advantages over the latter (Coleman 1990: 185). So, for example, wives, the self-employed, and the young may have less access to intermediaries than they need to establish credit. Moreover, various institutions that have no stake in my affairs may nevertheless be able to evaluate my trustworthiness and then to share their evaluations with others who do, at least potentially, have a stake in my affairs. Apart from such institutions, we also may establish, willingly or not, reputations that enable others to judge whether to risk dealing with us. Albert Breton and Ronald Wintrobe (1982: 69–70) suppose in addition that individuals must develop reasonably good instincts for assessing indicators of others' trustworthiness even absent institutions and reputations to certify them. Robert Frank (1988: 127–128) suggests that our capacities for being trustworthy may in part be genetic, as in uncontrolled blushing when we are being devious or are otherwise caught in embarrassing inconsistency.

And fourth, we commonly need to develop ongoing relationships so that we can spontaneously secure each other's trustworthiness. That is to say, we benefit if we establish ongoing relationships of trust and trustworthiness with other individuals.

In the following discussion, I will first quickly summarize the account of trust as encapsulated interest, which is the conception of trust that lies behind all the discussions here. Then I will turn to the contemporary thesis that what society needs if it is to go well is generalized or social trust, rather than trust in specific others, such as trust as encapsulated interest. As a counter to this thesis, I will then discuss the benefits of an atmosphere of trustworthiness. Thereafter I will take up issues in the workings of trust in the economy and in institutions. Then I will take up various problems in the working of trust in the larger society: logical limits on the extent of trusting, the relationship between cooperation and trust, the putative role of trust in the social structure, and parasitic abuses of trust. I will conclude briefly with comments on the scope of trust in society.

Trust as encapsulated interest

Ordinary trust can be analyzed and largely explained as an essentially three-part relationship grounded in encapsulated interest. The three parts are that A trusts B with respect to matters X. A does not very likely trust B with respect to everything. For example, I might trust you with respect to money matters and someone else with respect to more personal matters that I would want to keep confidential. And it is trust in you rather than merely expectations IF my expectation of your fulfilling what you are entrusted to do with respect to X depends on your taking my interests into account, so that your trustworthiness encapsulates my interest. It is easy to see how trust could be grounded in ongoing relationships in which both parties regularly exchange with each other over some range of matters. You and I could then be in a loosely structured iterated Prisoner's Dilemma, in which each of us has incentive to cooperate because taking the other's interests into account makes it in the other's interest to take our interests into account in similar ways. Even more loosely, I might have an interest in being cooperative with you because the reputation I build in my relations with you will affect other relationships that are valuable to me.

If we can develop such relationships, why, one might ask, do we need government or other institutions to govern our daily interactions? Of course, part of the answer is that we need government, as Hobbes argued, to protect us from miscreants who would intrude on and wreck the projects we achieve through mutually trusting relationships. But even in my relations with you, we may be better able to trust one another in some range of interactions or over certain matters if we are secured against endgame effects. In an endgame, or final interaction in our ongoing exchange relationship, we no longer have incentives for cooperation now from our previous concern to keep open the prospect of future exchanges with each other. We face endgame effects if our relationship is about to end or if it is about to have its stakes elevated to such a degree that one of us might be induced to cheat.

Consider one of the most important of our common relationships and the impact of endgame effects on it: marriage. Typically, when two people marry, their affections initially make it the case that their individual interests encapsulate the interests of the other. Hence, they are able to trust each other on the encapsulated interest account of trust. The endgame risk that each of them faces is the possibility that the other's affection will fade or fail entirely. Through much of history in Western societies, couples have de facto relied on the state or on the Catholic Church to block some of the worst implications of an endgame by making it illegal and severely punishable to end a marriage or even to engage in extramarital sexual relations.

Now that the law no longer coercively supports marriage in many nations, there are generally three possibilities. First, alternative institutions and practices might spontaneously arise to support marriage. Second, marriage might change its character, becoming far less stable and perhaps even ceasing to seem plausibly a lifetime arrangement. And third, many couples might sustain their marriages by maintaining their affections and, therefore, their trust.

At the moment, prenuptial agreements appear to be a spontaneously evolving institutional structure that depends on state backing through contract enforcement but does not otherwise depend on state sponsorship or creation. Many couples wish to guarantee themselves against financial disruptions that might result from divorce with prenuptial pacts that largely arrange divorce settlements in advance. That many marriages, and perhaps even the modal marriage, might simply be unstable could undercut the credibility of sustaining any marriage on mutual trust.

Expectations or inferences from such instability might also push more couples into using devices such as prenuptial agreements to protect themselves against some of the worst consequences of instability.

Many institutions do not work by reinforcing or backing trust but by making it unnecessary or, at least, less necessary. That is what the former regime of coercive fidelity did. In recent decades in the United States and in some other nations, the institution of marriage has changed in ways that make it more dependent on trust than it was earlier. The institution has changed from a relatively coercive regime to one in which divorce is relatively easy. It is commonplace to suppose that the increasing use of prenuptial agreements suggests that there is declining marital trust (*New York Times* 1986). Against that too quick conclusion, one should ask whether the increasing use of such agreements is evidence of declining trust or merely of declining confidence in a world in which incentives over the longer run have changed dramatically.

Compare my incentives in the two marital systems: coercive fidelity and easy divorce. If we change from the first to the second, my actual interests may change even though my concern for my spouse's interests might be no different from what it was before. Suppose my affections fail in either case. In the coercive regime I might stay faithful and we might therefore face no financial complications from a loss of affections. I do not stay married in the coercive system because of a concern for my spouse. I do so because of the coerciveness of laws that give me trouble if I leave my spouse or even if I commit adultery. I actually have my own personal interest in some degree of fidelity independent of specific concern for my spouse. Because my interests are different in the easy-divorce system, my spouse may wish to lock in certain benefits against the possibility that I might happen later to want a divorce – or even the possibility that my spouse might later want a divorce.

The confidence I have in my spouse in the coercive system is therefore not trust in the encapsulated interest sense but only confidence in the force of the institutions that back our fidelity. So long as my spouse has strong affection for me, I can trust her in this strong sense, however, because then it is in her interest to take account of my interests. What I cannot trust is that she will continue to have such affection for me. But this is true regardless of whether we live in the easy-divorce or the coercive-fidelity system.

If, however, we are like some of the characters in Jane Austen novels, I might even be able to trust my spouse to maintain her affection. For example, Darcy could probably trust Elizabeth not to lose her affection for him – once she belatedly discovered such affection. He could trust her because he was not merely Darcy, as she seemed to suppose when she first encountered him. Rather, he was the very wealthy Darcy, scion of a fine family and inheritor of a glorious estate. Elizabeth's discovery of that fact made him far more attractive than he had been before, so attractive as to be worthy of her great love. In the moment of Elizabeth's gazing on Darcy's portrait in his family manor, Jane Austen notes that "[t]here was certainly at this moment, in Elizabeth's mind, a more gentle sensation towards the original, than she had ever felt in the height of their acquaintance." (Austen 1952 [1813]: Chapter 43, p. 228). Both of them might change over the years, but Darcy's status would not, and the – apparently very large – part of Elizabeth's love for him that was grounded in his secure status would not fade.[2] (Of course, had their story been written by Lorenzo Da Ponte and composed by Mozart, all bets would be off.)

What the state could do in the coercive-fidelity regime was to reduce certain endgame effects. It could do some of that in other ways, at least for financial effects. Other institutions and widespread practices might also be able to do that. What the state presumably cannot do is enforce the maintenance of affections. But this is arguably the fundamental problem of marriage. The maintenance of affections also cannot be grounded in individual-level trust. It is not itself an iterated reciprocal exchange. I do not make a deal with you that I love you if you love me or that I like your company if you like mine. There may be choices involved in such affections, but the affections are not primarily a matter of choosing. Rather, like knowledge, suspicion, and many other states of mind and emotion, they simply happen to us.

Generalized or social trust

The bulk of the fast-growing literature on the value of trust in society seems to focus on the possibilities for social exchange that follow from *generally* trusting others (Luhmann 1980). So-called generalized or social trust is trust in random others or in social institutions without grounding in specific prior or subsequent relationships with those others and, as is often argued or implied, without taking into account the variable grounds for trusting particular others to different degrees. There is a substantial literature on such generalized trust, which is loosely seen as unspecific trust in generalized others, including strangers. At best, such

---

[2] Lord David Cecil puts Austen's view of marrying for money clearly: "It was wrong to marry for money, but it was silly to marry without it" (quoted in Blythe 1966: 12). Apparently, so long as money led to love, it was fine to marry in this way, for money one step removed.

generalized trust must be a matter of relatively positive expectations of others' trustworthiness, cooperativeness, or helpfulness. It is the stance of, for example, the child who has grown up in a very benign environment in which virtually everyone has always been trustworthy. That former child now faces others with relatively positive expectations by inductive generalization. The value of generalized trust is the value of such an upbringing: It gives us the sense of running little risk in cooperating with others, so that we may more readily enter relationships with others. Of course, this is again a value only if others are in fact relatively trustworthy.

One might wish to say that generalized trust is more than merely expectations about the trustworthiness of others, that it is genuinely trust in others. But it is very hard to say who is the B and what is the X in the relation A trusts B to do X if A's trust is truly generalized and not, as is usually the case, heavily limited and conditional. Hence, generalized or social trust seems to violate this paradigm of trust. But if generalized trust is, in a perhaps very complicated way, limited and conditional, what could it mean to call it generalized? In any real-world context, I trust some more than others, and I trust any given person more in some contexts than in others. I may be more optimistic in my expectations of others' trustworthiness than you are, but apart from such a general fact I do not have generalized trust. I may also typecast many people and consider some of the types very likely to be trustworthy and therefore worth the risk of cooperating with them, other types less so, and still others not at all. But this is far short of generalized trust. It is merely optimism about certain others (Hardin 1992). Such optimism from typecasting makes rational sense, just as typecasting of those one might employ makes rational sense as a first, crude indicator of competence or commitment.[3]

From various experimental studies and surveys, it is supposed by many social scientists that Americans have higher levels of generalized trust than do people in many other societies (Fukuyama 1995). Again, what is in fact needed if we want successful exchange is trustworthiness, which is likely to beget trust from learning of its utility in reputational and trial-and-error experience. But let us examine the claims for the value of generalized trust, even for its necessity. There is an explicit or implicit claim for the necessity of trust in many very current claims that American and other democratic societies face a crisis of declining trust. Claims of necessity that are causal rather than conceptual are among the strongest claims one can make in the social sciences, and among the most difficult to make

---

[3] As in the analysis of discrimination in hiring in Becker 1971.

compelling. Nevertheless, the claim of the necessity of generalized trust for social order is strikingly commonplace, as though it were beyond much serious doubt.

Many, maybe even most, claims for generalized trust can readily be restated as claims that, in contexts in which trust generally pays off, it makes sense to risk entering into exchanges even with those whom one cannot claim to trust in the encapsulated interest sense because one does not yet have an ongoing relationship with them nor does one have reasons of reputation to trust them. This is not a claim that one trusts those others, but only that one has relatively optimistic expectations of being able to build successful relationships with certain, perhaps numerous, others (although surely not with everyone). If the context is even slightly altered, this conclusion may be wrong, as it is in dealings with con artists who propose quick profit schemes or, often, with sellers in tourist traps. Hence, generalized trust seems likely to be nothing more than an optimistic assessment of trustworthiness and a willingness therefore to take small risks on dealing with others whom one does not yet know. That assessment would quickly be corrected if the optimism proved to be unwarranted because people or agencies in the relevant context proved to be untrustworthy.

Recent discussions of the crisis of declining (generalized) trust in society are grounded in contemporary survey data. Such data do not firmly establish any claim about levels of generalized trust because they are confounded with the encapsulated interest account of trust, and it is not clear that they tap so-called generalized trust. People respond to survey questions such as, Do you trust most people? or Are people generally trustworthy? Unfortunately, such questions are insufficiently articulated to distinguish trust as encapsulated interest from generalized trust. Suppose I trust most of the people I deal with at least in those matters over which I have dealings with them. This is, in part, because they *are* the people I deal with – had I not trusted them, I would have stopped dealing with them. Do I trust the vastly larger number of people with whom I have no dealings in those matters? No, presumably not. Most of these are people I do not even know and have no reason either to trust or to distrust. Unfortunately, if we begin to articulate our questions precisely enough to get at such discriminating differences, we may virtually have to explain what we are seeking to those we survey (or to those whom we put through experiments). We thereby give them theoretical understandings they did not have, and we in turn elicit answers or experimental responses to those understandings rather than to their normal experiences.

If we compare across nations, we find lower levels of generalized trust in some societies than in the United States. What questions are people in the United States answering when they say they trust most people? And what questions are those in certain other societies answering when they say they do not trust most people? Plausibly, they are answering different questions, perhaps because they are differentially alert to the problem of dealing with those with whom they do not have ongoing relationships, or perhaps because their background institutional structures differ in the scope of the interactions they protect. That is to say, they frame the questions differently.

Or consider variations over time in the responses to such questions within a single culture. Again, it is supposed that levels of generalized trust are in decline in many Western societies, especially in the United States. Such longitudinal claims are apt to be confounded with various other trends that might make the apparent trend in trust an artifact. For example, the level and extent of interactions a typical person has in the United States in the 1990s may be substantially greater than those a similar person had in the 1950s. On average, then, the later person would be less trusting of the whole – larger – class of those with whom she deals than the earlier person would have been. But she and the earlier person may be as trusting of any particular class of people, such as close friends, associates at work, relatives, neighbors, and so forth. Indeed, she may substantially trust more people in various matters than the earlier person would have, while still distrusting or lacking trust in more people in her dealings than the earlier person would have. To assess whether there is a meaningful decline in trust, one would need to have questions over the decades asking people how much they trust their close associates, random strangers, and so forth. Questions that do not control for context are too hopelessly under-articulated to yield the grand thesis that trust is in decline.

Has the scale of our interactions changed over the past four decades? The discussions of Robert Putnam and many others of the impact of television on the privatization of American life suggest that we interact less today than our peers did fifty years ago (Putnam 1995a, 1995b). But there is a similarly widely asserted thesis that increasing urbanization has produced more extensive interactions with people as compared with earlier small-town life. The truth of the latter thesis seems especially evident to the vast number of people who have moved from small to larger communities or who have prospered in ways their parents never knew. This number probably includes many, maybe even most, of the academic and other researchers who claim that generalized trust is in decline. The trend from small-scale organization of society and social relations in medieval times to the large-scale complexities of modern industrial states continues.

Even if we establish that there has been a meaningful decline in levels of optimism that others are trustworthy, controlling for types of others, we still have, unfortunately, data on only a short-term trend. As noted later, there have surely been many eras in which trust in others has suffered from the general faltering of institutional backings of trustworthiness. We do not know from mere survey data, which exist only for a few decades, whether there is a secular trend in trust or distrust. This particular era suffered from many episodic crises that might have undercut optimism about others' trustworthiness, and the effects of these crises might last the lifetime of a particular generation. But it is perversely ahistorical to suppose there were not even greater losses of optimism in earlier times. Yet, we seem to have survived into a richer social life than our predecessors knew.

Can we successfully live together without trust? Put somewhat differently, is trust necessary for social order? One might presume to answer this question by putting societies in a two-by-two matrix of the possible combinations of high and low trust on one side and high and low social order on the other. Suppose there were no cases of low trust and high social order. Unfortunately, this fact would not settle the issue *because social order provides the background conditions that facilitate trust* by creating the conditions for stable ongoing relationships and backing them with law to block the risk of massive losses from wrongly trusting someone. That is, social order might, as "The Anonymous Iamblichus" (1995 [an ancient Greek text]) asserts, produce trust as first among its benefits, after perhaps Hobbes's chief concern, namely survival.

Does social order grow out of trust? It might prosper better with widespread trust and trustworthiness, but it does not follow that it must initially be *grounded* in such trust. Consider the so-called velvet revolutions in Eastern Europe in 1989. Masses coordinated behind the expression of hostility to the prior regimes (Sztompka 1996). Distrust must have been endemic in, for example, East Germany at that time, with a very large fraction of the population implicated in the STASI (secret police) oversight of citizens at all levels. It was partly distrust that stimulated the quest for a new order. It would be odd to suppose that quest to have been grounded in trust. There might be instances in which fairly widespread trust has facilitated the move to civil society. And we might suppose that widespread trust is facilitated by civil society and that trust in turn supports social order.

But current writings go much further than this in their claims. For example, Adam Seligman (1997: 6) makes the somewhat restricted but still grand claim that generalized trust is *necessary* for the workings of civil society. Shmuel Eisenstadt and Luis Roniger (1984: 16–17) say that "There is the necessity for and the ubiquity of trust in human relations and the impossibility of building continuing social relations without some element of trust." Ubiquity? Yes or almost so.[4] Necessity? No. Impossibility? Maybe – but in a very different sense than that apparently intended by Eisenstadt and Roniger or by Seligman. That is to say, if we do build stable, continuing relations with others, we will almost necessarily have the conditions, including the relevant incentives, for trustworthiness and trust. It would be virtually, although not logically, impossible to escape the development, therefore, of some trust.

The claim that generalized trust is necessary is surely wrong on one count and undemonstrated and perhaps beyond demonstration on another count. First, it is merely widespread, not generalized, trust that even might be necessary. Second, while there might be a causal arrow from social order to trusting, and as well a causal arrow from trusting to enhanced social order, it may be beyond demonstration whether there is any necessary link. Furthermore, at least for initiation of social order and for mere maintenance of social order, widespread trust is not necessary, as is suggested by quite diverse cases, such as (1) Fredrik Barth's accounts of the Omani and Swat Pathan social orders (Hardin 1999b: Chapter 4), (2) social orders, including Nazi-ruled Czechoslovakia, that have been maintained nearly by pure force, and (3) the transitions from endemic distrust to social order in Eastern Europe from 1989 forward.

The atmosphere of trustworthiness

Kenneth Arrow (1974) supposes that normal economic relations require a background or atmosphere of normative commitments to be honest, to keep promises, and so forth. In a similar sense, we might suppose that social relations of many kinds require or at least are simplified by a background of trustworthiness, although this might be more nearly rationally than normatively motivated. This might yield an alternative account of what many scholars see as generalized trust. For example, children who grow up, especially from their earliest days, in a supportive environment have reason to suppose that people are trustworthy. They therefore have

---

[4] There is still the nagging possibility of Fredrik Barth's trustless societies of Oman and Swat. For discussion see Hardin 1999b, Chapter 4 on "Distrust."

reason to risk entering into relationships with others that will be beneficial to them if those others are trustworthy (Hardin 1992). They then give others reason to be trustworthy because those others can thereby develop beneficial relationships with them. Trustworthiness begets trust, which, perhaps to a lesser extent, begets trustworthiness.[5]

This general background or atmosphere of trustworthiness makes social life go much more smoothly than it would without such an atmosphere. Hence, life in a harsh ghetto or in a society that has broken down into violence and rabid self-seeking, as in Somalia at the end of the twentieth century, is hampered by the prudent lack of trust and by the disastrous lack of institutions to enable joint enterprises to proceed even without much trust. Introducing trust in such a context would be pointless. What is required for a constructive atmosphere is trustworthiness, which cannot easily be established by individuals across a whole society that has destroyed it. And, again, what is required first is institutional safeguards against the potential for disastrous consequences so that people can begin to take the risk of cooperating in ways that, if successful, would lead to trust relationships.

Unfortunately, trust and distrust may be asymmetric in the sense that the former is much harder to learn for someone coming from a prior background of untrustworthy relations than the latter is for someone coming from a prior background of trustworthy relations. Overcoming the experience of distrust may be extremely difficult. The benefit of trusting, when it is warranted, is that it opens up opportunities. Blocking the severe losses that might follow from misplaced trust might seem similarly to open up opportunities. But those who start from a prior background of justified distrust are not likely to seize those opportunities because they do not readily take risks on their potential partners in joint enterprises, and until they do take such risks, they cannot develop trusting relationships. Hence, "equalizing opportunities" does not equalize outcomes because those from the background of distrust may not seize the new opportunities (Hardin 1992).

Trust and the economy

One of the most important arenas of social life outside ordinary one-on-one individual relations and relations with the state is the economy. Any economy, including a complex market economy, may work in part through trust relationships, and it may also enable us to achieve things we could not achieve merely through relationships of trust. This is an

---

[5] For suggestive experimental evidence, see Yamagishi and Cook 1993.

enormous topic that is addressed in a massive literature that includes, illustratively, works already cited here or in discussions to follow by Arrow, Edward Banfield, Breton and Wintrobe, Francis Fukuyama, Ernest Gellner, and Niklas Luhmann. Most of that literature focuses on modern market economies and much of it on the nascent development of market relations in earlier times.[6]

Given the size and complexity of that literature, I will not attempt to organize it or seriously contribute to it here. Rather, I will merely note two issues of the role of trust: in the development of economic relations where they have been hampered and in a socialist, centrally planned economy, which one might suppose hampers economic relations. Both of these issues evidently involve institutional problems in securing trust or, alternatively, in eliminating the need for it. As already noted, institutions play a role in underwriting even interpersonal trust. As Hume says of contracts, if they "had only their own proper obligation, without the separate sanction of government, they wou'd have but little efficacy in [all large and civiliz'd] societies. This separates the boundaries of our public and private duties, and shews that the latter are more dependant on the former, than the former on the latter" (Hume 1978 [1739–40]: 546). Hobbes may have exaggerated the extent to which powerful institutional sanctions are required for grounding trust and promises, but he was not radically mistaken.

First consider an account of trust in the development of economic relations. Anthony Pagden supposes that the conditions of Neapolitan society under Spanish rule until the eighteenth century suggest answers to larger questions about the necessary conditions for economic growth and social development in the early modern world (Pagden 1988: 127). After the revolt of 1647, the Habsburgs deliberately worked to destroy trust relations in order to maintain control until Naples passed to Austria under Bourbon rule in 1724. Three Neapolitan political economists of the eighteenth century, Paolo Mattia Doria, Antonio Genovesi, and Gaetano Filangeri, attempted to explain how a working economy could be created on the ruins of the distrusting Spanish order.

Doria and Genovesi supposed that trust is the basis of the well-ordered republic. Doria wrote that trust "is the sole sustenance of states and leads to their stable maintenance" (quoted in Pagden 1988: 129). The Italian words are not exact equivalents of the English "trust." But we might suppose Doria's sense is roughly that of the encapsulated interest account discussed earlier, because for him trust is the motive to behave

---

[6] For a detailed account of the actual development of exchange relations in a context of international disorder and weak legal institutions, see Greif 1993.

toward members of the society at large in much the same way that one behaves toward members of one's own kin group, with whom, of course, one has ongoing reciprocal exchange relations (Pagden 1988: 138). This secular ethic of classical republicanism performs the role of Weber's Protestantism: It shatters the fetters of the kin. Hence, it runs against the view of community in Ibn Khaldun in his defense (to be discussed) of anarchic tribal Muslim communities in North Africa, communities that depend centrally on kin relations (Gellner 1988).

Filangeri supposed that confidence is the soul of commerce and that the credit it can generate should be regarded as a second species of money (Pagden 1988: 130). Doria argued that trade can flourish only under two conditions, "liberty and security in contracts, and this can only occur when trust and justice rule" (Pagden 1988: 137). It has so been taken for granted that contract enables cooperative dealings even absent trust that a recent literature has grown up to say that much of apparent contractual dealing is in fact regulated by informal devices (Macauley 1963).

Now turn briefly to problems of trust in a socialist economy. If the theses of Fukuyama (1995) and Seligman (1997) are correct, one might suppose that the chief problems of Eastern Europe and the Soviet Union before 1989 were the lack of trust in many relationships, especially in relationships with the government and its agents. Hence, centralization of the economy might have worked had there only been more trust. One might consider Sweden a partial example of the truth of this supposition.

Alternatively, one might suppose that centralization was a problem in addition to low levels of trust, or even that centralization tended to produce distrust or to reduce trust. Gellner says that, politically, a socialist government "needs to atomize society; economically it needs autonomous institutions" (Gellner 1988: 156). In the second part of this claim, he evidently supposes that an economy must be organized somewhat entrepreneurially, which is to say, somewhat as a market. Yet, if the first part of his claim is true, this need founders on the state's efforts to undermine trust relationships.

This last conclusion sounds plausible, although the causal relation might be opportunistic rather than inherent. That is, giving government power to regulate prices gives it power to do many other things as well, such as suppressing the symphonies and operas of Dmitri Shostakovich and the writings and political activities of more or less everyone. Any lousy official can abuse such power, and a Stalin at the top can abuse it grossly even though there need be no reason associated with the economic purposes of centralization to use the power in such ways.

Trust in institutions

If institutions are to be used to back up or substitute for trust relations, we may naturally wonder whether we can trust institutions. Many scholars claim that citizens trust government in some societies and, in the vernacular, we commonly speak of trusting institutions. Such vernacular use of the term "trust" might be a trivial and empty use, almost as trivial as when we say we trust the sun to rise tomorrow. We merely expect an institution to act in a certain way because it seemingly has always done so and we rely on that expectation. Such expectations are generally adequate to get us through most of life. Generalizing from past behavior or results raises the traditional formal problem of induction that bothers philosophers, although for most of us this may not be an obstacle to belief. Indeed, we – including philosophers – would find life impossible if we could not act on even weak inductive generalizations. Mere inductive reliance on organizations eliminates central concern with trust.

For lower-level institutions and organizations in society, we might make arguments generally analogous to those made about trust in government (Hardin 1998a, 1999a). That is, we might suppose that it is not typically possible to trust a government or a large organization *in a way analogous to the way we can trust one another*. It might, however, be possible for you meaningfully to say that *you* can trust *a particular institution* in the sense, discussed earlier, of encapsulated interest. You might know enough about a particular organization to be able to unpack it, to assess the motivations of individual organizational role holders and to judge how these fit together to produce organizational responses to your interests. Or if you could actually know of many of its officers that they act in relevant ways toward you because they have incentives to take your interests into account, you could say you trust the organization, although this would be a shorthand for the fuller account involved in unpacking that organization.

Most of us most of the time, however, cannot be in a position to claim in this strong sense to trust organizations that are important in our lives. Most of us cannot know enough about the incentive structures of organizations that matter to us even to judge which specific actions by role holders would be in our interest. Most obviously, moreover, most people cannot know many of the role holders in any of the institutions that matter to them and therefore cannot be said to be able to trust them in the way they might trust close associates or even local merchants. In sum, most people lack both the organizational theory and the personal knowledge to trust particular organizations.

Suppose we grant that it is not possible for our relations with institutions to be grounded in trust in the individual role holders in the institutions. Then how can we rely on those institutions to address our interests even in those cases in which they ostensibly have a mandate to do so? In part, role holders are made reliable in fulfilling their role requirements through the use of incentives, both rewards and sanctions, to induce cooperative behavior. But they are also (less overtly) made reliable by institutional roles that are designed to make it directly in the interest of role holders to do what the organization requires. In the heyday of Taylorism in the early years of this century, it was supposed that workers should simply do what they were told and that they would be monitored and paid according to what they did. Institutional control structures are typically far more subtle than Taylor's vision suggests. But the choice is not the simplistic one between monitoring and trust. The actual device in common use in organizations is matching interests and tasks through relevant structures (Hardin 1998b). This device functions so well in many organizations as to induce professional deformation, that is, excessively zealous effort on behalf of organizations and their goals. Such deformation leads to such dismal results as the Dreyfus affair in the French military, in which officers preferred to see an innocent man left with his dreadful punishment than to see the military embarrassed for mishandling his trial.

Hence, we may expect organizations often to be reasonably competent to do what they are supposed to do in serving our interests even though, at the micro-level of the people in the organizations, we could not explain why they do so. But those who have to deal with an organization need not trust it in any significant sense in order to depend on its apparent predictability. You may not know enough to be able to break the organization down into roles whose occupants you can judge and you may not be able to figure out the functional relation of the various roles to the things you want or expect from the organization. But you can possibly still know enough about the past history of the organization to have strong expectations of how it will respond with respect to your interests.

This general conclusion is strengthened by the fact that an institution sets up the possibility of sudden endgames for those who rely on trust. The person one trusts might move from one role or organization to another, ending the iterated play that grounded one's trust – through that person – in the organization itself. This problem can afflict both organization-client and intra-organizational relations. Many people with substantial careers in organizations can recount instances in which their reliance on the organization was in fact only reliance on a particular person, whose departure wrecked their expectations of trustworthy ful-fillment of some arrangement. Here the stakes need not change to produce endgame effects, which follow, rather, from a literal end of the game.

A major value of written rules and agreements in organizations is to stabilize expectations by connecting them to the organization rather than to its specific agents. This device entails a substitution of organizational mechanisms for personal trust and trustworthiness. Organizations face a de facto type-1 versus type-2 error problem. They can rely on inter-personal trust relations that may be unstable but that can be well crafted to fit cases. Or they can rely on bureaucratic devices that can be stable but that cannot be individually crafted. Larger, especially public, organi-zations tend to opt for the type-2 error and to avoid reliance on per-sonalistic relations. They need neither elicit nor depend on trust relationships with their clientele.

Although this claim lacks research, it seems likely that the develop-mental trend in organizations is away from reliance on trust toward reliance on structural and other incentives that substitute for trust. A perhaps minor, because special, case in point is the organization of modern banks. There is virtually no need to rely on trusting bank tellers because they are rigorously monitored and are structurally almost inca-pable of cheating their employers.

It is sometimes said in various contexts that monitoring depresses commitment and therefore reduces productivity. Bank tellers are an instance in which this claim seems conspicuously wrong. What seems more plausible is that monitoring that is generalized, relatively unob-trusive, and cheap works to enhance productivity by inducing productive behavior. Without the monitoring, you might be, as Hume says, "natu-rally carried to commit acts of injustice as well as me. Your example both pushes me forward in this way by imitation, and also affords me a new reason for any breach of equity, by shewing me, that I should be the cully of my integrity, if I alone shou'd impose on myself a severe restraint amidst the licentiousness of others" (Hume 1978: 535). Hence, monitor-ing that seems reasonable to all concerned might not depress commit-ment but might rather enhance commitment by securing expectations that others in similar roles will be kept in line and that none of us will think honesty or proper performance of our jobs foolish.

Of course, even if trusting is not central to all institutional arrange-ments, relationships of trust might still help to lubricate organizational actions, often indeed by violating bureaucratic rules that substitute for trust.

Logical limits in trusting

On the encapsulated interest account of trust, we obviously face episte-mological and time constraints that prevent us from having strong trust-ing relationships with many people. The constraint of time is clear enough if we must have ongoing exchange relations with others in order to build trust in them. The epistemological constraints even cut against the possibility that we can trust very large numbers of people through their reputations. In addition, in some contexts of dealing with groups rather than merely dyadically with individuals, the logic of encapsulated interest must be violated even if we have essentially ongoing relation-ships. Hence there are two ways in which we can come up against essen-tially numerical limits on trusting. First, unlike a medieval Icelander, whose world was tiny, we cannot trust more than a relatively small frac-tion of the individuals in our worlds (see further the discussion of Bodo's world in the section "Social Structure and Trust"). Second, we cannot trust large groups of individuals as such. We may be able to trust many or most of the members of a collectivity, but we cannot count on them as members of a group to encapsulate the interests of others in the group.

First, consider limits on how many individuals one can trust. Before getting to trust, note that someone who already has several friends may not think the risk of investing in developing another is worth it. This problem may explain at least part of the phenomenon of clique and friendship-group formation. It might also be part of the explanation of familism in contexts in which families are relatively large, that is, large enough to exhaust a substantial part of the resources any member might have for investing in rich relationships. In Breton and Wintrobe's termi-nology, members of cliques may concentrate their investments in exchange relations in a small number of intensive relationships and may shun others merely to avoid the difficulties of dealing with those with whom they do not have intensive relationships. Similarly, groups may actively develop exclusionary devices to keep their membership confined only to those they know well enough to trust (Hardin 1995: Chapters 4 and 6).

Both of these phenomena – clique formation and familism – turn on the epistemological limits, perhaps especially the limits of investments of time, on developing more than a modest number of close relation-ships. For example, the members of a family might wind up in conflict with other families primarily because they simply have no time for them while they are heavily engaged in daily life and toil with one another.[7] But this means that, because people are not having rich relationships with others beyond their cliques or their families, they are not even in a position to develop trusting relationships with those others because they do not have the ongoing exchange relationships in which to embed interests in trustworthiness. Hence, *it is the rational structure of the relationship of trust that blocks trusting more universally.* Trust as encapsulated interest rules out the possibility or coherence of generalized trust and even of very widespread trust by any individual.

Second, consider whether a collectivity can be trustworthy on the encapsulated interest account. Consider two very different strategically defined classes of groups: groups mobilized by coordination and groups mobilized for collective action (Hardin 1991a). Suppose a group is coordinated behind a leader, as happens with charismatic leaders, in response to what the leader wants it to do. Coordinators can commonly trust their leader because they will withdraw support if the leader violates their trust, making it generally in the leader's interest to fulfill their trust. Of course, the leader's interest in fulfilling can be trumped by changed incentives or preferences. But so long as the leader has an interest in pursuing the goals behind which the followers are coordinated, she can be trusted and she has power derived from the coordination of the followers. It is limited power in the sense that it cannot be used for just any purpose. Rather, it can only be used for the group's purposes (Hardin 1995: Chapter 3). Coordination power therefore fits very well with the three-part relational account of trust. The followers follow only insofar as the leader does X. If the leader attempts to change direction, the committed followers may quickly drop off, as in the extreme case of the Sabbatai Sevi, who lost his charisma when he submitted to conversion to Islam (Scholem 1973). Examples of such trustworthy leaders include certain political leaders of more or less single-issue parties, such as religious and poujadist parties.

In standard contexts of collective action that takes the form of a large-number Prisoner's Dilemma exchange, however, the group cannot be trustworthy. The members of the group might well share some set of interests that someone – call her a leader – has or that she would support for the sake of the collectivity's support of her. But if their support of her requires actions from each member of the group, their own interest might typically be to renege on acting, to free-ride on the efforts of others. Indeed, their own interest is to free-ride on the efforts of others even with respect to their own personal interest in the product of group

---

[7] As in the conditions in Edward C. Banfield's (1958) account of life in the fictionally named village of Montegrano in southern Italy.

effort. *Eo ipso*, their interest cannot encapsulate mine with respect to that joint product if it does not even include their own.

The difficulties of trusting a collectivity are not the whole story of the problem of trusting institutions, but they are an important part of it. I cannot trust a collectivity to act for my interests because their members cannot encapsulate my interests in their own. An institution or organization is in part a collection of people. If all of them are to act in my interests, it will not be because they are acting against the logic of collective action but because the institution has been structured to give them the relevant incentives. That leaves me, of course, with a severe epistemological problem of knowing enough about the organizational structure and incentive system to have reason to believe the people in the organization are acting in my interest.

Note a peculiar asymmetry in the possibilities for trust and distrust in such collectivities. The worst implication of the grand transition from a small-scale to a very large-scale, impersonal society might eventually, because of power differences and general cynicism, be to produce fairly *generalized distrust*, which might make sense in a way that generalized trust does not. For example, without much experience of government action toward me, my "distrust" of government might be little more than the sense that people with no connection to me are not likely to take my interests to heart and might even abuse them. At first hearing, this might sound unduly cynical. But this expectation is not as restricted a problem as it might at first seem. For example, suppose you hold stock in some company and you hear or come to expect that the company is in trouble and that its stock price will fall. You are likely to sell your stock *so that not you but someone else takes the loss*. If you are likely to seek benefit at cost to unknown others in this context, you might therefore expect others to do the same in various other contexts.

Now consider a more extreme grounding for distrust in government. For an easy case, consider an individual who has been abused by government in the past, as were the subjects of the notorious Tuskegee experiments designed to watch the progress of syphilis in untreated black southern prisoners, or the subjects of supposedly harmless exposure to radiation in various U.S. experiments by government agencies to find out how harmful such exposure might be (*New York Times Magazine* 1997). Such an individual has good personal reason to be wary of distant government officials, indeed to distrust them in a relatively unspecific and vague way that might have no counterpart in trust. As I generally should expect most people to act from their incentive to free-ride on various collective actions, therefore acting against my interests, I might similarly expect government officials to act in their interests and against mine in many contexts, especially when there are issues of which I am not even aware, as in the cases of the Tuskegee and radiation experiments.

This is the asymmetrical conclusion. I need not think it very likely that any official would be as brutally unconcerned with my interests as those officials were with respect to their experimental subjects. I need merely think it quite likely that officials will occasionally find it in their interests to violate my own, and that they will do so. Therefore, on the encapsulated interest account, I can sensibly distrust them even though I could not plausibly have any chance of being able to know enough to trust them – even in the event that they might be trustworthy toward me, as most of them might in fact be. The logical limits that block the possibility of trusting perversely enable us to distrust. I may believe that government generally benefits me, and I may be right in that belief. But that is merely an inductive generalization grounded in the vague sense that I am better off than I would be without government or the less vague sense that certain policies are actually in my interest. My weak distrust is grounded in a real understanding of the likely incentives that government officials sometimes face, including the perverse incentive, mentioned earlier, of professional deformation to protect their own agencies. That understanding is not merely an inductive generalization but rather a logical inference from normal human interests.

This dispiriting conclusion might be exacerbated by an unfortunate characteristic of many government policies, including many of the best understood and most important policies on economic benefits. If the populace is distributed along some rough continuum of preferences with respect to some policy arena, then any specific policy that is adopted will be very near the positions of only a fraction of the populace. Hence, most people might think that they fare relatively badly from any given policy. Hence they might not even reach the inductive generalization that an actual government does serve their interests adequately, that it typically trades off their interests for the interests of others. If I conjoin this pessimistic assessment with the inference that government agents may often have an interest in acting against my interests, I may now suppose the occasional instances of actions by officials who would merit distrust are not offset by the general good that government does for me.

Cooperation and trust

In the large contemporary literature on trust, the apparent point of wanting more trust is that trust eases the way to cooperative social relations, as is argued by Luhmann, Putnam, Fukuyama, and others

(Fukuyama 1995, Luhmann 1980, Putnam 1993). But it is hard to see just what is wanted. We want As to trust Bs to do Xs. When we think of this in its unpacked form, we immediately focus on specific devices to get the Bs to do Xs.[8] For example, the massive system of contract enforcement in any flourishing market society serves agents who do not genuinely trust each other with respect to anything in particular, who, indeed, need not even know each other well enough to be trusting without backing from the law. Yet, the system enables them to enter into very complex cooperative relations that are mutually beneficial. It would be odd to speak of generalized trust in such a case. If there is anything that can be called trust here, it is the very specific trust required to comply with a legal contract that is grounded in the system of contract enforcement. Alternatively, as is true in many ongoing business relations, it is the iterated interaction that gives the parties an incentive to behave well in this moment because they want the relationship to continue in future moments. At this point, however, the relationship is one of trust.

A working legal system that backs up contractual relations can enable parties to cooperate. Once they have successfully cooperated for a while, they may then be able to trust each other well enough not to require as extensive contractual regulation of their dealings. There are, of course, many contexts in which such successful contracting may have little or no chance of leading to trust. For example, our contract may cover what is for us a very unusual exchange, one that will not be repeated. And that exchange might involve very high stakes, as in the sale of a home by one of us to the other. In this case, the contract regime allows us to make a deal we could not otherwise make without grievous risks. But it need not induce either of us to trust the other, and we may have no further dealings with each other, even over matters on which we might benefit if only we did trust each other. What centrally matters to us in such an interaction is that we successfully cooperate in my selling the house to you, not that we cooperate because we trust each other or generally trust the larger society.

In sum, there are many and manifold instances of cooperation that need not and likely do not involve trust. Trust is merely one enabler of taking cooperative risks. And trustworthiness is merely one reason such risks can pay off. Cooperative relationships therefore comprise a larger – plausibly a much larger – category than trusting relationships.

---

[8] In some cases, the As are simultaneously Bs and the Bs are As, as in certain complex contractual relations.

Social structure and trust

The Hobbesian problem of dreadful disorder arises from the assumption that anarchy – the absence of enforcement – leads to distrust and social disintegration. Ibn Khaldun supposed that it is precisely anarchy that engenders trust or social cohesion (Gellner 1988: 143). The argument is somewhat circular. In anarchy there are, by definition, no institutional structures for regulating cooperative interactions. Hence, if there is unco-erced cooperation, it must typically require trust – although perhaps not always. That there is trust in instances of anarchic order therefore need not entail that such conditions engender trust, because trust is commonly constitutive of such order in anarchic conditions (that trust is not a nec-essary element of anarchic order is suggested by the example of the Swat Pathan, as noted at the end of the earlier discussion under Generalized or Social Trust).

Hobbes supposed, implausibly, that in the state of nature distrust would be so rampant that individuals would turn on other individuals. What is more plausible, and what is consistent with the vast literature on anarchy and on acephalous anthropological societies, is that there would be small-community organization. Individuals within small communities would have some protections that would make productive life possible. The small societies might, however, engage in hostilities with each other. As Gellner argues, in segmentary, pastoral society, there is only one means of protecting oneself against sudden onslaught from others: to gang up in a group (Gellner 1988: 144).

Khaldun says urban life is incompatible with trust and cohesion. Experimental work on Japanese and American societies suggests that reliance on a group builds trust relationships within the group but blocks or at least hinders the development of trust relationships more broadly (Yamagishi, Cook, and Watabe 1998). Khaldun's concern was with the transition from traditional, anarchic Muslim societies in North Africa to urban societies. The very fact that they are urban means that urban lineages accept governmental authority (Gellner 1988: 147). Hence, they cannot be anarchic, and it immediately follows that trust is at risk. Urban organization and economic specialization separate individuals from their relatives and immerse them in a larger, less knowable society. In Khaldun's vision, the city is comprised of specialists and, metaphorically speaking, a specialist has no cousins. In a tribal culture the specialist is despised. Every excellence is a form of specialization, and specialization precludes full citizenship. The unspecialized human being constitutes the moral norm. (Recall the peasant Chinese dictum that we should cut down the taller poppies, those who stand out and are not part of the ordinary mass – as though the standout violates some aesthetic principle.) The unspecialized can lose themselves in a solidary unit and gladly accept collective responsibility.

Against Khaldun's thesis we might argue that we would rather live in a society with the advantages of division of labor and scale than in one so small that there would be little division of labor (except perhaps the painfully traditional divisions by gender). Khaldun's moral thesis is that we would be better off in a small, close-knit community. This is a staggeringly complex and contestable normative claim, one that is partially shared by communitarian theorists of our time in the West – at least on paper, although not in their lives. None of those communitarian theorists would be able to live in a society such as Khaldun extols, nor, as an impressive social theorist, could Khaldun have fit into that society. Interestingly, however, the usual concern of communitarians is not with the richer relationships of trust in community, but rather with the origin of values in communal practice and knowledge (Hardin 1995: Chapter 7).[9] We may therefore face the sad prospect that the intellectual decline of communitarian argument may be at least temporarily interrupted by refocusing it on trust rather than on values.

Against the appeals of Khaldun's argument even on its own terms of communal engenderment of trust, and parallel to the trend toward division of labor, is a trend toward the reduction of the extremes of distrust that lead to violence in such small-scale societies as medieval Iceland and the traditional Muslim societies that concerned Khaldun. We can thank institutions for this change. Legal institutions replace the feud and the system of personal vengeance with police protections and replace the need for restrictive systems of barter with general exchange grounded in enforceable contracts and money. In contexts in which trust did not work earlier, because of pervasive distrust over certain matters, it is often no longer a concern that it still does not work, because we have far less need to rely on trustworthiness in order to engage in joint enterprises.

Part of the specialization that Khaldun disliked is specialization in the task of handling difficult interpersonal exchanges and other enterprises. And for such matters, we may be glad that no one of us relies on our cousins for managing those relationships. When your cousins now do play a strong role in mediating our relations, I have reason for distrust. This is, of course, the point of Max Weber's thesis on bureaucratization: that the resources and accounts of the individual get separated from those of

---

[9] It is the vision of Robert Putnam that the existence of smaller associations in a society is conducive to political participation, and, one might suppose, to trust in government. See Putnam 1993.

the firm. It was also the original point of anti-nepotism rules that are now increasingly in abeyance when the relative who might work for a firm is not a brother or male cousin but a woman, especially a spouse.

Even in a more complex society, some of Khaldun's conclusions about trust and distrust might still hold. Breton and Wintrobe (1982: 80) note that in an open, mobile, and relatively impersonal society, large investments in trust in a small number of intensive relationships are unusual. What we see instead are many contacts that are less intense. Breton and Wintrobe are presumably concerned with something roughly like commercial relationships, because we might still see substantial investments in trust and trustworthiness in close, intensive relationships with family and friends even in such a society as the United States. Indeed, Breton and Wintrobe themselves have had an admirably long and close collaborative academic relationship. The differences in the two patterns are, again, virtually a matter of arithmetic logic, because the development of intensive relationships requires substantial investments of time. If I must have relations with very large numbers of people, I cannot have intensive relations with many of them.

The change from traditional to modern industrial societies in this respect is radical. Axel Leijonhufvud (1995) compares the life of a village Frenchman, Bodo, who lived in the twelfth century, to that of a French professional living in Paris today. We can know very much about Bodo because he lived in the diocese of the church of St. Germain, which kept good records of his life. At that time, St. Germain was well outside Paris, but today it is near the center of the city, where our contemporary professional lives and works. Almost all of Bodo's consumption in his lifetime was derived either from his own efforts or from the efforts of about eighty people, all of whom he knew well on a nearly daily basis. The bit of his consumption that did not come from his small community would have been any spices he might have used and salt, which would have come from abroad and from the sea respectively, and which would have passed through several, perhaps many, hands on the way. His modern counterpart consumes things that have inputs from millions of people around the globe, most of whom the Frenchman would never know. There may be no one outside his family whom the professional knows as well as Bodo knew many of his fellow villagers.

Economic progress brings new classes into the center of society, making changes in culture and values much easier. A seeming concern of communitarians is to block such changes. They de facto argue for a society in which current dispensations as of some moment are turned into fairly rigidly determined positional goods. The implications of such a view are that we are either stuck relatively fast or finally overwhelmed by changes that come from outside the community. Khaldun would presumably have preferred Bodo's world to contemporary Paris, but he did not have a theory that would tell him or the communitarians how to secure that world.

As noted above, a continuing transition analogous to that from the twelfth to the twentieth century in Paris may explain some of the data that suggest that general levels of trust have been declining in the United States over the past few decades of survey research on the matter. As they stand, such data at best demonstrate episodic decline rather than secular decline. For example, one might suppose that, had similar surveys been done in the United States in the 1930s, the 1890s, the 1850s and 1860s, and the late 1830s, there would similarly have been declining levels of supposedly general trust. General declines in well-being and loss of grounds for expected stable economic and other relationships during those interludes must rightly have suggested to people that they, under prevailing conditions, could trust others less.

Parasitic abuses of trust

For a real-world society, in which there must be substantial variance on most social, intentional, cognitive (and so forth) measures, average levels of anything may be far less important than actual distributions, especially if individuals and societies have ways of selecting on the relevant dimension. So, for example, if we are in a society that is hierarchically organized for various purposes, it may often be more important that the most competent or trustworthy people be in certain hierarchical roles than that people of average competence or trustworthiness be in those roles. Even in a strictly egalitarian context, such as a working market, it is more important that there be highly trustworthy individuals in the system than that everyone be close to the average in trustworthiness.

But if the background norm is one of relatively trustworthy people in particular roles, the untrustworthy can take parasitic advantage of that background expectation. In a society in which the background standards are those of the con artist, stances toward others will generally be defensive and wariness might block most cooperative dealings, as in contexts of pervasive distrust and untrustworthiness. But in a much more cooperative society, which is likely to be either a very close society or one with relatively good institutional structures to protect various dealings, the typically correct stance will be one of openness rather than wariness.

I was once cheated by a small shop owner in downtown Chicago, who sold me a watch battery that was already dead, although it had recovered just enough to make my watch run for long enough to let me think it was okay. That shop owner's success was parasitic on the larger system of shops and stores that were more trustworthy, because my behavior in his shop was merely a generalization of my normal behavior in shops, most of which in my experience were trustworthy. In a particular shop that I might have used in my own neighborhood, I would not have needed to bother to check whether the shopkeeper opened a sealed package to take out a new battery. That shopkeeper depended on reputation for business by repeat customers. In the shop in downtown, I should have kept a more diligent eye on the shopkeeper because his business depended on casual traffic and not on repeat business or reputation.

Similarly, in a society in which personal relationships are generally not deviously exploitative, one can take a lot for granted on first meeting a new associate. Con artists, sexual exploiters, and many others have a field of play only because the background standards and expectations for behavior are relatively high.

Concluding remarks

Trust typically arises at the level of, and is grounded in, relatively small-scale interactions. It may not be merely a dyadic relationship, but it cannot be grounded in very large-number interactions, either one-to-one or one-to-many. Because most of us live in large-scale societies, we need devices other than trusting and trustworthiness to make many of our more or less cooperative activities go well. Typically, we can overcome the scale limits of direct trusting by relying on social constructions such as intermediary guarantors and reputations. But even these devices are commonly limited. To go much further, we must have strong institutional and especially legal backing that displaces the need for trust and reliance on others' doubtful trustworthiness. But such backing cannot be made to work efficiently, or even at all, in some contexts.

It may still be true that trust and trustworthiness are fundamentally important in making large-scale activities and, especially, large social institutions function. But to show how they do this requires substantial unpacking of the relationships in those institutions to understand how trust plays a role at the micro-level. Trust is inherently a micro-level phenomenon. It is individuals who trust, and it is individuals who, under institutional and other constraints, are trustworthy to a limited extent in particular contexts. Trust and trustworthiness may permeate the social structure, but they do so bit by bit.

References

"The Anonymous Iamblichi." 1995. Pages 290–295 in Michael Gagarin and Paul Woodruff, eds., *Early Greek Political Thought from Homer to the Sophists.* Cambridge: Cambridge University Press.

Arrow, Kenneth J. 1974. *The Limits of Organization.* New York: W. W. Norton.

Austen, Jane. [1813] 1952. *Pride and Prejudice.* London: Collins.

Banfield, Edward C. 1958. *The Moral Basis of a Backward Society.* New York: Free Press.

Becker, Gary. [1957] 1971. *The Economics of Discrimination.* Chicago: University of Chicago Press, 2nd edition.

Blythe, Ronald. 1966. "Introduction." In Jane Austen, *Emma.* London: Penguin.

Breton, Albert, and Ronald Wintrobe. 1982. *The Logic of Bureaucratic Conduct: An Economic Analysis of Competition, Exchange, and Efficiency in Private and Public Organizations.* Cambridge: Cambridge University Press.

Coleman, James S. 1990. *Foundations of Social Theory.* Cambridge, MA: Harvard University Press.

Dawson, John P. 1980. *Gifts and Promises: Continental and American Law Compared.* New Haven, CT: Yale University Press.

Eisenstadt, Shmuel N., and Luis Roniger. 1984. *Patrons, Clients and Friends.* Cambridge: Cambridge University Press.

Frank, Robert. 1988. *Passions within Reason: The Strategic Roles of the Emotions.* New York: Norton.

Fukuyama, Francis. 1995. *Trust: The Social Virtues and the Creation of Prosperity.* New York: Free Press.

Gellner, Ernest. 1988. "Trust, Cohesion, and the Social Order," Pages 142–157 in Diego Gambetta, ed., *Trust: Making and Breaking Cooperative Relations.* Oxford: Blackwell.

Greif, Avner. 1993. "Contract Enforceability and Economic Institutions in Early Trade: The Maghribi Traders' Coalition." *American Economic Review* 83 (June): 525–548.

Hardin, Russell. 1982. *Collective Action.* Baltimore, MD: Johns Hopkins University Press.

1988. *Morality within the Limits of Reason.* Chicago: University of Chicago Press.

1991a. "Acting Together, Contributing Together." *Rationality and Society* 3 (July): 365–380.

1991b. "Trusting Persons, Trusting Institutions." Pages 185–209 in Richard J. Zeckhauser, ed., *The Strategy of Choice.* Cambridge, MA: MIT Press.

1992. "The Street-Level Epistemology of Trust." *Analyse und Kritik* 14: 152–176. (Reprinted in *Politics and Society* 21 [1993]: 505–529.)

1995. *One for All: The Logic of Group Conflict.* Princeton, NJ: Princeton University Press.

1996. "Trustworthiness." *Ethics* 107 (October): 26–42.

1998a. "Trust in Government." Pages 9–27 in Valerie Braithwaite and Margaret Levi, eds., *Trust and Governance.* New York: Russell Sage Foundation.

1998b. "Institutional Commitment: Values or Incentives?" Pages 419–433 in Avner Ben Ner and Louis Putterman, eds., *Economics, Values, and Organization.* Cambridge: Cambridge University Press.

1999a. "Do We Want Trust in Government?" Pages 22–41 in Mark Warren, ed., *Democracy and Trust*. Cambridge University Press.

1999b. *Trust and Trustworthiness*. Unpublished manuscript, New York University.

Hertzberg, Lars. 1988. "On the Attitude of Trust." *Inquiry* 31: 307–322.

Hobbes, Thomas. [1642] 1983. *De Cive*. Oxford: Oxford University Press, ed. Howard Warrender (originally published in Latin).

1651. *Leviathan*. London: Andrew Cooke (or any standard edition).

Hume, David. [1739–40] 1978. *A Treatise of Human Nature*. Oxford: Oxford University Press, ed. L. A. Selby-Bigge and P. H. Nidditch.

Leijonhufvud, Axel. 1995. "The Individual, the Market and the Industrial Division of Labor." Pages 61–78 in Carlo Mongardini, ed., *L'Individuo e il mercato*. Rome: Bulzoi.

Luhmann, Niklas. 1980. Trust: A Mechanism for the Reduction of Social Complexity. Pages 4–103 in Luhmann, *Trust and Power*. New York: Wiley.

Macauley, Stewart. 1963. "Non-Contractual Relations in Business: A Preliminary Study." *American Sociological Review* 28 (February): 55–67.

New York Times. 1986. "Prenuptial Pacts Rise, Prenuptial Trust Fails" (19 November): 17–18.

New York Times Magazine. 1997 (31 August): [untitled] 41–42.

Pagden, Anthony. 1988. "The Destruction of Trust and Its Economic Consequences in the Case of Eighteenth-Century Naples." Pages 127–141 in Diego Gambetta, ed., *Trust: Making and Breaking Cooperative Relations*. Oxford: Blackwell.

Putnam, Robert D. 1993. *Making Democracy Work: Civic Traditions in Modern Italy*. Princeton, NJ: Princeton University Press.

1995a. "Bowling Alone: America's Declining Social Capital." *Journal of Democracy* 6 (January): 65–78.

1995b. "Tuning In, Tuning Out: The Strange Disappearance of Social Capital in America." *PS: Political Science and Politics* (December): 664–683.

Scholem, Gershom. 1973. *The Sabbatai Sevi*. Princeton, NJ: Princeton University Press.

Seligman, Adam B. 1997. *The Problem of Trust*. Princeton, NJ: Princeton University Press.

Sztompka, Piotr. 1996. "Trust and Emerging Democracy: Lessons from Poland." *International Sociology* 11 (March): 37–62.

Yamagishi, Toshio, and Karen S. Cook. 1993. "Generalized Exchange and Social Dilemmas." *Social Psychology Quarterly* 56: 235–248.

Yamagishi, Toshio, Karen S. Cook, and Motoki Watabe. 1998. "Uncertainty, Trust and Commitment Formation in the United States and Japan." *American Journal of Sociology* 104 (July): 165–194.

CHAPTER 2

Downsizing trust

Ronald Wintrobe

1 Introduction: The phenomenon of downsizing

One of the hallmarks of economic life in the 1980s and 1990s has been the phenomenon of downsizing: corporations and governments shed functions, reduced their budgets and employment, and in other ways attempted to do less than they had attempted previously. At least in North America and Britain, governments have attempted to balance their budgets and to give over functions to quasi-independent authorities such as central banks and to international ones like the European Economic Community. Superficially, the behavior of these governments can be explained as simply a response to the reality of accumulating budget deficits or debt. But if deficits or debt were the sole source of the problem, governments could solve it by simply raising taxes. Ultimately, then, downsizing cannot be related simply to the financial problems of governments, but must be traced to a disillusionment with the capacity of government to provide the goods, services, or regulations that citizens want.[1]

Perhaps the most extreme form of downsizing in the 1990s was that of communist governments. After all, the distinctive feature of the communist system was that, in it, governments took over and monopolized the production of goods and services in the economy. Thus one can conceive of the fall of communism as part of, and the ultimate example of, the 1990s trend toward downsizing. Again, there are many specific explanations or sets of explanations for what happened. Probably the most common one is simply the superiority of markets over planning. However, this approach doesn't explain why the communist system

---

[1] Hardin's chapter in this volume provides a valuable critical assessment of the evidence on the erosion of trust in governments.

47

didn't collapse much earlier! Another way to think about the problem is that these governments became corrupt, and ultimately lost the trust of the citizenry. Again, therefore, downsizing may be explained as a failure of trust.[2]

In this chapter, I focus on downsizing in business corporations, where much of the literature, and especially the empirical economic literature, has concentrated. Two explanations in particular have been extensively explored and tested: technology and trade. The first idea is that changes in technology, especially in computer technology, are skill-biased. The second line of thought is that globalization, interpreted as increased trade with underdeveloped countries, has resulted in the importation of products embodying relatively large amounts of unskilled labor. On either explanation, downsizing on the part of business firms is simply the rational response to a fall in the demand for unskilled labor. The problem with these widely held ideas is that, on the evidence which has accumulated so far, neither of them can satisfactorily account for the phenomenon. The evidence is that the magnitude of these changes is simply not large enough: American imports from underdeveloped countries are still quite small, and productivity growth from technical change is too meager.

In addition, there are some other puzzling aspects of corporate downsizing which escape these theories. Perhaps the most important of these is the fact that, at the same time that downsizing has taken place, and workers whose incomes are at the bottom end of the income distribution have been laid off, there has been a tremendous *increase* in the salaries of top executives and of others at the top end of the income distribution. Another puzzling fact is that much of the impact of downsizing has fallen on middle management, i.e., on supervisory and other nonproduction personnel. Yet, at the same time that such employees have been laid off in record numbers, the proportion of nonproduction personnel to direct labor has, at least on some readings of the evidence, continued to increase. This is how Gordon (1996) explains how American corporations have become *Fat and Mean*, to use the title of his book, which documents this picture of firms downsizing ("mean") yet at the same time becoming increasingly bloated with middle management ("fat").

I will begin by suggesting that the basic way to understand downsizing in corporations is to treat the corporation as a bureaucracy. As in any bureaucracy, relationships are primarily based on trust, since contracts are difficult to monitor and enforce within a hierarchy (Breton and

---

[2] This explanation is spelled out in more detail in Wintrobe (1998), Chapter 10.

Wintrobe 1982). I explain downsizing as a reduction in trust, which management can implement in one of two ways: as a *breach* of trust, or alternatively as a *repudiation* of it, motivated by changes (including globalization) that increase the elasticity of the firm's demand for labor and make trust within the hierarchy less valuable than before. Put differently, breach and repudiation of trust are both ways for management to renounce debts to employees. In the process, management compensation can increase. With breach of trust, this occurs as a reward for appropriating the rents of employees and transferring them to shareholders (as in the analysis of wage cuts stemming from corporate takeovers by Shleifer and Summers 1988). With repudiation of trust, management simply unilaterally removes one of the constraints on executive compensation. This chapter explains how these strategies work.

The outline of the chapter is particularly straightforward: the next section outlines the standard explanations of downsizing, and suggests some of their conceptual and empirical flaws. Section 3 develops the approach and the implications based on bureaucratic theory advanced here. Section 4 concludes the chapter.

2   Standard explanations of downsizing

The standard explanations of downsizing are that it is the result of either, or a combination of, (a) increased foreign competition, resulting from the opening of the global market to low-wage countries' manufactured products, and (b) skill-biased technological progress, particularly the widespread introduction of computers. Both of these changes result in the displacement of unskilled workers in the advanced countries. Downsizing is "necessary" from an efficiency point of view, in order to reduce costs in order to meet the threat of import competition, or of competition from domestic firms using new technologies.

On either of these theories, downsizing raises productivity. However, it is difficult to find evidence of productivity improvements as a consequence of downsizing. A careful study of downsizing by Baily et al. (1994) using plant-level data from the census of manufacturers in 1977 and 1987 failed to reveal any such correlation. They did find a substantial increase in productivity over this period (the average productivity of labor rose 33 percent), as well as evidence of downsizing in the aggregate (employment in those firms declined by 4.5 percent). However, they note that "plants that raised employment *and* productivity contributed almost as much to overall productivity growth in the 1980's as the plants that raised productivity at the expense of employment" (Baily et al. 1994, pp. 24–25).

With respect to the technology model, Gordon (1996, p. 182) points out that the timing is wrong: the big drop in employment shares for low-skilled workers took place during the recession of 1980–82; after that, their share of employment remained relatively constant. By contrast, the acceleration of computerization began only in 1983–4.

At a more general level, while no one can doubt the importance of the information revolution, there is little evidence that it has resulted in productivity growth. Blinder and Quandt (1997) note that the data show that the U.S. economy has experienced no increase in total-factor productivity for fifteen to twenty years (p. 26). Though they find the data "simply not believable" on this point (p. 26), they do conclude that advances in information technology have yielded only small gains in productivity so far (p. 31). They also discuss some of the reasons that the computer revolution may not have generated much in the way of productivity growth, including the usual carping about computer programs that do not work, obsolesce quickly, force people to be constantly learning new programs, and so on; note that computing and related equipment accounts for less than 10 percent of gross U.S. investment; and make some useful and sobering comparisons between computers and other inventions such as the telegraph and telephone. Oliner and Sichel (1994) develop baseline estimates of the contribution of computers to output growth in a Denison-style growth accounting framework. According to these models, the contribution of computer hardware to the growth of gross output between 1970 and 1992 was about .16 percentage point annually (p. 274), and the contribution to net output growth was much smaller. Adding in software and computer-services labor roughly doubles this number to one that is still tiny. Finally, with respect to the nonmanufacturing sector, Davis and Topel observe that "the meagre growth in labor productivity does not fit comfortably with an explanation for relative wage developments that postulate an important role for skill-biased technological change. We are left with a conundrum: If skill-biased technological change has been so important, why has labor productivity growth been so slow?" (Davis and Topel 1993, quoted in Gordon 1996, p. 184).

Turning to trade, the problem is, as most trade economists have acknowledged, that trade with low-wage countries, despite its growth, is still too small to have had a significant effect on labor market outcomes in the developed countries. Thus, for example, Lawrence and Slaughter conclude their careful study with the statement that "international factors contributed nothing to America's wage performance in the 1980's".[3]

Of course, this general conclusion has been disputed, and some argue that there are additional channels besides the ones discussed and measured through which trade with developing countries can widen the skill premium. For example, Wood (1994) argues that import competition has driven out many of the low-skill intensive activities that would otherwise have been present in the advanced countries. Cline (1997) surveys the large literature on this topic, and concludes that international influences contributed about 20 percent of the rising wage inequality in the 1980s (cited in Rodrik 1997, p. 15).

The standard trade or technology models also face some other difficulties: At the theoretical level, it is not obvious how "fat" could accumulate in a competitive firm in the first place. Such a firm minimizes costs, and has no place to "put" fat. So, if one starts with a model of the competitive firm, it is not obvious how this firm can become "leaner" as the result of increased trade, since it was never, by this assumption, overweight to begin with.

One odd bit of evidence is that, although there has been a dramatic increase in the insecurity of middle managers, and although many of the layoffs have been at this level, the data indicate that corporations have become *more*, not less, bureaucratic. That is, the proportion of nonproduction and supervisory personnel has continued to increase throughout the period of downsizing (Caves and Krepps 1993, Gordon 1996). Gordon refers to nonproduction personnel as "the bureaucratic burden"[4] and shows that this burden has "actually been growing, not contracting, through the mid 1990s. In 1948, it began as a postwar low of 12 percent of all private nonfarm employees. It increased substantially as the postwar period progressed, levelling off at roughly 19 percent in the 1980s" (1996, p. 35). During the period 1989–1994, when stories of downsizing were most widely reported, according to household survey data reported by Gordon the proportion of managers actually increased further (Gordon, p. 52).

Another puzzling fact is that, in America at least, where downsizing has been most common, at the same time that wages at the bottom end

---

[3] Lawrence and Slaughter, "Trade and U.S. Wages", quoted in Krugman (1994), p. 266.

[4] The reason that supervisory personnel constitute a "burden" is that, while from the firm's point of view monitoring and high wages are substitutes, from society's point of view supervision uses up real resources, while high wages are just a transfer from employers to employees. Hence, social welfare is increased whenever firms switch from the conflictual to the cooperative strategies.

of the corporate ladder have been stagnating, executive salaries have skyrocketed. After-tax CEO salaries increased by two-thirds over the 1980s, according to data from *The Economist*, reported by Gordon (p. 34). The overall result is that the inequality of income greatly worsened for the first time on a sustained basis in the twentieth century. At the bottom end, what Freeman (1996) calls "an economic disaster" has befallen low-skill Americans: "The real hourly wages of young males with 12 or fewer years of schooling has dropped by more than 20 percent in the last two decades" (Freeman 1996, p. 2). In Europe, unskilled wages have risen, but unemployment has soared. Now, it is possible to advance the technology or trade explanations to explain what has happened to the bottom fifth. But how does increased import competition or computerization raise the salaries of the top group? Thus, although Krugman (1996, pp. 197–199) concludes that technology explains one-half of the changes in inequality, he also notes that "[t]he professions that have seen the largest increases in incomes since the 1970's have been in fields whose practitioners are not obviously placed in greater demand by computers: lawyers, doctors and above all, corporate executives"[5] Moreover, he notes that there has also been a "fractal" quality to the changes in inequality; within any skill group, (e.g., *among* lawyers or doctors) there is more inequality in earnings than before. For these reasons, Krugman also favors the "winner-take-all" hypothesis advanced most notably by Robert Frank and Philip Cook (1995). However, it is worth pointing out that one reason for the increased number of winner-take-all markets is precisely the spread of globalization. This suggests that globalization may work in different ways than those specified in the standard models, a theme to which we return in the next section.

To summarize, the standard models cannot explain how fat accumulates in competitive firms in the first place, and have difficulty accounting for the apparent lack of increased productivity as a result of downsizing. They cannot explain the apparent increase in the proportion of nonproduction or supervisory personnel throughout the 1980s and into the 1990s. There is an increase in wealth which has mainly fallen on the upper classes, but this is not part of the story. So the increase in executive salaries at the top appears, on either of the standard explanations, to be an entirely different phenomenon than the stagnating or falling wages and the displacement of workers at the bottom. The following section addresses these issues. I suggest that it is first necessary to understand the typical corporation as a bureaucracy. I then describe some other channels through which globalization operates (following

[5] Krugman (1996), p. 199.

recent work by Rodrik 1997). I then show how this and other changes act to reduce the demand for trust within the firm, and how this provides an alternative explanation for downsizing, increases in executive compensation, and the growth in the proportion of nonproduction employees.

3 Breach and repudiation of trust in bureaucracy

To begin with, I suggest that the modern corporation is best understood, at least in part, as a bureaucracy. Here are some reasons:

1. The firm is typically not managed by its owner(s) but by a hired manager or chief executive officer (CEO), who is directly responsible not to the shareholders, but to a board of directors. Typically, monitoring by the board is fairly lax, so the manager has considerable freedom to exercise discretion.
2. The performance of the CEO is difficult to evaluate. The firm may be doing well, or badly, but how can a shareholder know to what extent either result is due to the CEO's efforts and strategies? Accordingly, proxies for his or her unmeasured productivity must be found. One common proxy is the size or rate of growth of the firm. For this and other reasons, Dial and Murphy (1995) suggest that the usual executive incentive packages do not provide effective incentives to downsize. Instead, they argue that managerial compensation is typically tied to firm size, that the nonmonetary compensation of executives – including power, prestige, and community standing – tends to be linked to firm size and survivability and not to wealth creation, and that managers often embrace survival and not value creation as the ultimate objective of the organization. These arguments are precisely those usually advanced to justify the hypothesis of size or budget maximization in government bureaus (Niskanen 1971).
3. Because both in relationships with outsiders (e.g., contractors and suppliers) and especially within the firm, contracts are difficult to monitor and/or unenforceable, relationships are typically based on loyalty or trust rather than on formal contractual relations. Where relationships are based on trust, rents are typically involved, since the distribution of rents is the basic way to accumulate trust or loyalty. Loyalty is the hallmark of bureaucratic relations.

Now, there are a number of different ways to analyze bureaucracy. One of these is Niskanen's (1971) model, in which bureaucrats, for reasons similar to those just listed, are assumed to maximize the size of the budget under their control. Caves and Krepps (1993) explicitly base their tests of downsizing on a version of Niskanen's hypothesis. Their hypothesis is that increased import competition and hostile takeovers act to reduce the rents available to be redistributed to employees and thus cause downsizing. However, they do not explain how either of these changes can cause a budget maximizer to downsize. This can result only from a change either in demand (which would cause any organization to downsize) or in control costs. In other words, they don't explain the internal mechanism by which a change in import competition or a takeover results in a change in behavior on the part of the firm's CEO. Otherwise, downsizing can occur if and only if the connection between the size of the organization and the manager's salary, prestige, and other executive emoluments is broken.

A second approach to analyzing bureaucracy originates in efficiency wage theory (e.g., Shapiro and Stiglitz 1984) and has recently been applied to the problem of downsizing by Gordon (1996). According to this line of thought, there are basically two ways to solve the problem of the divergence in incentives between employees and employers that arises whenever the performance of employees is difficult to monitor: the "cooperative" strategy, in which the loyalty of employees is bought through granting them high ("efficiency" or "no-shirking" wages), and the "conflictual" or "stick" strategy, in which employees are paid a wage just above their marginal products and monitored intensively to prevent shirking and other forms of disobedience to the "implicit" contract. Gordon suggests that countries typically develop industrial labor systems that can usefully be classified into two types corresponding to these two strategies.

The evidence cited by Gordon, as well as casual observation, certainly point to the existence of two forms of industrial systems. For example, the international labor organization (ILO) provides international data for the number and relative proportions of employees in "administrative and managerial" occupations (the "bureaucratic burden"). Comparing data for 1989, the bureaucratic burden was 13.0 percent in the U.S. and 12.9 percent in Canada. On the other hand, in Sweden it was 2.6 percent, in Norway 6.8, the Netherlands 4.3, Japan 4.2, Germany 3.9, Denmark 4.5, and Belgium 4.5 (cited in Gordon, p. 43). So the bureaucratic burden in the U.S. was the highest among countries compared, and there is a substantial difference in the ratio between Anglo-American or "stick" countries and the European or Japanese ("carrot") models.

Gordon explains downsizing as the increasing conversion, in the U.S., from the "carrot" to the "stick" strategy of industrial relations management. But a major problem with the analysis is that it doesn't explain why the U.S. companies waited until the 1980s to implement the change in strategy. What made the "stick" strategy more profitable in the 1980s, compared to, say, the 1950s? This point is addressed in the next section.

A third approach to understanding bureaucratic behavior focuses on trust within the firm or bureau (Breton and Wintrobe 1982; Wintrobe and Breton 1986). The importance of trust arises from the limits on formal contracting within organizations: contracts are typically too costly to specify in detail, and too difficult to enforce. The recognition of this point has become increasingly common in recent literature (e.g., La Porta et al. 1997). The special aspect of the Breton-Wintrobe model is its emphasis on the distribution of trust. In that model, some forms of trust reduce productivity within the firm (e.g., "horizontal" alliances among subordinates, which permit collusion among subordinates against their superiors). Other forms ("vertical" trust between superiors and subordinates) increase it. So firm productivity depends on the distribution of trust within the firm and not merely its level.

How would such changes as globalization or new technology affect trust relationships within the firm? To begin with globalization, it appears that the standard account described above leaves out some important aspects of this phenomenon that have featured prominently in many of the policy-oriented discussions of the issue. Dani Rodrik has recently suggested as much in his book *Has Globalization Gone Too Far?* (1997). He points out that it is not just trade with underdeveloped countries that advances with globalization, but also the possibility of importing from developed countries or of outsourcing anywhere. Competition comes not only from low-wage "emerging" markets but also from developed markets, rendering every firm"s market share less secure. Thus, Rodrik quotes Bhagwati's (1996) statement that

> what we're facing now is a new and steadily encroaching reality where the nature of comparative advantage is becoming thin, volatile, kaleidoscopic . . . The margins of competitive advantage have become thinner: a small shift in costs somewhere can now be deadly to your competitiveness. (Bhagwati 1996, cited in Rodrik 1997, p. 23)

Analytically, therefore, it is not so much the fall in demand for the products of developed countries as a result of imports from underdeveloped countries that is important, but *the increase in the elasticity of demand* that arises from the possibility of importing from, or outsourcing, *anywhere*. The evidence on trade described above does not include these effects, and so misses what might be the most important element in globalization.

The volatility of product demand curves as a consequence of globalization also results in greater volatility or instability in labor market outcomes (Rodrik 1997, pp. 19, 20). An increase in volatility in labor market outcomes has been well documented in the United States. Gottschalk and Moffitt (1994) show that one-third to one-half of the widening wage distribution from the 1970s to the 1990s can be attributed to the increase in the short-term variance in earnings (p. 218). Slaughter (1996) documents that the demand for labor in the United States has become more elastic since the 1960s in most two-digit manufacturing industries and that the elasticity of labor demand tends to be higher in industries that exhibit greater levels of international integration. Note that the relevant measure of openness in this context is not the volume of trade or investment but the ease with which international transactions can be carried out. So this hypothesis explains some, perhaps a substantial part, of the increased insecurity of workers as well as the fall in demand for the less skilled (who are most easily substituted for).

But while globalization is important in having these effects, other forces may operate in the same ways. Consider the recent analysis by Jensen (1993), who compares the current environment to the historical industrial revolution. He suggests that the scope and pace of the changes over the past two decades qualify the current situation as "a modern industrial revolution." The changes include deregulation, technology, organizational innovation (changes in telecommunications, including computer networks, e-mail, fax, etc.), globalization of trade, and the revolution of political economy (the conversion of formally closed, centrally planned socialist and communist economies to capitalism).

Now many of these changes, as well as some others (e.g., the spread of privatization), have the same implication as globalization, that is, they also cause an increase in the firm's elasticity of demand for its products, and therefore in the firm's elasticity of demand for labor. Increased competition means that every firm's market share is more insecure. Gottschalk and Moffit (1994), for example, speculate that the increase in earnings instability in the U.S. labor market is likely the result of such factors as the decline in regulation, the decline in unionization, the disappearance of administered prices, and general increases in both domestic and foreign competition (pp. 218–9).

For our purposes, the central question is the following one: What effects do such changes in import competition, technology, and deregulation have on trust relationships? The answer is straightforward: All of them imply that trust within the firm and with suppliers and customers is less valuable than before. The reason is that they all imply that expectations about a future relationship with employees (crucial to the maintenance of trust) are more tenuous, implying that employers will desire to invest less in trust capital with their employees. In short, the increase in competition resulting from stabilization, deregulation, and the other changes discussed here reduces the value of trust within the firm.

The fall in the value of trust within the firm raises a more subtle question: what happens to the trust capital that has already accumulated within the firm? As a result of the fall in the value of trust, the manager is free to appropriate the capital value of the existing trust assets, which were jointly held by the employer and the employees, and to appropriate these rents (the yield on these assets) to himself or redistribute them to shareholders. Downsizing facilitates this operation.[6] On this way of thinking, downsizing implies the shedding of unprofitable relationships with employees; it means *breaching* or *repudiating* trust, or to put it differently, breaking the implicit contract with employees whereby their loyal behavior in the past would ultimately have been rewarded with a share in the profits of the firm.[7] To illustrate this point, assume that at least some employees had accepted a wage less than their marginal productivity when they were young, in the expectation that they would receive wages in excess of productivity when they are older. Now the manager is in a position where it serves his interest to cheat on this promise. The firm no longer needs their loyalty; hence the collapse of loyalty which will result from the breach of trust is an acceptable price to pay for the windfall gains that will accrue from the repudiation of debt.[8] This explains why no increase in productivity is observed in downsizing firms: the breaching of trust destroys employee morale.[9]

Some documentation of the fall in morale can be found in surveys of

---

[6] Another way to breach trust is to reduce wages, as in the analysis of breach of trust in corporate takeovers by Shleifer and Summers (1988).

[7] Robert B. Reich, as U.S. secretary of labor, suggested that business has breached an "implicit social contract": "The most important part of the contract is that if the worker is reliable and if the company is making money, that worker keeps his or her job. The second principle is enjoying rising wages and benefits as a company"s profits improve. This social contract is no longer with us." (Quoted in Gordon, pp. 64–5)

[8] An additional implication of globalization that reinforces this implication is that the people at upper levels are themselves more mobile, and have less reason to be loyal to their communities and to their workforces, as discussed by Christopher Lasch (1995). The increased mobility of managers reinforces the decline in the need for trust with their labor force, and the incentive to cheat on the implicit contract.

[9] Jensen (1993) admits that breach of trust can have negative productivity implications but never addresses the implications of this point directly, except to assert that sometimes contracts should be broken.

the effects of downsizing by the American Management Association in 1994, reported by Gordon, who notes that

> Only a third of corporations reported that their downsizing had actually resulted in productivity gains: fully 30 percent reported that productivity had declined.... Far from generating uniform improvements in performance, one of the surveys concluded, "the surest after-effect of downsizing is a negative impact on employee morale"; 83 percent of corporations which had downsized between 1989 and 1991 reported that "employee morale had declined in 1994."[10]

In addition, it is worth pointing out that although there is very little evidence that the revolution in information technology has raised productivity, this does not mean it has not had important effects. In particular, one implication of the spread of fax, e-mail, and the world wide web is that it has become more difficult for those in authority to keep information secret, and much easier for those not in authority to provide information to each other and to the public. In politics, this fosters the expansion of civil society, and makes it more difficult for dictators and other politicians to govern through deceit. Within the firm, the spread of these technologies may be expected to have similar effects, that is, they foster the accumulation of trust among employees (horizontal trust) and make the accumulation and maintenance of trust with superiors (vertical trust) more difficult. This provides an additional reason for downsizing trust within the firm: in the future, it is rational to expect trust relationships to be different, and to contribute less to productivity, than in the past. And it supplies an explanation for why recent changes in technology have failed to increase productivity.

But what profit is there for the manager in breaching implicit contracts? I suggest that two avenues leading to increased executive compensation are opened up by the implementation of this strategy. One of these is related to that suggested by Shleifer and Summers in their analysis of wage cuts in takeovers. They explain hostile takeovers as a way of breaching (now unprofitable) implicit contracts. The takeover artist is capable of introducing wage cuts that the old manager could not, because the new CEO is not bound by the implicit contracts entered into by previous management. By imposing wage cuts, the new manager can transfer the rents of employees to shareholders: hence the share price of the firm may be expected to rise. The new manager will be motivated to do this to the extent that the basis for the new manager's compensation is or can be switched, so that, rather than being related to the size of the

---

[10] Gordon (1996), p. 59, survey quoted from Hedrick Smith, *Rethinking America* (New York: Random House, 1995).

firm, it is based on the firm's stock price via shares, stock options, and so forth.

Alternatively, instead of imposing wage cuts, management could downsize the firm. On this scenario, rents are redistributed from employees and customers to shareholders, with the manager taking his cut. With either wage cuts or downsizing, the stock price can be expected to rise, even though there is no increase in productivity. However, the change in the firm's stock price does not factor in the losses to workers of their rents, or to the community if relation-specific capital is lost. Consequently, the analysis implies that the increase in the stock price of the target firm, usually quite large in hostile takeovers,[11] is not an appropriate indicator of the change in social value, which may in fact be negative if workers and the community lose more than shareholders gain.

Now there is another, simpler scenario that does not require the stock price to increase at all for downsizing to be an attractive strategy to managers. The basic idea is that one constraint on executive compensation is that unseemly increases in executive compensation, for example, those granted at the same time as the wages of employees are being cut, or when employees are being laid off, would tend to reduce trust within the firm. Consequently, to the extent that the manager wishes to preserve productivity, trust with his or her employees constrains executive compensation. This constraint disappears as trust within the firm is dispensed with.

To see how this strategy – which will be referred to as *repudiation of trust* – works, start with the fact that an implicit contract between managers and employees means that both managers and employees expect to share in the fortunes of the firm: they both expect to see their compensation increase in good times, and decline in bad times. The convention of tying the compensation of executives and employees to the size or growth rate of the firm, however imperfect these indexes may be as proxies for actual productivity, is one way of implementing this contract. Moreover, from the point of view of shareholders, linking executive compensation to size or growth provides a control over the compensation of executives, since it provides an objective benchmark to "meter" their productivity. In the absence of simple indices like size, what prevents executives from unilaterally increasing their own compensation? The board of directors will have to ratify any new compensation package, but, in most U.S. companies at least, the board is largely passive, in the pocket

---

[11] Estimates of the premium paid in hostile takeovers for shares of the target firm are very large, in the range of 20 to 30 percent. See, for example, the pioneering studies by Bradley (1980) and Roll (1986), confirmed by subsequent studies, e.g., Varian (1988).

of the manager, and does not pose much of a constraint.[12] The opposition of shareholders is unlikely to pose a problem, especially if the firm is widely held, but possibly even if it is not, since even a doubling or tripling of the compensation of a handful of senior executives would not reduce the value of the firm by much, and is easily justified if it can be argued that the resulting increase in executive motivation might result in the share price rising by even a small percentage over what it would have done otherwise. Of course, in widely held firms, even if shareholders were opposed, there would be very little they could do about it.

Matters are very different when changes in executive compensation act as a "signal" for changes in the compensation of a large number of employees, as an implicit contract in effect specifies. Making size a proxy for the compensation of all employees is a simple way to implement this contract.[13]

[12] See, for example, Jensen's comments (1993, p. 850 and pp. 852–4) and his extensive list of references (p. 850) on the failure of internal control systems headed by boards of directors.

[13] One interesting case of downsizing is that of General Dynamics, discussed in Dial and Murphy (1995). Their article describes how, in 1991, defense contractor General Dynamics engaged a new management team that adopted an explicit corporate objective of creating "shareholder value." The key was appointing the ex-astronaut William Anders to the position of CEO. Anders first negotiated a compensation package for himself, and then a package to stimulate the interests of top executives in downsizing. For the twenty-five top executives, the so-called "gain-sharing plan" meant they would get cash bonuses for each ten-dollar increase in the company stock price equal to 100 percent of their base salaries if the stock price stayed at or above this level for ten consecutive trading days. For each subsequent ten-dollar increase sustained for ten consecutive trading days the executives would receive additional bonuses equal to 200 percent of their base salaries. This package for executives in place, the corporation was downsized, to the extent of laying off 73 percent of its workforce over the next three years.

Paying large executive cash bonuses amid massive layoffs ignited controversy. As one commentator put it, "The CEO of General Dynamics must be the laziest man in the world. Look at all the incentive plans they have to give him to go to work in the morning." (Alison Leigh Cowan, "The Gadfly CEO's Want to Swat," *New York Times*, February 2, 1992, quoted in Dial and Murphy, p. 282).

By 1993 shareholders realized gains approaching 4.5 billion dollars, representing a dividend-reinvested return of 553 percent. Dial and Murphy assert that the study "demonstrates that even firms in declining industries have substantial opportunities for value creation." But the story is also consistent with the idea that value is being redistributed rather than created as in the Shleifer-Summers hypothesis. And in some aspects, in particular, in the behavior of its CEO the story fits the repudiation hypothesis. Thus, in agreeing to take his position, "One of Anders' chief concerns was to secure his independence from General Dynamics' largest shareholder, the Crown family, which held 22 percent of the outstanding shares. Anders viewed the existence of the major shareholder as an obstacle rather than a benefit. . . . He secured a contract which, in his words, would make him able to "retire on the day I walked in here." (Dial and Murphy, p. 269). This is not the usual way to establish a trust relationship.

In short, the implicit contract between employers and employees also acts as a constraint on executive compensation. Once the link between the compensation of executives and the compensation of employees is broken, executives are free to exploit their bargaining power vis-à-vis shareholders. They no longer have to worry about adverse effects on productivity from the loss of trust with employees, nor about automatically triggering generalized wage increases which could have adverse effects on stock prices or for other reasons attract the concern of shareholders. On this account, downsizing frees the manager to exploit further his discretionary power vis-à-vis shareholders.[14]

> Another way to look at it is to imagine what would have happened to productivity if bonuses comparable to those given to executives had been made available to employees generally. It is also worth mentioning that defense contractor General Dynamics is not exactly the prototype of an industry selling in a competitive market, and with no connections to the government. Anders was named CEO on January 1, 1991. In early February 1991, the federal government allowed General Dynamics and McDonnell Douglas to delay repayment of 1.4 billion dollars in liquidated progress payments made on the cancelled A12 plane. The company had claimed that repayment would cause "extreme financial pressures," a claim that many downsized employees presumably would have liked to assert to General Dynamics. The Gulf War began in the air on January 17, and the four-day ground war on February 24. Dial and Murphy note that "GD's marquee products, 'Tomahawk' cruise missiles, F-16 fighters, and M-1 'Abrams' tanks performed spectacularly." It would be interesting to know if their performance was as inflated by the Pentagon as that of the Patriot missile proved to have been.

[14] Since this paper was written and circulated (March 1998), a new and important article has appeared (Hallock 1998) that provides some empirical evidence on some of the issues discussed here. Hallock tests the relationship between layoffs, executive pay, and stock prices for a sample of 550 of America's top-paid executives over the period 1989–95. Consistent with the argument of this paper, CEOs heading firms with recent layoff announcements do enjoy substantially larger pay increases than those who do not. However, Hallock argues that this result is artificial. The fact that there is a correlation between layoffs and CEO pay does not imply causation. In particular, he notes that large firms tend to pay their executives more and also to have higher layoffs. Including the size effect and a number of other firm-specific effects, Hallock argues, removes the correlation between CEO pay and layoffs. Interestingly, Hallock also finds, consistent with previous studies, that the stock market reacts negatively to the announcement of layoffs. However, he provides no explanation for the negative evaluation by the stock market. It is clearly consistent with the repudiation of trust hypothesis advanced here (though not with the breach hypothesis). It is inconsistent with the hypothesis that layoffs raise productivity. Nor does Hallock provide a theory as to why large firms pay more. In fact, *all* employee salaries tend to be larger in larger firms, not just that of the CEO. From the point of view of the repudiation of trust hypothesis advanced here, it is precisely the large firms where we would expect managers to be most interested in breaking the connections between their own salary and variables such as the size of the firm and the salaries of junior employees. So these are not fixed effects which have no relationship to causation, which is the way Hallock interprets them. They are constraints on executive compensation. The larger the firm, the more likely repudiation of trust will

To summarize, I have suggested two strategies whereby managers can increase their compensation: (1) breaching trust to the advantage of shareholders, and (2) repudiating trust with both employees and shareholders. The remaining question is that posed and answered in general by efficiency wage theory and specifically by Gordon: in the absence of trust, how does the organization function? As Gordon suggests, there is an alternative: the "stick" strategy. The firm substitutes more careful monitoring for trust. This would explain the continued growth in the bureaucratic burden over the period of downsizing: supervisors and other personnel are now required to police employees who formerly were trusted to perform their tasks. It also explains the timing of the "norm shift" in wage determination in the 1980s discussed by Gordon and referred to by many other observers of corporate behavior, including Mitchell (1985) and Howell (1994). It is a consequence of the fall in the value of trust within organizations generated by all the forces discussed here, notably deregulation, globalization, and technological change.

With respect to technology, it is worth emphasizing that there is a big difference between the explanation advanced here of how technological change can cause downsizing and the usual one, which focuses on skill-biased technological change. Thus, Krugman finds the following to be compelling evidence in favor of the standard technology story:

> In 1979, a young man with a college degree and five years on the job earned only 30 percent more than one with similar experience and a high school degree; by 1989, the premium had jumped to 74 percent. If the technology of the economy had not changed, this sharp increase in the relative cost of skilled workers would have given employers a strong incentive to cut back and substitute less-skilled workers where they could. In fact, exactly the opposite happened. Across the board, employers *raised* the average skill level of their work forces.[15]

On this account, the change in employment patterns is simply a rational response to technological change, and is somehow inevitable. Technological change is all there is to it. The account proposed here is different: technological change can be responded to in a number of different ways, *one* of which is by breaching or repudiating

be an attractive strategy for CEOs. Similarly, the more "bureaucratic" the firm, i.e., the tighter the link between the salary of the CEO and that of his employees, the more eager an ambitious CEO, chafing at the constraint on his compensation package, will be to break the link between his salary and theirs by adopting the repudiation of trust strategy.

[15] Krugman (1996), p. 197.

trust, that is, by breaking the implicit contract with unskilled workers, downsizing, and substituting supervision of those remaining for a trust relationship.

Moreover, the implications of the theories differ. The key piece of evidence that would make the standard story compelling is evidence of productivity growth. Again, this has yet to be produced. The breach of trust hypothesis, applied to downsizing, does not imply an initial increase in productivity, and in the long run it is consistent with a fall in productivity, as employees become distrustful of their employers and unwilling to invest in relation-specific capital within the company. With respect to the repudiation of trust, this argument implies that trust falls throughout the company. The effect of this change on productivity depends, in the Breton-Wintrobe model, on the character of the trust relationships within the firm. Productivity will *fall* if trust was primarily vertical in the first place, and *rise* otherwise. Consequently, the repudiation hypothesis implies an inverse correlation between the *change in productivity* in downsizing firms and their *initial productivity*. That is, productivity in highly productive firms will fall as a result of downsizing, while the fortunes of low-productivity firms would more likely improve as a result of the process. So the three theories have very different implications with respect to productivity, and could be confronted with the evidence on this question.

Finally, it is worth pointing out that there are some other ways in which the "modern industrial revolution" reduces trust in society, for example, through the political process. Rodrik (1997, pp. 24–25) points out that a key component of the implicit social bargain in the advanced industrial countries has been the provision of social insurance and safety nets at home (unemployment compensation, severance payments, and adjustment assistance, for example) in exchange for the adoption of freer trade policies. He provides some evidence for this point of view by showing that there has been a strong correlation between a country"s openness to international trade and the size of its government. To illustrate the point, it is in the most open countries, such as Denmark, the Netherlands, and Sweden, that spending on income transfers has expanded the most.

As already explained, both the increased elasticity of demand for labor and the enhanced global mobility of managers make them less dependent on the goodwill of the local workforce. This reduces the demand for trust through the political process, as well as within the firm, and undermines the willingness of employers to assist their employees through the tax-transfer system. In the same way, increased trade and investment opportunities make it more costly for workers to achieve a high level of labor standards and benefits. These changes reinforce the effects discussed previously in lowering the demand for trust throughout society.

4   Conclusion

In this chapter, I first considered the standard explanations of downsizing, namely, that it is the result of increased trade with low-wage countries or of skill-biased technological change, and suggested that both of these explanations are flawed. I then advanced the notion that the phenomenon of downsizing is best understood by considering the firm as a bureaucracy, and in particular by looking at the firm as an organization in which relationships are based on trust, as they are in any bureaucracy. Globalization, technological change, and deregulation make trust relationships within the firm more dispensable. Downsizing is then analyzed as a way either of breaching trust once it is no longer profitable, and transferring the rents earned from it to shareholders, or simply of repudiating it, a way of freeing the manager from constraints on executive compensation. On either the repudiation or the breach of trust hypothesis about downsizing, the fall in the incomes of low-wage Americans and the increase in executive compensation are directly related, and not separate phenomena, as is implicit in standard theories. On the hypotheses advanced here, downsizing is precisely a strategy for raising executive compensation.

The effects on productivity are also different from those given by the standard (efficiency driven) hypothesis: For example, on the repudiation of trust hypothesis, downsizing simply lowers trust within the firm, and will therefore lower productivity in firms where trust relationships are primarily productive (vertical), and raise it where the opposite is the case. Seen in this light, the forces motivating downsizing are all of those forces that reduce the value of trust, such as globalization and computerization. These forces make it more difficult or less profitable to accumulate and maintain the forms of trust that are productive from the organization's point of view, and open up the possibility for executives to raise their salaries by firing their employees.

References

Baily, Martin Neil, Eric J. Bartelsman, and John Haltiwanger, "Downsizing and Productivity Growth: Myth or Reality?", National Bureau of Economic Research Working Paper No. 4741, 1994.

Blinder, Alan S., and Richard E. Quandt, "Technology: The Computer and the Economy," *Altantic Monthly*, 280, no. 6 (December 1997): 26–32.

Bradley, M., "Interfirm Offers and the Market for Corporate Control," *Journal of Business*, 53(1980): 345–376.

Breton, Albert, and Ronald Wintrobe, *The Logic of Bureaucratic Conduct.* New York: Cambridge University Press, 1982.

Caves, Richard, and Matthew Krepps, "Fat: The Displacement of Nonproduction Workers from U.S. Manufacturing Industries," *Brookings Papers on Economic Activity*, 1993(2): 227–273.

Cline, William R. *Trade and Wage Inequality.* Washington, D.C.: Institute for International Economics, 1997.

Davis, Steven J., and Robert H. Topel, "Comment," *Brookings Papers on Economic Activity*, 1993(2): 214–221.

Dial, J., and K. J. Murphy, "Incentives, Downsizing and Value Creation at General Dynamics," *Journal of Financial Economics*, 37(1995): 261–314.

Frank, Robert, and Philip J. Cook, *The Winner Take All Society.* New York: The Free Press, 1995.

Freeman, Richard, "Will Globalization Dominate U.S. Market Outcomes?", in Susan Collins, *Imports, Exports, and the American Worker.* Washington: Brookings Institution, 1996.

Gordon, David, *Fat and Mean: The Corporate Squeeze of Working Americans and the Myth of Managerial Downsizing.* New York: Simon and Schuster, 1996.

Gottschalk, Peter, and Robert Moffitt, "The Growth of Earnings Instability in the U.S. Labor Market," *Brookings Papers on Economic Activity,* 2(1994): 217–273.

Hallock, Kevin F., "Layoffs, Top Executive Pay, and Firm Performance," *American Economic Review*, 88(1998): 711–723.

Howell, David R., "The Skills Myth" *American Prospect*, Summer 1994: 81–89.

Jensen, Michael C., "Presidential Address: The Modern Industrial Revolution, Exit, and the Failure of Internal Control Systems," *Journal of Finance,* 48(1993): 831–880.

Krugman, Paul, *Peddling Prosperity.* New York: Norton, 1994.

Pop Internationalism. Boston: MIT Press, 1996.

La Porta, Rafael, Florencio Lopez-de Silanes, Andrei Shleifer, and Robert W. Vishny, "Trust in Large Organizations," *American Economic Review*, 87, no. 2 (1997): 333–338.

Lasch, Christopher, *The Revolt of the Elites and the Betrayal of Democracy.* New York: Norton, 1995.

Lawrence, Robert Z., and Matthew Slaughter. "Trade and U.S. Wages in the 1980s: Giant Sucking Sound or Small Hiccup?" *Brookings Papers on Economic Activity (Microeconomics)* (1993): 161–210.

Mitchell, Daniel A. B., "Shifting Norms in Wage Determination," *Brookings Papers on Economic Activity*, 2(1985): 575–599.

Niskanen, William, *Bureaucracy and Representative Government.* New York: Aldine-Atherton, 1971.

Oliner, Stephen D., and Daniel E. Sichel, "Computers and Output Growth: How Big is the Puzzle?" *Brookings Papers on Economic Activity*, 1994(2): 273–317.

Rodrik, Dani, *Has Globalizaton Gone Too Far?* Washington, D.C.: Institute for International Economics, 1997.

Roll, R., "The Hubris Hypothesis of Corporate Takeovers," *Journal of Business*, 59(1986):197–216.

Shapiro, Carl, and Joseph Stiglitz. "Equilibrium Unemployment as a Worker Discipline Device," *American Economic Review*, 74 (June 1984): 433–444.

Shleifer, Andrei, and Lawrence Summers, "Breach of Trust in Hostile Takeovers," in Alan J. Auerbach, *Corporate Takeovers: Causes and Consequences.* Chicago: University of Chicago Press, 1988.

Slaughter, Matthew. "International Trade and Labor-Demand Elasticities," unpublished paper, Dartmouth College, 1996.

Varian, H. (ed.), "Symposium on Takeovers," *Journal of Economic Perspectives*, 2(1988).

Wintrobe, Ronald, "Modern Bureaucratic Theory," in Dennis Mueller, ed., *Perspectives in Public Choice.* New York: Cambridge University Press, 1997.

  The Political Economy of Dictatorship, New York: Cambridge University Press, 1998.

  and Albert Breton, "Organizational Structure and Productivity," *American Economic Review*, 76(1986): 530–538.

Wood, Adrian. *North-South Trade, Employment, and Inequality: Changing Fortunes in a Skill-Driven World*. Oxford: Clarendon Press, 1994.

CHAPTER 3

Information and political decision makers

Jean-Dominique Lafay

Governing politicians (GPs) essentially produce decisions.[1] And they are often maintained in power (voted for in a democracy) on the basis of the perceived quality of these decisions. We shall consider here two polar decision processes between which the GPs may choose: a *self-decision-making* process, and a *delegation* process. In the first case, the GPs take decisions by themselves, based on their already held or specially acquired information. Decisions are transmitted through precise orders to the implementing bureaucracies. Indeed, some difficulties may appear at the level of this transmission process, but the main problem remains, as for any central planner, how to obtain sufficient and relevant information, from bureaucracies, from experts, or from any other source.

In the second, delegation case, the GP behaves as a principal, and only reveals broad preferences (or objectives) and specific constraints to a bureaucratic agent, who is then delegated the decision responsibility. The information costs are clearly minimized here. However, the price to pay is that the GP now faces an agency problem, which originates in the resulting asymmetric information.[2]

On the basis of the economic theory of bureaucracy (Blais and Dion eds. 1991, Breton 1996), or of the theory of incentives and decentralization (Caillaud, Jullien, and Picard 1996, Gilbert and Picard 1996), theoretical developments have focused more on the agency problem (how an

---

[1] Cf. Boulding (1966): "The problem of government policy is just a problem in decision-making."

[2] Another important case is the *decentralization* process. It presents some aspects of a delegation process, but it also has its own characteristics. First, the decentralized decision makers have to respect central constraints rather than follow central discretionary objectives. Second, the decentralized decision makers, who are generally elected, at least in democracies, are directly accountable to public opinion. To simplify matters, the decentralization case will be ignored here.

uninformed principal controls – or does not control – the final output of his agents) than on the mere activity of the bureaucracy as a producer of informational inputs (i.e., intermediate goods) for political decisions. Indeed, information is central in both cases, but its role is very different. In the delegation case, the bureaucracy is an agent producing final public goods. The aim of the GPs, as of any principal, is to obtain information about what the agent *does* – about his productive efficiency – and/or about the rent he earns, through direct control, bureaucratic competition, or supervisors' reports. In the self-decision-making case, the bureaucracy *produces* information as an input necessary for adequate decisions. The central problem involves the adequacy, the quality, and the cost of what the bureaucracy provides to the GPs, rather than the way it is produced.

As a matter of fact, many public policies are of a nondelegated nature, that is, they are submitted to direct decision making by governing politicians. For example, most foreign policy decisions and emergency interventions fall into this category. Many decisions concerning public communication, which aim at producing politically efficient information to the electorate, to interest groups, to national and foreign institutions, and so forth, are also concerned.

The first section of this chapter studies policies resulting from self-decision-making by the GPs and the question of the choice between self-decision-making and delegation. The second section examines the type of information which is used by the GPs, the possible biases contained in it, and how these biases can be remedied. The third section summarizes.

I   Information for self-decision-making politicians, and comparison to the delegation option

In the following analysis, "information" is assumed to be a simple contingent good, which permits to revise a decision. The value of this information depends on the expected gains from this decision, evaluated on the basis of the updated beliefs (and given that the value of any information depends on the stock of knowledge previously accumulated by the decision maker – cf. Aidt 1998 on this point).

I-1   *The optimal degree of information*

We consider a simplified public sector, with a single unified group of political decision makers (the GPs) and a single bureaucracy (B), which is assumed to be their only source of external "private" information. The *degree of information* of the GPs, *i*, varies between 0 – no external private information – and 1 – full information. It is supposed to vary continuously between these two extreme values and to be twice differentiable. The variable *i* measures the degree of efficient information, that is, information checked, selected, and adequately processed. Indeed, a significant share of crude information is systematically biased, either because of deliberate manipulation by the providers or because of some idiosyncratic factors. It is assumed that adequate corrections are made before computing the value of *i*.

The technical *quality of the decision* depends on the degree of information gathered to take it: $d = d(i)$. *d* is normalized between 0 and 1. $d(1) = 1$ corresponds to the full information case, and $d(0) = 0$ to a decision made with no information except free common knowledge and the private information already acquired by the GPs (drawn from their own informational capital, from the existing political channels, or from interest-group demands).

The benefits brought by a given project are assumed to depend only on its scale (*H* being the scale factor) and on the quality of the decision (which depends in turn on *i*):

$$B = B(d(i), H) - B(d(0), H) \tag{1}$$

(The marginal impact of *i* on d – $\delta d/\delta i$ – and the marginal benefit of a higher decision quality – $\delta B/\delta d$ – are assumed to be positive and decreasing.)

Benefits depend on the shape of the utility function of the GPs. This shape need not be more detailed here: politicians may be benevolent welfarists as well as egoistic maximizers, trying to get reelected, or to increase the rents associated with their present and future positions.

The total cost function for a decision of quality *d* concerning a project of size *H* is continuous and twice differentiable, as follows:

$$C = C(i, H), \text{ with } C(0, H) = 0 \tag{2}$$

(The marginal cost of *i* is assumed positive and increasing.) Information corresponds then to "ready-to-use" information, so that the decision maker does not bear any costs other than those displayed in (2), except perhaps the (negligible) costs associated with the formal calculus necessary to determinate the corresponding optimum decision. For simplicity's sake, and without loss of generality, we suppose that private information is provided exclusively by the bureaucracy (the GPs don't resort to private providers for this particular good). Information corresponds to any piece of information that is acquired at a positive opportunity cost, including the time spent to gather and process it (i.e., information not already owned by GPs and that is not common knowledge). $d(1) = 1$ is assumed to be an upper limit for the quality of decisions. This means that no other institutional system, notably no delegation of the decision-making responsibility, can lead to better decisions than those made by perfectly informed GPs. This corresponds to the Revelation Principle (Myerson 1979), which says that a centralized decision-making system weakly dominates a decentralized one under perfect information.

The optimal value of i (degree of information) is the value that maximizes (1) minus (2), with the usual first-order conditions:

$$(\delta B/\delta d) \cdot (\delta d/\delta i) = \delta C/\delta i \qquad (3)$$

For a given value of H (the scale variable), (3) corresponds to i^* and d^* in Figure 3.1.

As Figure 3.1 illustrates, the information demand of the GPs on the bureaucracy may vary considerably, according to the shape of the cost and benefit functions. Some decisions may correspond to a very low optimal degree of information:

- The benefits of a better decision may be low. If, for example, rationally uninformed voters are unable to detect the true effects of a decision, investment in pure persuasion (in framing and "marketing" the announced policy) tends to be more politically efficient than investment in information.
- The speed of a given decision may sometimes be crucial. Hence the delay necessary to collect all the relevant data will quickly become prohibitive.
- When information is too costly and/or too technical, simplifying methods ("satisficing" criteria, rules of thumb, or even random choice) will dominate theoretical ones.

This could explain why many economists engaged in governmental advising feel disappointed. But this disappointment simply reveals that (1) they underestimate the information costs and delays required by a technically adequate answer according to their own standards, and that (2) their so-called *scientific* analysis is perhaps not so scientific, inasmuch as it ignores the potential conflict between "economic" and "political" objectives.[3]

---

[3] Tollison's argument, that the practical role of economic advisers is not much more than to avoid a few decisions that "are totally stupid, simply totally stupid" (Tollison in Allen 1977:81), is perhaps not as provocative as it looks. It may simply reflect their systematic ignorance of the true utility functions of the political decision makers.

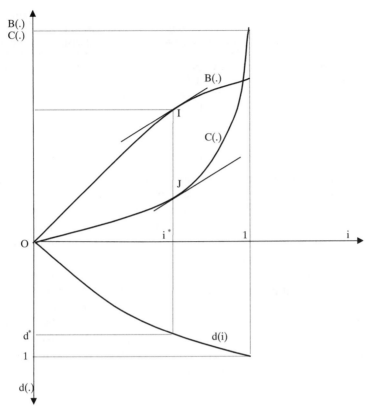

Figure 3.1. The optimal degree of information for a nondelegated decision and the resulting quality of this decision.

$B(.) = B(d(i),H) - B(d(0),H)$ are the benefits provided by a decision of quality d, for a project of scale H.

$C(.) = C(i,H)$ are the costs for a degree of information i and a project of scale H (nondelegated decision).

$d(.) = d(i)$ determines the quality of a nondelegated decision as a function of the degree of information.

I-2   *Self-decision-making by governing politicians versus delegating decisions*

Instead of collecting the relevant information and making decisions on their own, the GPs can delegate some decision rights to the bureaucracy. In fact, they may choose between three types of decision processes:

	Accountability for the decision	Responsibility for the decision	Information relevant for the decision
Self-decision-making	Governing politicians	Governing politicians	Bureaucracy
Delegation	Governing politicians	Bureaucracy	Bureaucracy
Decentralization	Local governments	Bureaucracy or local governments	Bureaucracy

Because we don't treat the question of political decentralization, the GPs always remain politically accountable for all the decisions considered in our analysis, even those taken at lower bureaucratic tiers (while, in a decentralized process, political accountability concerns, at least to a large extent, the elected local decision makers – local GPs – and no longer the central authorities – national GPs).

Also, the analysis is limited to the two polar cases (full self-decision-making or full delegation) only for simplicity's sake. Actually, there are several possible degrees of delegation, if not a continuum. Delegation can be limited to "small" or "medium" decisions, the GPs returning to a self-decision-making system for the "important" ones (for example, the delegate is allowed to decide and to pay without special authorization only up to a certain threshold).

Figure 3.2 illustrates the case where the GPs delegate the decision-making capacity to the bureaucracy, and compares it to the self-decision-making situation.

Benefits: The *B* curve is the same as in Figure 3.1, for a similar project of similar (and given) *H* size. The benefits of decisions accrue to the GPs, no matter who makes them. Moreover, the GPs are judged on the basis of the "quality" of the decisions, no matter who makes them in reality.[4]

Costs: From the point of view of the GPs, delegation is a double source of costs: (1) it implies a larger budget for the bureaucracy, in order to pay for the costs of decisions that it now makes, and (2) the GPs have to communicate information to the delegated bureaucracy about their preferences, their objectives, and about some constraints initially unknown to the bureaucrats (these latter costs are mainly political costs – i.e., the GPs must reveal information that they would prefer to keep

---

[4] This means among other things that we disregard the possibility of a "scapegoat effect," in which the government can escape part of its responsibility by attributing bad decisions to the delegated bureaucracy.

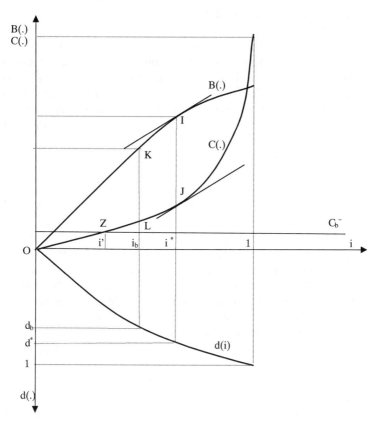

Figure 3.2. Choice between delegated and nondelegated decisions.
$B(.) = B(d(i),H) - B(d(0),H)$ are the benefits provided by a decision of quality
d, for a project of scale H.
$C(.) = C(i,H)$ are the costs for a degree of information i and a project of scale
H (nondelegated decision).
$C_b = C_b\tilde{\ }$ are the (fixed) budgetary costs of delegating a decision to the bureaucracy.
$d(.) = d(i)$ determines the quality of a nondelegated decision as a function of the
degree of information.

secret). Without loss of generality, these costs are assumed to be fixed
$(C_b = C_b\tilde{\ })$ – as if the politicians were paying a given fee for being
discharged of specific decision making. The former $C(.)$ curve in Figure
3.1 is also drawn on Figure 3.2 to have a measure of the opportunity
costs of delegation: if the delegated bureaucracy makes a decision of
quality d_b, the GPs would have to benefit from a degree of information

$i = d^{-1}(d_b)$, with a cost $C(i,H)$, to obtain the same quality through self-decision-making.

Bureaucratic equilibrium: In the delegation case, the bureaucracy – not the GPs – chooses the decision quality d_b for a given project. This choice is a function of its utility function and of its capacity to extract an agency rent from its principal. How d_b is determined is not explicitly derived here. It is, however, clear that (1) d_b is (weakly) inferior to 1 (revelation principle), and that (2) d_b can be higher or lower than d^*, according to the shape of the different curves. This second point means that bureaucratic delegation can lead to higher- as well as lower-quality decisions than self-made decisions by GPs.

Choice between options: Two steps may be distinguished in the choice between delegation and self-decision-making. In a first step, the GPs check whether the (expected) level of quality, d_b, retained by the delegated bureaucracy can be obtained at lower cost by self-decision-making (i.e., whether $C(d^{-1}(d_b),H) < C_b^\sim$). If i' is the value for which $C(d^{-1}(d_b),H) = C_b^\sim$ (point Z in Figure 3.2), the delegation solution is dominated for any $i = d^{-1}(d_b)$ between 0 and i'. But, if $i = d^{-1}(d_b)$ is to the right of i', the choice between the two options can be made only in a second step, by comparing the values of the respective net benefits. For example, in Figure 3.2, IJ is (slightly) larger than KL, so that the self-decision-making solution wins, but indeed the reverse could have been true.

Several economists, after Friedrich Hayek, have raised doubts about the capacity of centralized decision makers, politicians, and bureaucratic planners to gather and use efficiently all the necessary information, particularly information on allocative effects. They give strong arguments for limiting the responsibilities of big, centralized governments, and for promoting delegation (and federalism, and decentralization). From a strictly technical point of view, the evidence is not so one-sided:

1. Centralization indeed increases the costs of information transmission, but it also decreases the costs of information processing. Moreover, it economizes on an important type of information cost, that is, the cost associated with the obligation of the GPs to reveal their preferences, objectives, and some constraints initially unknown to the bureaucracy.

2. If delegation increases the total communication capacity of the public system, by using a more efficient aggregation of information incorporated in final decisions, it is for the GPs at the cost of losing control on the delegated agency (Caillaud, Jullien, and Picard 1996). From a social welfare point of view, this loss of control may have advantages, improving checks and balances

and reinforcing the division of power. But, for the GPs, it is generally a cost, simply because it makes their political destiny more or less dependent on choices in which they don't participate (though with a partial compensation, the possibility for the GPs to take the delegated bureaus as scapegoats).

3. For some decisions, the GPs have much more private information than the bureaucracy, so that the information costs are at the disadvantage of the latter. This is generally true for all questions concerning general coordination (the potential external effects of a decision and the impact of other expected decisions on it). Also, the GPs are in a much better position to obtain at low cost highly relevant information about the preferences and reactions of public opinion, through political channels or thanks to information delivered at no cost by interest groups.[5]

4. An often-advanced advantage of centralized organizations is their higher speed of reaction and their reliability in coordination (Bolton and Farrell 1990). This point, though it concerns more the capacity to decide (i.e., the shape of the $d(i)$ curve in Figures 3.1 and 3.2) than the strict capacity to provide quickly relevant information, may be crucial for several categories of decisions. As a general rule, delegation is more efficient in situations with less urgency.

5. As the "peak-decision unit," GPs benefit from their legitimacy. This allows them to obtain bargaining solutions more quickly and to implement them more easily. Indeed, this last aspect is less important if the political regime is unstable and/or if the political class is discredited. Bureaucracy then has a tendency to replace the GPs as the legitimate authority, as during the French Fourth Republic (1945–1958).

6. The GPs may finally have an absolute preference for making "big decisions" themselves, simply because almost everyone usually prefers to be at the helm when his or her basic interests are concerned.

The choice will also crucially depend on the distance between the preferences of the GPs and those of the bureaucratic agent, at least as this is perceived by the GPs. If this distance is small, then d' (the bureaucratic decision) will not differ much from d^* (the best self-made decision from the point of view of the GPs, after collecting the adequate information). Hence, because the GPs do not incur specific information

---

[5] Indeed, it has a cost for the interest group that sends the message, but this cost is also in itself a means to signal his preferences (cf. Potters and van Winden 1990).

costs, delegation will generally dominate self-decision-making. This situation may happen "spontaneously," or because the incentive structure and/or the control mechanisms work efficiently (through bureau or public manager competition, for example; see Breton and Wintrobe 1982 and Breton 1996). In a sense, the "spoils system" that some countries practice systematically and extensively can be seen as a means to reduce the distance between the GPs and the (delegated) bureaucratic agents.

In some cases, the delegation can easily be reversed, so that the threat of putting an end to the delegation of a given bureau, if it exploits its agency position too much, is credible. A kind of institutional contestability may be at work there. There is always a clear limit to the "low" quality of delegated decisions: it corresponds to the point below which the self-decision mechanism appears more beneficial (despite its higher informational costs). This neglected form of bureaucratic control certainly has more practical influence than is generally supposed.

II   Information required for policy decisions: Possible biases and possible remedies

II-1   *Information for policy making*

As a general rule, private decentralized decisions in the marketplace demand much less private information than public decisions. There is no need for any public revelation of individual preferences, and the price system provides at no or low cost most of the relevant information. On the contrary, public decisions, whatever their objectives may be, generally necessitate a huge amount of private information, and this information is dispersed among all the individuals in the society.

Economic policy decisions, for example, necessitate detailed information not only about their expected effects in the three Musgravian technical domains (stabilization, allocation, and redistribution), but also about the possible reactions of public opinion and market participants, because of the major role played by expectations, in both the economic *and* political spheres. Finally, if errors are very costly and/or if the decision is easy to reverse, it will be judicious to gather detailed and up-to-date information about the implementation process regarding a given policy.

Information on stabilizing effects: Most governments have bureaus and advisers specialized in macroeconomic analysis that are able to inform them at low cost about the stabilizing (or destabilizing) effects of a given decision. Though the quality of this information is uneven (depending on the quality of the models used, on the capacity to gather information quickly, and on the ability to implement the decided policy quickly), the situation here is similar to the one observed in any firm.[6]

Information on allocative effects: The allocative aspects of public decisions are very different from those observed in private firms. Rational allocation of public goods and the correction of externalities require a detailed knowledge of the marginal rates of substitution of all the citizens.[7] The information task is demanding here, because of the large number of citizens, and more importantly, because of the free-riding problem that impedes voluntary revelation of individual preferences. This information problem concerns all politicians – those who, as welfarists, spontaneously aim at establishing better "Wicksellian connections" (Breton 1996), as well as self-interested politicians who, in order to stay in power, need to have an idea of the distance between what they decide and individual "bliss points".[8] One must recognize, however, that the information problem in public decision making is often overstated (Milgrom and Weber 1983). Simple techniques may strongly reduce information costs. Statistical sampling permits, for example, much low-cost learning about a large population. Another cost-reducing technique is to choose at random a few "benchmark" individuals, to subsidize them for revelation of private information, and to observe what is feasible for the remaining population. Notwithstanding, information in the allocative domain remains the most difficult to obtain, and many policy decisions,

---

[6] Some macroeconomic predictive errors may have huge political consequences. For example, President Chirac's decision (in April 1997) to dissolve the French Parliament (where the right-wing coalition had a majority) was largely inspired by a report made at the beginning of 1997 by the French treasury. The conclusion of this report was that the French government could not avoid tax increases and restrictive measures if it were to respect the European 3 percent limit on national fiscal deficits in 1998. Because of this expected worsening of the economic situation, advanced general elections in May 1997 were judged a less bad choice than general elections at their normal date (March 1998). Not only were the elections lost, but income growth, and hence tax receipts, were much higher than predicted, so that the 1998 governmental public budget has been in fact very easy to build for the new left-wing government.

[7] Equalizing the relative prices of public and private goods with the *sum* of individual marginal rates of substitution, as Samuelson's theorem implies, requires a knowledge of all these individual marginal rates.

[8] One may think that, in a median voter framework, politicians who seek to be elected only have to know the preferences of this median voter. However, (1) they have to incur costs to know who exactly is the median, and (2) if their information about the positions of individual "bliss points" is imperfect – if voting is "probabilistic" from their point of view – then they must take into account the preferences of all the electorate (on probabilistic voting, cf. Lafay 1993).

because they have to be taken quickly and at reasonable costs, have limited scope in this domain.

Information on distributional effects: Knowledge about the distributive effects of a policy is central in political decision making, no matter whether the objective is to promote altruistic "social justice" or to pursue more egoistic political advantages (through adequately targeted programs benefiting, for example, the inhabitants of a specific constituency). Distributional information – at least if it remains private – may help governing politicians in avoiding social trouble, in finding a consensus, or in building a majority. The information task is often simplified because (1) the population can generally be clustered into homogeneous groups, and (2) the politicians benefit from good private information at low cost, less through the bureaucracy than through political channels, opinion surveys, voting, interest-group pressures, public demonstrations, strikes, and so on.

Information on expectational and public opinion effects: Public decisions are not only technical measures. They supply information to the public, as a joint product, and this, in turn, influences individual expectations and reactions. As consumers and producers, individuals are considered to have well-informed rational expectations, hence the weight given to credibility and time consistency in the theory of economic policy. On the contrary, in the political domain, because of the high costs of information compared to the expected benefits of voting or participating in collective actions, the citizens are often seen as rationally ignorant.[9] Moreover, these deliberately uninformed citizens may rationally choose to follow some political leader (to be "deferent" – Buchanan and Vanberg 1989). Then, it may be worthwhile for a political leader to invest in trust capital on the political market (Coleman 1990, Breton and Wintrobe 1982).[10] Because of the contrast between informed and rational individual reactions on the economic markets, and uninformed and deferential behavior on the political market, the communication aspects of public policies are relatively complex. On one hand, information supplied to the public has to take into account the enlightened microeconomic expectations of individuals when they act on markets (especially on financial markets). This means credible precommitments and time-

---

[9] Or, at least, they will process information roughly, through heuristics, short-cuts, rules of thumb, etc.

[10] Huge information asymmetries will also exist between citizens who have specific interests and/or preacquired private information on a specific question, and others who are totally ignorant and uninterested. This results in large capacities for fiscal illusion, or others forms of governmental manipulation (through rent giving or politically motivated redistribution to targeted interest groups).

consistent decisions. On the other hand, the political decision makers have strong incentives to exploit the low degree of political information of the population and to lean on their capital of "deference," sending either biased messages (underestimating constraints and overvaluing results, through rosy scenarios, half-truths, false comparisons, etc.) or persuasive messages (trying to change the preferences of the electorate by psychological manipulation of individual emotions, or by rallying the voters to their claimed intentions, values, or ideology).

Information on implementation: Policies that are highly reversible, such as, for example, economic sanctions against a given country, necessitate a narrow control of their implementation from a technical point of view. At any time, the GPs need to know whether to stop, to adapt, or to pursue. Asking for information about implementation is also a means of controlling the bureaucracy (to signal that its action may be assessed at any moment). However, if reversibility is not central, the GPs will not have much pressure from their rationally ignorant citizens to verify whether an announced policy has been implemented in detail and really works.[11]

II-2   *Biases in the information produced by the bureaucracy*

Bureaucracy, as well as the other producers of information for the GPs (notably interest groups), will try to distort this information in order to maximize their expected utility. Several biases may result from this situation:

Bias due to an insufficient focus of the GPs on allocative aspects: The GPs' informational demand about the allocative effects of a given *political* decision is likely to be much weaker than in the three other domains (stabilization, redistribution, and expectations/public opinion), at least if the length of their mandate is limited and if voters are myopic. Gathering the necessary information is very costly. Moreover, it is not highly rewarding in the short term from a political point of view. Hence, there are generally few debates on the allocative aspects of proposals of the bureaucracy. Contrary to politicians, bureaucracy has a strong interest in these matters, because of its much longer time horizon. If its allocative advice is taken for granted, without deep discussion and checking, then strong biases toward its own bureaucratic preferences are likely to

---

[11] The model proposed by Canzoneri (1985) for monetary authorities can easily be generalized here: the individuals have no incentive to bear the costs of verifying that the government has done its best. So they tolerate a given error margin above which the government loses its credibility.

occur (with notably oversized projects and an excessive technological level).

Evaluation of implementation costs: Some policies have very short-term distributional and expectational/public opinion effects. Because of their specific, electorally constrained rate of time preference, politicians tend to overestimate implementation costs (and to advance arguments on the "political impossibility" of otherwise desirable measures). By contrast, economic experts, because they emphasize economic aspects, tend to underestimate the implementation costs (to ignore, for example, the political troubles that can be triggered by adjustment programs in LDCs).[12] The bureaucracy has an intermediate position: on one hand, its rate of time preference is lower, so that its implementation costs are negligible, compared to the actualized sum of benefits. But, on the other hand, its risk-averse preference for the status quo (or for small incremental changes) creates an incentive to overvalue implementation costs. As a result, the direction and the size of the final bias are uncertain.

Strategic manipulation: A bureaucracy that produces information has a better *ex ante* knowledge of the quality of the information it transmits. Thus it may manipulate its output to its advantage in three different ways (Tirole 1986): by concealing evidence (relevant information is not reported), by distorting evidence, and by not searching for evidence. For the same reasons that it does not reveal its true cost function in the Niskanenian theory, the bureaucracy gives biased responses to the information demand of the GPs. The bias could be, for example, an optimistic one, simply because the message that "the policy is wrong" is much more costly to send than the message that "the policy is marvelously efficient."[13] And, if the GPs do not control for this information bias, it will transform itself into a decision bias. However, credibility constraints, competition between information suppliers, and ex post evaluations set limits to the manipulation possibilities. Also, the GPs always have the opportunity to ignore the supposedly manipulated information and to make decisions on the sole basis of their existing knowledge and experience, according to systematic rules, or even at random.

---

[12] Cf. Lafay and Lecaillon (1993) and Haggard, Lafay, and Morrisson (1995).

[13] On the accuracy of supervisors' reports and evaluations cf. Prendergast and Topel (1996), and also Jean Molinet, a fifteenth-century chronicler, about Charles le Téméraire: "et, pour cette raison, chacun craignait de l'avertir de chose susceptible de provoquer son déplaisir" (and, for this reason, everybody was afraid of announcing to him something that could induce his displeasure), in Régnier-Bohler ed. (1995:963). On the more general question of the deviating behavior of the bureaucracy in the transmission of information, cf. Harnay and Vigouroux (1996).

II-3   *Limiting the biases and improving the efficiency of the bureaucratic production of information*

Efficiency is examined here from the point of view of the GPs, not from a social welfare, normative point of view. It is essentially seen as a problem of bureaucratic monitoring. This problem is easier to address when informational demands by the GPs are well specified, that is, when the informational output of the bureaucracy is *demand-driven*. Adequate formal incentive systems can be implemented relatively easily. A simple carrot-and-stick mechanism or the exploitation of the internal competition between bureaucracies and/or bureaucrats may be sufficient. The main problem for the GPs is how to oblige the bureaucracy to take into account their generally much shorter time horizon, their specific "(political) survival constraints," and the resulting necessity to adequately react to the pressures of public opinion. The capacity of the information-producing bureaucracy to respond quickly and efficiently to specific demands is also important. A technique often used by the GPs in this domain is to put their high bureaucrats under constant emergency demands, even if those demands are not true emergencies, just for training and testing their capacities in this domain.

However, a large part of bureaucratic informational production is not a response to specific demands. It is *supply-driven*: the bureaucrats select, collect, and transmit information on their own initiative. Then the bureaucrats, even if they are perfect Weberian civil servants, need to know what type of information could be relevant for the GPs. Three serious difficulties arise here:

1. The bureaucracy may remain reluctant to transmit unbiased information if the transmission implies high potential costs for it (for example, several alarm signals are not correctly transmitted because they could raise doubts about the management capacities or the integrity of the reporting bureaucrats).
2. It may be technically very difficult and costly for the GPs to inform the bureaucrats about their detailed preferences and objectives. These are too complex and too multidimensional to be easily formulated and transmitted (there is no unique and objective maximand, such as profits in a private firm). At best, preferences and objectives can be summarized through a short list of broad "ideological" orientations. But this kind of information can be deeply misunderstood in some decisive circumstances, and, as a consequence, do more harm than good.
3. It is generally not optimal from the point of view of the GPs to

give true information about both their preferences and their constraints. This is linked to the problem of *private truths versus public lies* (Kuran 1995). Efficiency as well as interest may command rationing, manipulating, or keeping secret some information. Moreover, distortion of information is sometimes an *efficient* policy, for example, to protect external sources of information or to preserve or gain a position in bargaining situations or in negotiations. Secrecy regarding distributional effects may also be useful, as an artificial veil of ignorance, in order to obtain more easily a consensus or at least stable majoritarian choices (Congleton and Sweetser 1992). Also, when the speed of reaction is decisive, time is not sufficient to fully explain the reasons for a given decision, and secrecy will often dominate partial or imperfect information, which could make the decision appear inconsistent. Similarly, disclosure of policy intentions may be understood as irrevocable commitment, resulting in a lack of flexibility vis-à-vis future policy. It may also generate false beliefs or expectations, and erratic reactions and panics.[14] These questions have been studied at length in the context of monetary policy and financial markets (Goodfriend 1986). Furthermore, the GPs seldom have an *interest* in revealing too explicitly their true private preferences and constraints. On one hand, these may not be ethically, ideologically, or politically acceptable to public opinion. On the other hand, the GPs have much less leeway after such a revelation. Revealing later different public preferences or even choosing a "strategy of ambiguity" (Shepsle 1972) may become almost impossible. More fundamentally, concealing their preferences brings strategic advantages to the GPs as principals of the bureaucratic agent: bureaucratic agents are then forced to reveal the true cost of their output (Miller and Moe 1983).[15]

Finally, from an organizational point of view, there is a clear advantage in specializing as much as possible the bureaus in charge of the production of "ordinary public goods and services" and the bureaus in charge of information production. First, information production will be considered less a complementary and secondary task. Second, there will

---

[14] For these reasons, the French government kept secret, for example, the fact that the radioactive cloud of Chernobyl passed over the country in 1986 (and did not stop at the border, as was officially said at that time).

[15] While, in the traditional Niskanenian theory, the bureaucratic agent is assumed to know the utility function of his principal and, as a result, is in a position to obtain a rent.

be a lower risk that nonspecialized bureaus will ration information, because they consider it a means to supervise their other activities. Third, a specialized bureau has, by definition, no temptation to manipulate information in order to serve the expansion of the other activities of the bureau. Its long-term survival and expansion implies the provision of information in sufficient quantity and quality to its unique customer, the government.

A practical solution would be to create in each large ministry such a bureau, reporting directly to the minister, with a significant capability of inquiry. This bureau would be different from the ministers' cabinets and discharged from any executive responsibilities. A cumulative effect could be expected here: as the ordinary bureaus know that the minister is informed by a competitive source, they will have a strong incentive to manipulate less their own production of information and to improve its general quality.

But specialization is not relevant to solving the problem of quality of supply-driven information, simply because bureaucrats generally know little about the true objectives and constraints of the GPs. Formal incentive systems are helpless here, or at least strongly dominated by establishment of trust relationships and selection methods based on ideological or psychological proximity of the minister's staff and the bureaucrats and experts in charge of the information-producing bureau. Indeed, this means that positions in the information bureau will not be permanent, and that a minister can change, when and as often as he wants, the top bureaucrats and experts in it. Indeed, this management method presents an instability cost, but, from the point of view of the GPs, it has also an important advantage: it reduces the discrepancy between their time preference and the usually much longer time preference of the information-producing bureaucrats.

III   Conclusion and organizational perspectives

The choice between self-decision-making by governing politicians and delegation to the bureaucracy is not only a long-term institutional question, but also a practical day-to-day organizational problem. Any superior is regularly faced with this kind of choice. If the political superior makes the decision on his own, then the bureaucracy fundamentally becomes a producer of information, and the problem is how much to demand for this input and how to control for its quality. If the decision is delegated, and as long as the political superior is interested in it and/or accountable for it, the bureaucracy becomes an agent, with the corresponding agency problem. Economic theories of bureaucracy have focused on this last aspect, but, as the evidence shows, many public decisions are of the nondelegated type, that is, they reflect the situation where bureaucracies are providers rather than agents of the GPs. We have presented here a simple framework to deal with the nondelegated case and the associated question of the choice between self-decision-making and delegation. As the analysis shows, the cost of revealing their true preferences and true constraints is central for the GPs. In the delegation case, the GPs must give much more information to the bureaucracy about what they want and what is feasible. Such a revelation implies important technical, strategic, and political costs, which are generally ignored in the literature.

Indeed, the actual balance between these two decision processes is a choice depending on the preferences of the politicians. This means that it is not necessarily "socially optimal" from a normative point of view (whatever the definition of social optimality may be). If the costs to politicians of revealing their preferences and constraints are high, then we should observe a general tendency to underdelegate and to underinvest in information, that is, to make hard decisions with soft information. Moreover, one could consider the nonrevelation of governmental preferences and constraints a social cost in itself (though this point is debatable). Consequently, a more systematic delegation of decisions to agencies could be seen as welfare-improving. But, on the other hand, it is likely to increase the rent extraction power of the bureaucracy. For this reason and others, it would be naive to believe that centralized decisions should be seen as an outdated mode of political governance.

References

Aidt T. S. (1998), "Economic Voting and Information," mimeo, University of Aarhus.

Allen W. R. (1977), "Economics, Economists, and Economic Policy: Modern American Experiences," *Historical Political Economy*, 9:48–88.

Blais A. and Dion S. eds. (1991), *The Budget-Maximizing Bureaucrats: Appraisals and Evidence*, Pittsburgh: University of Pittsburgh Press.

Bolton P. and Farrell J. (1990), "Decentralization, Duplication, and Delay," *Journal of Political Economy*, 98:803–826.

Boulding K. E. (1966), "The Economics of Knowledge and the Knowledge of Economics," *American Economic Review*, Papers and Proceedings, 56:12.

Breton A. (1996), *Competitive Governments: An Economic Theory of Politics and Public Finance*, Cambridge: Cambridge University Press.

Breton A., Galeotti G., Salmon P., and Wintrobe R. eds. (1993), *Preferences and Democracy*, Dordrecht: Kluwer Academic Publishers.

Breton A. and Wintrobe R. (1982), *The Logic of Bureaucratic Conduct*, Cambridge: Cambridge University Press.

Buchanan J. M. and Vanberg V. (1989), "A Theory of Leadership and Deference in Constitutional Construction," *Public Choice*, 61(1):15–27.

Caillaud B., Jullien B., and Picard P. (1996), "Hierarchical Organization and Incentives," *European Economic Review*, 40:687–695.

Canzoneri M. (1985), "Monetary Policy Games and the Role of Private Information," *American Economic Review*, 75:1056–1070.

Coleman J. (1990), *Foundations of Social Theory*, Cambridge: The Belknap Press of Harvard University Press.

Congleton R. D. and Sweetser W. (1992), "Political Deadlocks and Distributional Information: The Value of the Veil," *Public Choice*, 73(1):1–20.

Gilbert G. and Picard P. (1996), "Incentives and the Optimal Size of Local Territories," *European Economic Review*, 40(1):19–41.

Goodfriend M. (1986), "Monetary Mystique: Secrecy and Central Banking," *Journal of Monetary Economics*, 17(January):63–92.

Haggard S., Lafay J. D., and Morrisson C. (1995), *The Political Feasibility of Adjustment in Developing Countries*, Paris: OECD.

Harnay S. and Vigouroux I. (1996), "Offre d'information dans la relation d'agence politico-administrative: de la pression à la persuasion," miméo, LAEP, Université de Paris I.

Kuran T. (1995), *Private Truths, Public Lies: The Social Consequences of Preference Falsification*, Cambride: Harvard University Press.

Lafay J. D. (1993), "The Silent Revolution of Probabilistic Voting," in Breton, Galeotti, Salmon, and Wintrobe eds.

Lafay J. D. and Lecaillon J. (1993), *The Political Dimension of Economic Adjustment*, Paris: OECD.

Milgrom P. and Weber P. (1983), "Organizing Production in a Large Economy with Costly Communication," Cowles Foundation Discussion Papers No. 672, Yale University.

Miller G. J. and Moe T. M. (1983), "Bureaucrats, Legislators, and the Size of Government," *American Political Science Review*, 77(2):297–322.

Myerson R. (1979), "Incentive Compatibility and the Bargaining Problem," *Econometrica* 47:61–73.

Potters J. and van Widen F. (1990), "Modelling Political Pressure as Transmission of Information," *European Journal of Political Economy*, 61(1):61–88.

Prendergast C. and Topel R. H. (1996), "Favoritism in Organizations," *Journal of Political Economy*, 104(5):958–978.

Régnier-Bohler D. ed. (1995), *Splendeurs de la cour de Bourgogne, récits et chroniques*, Collection Bouquins, Paris: Robert Laffont.

Shepsle K. A. (1972), "The Strategy of Ambiguity: Uncertainty and Electoral Competition," *American Political Science Review*, 66:555–568.

Tirole J. (1986), "Hierarchies and Bureaucracies: The Role of Collusion in Organizations," *Journal of Law, Economics, and Organization*, 2(2):181–214.

PART II

Competition and collusion in government

CHAPTER 4

Divisible versus indivisible policies: An exploration of clientelistic politics

Giorgio Brosio

Introduction

This chapter is a brief exploration of clientelistic politics. Clientelistic, also referred to as patron-client, politics is characterized by vertical ties – that is, distinct individual transactions – between clients/voters and their representatives/patrons. Clientelistic politics specializes in individualistic benefits to the exclusion of collective programs, unless the latter can clearly be translated into benefits for individual voters and political leaders. Patron-client systems are contrasted to democratic systems, based on universalistic rules and legal entitlements – the "legal-rational systems" in Weberian terminology – which are considered to be superior to them.

In infant democratic systems clientelistic politics is seen as a hindrance to their proper evolution. In mature democracies, it is seen as a risky venture, which may erode legality and/or easily degenerate into an authoritarian régime. According to historians and political scientists (see Eisenstadt and Lemarchand 1981; Graziano 1973; Tarrow 1977) patron-client politics is mostly typical of early phases of democratic systems and is bound to disappear as democracies mature. They admit also a few cases of mature democratic systems, where governments have turned to clientelistic practices to forestall strong declines in their popularity due to wrong policies or strategies. In both cases, however, clientelism is meant to be a transient phenomenon. When infant democracies come of age, or when mature democracies solve their problems, vertical ties between patrons and clients are replaced by horizontal ones. Shefter (1994) has defined this literature as the "Neoclassical theory of patronage".

These views on clientelistic politics conflict with the observation that mature democratic societies are permeated, to a widely varying extent, by clientelistic practices. Politicians need support to achieve and to maintain their positions. They can, and in fact do, shift selectively from clientelistic practices to nonclientelistic practices according to situations and opportunities. In other words, clientelism seems to be somewhat intrinsic to the working of democratic systems.

On the demand side, one can easily envisage situations where patron-client politics is more advantageous to a relevant share of the population than a democratic system based on legal, universalistic rules for the distribution of benefits and costs of public action. In fact, these rules do not exclude per se the exploitation of a considerable fraction of the population by the majority, while there are situations where patron-clients politics allows voters to extract the most from their political capital.

Clientelistic politics need not be initiated by dishonest or corrupt politicians. Nor does its elimination require ideologically oriented mass parties and voters, as is frequently claimed.

Patterns of clientelistic politics

In general terms, a clientele is a network of implicit contracts between a patron and his clients. The patron has a collective resource to distribute. It can be land, jobs, public goods, or public policies; in other words, this resource has more than one potential user. Clients pay with their own economic and political resources. Clienteles are never totally private organizations, because of the nature of the resource that is being distributed. They may become totally public, as when a democratic system conforms its way of governing to clientelistic patterns.

Indian clienteles, such as those modeled by Platteau (1995), are a network of contracts between a landlord and a group of poor farmers. The latter are required to work on their patron's land and receive in exchange the use of a small plot of land and a minimum subsistence wage, which will allow them to avoid starving in bad years. Poor farmers may also be mobilized by their patrons to ensure them positions of power in local and/or national politics. Here resides the political ingredient of this mainly private clientele.

Scott (1972a, 1972b) distinguishes three phases in the evolution of clientelistic politics in democratic systems. The early phase is typical of preindustrial or early industrial settings, such as English rural constituencies in the first half of the nineteenth century, or southern Italy in the second half. Here, constituencies were controlled by dominant landowning families and voters' decisions were virtually predetermined by the existing economic arrangements. For example, smallholders, who frequently needed to rent a portion of their land, wished to maintain good relations with the local élite, whereas tenants were brought into line by economic pressures exerted by their landlords. Traditional patterns of deference towards the established authorities helped to bring down the cost of votes.

This early phase was disrupted by the advent of industrialization and urbanization and the extension of the franchise to the entire adult population. Traditional social ties were severed and voters saw an increase in their bargaining power. Thus, political machines supplanted traditional patron-client relations. A political machine is an electoral organization capable of regularly winning elections. Votes are controlled by giving particularistic material rewards to electors. Setting up a political machine was a costly business and required a firm control over public resources. In European countries, such as in Italy, especially during Giolitti's premiership, and in France under Napoleon III, the political machine was a central government initiative. The Ministry of the Interior used its provincial ramifications, the prefectures, to enhance the government's electoral positions. Within this system, prefects became powerful, disciplined local bosses, who deprived the traditional ruling class of its former patronage resources.

The development of the political machine in American cities during the last century followed a different pattern of evolution. Here, the decentralized system of government put resources at the disposal of those who were able to control local governments. New immigrants constituted a deep reservoir of votes for those who were able to organize them. Ethnic and cultural cleavages favored the development of vertical ties and the provision of distinct rewards for electoral loyalty to individuals and families.

Clientelistic politics in third world countries after their liberation from colonial powers is a mixture of the two previous variants. Centralization of power provided the resources to reward clients, whereas clanic ties made the organization of voters much easier.

The third phase is that of the dissolution of the political machine. Here, vertical ties between patrons and clients are replaced by horizontal ones between voters. New loyalties emerge in the process of sustained economic growth, loyalties that stress class or occupational ties. Workers and businesses come to appreciate their broader long-run interests and require general legislation and general policies. Political parties become more ideologically oriented. Voters' inducements become general, leading to the progressive dismantling of clientelistic politics.[1]

---

[1] Banfield and Wilson (1963), in their famous book about the "political machine" in American cities, present a similar view of the dissolution of clientelistic politics. The machine started to wane when reform movements came onto the local political scene, representing the attempt of the middle classes to take control of city administrations.

Scott's view – which is typical of most political scientists, with the notable exceptions of Lemarchand and Legg (1972) and Clapham (1982) – is contradicted by the observation of the working of modern representative democracies. Here, officials and politicians are far from always acting on the basis of impersonal bonds with their electorate. Instead, they try sometimes to acquire the loyalty of voters by supplying particularistic, individually tailored goods and services, instead of general public policies and legislation. For example, the entire political system is deeply embedded in clientelistic practices in the South of Italy. These same practices frequently permeate local government operations in a number of clearly mature democratic countries, such as France and the U.S. In most democratic countries members of Parliament entertain clientelistic ties with their constituencies. American presidents, when elected, do not abstain from using the spoils system, distributing a few thousand of the better positions to their electoral supporters. The last example shows a peculiar feature of patron-client politics: namely, that the presence of clientelistic practices in some areas of government, such as the executive branch, is compatible with their absence in other areas, such as the legislative branch.

A model of supply of clientelistic politics

Let us illustrate the basic features of a clientelistic system with the help of an example. A city has to rehabilitate its water provision system, now completely worn out and unreliable. There are two solutions at hand. The first is to rebuild the entire network and replace the old, leaking pipes with new ones. The second is to provide every household with a special filter, to make water safe to drink. The first is the typical collective solution. The second is the public provision of a private good or service. This is not enough to characterize a system as clientelistic. One has to introduce discrimination: more precisely, the extent of discrimination and the legal basis for it.

In liberal/democratic institutional settings, legal or constitutional rights forbid outright discrimination between users based on straight idiosyncratic characteristics. This means, in our example, that every household has the right to be connected to the water provision network, or has the right to be provided with a filtering system. A liberal/democratic democracy should, however, not only allow but even foster proper discrimination. That is, governments should tailor their policies to the individual demands of the citizens (see Breton 1996, especially Chapter 2, for an explanation of this point). The point can be illustrated with reference to Lindahl's model of taxation. The first best solution requires perfectly discriminated – that is, tailored to individual willingness to pay – tax prices to finance public goods. Real world uniform tax rates and provisions are justified only on information problems.

Discrimination, however, may be perfected on a legal basis: that is, by means of impersonal rules that detail all the characteristics of taxpayers and that are relevant for the application of individually tailored prices. Or it may be left to politicians' discretion. This is precisely the case with clientelistic politics. But even in democratic/legalistic settings, politicians may be tempted to build personal ties with their voters by using subtle forms of discrimination allowed by the constitutional and legal system. Coming back to our example, some users may receive the filter before others, some may receive speedier maintenance when the system goes wrong, and so on. Discrimination may even be purely alleged. For example, the mayor may send a letter to every citizen pointing out the special consideration given to their needs. In other words, the public provision of a private good creates an opportunity for setting up a clientele. If this is true, the private good solution should be more productive of votes and of political consent. More precisely, ceteris paribus in terms of price and quality, it should increase the expected number of votes obtained by the politician who is responsible for the service and/or by those whose electoral fortunes depend on this decision, such as the incumbent mayor.

As to supply conditions, individual goods and services are usually costlier than collective goods, assuming ceteris paribus in terms of consumer satisfaction. The first and obvious reason is simply the difficulty of obtaining economies of scale in their provision. In fact, one of the main motives for the existence of a public sector – that is, of a system of collective provision of goods and services – is precisely the savings in costs associated with the larger scale.

A second reason is higher transaction costs. Discrimination, especially subtle discrimination, is costly in terms of information costs and communication systems.

Let us finally assume that users – that is, voters – are indifferent to the technical way in which their needs are satisfied, provided that the price and the quality of the various solutions are the same. (This does not imply, however, that they are also indifferent to the nature of the relationships they entertain with politicians.)

We can now clarify, with the help of Figure 4.1, the choices open to our incumbent mayor.

Supply conditions are represented by simple linear marginal cost curves. The slope of the cost curve is higher in the case of the provision of an individual good. The citizens' demand for the water service is rep-

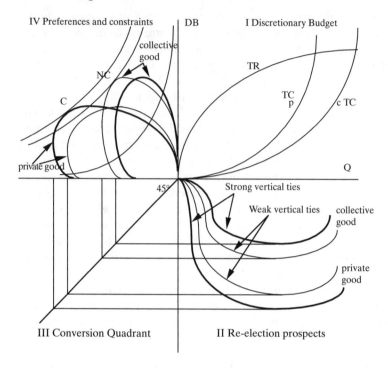

Figure 4.1. Policy choices in clientelistic and nonclientelistic systems.

resented by a simple linear aggregate demand curve. To simplify, the possibility of discrimination on the revenue side is not allowed for here. Every citizen pays the same price, which is equal to the total cost divided by the number of citizens. These cost and revenue conditions are presented in quadrant I.

Relations between citizens and politicians in every system are characterized by information asymmetries. In the case in point, this means that the contribution/price asked may be higher than the cost of providing an efficient service. The difference between total revenue and minimum total cost creates a discretionary budget, DB, which the politician in charge can retain and spend for his own purposes.

A reasonable behavioral hypothesis about politicians is that they maximize a utility function with two arguments: namely, political survival (that is, re-election) and the discretionary budget, as follows:

$$U = u[eE(Q,T), S, DB]$$

where S is the value for the politician in question of his political survival; and $eE(Q,T)$ is the probability of reelection, which in turn depends on the amount of the good provided, Q, and the ties, T, between politicians and citizens/voters.

A short illustration of $eE(Q,T)$ is needed. The probability of reelection is related to the probability that each voter will grant his or her consent to the incumbent politician. In turn, this probability is a function of the utility of each voter. Mueller (1989) provides a good summary of, and references to, the literature on voting under conditions of uncertainty. For simplicity, we assume that the utility function has only two arguments. The first is vertical ties with the politician. It seems, in fact, reasonable to assume that in every context voters do value positively the possibility of having direct access to their representative. The second argument is the publicly provided good. Since the price is fixed and equal for all, utility gains amount to the consumer surplus, which in turns depends on the quantity of Q. In a median voter framework with competing candidates, the probabilities of reelection are at a maximum – for a given level of T – when the incumbent chooses the level of Q which corresponds to his estimate of that preferred by the median voter.

The probability of reelection as a function of Q is reported in quadrant II of Figure 4.1. The probability of reelection increases as Q increases until the quantity preferred by the median voter is reached;[2] thereafter it decreases. The function initially shows increasing returns in the quantity of Q, followed by decreasing returns. There is a different maximum for each of the two options: namely, the provision of a private or of a collective good.

Since the provision of the private good makes it possible to keep, or to create, vertical ties, reelection probabilities are, for the same quantity of Q, higher than those related to the provision of the collective good. The relationship between reelection and discretionary budget is reported in quadrant IV. There are two transformation curves. The one referring to the provision of a collective good allows the politician to reach a larger discretionary budget, but gives him lower reelection probabilities than the provision of the private good. The second curve shows higher reelection probabilities and a lower discretionary budget. The choice, as usual, depends on preferences, that is, on the weights assigned by the politician to the arguments in his utility function.

The preferences are portrayed in the same quadrant. When S is given

---

[2] If preferences for the good in question are normally distributed, a quantity Q^* (not indicated in the figures) is the one that corresponds to the social optimum, where the discretionary budget is also at its maximum. This is, however, irrelevant to our problem.

a value of 1, the shape corresponds to the utility function $[eE(Q,T), 1, DB] = eE \times DB$, meaning that indifference curves are convex to the origin and implying a diminishing marginal rate of substitution between reelection prospects and discretionary budget.

The case is reported in quadrants II and IV of Figure 4.1, where the bold curves illustrate the early phases of clientelistic systems, when voters are poorly organized across class or interest lines and there are strong vertical ties between voters and politicians. Thus, the provision of a private good is more productive in electoral terms than the provision of a collective good. Given the shape of the indifference curves, the politician prefers to supply the private good, as shown by equilibrium point C in quadrant IV. His electoral prospects are clearly brighter. Moreover, he can continue to maintain his clientelistic ties more easily.

Shifting away from and toward clientelistic systems

As we have seen, political modernization implies, according to most of the literature, the gradual dissolution of the political machine. Urbanization and industrialization produce class cleavages, and trade unions and mass parties start to be organized. New loyalties emerge in this process. Workers and businesses come to appreciate their broader long-run interests and consequently universalistic legislation, general policies, and administrative honesty as well. Political parties become ideologically oriented. Voter inducements become more general, posing a serious threat to the survival of political machines.

This new societal context is represented with plain lines in quadrants II and IV of Figure 4.1. Since voters attach more utility than before to the establishment of horizontal ties, vertical ties become less productive in electoral terms. The reelection function curve associated to the provision of the private good now has lower values, whereas the same function associated to the collective good is steeper. Transformation curves of quadrant IV now have a different shape, which reflects the new combinations of reelection prospects and discretionary budget. In the case shown in the figure (equilibrium point NC), the provision of a collective good is now more worthwhile for the politician, meaning that the clientelistic system is bound to disappear.

History shows in fact that patron-client politics has disappeared in many, possibly in most, mature democracies. However, contemporary politically modernized societies offer many counterexamples of cases in which patron-client politics has survived. Clienteles do not (always) react passively to their dissolution; they may and do resist threats to their survival by using different tactics and means, such as the use of external financing and the formation of ideological ties between patrons and clients.

External financing may be derived from a variety of sources, both legal and illegal. It may come from the national government. In fact, in many countries, at different stages of their histories, clienteles have thrived at local government level by benefiting from central government transfers. It may also come from other areas of the same country, as happens frequently in developing countries, where urban clienteles are financed by the exploitation of rural areas. It may even come from other segments of the society in the same area. For example, in limited franchise systems, fiscal exploitation of nonvoters has been an important source for the financing of the ruling élite.

External financing, as mentioned, may also be illegal. This is the case when funds from a criminal organization are offered in exchange for politicians' closing their eyes to its operation. Recent Italian history – documented by the various *Mani Pulite* (Clean Hands) trials (see, among others, Barbagallo 1997) provides plenty of evidence of this kind. American and Latin American history provides another rich source of evidence. Mexico is a contemporary case in point: "Legislative and administrative reforms have made it much easier for the opposition to control the PRI's spending, for example, but the obvious and urgent concern is whether the PRI is turning to the drug trade as an alternate source of funds" (Guillermoprieto 1996, p. 35).

The other tactic is the recourse to ideological, political, ethnic, or even religious ties between patron and clients. This results in a reduced incidence of transaction costs in the keeping of the clientele system. The economic impact of this kind of politician-voter relationship is clearly illustrated in the literature (see Breton 1996, especially Chapter 5).[3]

While external financing adds to total revenue, the introduction of ideological ties reduces the total cost of service provision. Ideological affinities may also be used as an instrument for creating access to exter-

---

[3] There is also plenty of historical and contemporary evidence about parties infiltrated by clienteles or clienteles that infiltrate political organizations. We may cite the so-called Georgian Mafia in the former Soviet Union and the transformation of the Mexican PRI into a network of clienteles. Italy again provides plenty of evidence. During the First Republic, clienteles entered the Socialist Party and used its political slogans to foster ties between bosses and clients. A similar phenomenon took place very recently. The 1994 national election witnessed a massive shift of votes from the Christian Democratic Party to Berlusconi's newly formed Forza Italia. According to most commentators, clienteles made this shift possible; local notables saw Berlusconi's party as the new holder of power at the national level, and patrons channeled the votes of their clients toward it.

nal financing, for example from the central government. Thus, the economic impact of both tactics is the same: they increase the discretionary budget. This is shown in a unified way in Figure 4.2, where the same cost conditions are reported, but the revenue from citizens' pockets is supplemented by a grant. For the sake of simplicity, this grant is a lump sum transfer. No variation in reelection prospects is assumed here as a consequence of the grant.

The new transformation curves are represented in quadrant IV. They look bumpier than the former ones, as there is now a higher discretionary budget for every reelection prospect. The provision of the private good – shown by equilibrium point C in quadrant IV – that allows the clientelistic system to survive is again the best choice for politicians. Obviously, this may appear as an ad hoc explanation: that is, the result may appear as dependent on the shape of the various curves. The point I want to make, however, is simply that as the grant increases, so the provision of the private good becomes increasingly worthwhile to politicians. This has an immediate economic explanation. Since reelection prospects and discretionary budget are poor substitutes, as the latter increases in relation to the former due to the grant, politicians will substitute for the same amount of the grant with increasing doses of reelection prospects, thus preferring those combinations that lie on the transformation curve to the private good.

We can also imagine and observe the reverse shift: that is, from non-clientelistic to clientelistic politics. Governing parties, or politicians, may be tempted to use clientelistic practices when competition from opposition parties that use ideological appeals becomes too strong to sustain. In terms of our model, such a shift is based on the assumption that voters will be tempted to keep their support for the party in power when they appreciate the (immediate) benefits from the establishment of vertical ties with politicians. Post–Second World War politics at all levels of government in the South of Italy provides some evidence of this shift. When left-wing parties, which offered a platform of radical land reform and wealth redistribution that looked quite attractive to the poor strata of the electorate, came to represent a concrete threat to the moderate governing parties, the latter increased the intensity of their clientelistic policies, such as the creation of public-sector jobs, easy promotions, and the distribution of the so-called "disability" pensions based on highly discretional eligibility criteria at all levels of government (see Zuckerman 1979 for a clear illustration of the process, and Chubb 1982 and Walston 1988 for a detailed description of these practices). This reaction proved to be quite successful in terms of electoral results, even if it has strained the finances of both the central and local governments.

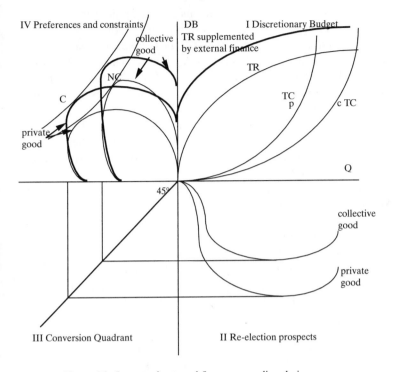

Figure 4.2. Impact of external finance on policy choices.

In terms of our model, we have only to make the reverse step in quadrant II of Figure 4.1, moving this time from equilibrium point *NC* to equilibrium point *C*. Since voters' loyalty is bought by the provision of individually tailored services, vertical ties become more productive in electoral terms. The reelection function curve associated to the provision of the private good now has higher values, whereas the same function associated to the collective good has a lower slope.

Costs and benefits of patron-client politics

On normative grounds, patron-client systems are considered (a) to represent a hindrance to political competition, and (b) to operate too close to (or even across) the borderline that separates legality from plain corruption.

Hindrance to competition has many aspects. The first is that, being based on the lack of general, enforceable rules, patron-client politics may put citizens/clients at the mercy of patrons. Put in a milder form, it gives to suppliers of policies a greater negotiating power than they have in a democratic system based on universal rules. A second aspect is the increased stickiness of political markets. A client who has received some kind of benefit from his patron on the basis of the discretionary power of the latter and not on clear legal grounds will clearly hesitate, for fear of losing his benefit, to give his vote to a competing party, even if the electoral platform of this party looks very attractive. A third aspect, which is typical of political machines (see Ostrom 1987), is the potential for collusion among centers of power, using Breton's (1996) terminology, which is increased when politics is dominated by clienteles.

While fully recognizing the validity of these statements, one has to take into account other features that run in the opposite direction. The most important of these is that patron-client politics may bring out the value of clients' political capital. That is, it can increase the value of citizens' voting rights and of the consent that they can grant to politicians. This advantage is in operation when rule-based democratic systems are scarcely competitive, or when some segments of the population are denied political rights or discriminated against in their entitlements.

Take the case, for example, of the New York political machines of the last century. They were created by offering some benefits to new immigrants whose political support capital was not exploited by the existing political organizations. Clienteles may also thrive in those democratic systems which offer little protection to minority segments of their population. This may be the case of democratic systems with few checks and balances. For example, one can imagine a system of responsible government with a great concentration of power in the Parliament. The Parliament is dominated by a single party, which frequently colludes with the opposition. Segments of the population that are not represented by the parties will have little protection, a situation favoring the creation of politicians/patrons, who will act as political brokers between these segments and the parties. This will increase the amount of political competition. That is, a system with (a plurality of) clienteles may give more bargaining power to citizens/clients than a rule-based democratic system with a small endowment of checks and balances.

The relationship between clientelistic politics and corruption is a typical Occam's razor question. It goes, however, to the heart of the ethics of democratic politics – namely, what are the correct means for the acquisition of political consent?

Surely, according to current definitions, clientelism and corruption are two distinct phenomena. Clients give their votes and/or political support in exchange for public sector benefits, while corruption implies direct payments to politicians for getting the same (or other) benefits. In reality, the problem is much more subtle. For example, most democratic systems strictly forbid the sale of votes for plain money. But where is the divide between plain money and money benefits from public policies? The imposition of legal rules and constraints upon the distribution of money benefits does not solve every problem, due to the possibility of tailoring them to individual voters, who might happen to be those who have voted for the politicians in power.

Clearly, clientelistic politics has a built-in potential for generating corruption through its constant erosion of the legal system. The patron-client relation is based on an implicit contract according to which consent and votes are exchanged for private goods. Considering that the abuse of the law or the nonpunishment of malfeasance are perfect examples of private goods (which can easily be delivered by a politician with strong connections to the bureaucracy and the judiciary), it is easily understood why clientelism may degenerate into a machine that produces, "regulates," and protects illegal behaviors, especially if resources to finance ongoing policies stop flowing in. The system thrives on consuming the capital of "the rule of law" and the associated trust. Welfare benefits, auctions, public works, public jobs, court trials, public controls and monitoring are typical instances that allow the emergence of a private good, which may take the form of abusing laws and/or regulations or simply the nonprosecution of offenders.

Conclusions

Clientelistic politics is usually dismissed by social scientists as a (happily) transient phase in the evolution of democratic systems. It is considered to be a political system that is expensive to run, a threat to the legal basis of democracy, and a serious hindrance to political competition.

All of these charges are basically true. In spite of them, clientelistic politics shows a remarkable resilience. Its transience is seriously questioned by both historical and contemporary evidence. In fact, clientelistic politics is almost intrinsic to the working of democratic systems. Politicians may have recourse to clientelistic practices whenever other policies do not provide enough support or benefits for them.

This chapter has presented a simple but quite general model of supply of clientelistic politics. It illustrates the choice that politicians may face between clientelistic policies based on vertical ties between politicians and voters and the delivery of private goods to the latter, and nonclientelistic policies where collective goods are provided and vertical ties fade out. The model may be used to illustrate the selective behavior of politicians, who may shift from or toward clienteles according to the availability of resources and the productivity of such policies in terms of consent.

The chapter has also briefly explored the connection between clientelistic politics and competition. It has been shown there there are situations where clienteles increase the intensity of competition by raising the supply price of voters' consent.

Finally, one has to take into account that a protracted use of clientelistic practices may seriously erode the legal basis of democratic systems. Thus, constitutional provisions should foster political competition in the system by increasing the number and effectiveness of its checks and balances.

References

E. C. Banfield and J. Q. Wilson, *City Politics*, New York, Vintage Books, 1963.

F. Barbagallo, *Napoli Fine Novecento*, Torino, Einaudi, 1997.

A. Breton, *Competitive Governments: An Economic Theory of Politics and Public Finance*, Cambridge University Press, 1996.

J. Chubb, *Patronage, Power and Poverty in Southern Italy: A Tale of Two Cities*, Cambridge University Press, 1982.

C. Clapham, *Private Patronage and Public Power: Political Clientelism in the Modern State*, London, Frances Pinter, 1982.

S. N. Eisenstadt and R. Lemarchand (eds), *Political Clientelism, Patronage and Development*, London, Sage, 1981.

L. Graziano, "Patron-Client Relationships in Southern Italy," *European Journal of Political Research*, vol. 1 (1973), pp. 3–34.

A. Guillermoprieto, "Mexico: Murder Without Justice," *New York Review of Books*, October 3, 1996.

R. Lemarchand and K. Legg, "Political Clientelism an Development," *Comparative Politics* (1972), pp. 149–78.

D. C. Mueller, *Public Choice II*, Cambridge University Press, 1989.

V. Ostrom, *The Political Theory of a Compound Republic: Designing the American Experiment*, 2nd rev. ed. Oakland, ICS Press, 1987.

J. P. Platteau, "An Indian Model of Aristocratic Patronage," *Oxford Economic Papers*, vol. 47 (1995), pp. 636–662.

J. C. Scott (1972a), "Patron-Client Politics and Political Change in Southeast Asia," *American Political Science Review*, vol. 66 (1972), pp. 91–113.

J. C. Scott (1972b), *Comparative Political Corruption*, Englewood Cliffs, N.J., Prentice-Hall, 1972.

M. Shefter, *Political Parties and the State: The American Historical Experience*, Princeton, Princeton University Press, 1994.

S. Tarrow, *Between Center and Periphery: Grassroots Politicians in France and Italy*, New Haven, Yale University Press, 1977.

J. Walston, *Mafia and Clientelism: Roads to Rome in Post-war Calabria*, London, Routledge, 1988.

A. Zuckerman, *The Politics of Faction*, New Haven, Yale University Press, 1979.

CHAPTER 5

Founding Fathers versus Rotten Kids: A positive approach to constitutional politics

Gianluigi Galeotti

1   Constitutional puzzles[1]

When dealing with constitutional matters, economists tend to over-emphasize the role of demand and assume an alert citizenship striving to restrain future Leviathans. Whatever the aims and merits of the con-tractarian interpretations, it seems important to follow a basic tenet of economics and consider political demands fulfilled indirectly as a by-product of the competition among the leaders, as it is the case with economic demands in the marketplace. That tenet is consistent with the historical constitutions arranged, rearranged, and rebuilt by aristo-crats, clerics, officials, and politicians of less or more democratic vintages, engaged in their struggle for power. Contrasted with that evidence, the contractarian framework generates three puzzles: the "mystery" of constitutional enforcement (Peter Ordeshook, 1992); the emergence of individual freedoms (Ejan Mackaay, 1997); and the maintenance of modern constitutions in the presence of extra-constitutional changes (William Niskanen, 1990). This chapter faces those puzzles in terms of the positive line of inquiry pursued by Albert Breton and tries to elucidate the role of political struggles in molding constitutional evolution.

Within a positive perspective, the main theme is not the origin of the constitutional compact – a subject on which we know little beyond fas-cinating stories of mythical advisers; it is rather systematic *continuous adjustments* and its relatively few *discontinuous changes*. If adjustments and changes are under the control of those who should be controlled, the puzzles can be reformulated by asking: how can constitutional polit-

[1] The author is grateful to Luisa Giuriato and Ron Wintrobe for early exchanges on the subject, to Elena Granaglia and to an anonymous referee for their comments, and to Vani Borooah for his comments and suggestions.

104

ical struggles be distinguished from "ordinary" ones? How does constitutional politics come to affect citizens' freedom and property? Why are constitutional adjustments mostly not sanctioned by formal revisions? The contractarian view handles the first question in terms of definitions (decisions on constraints versus decisions within constraints), solves the second via ad hoc constitutional provisos (assuming their automatic enforcement), and leaves the last one unanswered, though disputing the legitimacy of the changes. The tentative replies explored in this chapter move from the early analysis of Kenneth Wheare (1951), make use of Breton's 1996 array of formal and informal centers of power, and view constitutions as coordinating devices (Russell Hardin, 1989). In leaders' struggles for political influence we look for the guarantor of individual freedoms and the spring of the democratic evolution of politics.

The aim of the chapter is to suggest a line of research more than to present a fully developed model. Though lacking in systematic historical and contemporary evidence, our exploration should help to orient the search for that evidence. As a preliminary caveat, let us underline that some of our definitions are different from the conventional ones: constitutions are intended as sets of rules superintending the working of the supply side of politics; that supply side includes both power-holders and political entrepreneurs, and it is subject to collusive and competitive pressures that resemble an oligopolistic setting. Section 2 deals with those definitions and shows the role of legitimacy in making a constitutional order stable. Section 3 is more historically oriented. It moves from a remark suggested by Machiavelli on political conflicts as the seed of liberty and tries to account for two traits of the evolution of political constitutions: the internalization of dissent and the regulation of conflicts via the allocation of powers. The analysis is then applied in Section 4 to describe the main feature of modern democratic constitutions (citizens' rights as points of reference to orient the political competition) and in Section 5 to interpret the issue of constitutional maintenance. There we distinguish constitutional adjustments – changes which keep the existing balance of power – from the changes which modify that balance and require the normal procedures of amendment. Section 6 concludes the paper by stressing the role of constitutional changes in coping with leaders' opportunism.[2]

---

[2] The author's limits of knowledge are responsible for the strong Western afflatus of the analysis. Though affected by internal and external conflicts, non-Western societies seem to have followed a different pattern of evolution. It would be interesting to investigate the reasons for such a difference. We wonder whether it could be related to the medieval struggles (of a competitive nature) between the church and the political authorities.

2   The stability of the constitutional order

Modern constitutional documents cover three areas, one stating social goals and individual rights; one sanctioning powers, duties, and interactions of the various branches of government; and a third one dictating the procedures for amending the document itself. The last area is the real innovation, as the substance of the first two has always been a feature of the de facto constitutions of any polity. In terms of powers, remember Aristotle's notion of a constitution as of the set of rules defining a community's political institutions (in a way replicated by Dennis Mueller, 1996, 43). In terms of principles, the acquiescence to legitimate authorities was always based upon shared values – Randall Calvert's (1995) ideologies – somehow reassuring citizens and setting limits, however broad, upon the public decision makers (think of the distinction between private economic relations and state action respected for centuries in medieval Europe). The notion of shared values may sound odd to those who consider all nondemocratic regimes as synonymous with absolute power and the prototypal embodiment of force, but "no leadership is absolute" (North, 1981) and both consent and coercion are necessary to keep any social system working (Ronald Wintrobe, 1998).

Therefore let us define in broad terms a constitutional order as *the set of socially recognized rules, behaviors, and expectations which identify political leaders (power holders and political entrepreneurs), and structure their relations in view of the provision of what is expedient to the public action.* Such a definition recognizes the higher status of that order over the institutions which it identifies, and underlines its functional dimensions: the regulation of political supply and, implicitly, the notion of legitimacy and the reference to citizens' expectations. Those dimensions will be analyzed in the following sections in order to recognize continuity and novelty in modern constitutions. This section lingers over the distinction between the supply- and the demand-side of political markets and introduces the notion of political legitimacy as the variable linking together those two sides in the self-enforcing way that makes the political markets stable.

The role of political supply

The contemporary normative concern with the aggregation of peoples' preferences seems at times to overshadow the role of supply in materializing people's demand. "Even if strong and definite [people's volitions] remain latent, often for decades, until they are called to life by some political leader who turns them into political factors." Schumpeter's well-known words underline how people's needs and expectations represent a raw material that leadership is to transform into an input, both in conventional and in political markets. Any political demand comes to be true only when expressed by someone, and that someone is by definition a political leader. That identification gets obfuscated in the political field for two reasons. First, because those leaders – think of an agitator, a lobbyist, an MP, or a minister – occupy opposite positions in the two exchanges in which they are necessarily engaged by virtue of their activity: they "supply" when providing their constituencies with services which consist in "demand" on their behalf, and the two relationships are mixed up in processes consisting of asking and accepting, conceding and compromising on the characteristics of the goods and services to be provided.

The second reason relates to the fact that political leadership includes both those in charge of formal positions (power holders) and other leaders who, competing or not for those positions, are active in supplying information or advancing interests. The latter group – the political entrepreneurs – is a species including influential wise men, respected warriors or king's courtesans of the past, and the influential columnists, conveners, and party leaders of today. In terms of substance, the trait common to both species is the influence they exert upon decision making. Therefore we consider both groups as political leaders animating the supply side of the market for political influence. That influence is a variable measurable in terms of how much their positions have to be taken into account – even when not accepted – by other leaders in designing policies and enforcing decisions. As in the marketplace, political leaders can be more or less successful in advocating or opposing policies, depending on the impact and echoes they stir up among the people. And it is the eventual impact that makes the difference between Oliver Cromwell, José de San Martin, Patrick Henry, Cola di Rienzi, and an unheeded speaker at the Hyde Park Corner in London.

The relevance of political entrepreneurs – whether influential leaders or simple mouthpieces for others' grievance – is confirmed by their being the first target of political repression. In that sense the Bill of Rights is a supply-side concern. Freedoms such as those of association, assembly, and expression are indeed individual rights, but their ultimate value is to reduce the costs of entry for political entrepreneurs.[3] As we are going to see, a crucial trait of the constitutional evolution is that of improving the

---

[3] The drafters of military codes permit individual complaints, but consider the making of the same complaint by two or more people to be insubordination: their purpose is to strip the demand rights of a soldier of any "supply" implication.

contestability of the market for political influence. Should we be amazed by the idea of autocrats competing for consent or ready to compromise, we have to consider how consent has always been a source of influence, and policy decisions a ubiquitous medium of political exchange (see Michael Foley's 1989 comparison of the crises of the early Stuart constitution in England with what occurred in the U.S. in President Nixon's times). The exercise of power, however, is influenced by people's attitudes, and that calls in the role of political legitimization in the workings of the constitutional order.

People's acquiescence and constitutional legitimacy

When not a consequence of wars, major constitutional changes see people as the pivotal factor, though it is again the leadership that makes the difference between a revolution and a stampede. But what about people's role in the ordinary working of a constitutional order? Here, a constant feature is represented by their acquiescence, not a synonym for indifference but an attitude – compliance without protest – that can go from full support to dissatisfaction and dissent. We agree with those who consider a constitution to be a "massive act of coordination" (Hardin, 1989), where acquiescence is more important than agreement in generating a set of stable and self-enforcing expectations (Ordeshook, 1992). More specifically, it can be submitted that people's expectations and leaders' rational behavior are knit together thanks to the notion of constitutional legitimacy.[4]

Hardin (1989, 102) affirms that a constitution cannot be a contract because it does not solve a strategic interaction of "the prisoner's dilemma" nature, but solves a prior problem of collective coordination. It is maintained by mutual expectations and it is backed not "by external sanctions . . . [but] by default, by the difficulty of recoordinating on an alternative arrangement." The fact, however, that there is no alternative does not mean indifference to how the coordination is arranged. As in any multiple equilibria game, a focal point is needed to stabilize the expectations of both people and political leaders. Precedence seems important on this account; either we follow Aristotle's

---

[4] Many scholars identify legitimacy with political support. However, to take into account that discontent with a decision does not translate automatically into alienation from the existing order, it seems preferable to distinguish constitutional legitimacy from political legitimacy of a more occasional nature.

reconstruction[5] or consider the longing for continuity required by many new masters.

The obedience to the authority – however culturally induced, influenced by personal experiences or other people's attitudes – was probably at first nurtured by personal trust in the appointee; but when that authority grew in articulation and complexity a more institutionally oriented substitute was required. A constitutional order represents that substitute by signaling legitimate powers through simple rules or more elaborated institutions.[6] Legitimacy allows a smooth working of the constitutional order: by "making lawful" the acts of those empowered to operate, it is a cost-saving device for the citizens (it reverses the burden of proof in terms of expectations); by making compliance easier, it reduces the costs of the exercise of power. The meaning and value of people's acquiescence is greater, the lower the costs of voicing dissent, and that in turn affects the stability of the constitutional order and the strength of the collusive links holding together the leadership itself. Before discussing the role of legitimacy in orienting leaders' behavior, we consider how political conflicts have helped to reduce those costs thanks to the affirmation of political freedom.

3　The rise of citizens' rights and the regulation of competition

By assuming that "at the beginning was the state," we avoid the debate on the origin of political institutions, but for the remark that the contractarian view exceeds, and the predatory view falls short of, what is required to account for the mix of consent and coercion that characterizes any constitutional order. As for the former view, the veil of uncertainty behind which the "Founding Fathers" are purported to accomplish their job is an implicit admission of the impossibility of designing a complete constitutional contract (Jean-Jacques Laffont and Jean Tirole, 1990). At most, we would have a vague mandate allotting to future "Rotten Kids" the authority to replenish whatever might be required at the proper occurrence, with the related manipulations that are functional to the pursuit of their own interests (Avinash Dixit, 1996) – a conclusion not substantially different from that reached by a predatory

---

[5] From the hierarchy of the household to that of the village, a coalescence of households, and to that of the state, a coalescence of villages (Trevor Saunders, 1981). Remember that the Roman paterfamilias had the right of life and death over his household.

[6] Hardin (1998) argues that "the law, as opposed to the mere practice, of promise-keeping is an instance of the substitution of institutions for trust relationship . . . The law takes over those areas in which trust-worthiness would be inherently less reliable."

interpretation cast in the proper time horizon. The two views converge, therefore, in pointing out that whoever is in control of the coercion is tempted to extract political rents[7] at the expenses of the public. Our purpose is to explain how the struggles and bargains over those rents engendered a constitutional evolution that reduced the space for that extraction.

Modeling the apparatus of government in terms of a monopoly has the virtue of catching its stylized essentials. But it holds under stringent assumptions of perfect information on people's demand, perfect internal coordination, no influence and enforcement costs. In other terms, it is a black box leaving out the substance of asymmetric influence, the competition for and within the power positions, the struggles over features and characteristics of the goods and services to be provided, and the presence of other institutions of supply (Breton, 1996). To account for that complexity we have to travel backward the route that led to a better understanding of the influence of (private) transaction costs in shaping the different institutions superintending human interaction. We need a symmetrical reflection on the role of (political) transaction costs in going from "at the beginning was the state" to the separation and articulation of public powers, in a paradoxical reversal of the old *divide et impera* rule.

Once the malleable features of what is publicly provided – be they private or public goods and services – are combined with people's heterogeneous expectations, hidden information and hidden action problems plague any collusive agreement. The costs of knowing people's expectations and of controlling the behavior of those supervising the delivery engender the market for political influence, as intermediaries and agents manage information and performance at a price, cashable by both sides of the transactions they are involved in. The nature of that market – centered around the hierarchical lines of formal authority outlined by the constitution – is captured by two apparently contradictory remarks: political institutions express ex ante agreements among political leaders (North, 1981); no autocrat goes unconstrained because of the presence of potential *rivals* and the claims of its *agents* (North, 1990). Why the need for agreement? and why its "flawed" working? An oligopolistic setting seems to express the contrasting pressures on political leaders stretched between the centripetal lure to collude and

---

[7] Accumulation of wealth, amenities of power, and whatever may be included under the label of political rent, a label vague and useful, like that of profit, to interpret market behaviors. As for political entrepreneurs, we refer to Breton's 1996 interpretation of rent seeking (65–66).

the centrifugal strain to compete. A perfect collusive coordination would allow them to maximize their total rent, but collusion has inbuilt incentives to strive after the higher share made available to each leader by what he controls in terms of privileged information and unchecked behavior.

Without attempting a systematic analysis, we need only mention how the oligopolistic setting accounts for a number of institutional features and their evolution. Thus, the fact that collusion is relatively more effective against small rather than large "buyers" is consistent with the stronger links to power of the higher echelons of society and with the competition to get the support of those (small "buyers") who can shift their alignments more easily.[8] The feudal pyramid of power as well as the corporatist political representation by trade or profession is an attempt to "allocate buyers" to political leaders, and party whips in Parliament or the committee system in Congress show the stronger grip on political entrepreneurs when their behavior is more easily detected. Other devices have been concocted first to control the access into the market of influence and then to constrain behaviors through elaborate webs along clan, ethnic, religious, class, or ideological lines. However, the costs of those controls leave always opportunities to better individual positions at the expense of collective interests, and the different "cost structures" of political entrepreneurs create endemic tensions to violate the collusive rules.

Machiavelli's remark

Niccolò Machiavelli seems to have been the first to link those struggles for and within power to the affirmation of political freedom. Commenting on the events of republican Rome he observed that "in every republic there are two different inclinations: that of the people and that of the upper class, and all the laws which are made in favor of liberty are born of the conflict between the two . . . Good laws are born . . . from those quarrels which many condemn without due consideration" (*Discourses on the First Ten Books of Titus Livius*, Book 1, Chapter 4 [1531]: Viking Penguin, 1979, 183). What Machiavelli was describing is not a one-shot game, since the reference to "laws" implies a more substantial impact of how the "quarrels" internal to the leadership – of oligarchic nature not only in the case of the Gracchi – turn to the advantage of a third side, citizens' freedom. It can be submitted that the contrasting pushes to collude and to compete can explain a constitutional evolution that

---

[8] We are following the analysis of George Stigler (1964).

internalized those very conflicts and lowered the cost of entry into the market of influence. It follows first that Machiavelli's remark should be prominent among the factors that help to solve the puzzle of the emergence of constitutional rights (why do power holders grant those rights instead of favoring themselves or those on whom they rely to stay in power?).[9] Second, the institutionalization of those quarrels through the constitutional division of powers has to be viewed not as a sudden revolutionary outcome, but as the fruit of an old and slow evolution still in progress.

We mentioned how the market for influence is held in equilibrium by the focal point that constitutional legitimacy represents for leaders. In normal circumstances, both too much collusion and too much competition can put at risk the survival of the constitutional order. In the first instance, leaders' free-riding on collusive agreements would be more tempting, and in the second the erosion of legitimacy would dampen the working of the political machine. In both instances, the formal breaking of the collusive rules would amount to self-exclusion because of "the difficulty of re-coordinating on an alternative arrangement." In the long run, the adaptation of the existing rules is the only available option. Why and how did the oligopolistic struggles for influence engender an evolution that reduced the cost of dissent and brought about the more regulated competition implicit in the division of powers?[10]

The internalization of dissent

As for the "why," we can first interpret the reduction in the costs of dissent as an attempt to take into account the heterogeneity of demands, as "disregard of differences among buyers proves to be equivalent to imposing an excise tax upon them, but one which is not collected by the monopolist" (Stigler, 1964). At the same time economic and social changes require new alignments, and the rules of oligopolistic collusion have to adapt: new "large buyers" appear on the social scene and new entrepreneurs compete for their support. Second, the combination of dif-

---

[9] Mackaay's 1997 reply considers a number of conditions defining the climate that has accompanied that emergence: accumulation of wealth, widespread abuse of power, absence of external threats, and coalitions of dissenting groups. It is only in relation to the phenomenon of international imitation that the competitive pluralism of rulers is mentioned.

[10] In this preliminary analysis of ours, we refer only to the division of powers without discussing explicitly its more articulated variant represented by the "checks and balances" version.

ferent demands and the plurality of the goods and services provided make the rivalry multidimensional and the oligopolistic coordination more complex. The traditional assignment of old and new "buyers" along geographic jurisdictions was complemented by more functional and specialized lines of activity that sanctioned the interdependency of influence, and combined the reciprocal control of behaviors with the need for agreements where those lines overlap. This point relates to the "how" and requires precise attention.

The interdependence among the actions of the various leaders – power holders and connected entrepreneurs – requires that each be able to form expectations that can be reasonably held in dealings with the others to avoid struggles and warfare. Whatever the "simple" nature of early political power, changes in technology and in relative prices open new opportunities for political actions that some entrepreneurs are quicker than others to pick up and use to improve their own positions. Uncertainty arises – which initiatives is each empowered to take, and within which limits, which procedural rules have to be followed, how to solve disputes – and the definition of new sets of rights (powers or "constitutional entitlements") is needed to reduce conflicts. If we interpret interference and interactions among political leaders in terms of externalities, Demsetz's 1967 analysis of the origin of rights comes to have its constitutional counterpart. The growing articulation of constitutional rules is a response to the need to internalize those externalities by transforming them into formal powers and constitutional procedures. The executive has always had an advantage in the process: the same Cromwell dissolved the Parliament three times and in his *Instrument of Government* sketched a division of powers, while preserving a strong executive. More generally, the division of powers and political entrepreneurs' rights come to make possible and to underpin future dealings exploiting the opportunities for new benefit-cost possibilities. If competition is "rivalry subdued into organization by rules of the game" (Walton E. Hamilton, 1934), the role of the constitution is to provide for those rules and their evolution. Therefore, we can rephrase Demsetz by saying that constitutional powers develop to internalize political externalities when the gains of internalization for political leaders become larger than the cost of the constitutional internalization.

The process is still going on, as discussed in section 5 in terms of the maintenance of modern constitutions. But it is important to stress that it started before the enactment of formal constitutions, and the emphasis on specific turning points – such as the French or U.S. constitutional revolutions – should not discourage more careful historical research on the matter.[11] For the moment let us observe how the constitutional entrenchment of the division of powers, the proceduralization of conflicts, and the disaggregation of people's demand among the separate institutions internalized dissent and made it functional for the stability of the constitutional order. At the same time, the constitutional settlement of political leaders' rights defines the effective amplitude of citizens' liberties indirectly, almost as a by-product of the defense of their own prerogatives. As with Machiavelli's political struggles, the protection of ordinary citizens tends to be a residual variable. That remark should sound less reductive than it appears, as the success of constitutional innovations depends ultimately on people's acquiescence. And people's legitimization of authority tends to sanction outcomes, not duly followed procedures. The ratification to the U.S. Constitution of 1787 violated the Articles of Confederation of 1781, but it remained; and the main basis of the British Constitution was a coup d'état. The same Glorious Revolution introduced both the *Instrument of Government* (1653) and the *Bill of Rights* of 1689: the former vanished even before the restoration of the monarchy in 1660, but the latter survived (Peter Madgwick and Diana Woodhouse, 1995).

4   The two keystones of the modern constitutions

Has the U.S. Constitution proven to be more effective in preserving political property rights rather than in protecting economic property rights (Niskanen, 1990)? Some scholars (Richard Posner, 1987, 25) seem to lean toward the opposite view, and an examination of how constitutional rights translate into effective protection can help us to face the issue.

Let us start by remarking that the modern constitutional enunciation of a right is of a rather general nature, most of the time combined with a qualification relating its exercise to "the framework of the laws that

---

[11] After all, the Magna Carta could provide for the habeas corpus only in the presence of an independent judiciary, a protection unavailable in many European countries of the twentieth century. The role of the medieval representative assemblies – "the great political invention of the middle ages" (Sammy Finer, 1997, vol. 2, p. 1024) – deserves attention. The electoral evolution of the British Parliament in the period 1620–1680 shows how the Glorious Revolution broke apart the identity of interest within the ruling classes and how divisions "arose from the competition within the elite for control of boroughs or the voices of country freeholders" (Mark Kishlansky, 1986, pp. 227–8).

govern it"![12] The reasons for that combination relate to the uncertainty of the future. To allow the permanence of the statements and to foster the effectiveness of future public action, the constitutional declaration has to be clear on principle, leaving the contents to future legislation. That interpretation is consistent, first, with the early introduction of the Bill of Rights as related to the need for establishing the legitimacy of a new leadership after major displacements of power.[13] Second, those rights are necessary complements of the division of powers. However vague, they represent points of reference to orient the policy decisions of the various powers and, in a competitive setting, benchmarks for their reciprocal checking. Therefore, the recognition of the programmatic value of constitutional statements does not imply their irrelevance, but puts emphasis on the role played by the division of powers in transforming them into effective action. The U.S. "commercial clause" shows the flexibility of such statements in adapting to evolving circumstances.[14]

A second remark, more in the nature of a caveat, concerns the fact that economists seem to fall sometimes into the verbal trap of considering constitutional rights at their face value, as if they should work by fiat. In an interesting reversal of roles, legal experts warn us against the "tendency to think that constitutional rules execute themselves" (Robert Bork, 1984). It follows that the arrangement through which modern constitutional orders strive after their purposes rests on two keystones: the political and economic rights stated in the ideological part of the document, and the powers and duties of the various public authorities regulated in the second part. As guidelines for future action, principles count insofar as they are translated into effective action by what occurs inside the supply side, within its two crucial dimensions: division of powers and

---

[12] As stated in the constitution of the Fourth French Republic. The standard U.S. clause says that "the Congress shall have the power to enforce this article by appropriate legislation," while the otherwise quite detailed German constitution says that the "details shall be the subject of a federal law."

[13] The "war of words" that characterizes the drafting of a constitution signals the need for a new "social paradigm." Those "words" are the pledge of a new leadership that has to consolidate people's expectations. Charles Epp (1996) argues that the adoption of the Canadian Charter of Rights and Freedoms in 1982 did not bring about any effective innovation: in our view, it was an important symbolic part of the package related to the repatriation of the Canadian constitution.

[14] Its "principle" did not need any "amendment of the constitution to adjust the powers of Congress in economic affairs to the needs of the U.S. today. It is indeed remarkable that powers granted over 150 years ago to an agricultural country with a few million people should be adapted to the needs of a great industrial power with 50 times that population" (Wheare, 1951, 109).

people's reactions. A constitutional equilibrium implies a degree of consent among the centers of influence on lines of actions that foster or weaken their legitimacy because of their correspondence with popular expectations. For better or for worse, people's attitudes come to complement the working of the division of powers.

In conclusion, it is not the written words that confer rights, but the substantive support provided by what occurs inside the supply side in transforming Madison's parchment barriers into effective ones. Therefore, it is not to the words of a document that we have to look for the enforcement of rights, but to the efficacy of the contraposition of interests enacted on a stage and watched by the subjects. Western political history shows how the struggles for political influence represent the real support for freedom, and how the search for legitimacy has led to a growing emphasis on popular consent. From the charter granted by King John at Runnymede onward, the notion of a contractarian agreement has had a rhetoric appeal. But the real enforcing guaranty is provided by the equilibrium of the political forces involved, as shown by the ill-fated constitutions of the past (from the Polish of 1791 to the Prussian of 1848) and of the present, in societies where the formal statement of individual rights does not imply their effective protection.

The role of elections and the risk of collusion

The competition we are referring to is the competition studied and described at length by Breton (1996): it includes but is not limited to party competition. In the contemporary world, however, political parties deserve attention for the way in which they can improve or reduce the competition of the system. That granted, we should ask why the electoral system is not dealt with explicitly in the constitution (Belgium, Denmark, and Sweden are among the few exceptions). We do not maintain that it should be, but find that omission surprising not so much because of the risk of manipulation by the majority (think of gerrymandering), but because the rhetoric of people's sovereignty should imply that it be at the heart of the constitution. It can be submitted that the omission is an indirect proof of the latent feeling that the real guarantee of freedom is not in the details of any electoral law but in the division of powers and in the competitiveness of the entire system. It should follow that the ultimate constitutional role of elections is not that of representing the people – a random selection would be more efficient – but that of providing a periodic and explicit check on the legitimacy of the constitutional order (Bernard Manin, 1997). It counts not for the details of the statutory rules, but for its recognition of the low cost of expressing dissent and for its explicit reference to people's attitudes. At the same time, it cannot be excluded that the original omission was discovered too late, so to say, when party politics was already very pervasive and watchful of keeping its influence to decide the matter. That remark calls attention to the danger that party politics represent for the enforcement of collusive agreements apt to reduce the internal competitiveness of the public machine. That is confirmed by the fact that Adolf Hitler and Benito Mussolini never changed the liberal constitutions that brought them to power. It was thanks to strong collusive ties that they were able to change the substance while keeping the formality of the old order. And that confirms how even a perfect constitution is useless if not sustained by effective competition.

5   The issue of constitutional maintenance

Has the public action that followed the Great Depression "wrought several lasting alterations in the constitutional structure" of the U.S. (Clinton L. Rossiter, 1948)? Considering the growth of public action occurring in the last century under democratic constitutions, it is easy to understand why many people wonder about the notion of constitutional boundaries to public action. If today the tide is for slimmer governments, there are those who favor the status quo, and the constitutional debate is always intense. Constitutional changes can be ubiquitous or nonexistent depending on the eyes (and the pocket) of the beholder, and the issue at stake is not the need for or occurrence of changes – when the world changes the contents of no rule at any level can remain the same – but rather the fact that the procedures for amendment are much less used than we would expect. If Niskanen (1990) speaks of extraconstitutional changes, other authors express harsher judgments to the point of asking why "nonconsensual constitutional revisions [are] often the rule rather than the exception" (Charlotte Twight, 1992).

That "nonconsensual" label calls to mind authoritarianism, conspiracy, or deception, and therefore posits a dilemma. If there is real dissent, the failure of political competition to avert plots and swindles is a failure of democracy itself. Should, however, the democratic system work reasonably well, the fact that those innovations went unchallenged on constitutional grounds shows that the label is inappropriate.[15] To handle the puzzle of constitutional maintenance – in the literal meaning of keeping

---

[15] Peter Aranson (1988) suggests the case of power holders serving the interests of subtle rent seekers. According to Twight (1992), politicians would be able to modify citizens' rights by manipulating political transaction costs so to reduce opposition to the change. The notion of endogenous transaction costs applied to public decision making recalls Puviani's illusions, and shares the same difficulty in terms of refutability.

it in a good order – we need a criterion to identify a constitutional change before asking why it is adopted in an informal way. In terms of our discussion, a change can affect either the ideological first part or the distribution of powers regulated in the second part of a constitution. Sanctioned rights can fall into oblivion or new rights can be protected even without formal enactment. The Fifteenth Amendment to the U.S. constitution – adopted in 1870 in a singularly "clear and absolute form" (Wheare, 1951) – was made effective almost a century later; the protection of minorities' rights is often the fruit of a more sensitive reading of "old" rights. Powers can be reassigned across jurisdictions without any constitutional modification (see Stan Winer's contribution to this volume). If Wheare (1951) detected a process of centralization of public decision making, today in many European countries the reverse is occurring vis-à-vis the European Union, though few national constitutions provide explicitly for that implicit limitation of sovereignty. Therefore it seems important to concentrate attention on how ideological and structural changes affect the balance of power and to develop Wheare's remark that the very *processes* by which those changes occur *adapt to changing conditions*.

To simplify, we disregard the amendments of more or less symbolic value or of formal necessity (those concerning the colors of the flag or the republican form of government, say) and point out the difficult distinction between a new initiative of a legitimate power and a genuine new area of public action. Any move of a political leader (a political entrepreneur's initiative, a parliamentary deliberation, a ministerial action, an innovative bureaucratic program, a judge's decision) brings with it its own constitutional dimension. Its contents are scrutinized by other leaders and assessed for what it implies for their own positions and in terms of people's reactions. At times, a constitutional innovation implicit in an action can be considered expedient, and at other times the exercise of a proper power can appear controversial. In all instances, what matters is not the formal attribution of a power so much as what is made explicit by its exercise, a matter influenced by what is politically relevant: the growing influence of the British Parliament in the fifteenth century, Alexander Hamilton trying new federal powers when organizing an army in 1794 to fight the "war of the whiskey," the Italian judges reversing their historical meekness towards politicians. Wheare (1951) discusses at length the factors – technological changes (from the development of weapons to the methods of tax collection), economic crises, war emergency, and the very rules of politics – which *cause the constitution to mean something different* from what it used to mean or which *disturb its balance*.

Constitutional coordination means that, in equilibrium, each center of influence possesses the consent of the other centers to act in a given area. That does not eliminate conflicts, but identifies how other power holders come to be benefited or harmed by any modification. If anybody crosses a boundary and infringes upon others, the negatively affected ones – be they political entrepreneurs or formal centers of influence – will take initiatives to oppose the change. As we have seen, constitutional powers count in two complementary ways: first, in terms of how they are balanced by the related "entitlements" of other centers; second, in terms of the impact on people's welfare. Those two aspects are relevant to the calculus of any center, say A, when assessing the value of a modification in the power entitlement of another center, say B. In deciding whether or not to grant its assent to the modification, center A weighs the expected gains and losses affecting its own capacity to deal with other centers and with its constituencies. And there is little room for exchange when popular pressure is strong and legitimacy is at stake. Examples abound. In 1905 the U.S. Supreme Court declared a statutory limit on the number of daily hours of work invalid, and in 1908 unanimously sustained that same limit (see note 18); in 1994 German participation in military operations outside the territory of NATO countries was excluded because of article 87a of the Basic Law,[16] and in 1998 over two thousand German troops were in Bosnia. In a changing environment, competitive pressures react to the occurrence of suboptimal outcomes by stimulating wider or narrower lines of public action.

A constitutional change implies a redefinition of powers in terms of new, wider or narrower lines of action. And it is the reaction of other centers that draws the line between *adjustments* and *innovations*. When all political leaders agree – or acquiesce to the change – we can deduce that the change has been adjusted, leaving the eventual balance of power unaffected. When that consent is lacking, we can infer that the constitutional balance of influence is considered to be under threat, and we face an innovation requiring the amending procedures. The presence of contrasting evaluations among political leaders – including invalidation by the courts, as discussed later – either stops the proposed change[17] or puts in motion the formal procedure for amending the constitution. In a positive analytical framework that recourse reveals the lack of consent:

---

[16] "The Federation shall establish armed forces for defense purposes." In 1995 a German technician was prohibited from participating in flying missions for NATO over Bosnia.

[17] A polar case occurred in Canada, when the Meech Lake Accord – a package of amendments to the constitution contrived to induce Quebec to sign the 1982 constitution – collapsed on June 23, 1990, because of the opposition of Elijah Harper, the only representative of Native Indians in the legislature of Manitoba.

when it is difficult to agree on substance, the solution is to resort to procedures. In that sense, the early proposition of *The Calculus of Consent* is vindicated – only unanimity is a characteristic of constitutional changes, and when that unanimity is lacking, the issue becomes a qualified political decision. Our approach would suggest, however, that the purpose of the amending procedures is that of making the adoption of changes not meeting the unanimous consent of political leaders more difficult. Does it follow that the more demanding those formal procedures, the stronger the veto power of each center of political influence and the greater therefore the risk of collusion? If so, those afraid of extra-constitutional changes should invoke the simplification of those very procedures! As for collusion, any definite conclusion is premature if we do not consider the cost of entry into the market of political influence. But let us first consider the growing complexity of the public machine.

Complexity and collusion

Constitutional changes conditional upon the degree of consent of the political leadership – including those entrepreneurs of an extra-constitutional variety made influential by an adequate popular support – can explain the growing complexity of the public machinery. In itself, the complexity of modern governments could be the price to be paid in order to keep the balance of power, but the efficiency of that price depends on the absence of collusion. The expansion of the public sector during this century has been accompanied by the formation of new centers of influence, and by new powers granted to the old ones. Indeed, independent public agencies, ombudsmen, easier access to traditional and to new administrative courts, police accountability, "government by committee" (Wheare, 1955), delegation of powers, and other institutions of the same kind appear to contradict the logic of parliamentary representation. In the suggested approach, however, they are instrumental to the articulation of the public machinery required to keep the constitutional balance of power. But that price could be too high in the presence of collusion: even worse, could that inefficient complexity encourage further collusion?

Collusion is positively related to cost of expressing dissent, that is, to the cost of finding a political leader expressing dissatisfaction. A more articulated division of powers is a guarantee of responsiveness if it encourages the attention of new and more specialized political entrepreneurs. Insofar as any meaningful opposition can find a leader, the cost of collusion is reduced. The relevance of that constraint requires an adequate empirical testing. Let us underline, however, that when competition is absent – because of repression, corruption, or for some other reason – there is no viable alternative to assess consent, and no constitutional rule can perform miracles. The same appeal to people's votes could be equivocal, as its meaning always depends on the cost of expressing dissent, that is, on the same condition that makes credible the consent of political leaders.

The constitutional courts

The role of courts in the building of modern constitutions has been important. Think of the English historical experience during Tudor times or of Alexis de Tocqueville defining U.S. federal judges as "statesmen-politicians." Today, the judicial influence within the modern division of powers is an accepted reality, and constitutional judges are active participants in the process of constitutional adjustment. Their nonpartisan status – in terms of a technically qualified and reasonably independent contribution – helps to reduce the space for conflicts, to speed up such adjustments, and to single out the areas of constitutional innovation. If it is easy to agree that their influence is substantial – in the U.S., the "First Amendment is almost entirely judge-made law" (Bork, 1984, 230) – the fact that they have to pay attention to their own legitimacy could appear more controversial.

Laffont and Tirole (1990) underline that when constitutional judges act on the basis of soft information (what else is available?) "they have discretionary power and compete with the legislative and executive branches in filling unforeseen contingencies," and the search for their own legitimacy is the only solution to the old worry, *quis custodiet ipsos custodes?* Wheare (1951) supports that point empirically,[18] and Madgwick and Woodhouse (1995, 7) observe that "the interpretation of a constitution by the judges is part of the political process." Finally, two legal scholars (Louis Fisher and Neal Devins, 1992, 2) make a point worthy of full quotation for its consistency with what we have been dis-

---

[18] The U.S. Supreme Court "has not been unaffected by the changes in opinion in that country during the first half of the twentieth century. In 1905 the Court declared that a statute of New York State which had fixed a maximum of sixty hours per week and ten hours per day for bakers was invalid, on the ground that it violated the liberty of the citizen to work as long as he liked. The right to sell or purchase labour, the Court said, was part of the liberty which the Constitution guaranteed . . . In 1908, however, the Court unanimously sustained an act of the State of Oregon fixing a maximum of ten hours a day for women workers in certain employment . . . and in 1917 . . . it sustained an act of the same state extending the maximum of ten hours to men" (Wheare, 1951, 46).

cussing so far: "The historical record demonstrates that the judiciary often accepts the political boundaries of its times. Attempts to defy those boundaries and invalidate the policies of elected leaders create substantial risks for the legitimacy and effectiveness of the judicial system. Abstract legal analysis is tempered by a sense of pragmatism and statesmanship among judges . . . Courts are not the sole participants in the process of shaping and declaring constitutional values. They share the task with other political institutions at the national and state level."

6   Conclusion: Controlling political leadership

Like Janus, a constitutional order has two faces: it has to be imposed on the people and it has to be accepted by the people. The ancients softened the first face by insisting on the mythical origin of that order; the moderns claim that self-imposed coercion follows from the contractarian basis of the constitution itself. Could the change of emphasis be attributed to the growing costs of holding sway? The effective protection of individual liberties could make the contractarian claim plausible, but the many constitutional declamations that remain dead letters bring into question how that contract is enforced and why those liberties emerged in the first place. This chapter urges that a positive line of inquiry – still in its infancy (Stefan Voigt, 1997) – should replace the farsighted Founding Fathers with more mundane Rotten and normally sighted Kids and consider a constitution as the set of rules superintending the interactions of political leaders, in a setting made stable by people's acquiescence. Constitutional legitimacy is the focal point allowing the coordination of leaders' and citizens' expectations.

Oligopolistic collusion among the political leaders (power holders and political entrepreneurs) is tempered by competitive pressures, as first remarked by Machiavelli. By generalizing that point, we submit that political conflicts reduced the cost of dissent, regulated leaders' competition, and improved the position of ordinary citizens, the passive but still prevailing side of the constitutional game. Constitutions may be more or less well written documents, but their vitality depends on the effectiveness of politicians' competitive struggle in transforming constitutional "principles" into effective rights. As for maintenance, constitutional changes are chapters of an unceasing struggle fought on two fronts: influence and legitimacy. Political leaders evaluate how any change impinges on their formal or informal powers directly and in terms of their legitimacy before the people. Effective constitutional adjustments are those that meet the unanimous consent of the formal centers of powers and of informal centers of influence. It is the competitiveness of the system that protects against collusion, and the cost of expressing dissent meaning to people's acquiescence. Is there any limit to the proc constitutional adjustment? How far can the effective constitution _ from the written one? If we accept the two pillars sustaining the constitutional vault – principles (Bill of Rights) and regulated competition (division of powers) – it is difficult to identify any conceptual limit different from what is accepted by the political consensus of the formal and informal centers of power.[19] Of course, there is the risk of collusion, but that is the risk of the democratic order itself. In that sense, the only insurmountable limit is the one (unsuccessfully) argued by Carl Schmitt in early 1932: not to allow those candidates who are against the democratic method itself to run for office (Finn, 1991, 172).

An interesting implication of our analysis refers to the efficiency of constitutional flexibility. Because of the rational propensity to respond to any constraint by adjusting themselves at the margins still under their control (Thràinn Eggertsson, 1995, 202), political leaders can always find new ways to reap their rents. It is therefore necessary to adjust those constraints as soon as a way is found to bypass the old ones. But it is only the "animal" spirit of political entrepreneurs that can devise how to beat the analogous spirit of their fellow entrepreneurs. Low costs of expressing dissent thanks to fundamental freedoms, and the political competition developing within the division of powers, are the necessary and sufficient conditions to make the flexibility of constitutional rules instrumental to the control of political opportunism.

References

Aranson, Peter H., 1988, "Procedural and substantive constitutional protection of economic liberties," in James D. Gwartney and Richard E. Wagner (Eds.), *Public Choice and Constitutional Economics*, Jai Press, 285–313.

Bork, Robert H., 1984, "A lawyer's view of constitutional economics," in Richard B. McKenzie (Ed.), *Constitutional Economics: Containing the Economic Powers of Government*, Lexington Books, 227–235.

Breton, Albert, 1996, *Competitive Governments: An Economic Theory of Politics and Public Finance*, Cambridge University Press.

Calvert, Randall, 1995, "The rational choice theory of social institutions: coop-

---

[19] For a recent example, consider the deal struck by a number of U.S. attorneys general with tobacco companies to settle all state lawsuits against them, following the failure of a similar proposal in Congress. *The Economist* (47/1998) considered the deal "an abuse of the legal process and an evasion of democratic accountability." If nobody in the U.S. raised the issue and *The Economist* were right, we would have an instance of constitutional adjustment.

eration, coordination and communication," in Jeffrey S. Banks and Eric A. Hanushek (Eds.), *Modern Political Economy*, Cambridge University Press, 216–267.

Demsetz, Harold, 1967, "Toward a theory of property rights," *American Economic Review* 57, 347–354.

Dixit, Avinash, 1996, *The Making of Economic Policy: A Transaction-cost Politics Perspective*, MIT Press.

Eggertsson, Thràinn, 1995, "On the Economics of Economics," *Kyklos* 48, 201–210.

Epp, Charles R., 1996, "Do Bills of Rights matter? The Canadian Charter of Rights and Freedoms," *American Political Science Review* 90, 765–779.

Finer, Sammy E., 1997, *The History of Government from the Earliest Times*, Oxford University Press.

Finn, John E., 1991, *Constitutions in Crisis: Political Violence and the Rule of Law*, Oxford University Press.

Fisher, Louis, and Neal Devins, 1992, *Political Dynamics of Constitutional Law*, West Publishing.

Foley, Michael, 1989, *The Silence of Constitutions*, Routledge.

Hamilton, Walton E., 1934, "Competition," *Encyclopaedia of the Social Sciences*, MacMillan.

Hardin, Russell, 1989, "Why a Constitution?," in B. Grofman and B. Wittman (Eds.), *The Federalist Papers and the New Institutionalism*, Agathon Press, 100–123.

Hardin, Russell, 1998, "Trust," *The New Palgrave of Law and Economics*, MacMillan Reference Limited.

Kishlansky, Mark A., 1986, *Parliamentary Selection: Social and Political Choices in Early Modern England*, Cambridge University Press.

Laffont, Jean-Jacques, and Jean Tirole, 1990, "The politics of government decision making: regulatory institutions," *Journal of Law, Economics and Organizations* 6, 1–31.

Mackaay, Ejan, 1997, "The emergence of constitutional rights," *Constitutional Political Economy* 8, 15–36.

Madgwick, Peter, and Diana Woodhouse, 1995, *The Law and Politics of the Constitution of the United Kingdom*, Harvester Wheatsheaf.

Manin, Bernard, 1997, *The Principles of Representative Government*, Cambridge University Press.

Mueller, Dennis, 1996, *Constitutional Democracy*, Oxford University Press.

Niskanen, William A., 1990, "Conditions affecting the survival of constitutional rules," *Constitutional Political Economy* 1, 53–62.

North, Douglass, 1981, *Structure and Change in Economic History*, Norton.

North, Douglass, 1990, *Institutions, Institutional Change and Economic Performance*, Cambridge University Press.

Ordeshook, Peter C., 1992, "Constitutional Stability," *Constitutional Political Economy* 3, 137–175.

Posner, Richard A., 1987, "The constitution as an economic document," *The George Washington Law Review* 56, 4–38.

Rosster, Clinton, 1948, *Constitutional Dictatorship: Crisis Government in the Modern Democracies*, Princeton University Press.

Saunders, Trevor J., 1981, *Aristotle: The Politics*, Penguin Classics.

Stigler, George, 1964, "A theory of oligopoly," *Journal of Political Economy* 72, 44–61.

Twight, Charlotte, 1992, "Constitutional renegotiation: impediments to consensual revision," *Constitutional Political Economy* 3, 89–114.

Voigt, Stefan, 1997, "Positive constitutional economics: a survey," *Public Choice* 90, 11–53.

Wheare, Kenneth C., 1951, *Modern Constitutions*, Oxford University Press.

Wheare, Kenneth C., 1955, *Government by Committee: An Essay on the British Constitution*, Oxford at the Clarendon Press.

Wintrobe, Ronald, 1998, *The Political Economy of Dictatorship*, Cambridge University Press.

Decentralization and federalism

CHAPTER 6

Fiscal decentralization and competitive governments

Richard M. Bird

Fiscal decentralization has recently become a matter of considerable policy importance to governments around the world, not least in developing and transitional countries.[1] It is thus natural to ask whether the multitiered governments now in existence in many countries are "competitive" in the sense in which Albert Breton (1996) uses the term. How relevant is his stimulating analysis to one concerned with the immense variety of real-world institutions and problems encompassed by the general term "fiscal decentralization"? In an earlier paper (Bird, 1993) I argued that most of the fiscal decentralization taking place around the world could best be analyzed using a "principal-agent" framework. Yet Breton has explicitly ruled out this approach as irrelevant to the central issues concerning him.[2] How, if at all, can these apparently directly opposing viewpoints be reconciled? This is the question that I pose and attempt to answer, at least provisionally, in this chapter.

I shall proceed as follows. In the next section, I define some key terms employed in the subsequent discussion. I then outline the essence of the decentralization issue as it emerges in practice, emphasizing that several quite different problems and approaches are often confusingly subsumed under this general heading. Finally, I set out briefly a first attempt at understanding how Breton's competitiveness approach helps in the

I am grateful for the hospitality of the Fiscal Affairs Department of the International Monetary Fund, where I was a visiting scholar at the time this paper was finished. I am also grateful to Robert Inman and Wayne Thirsk for helpful comments on an earlier draft and to Albert Breton for helpful discussions of some of the material.

[1] For extended discussion, see Bird, Ebel, and Wallich (1995) and Bird and Vaillancourt (1998). Some parts of this chapter are based on the introductory chapter to the latter book as well as on ideas set out in more detail in Bird (1993, 1995) and Bird and Chen (1998a).

[2] See Breton, Cassone, and Fraschini (1998) and Breton (1996), Chapter 6.

analysis of these problems. It turns out that at one level, it does not, essentially because it is for the most part concerned with a more fundamental question that is less immediately relevant than some other aspects of decentralization in the less than perfectly democratic states that make up most of the world. Nonetheless, I shall conclude by arguing that the main policy-relevant implication of the competitive-government approach appears, perhaps surprisingly, to be similar to that of the information-theoretic approach which is slowly attempting to fill some of the gaps in the conventional "fiscal federalism" literature (Boadway, 1997). At a theoretical level, Breton, Cassone, and Fraschini (1998) are undoubtedly correct in pointing out the fundamental differences between even the newest varieties of fiscal federalism and the competitive-government approach. At the level of policy, however, I suggest that these differences are perhaps less significant than the strong emphasis that each approach places – albeit for very different reasons – on the key role of information in determining outcomes.

Types of decentralization

One reason decentralization is not easily understood is because it is a complex phenomenon that takes many forms and has several dimensions. A wide variety of institutional restructurings may be encompassed by this label. Useful distinctions may be drawn among concepts I have elsewhere (Bird, 1993) labeled deconcentration, delegation, and devolution.

Deconcentration covers cases in which, in effect, the central government disperses some responsibilities to regional branch offices, which may in turn be grouped on a territorial basis. This is the form of decentralization that prevailed in Eastern Europe until recently, for example (Bird, Ebel, and Wallich, 1995). The limited decentralization found in Sri Lanka and in some African countries may also be characterized as deconcentration. A centrally designated district officer (regional representative of the central government) is charged with coordinating the local activities of various central government agencies, but has no formal or direct responsibility to local residents. Regrouping functions territorially in this fashion is no different in principle from other possible ways of reorganizing central governments to improve their efficiency and effectiveness. Hence, it raises none of the special problems often associated with decentralization and is not further discussed here. Occasionally, deconcentration in this sense may be somewhat awkwardly coupled with a more delegated (or even devolved) form of decentralization.[3] Conceptually, however, de-concentration (whether functional or territorial) remains distinct from "real" decentralization because it is in principle concerned solely with the more efficient and effective delivery of central government policies, and not at all with fostering or accommodating local inputs into those policies.

In contrast, the central issue with respect to both delegation and devolution relates to the balancing of central and local interests. *Delegation* refers to a situation in which local governments in effect act as agents for the center, executing certain functions on its behalf. In principle, what is to be done by the local government is determined by the center, but in fact *what* is actually done and *how* it is done is often determined largely by local practice. I have argued elsewhere (Bird, 1993) that this form of decentralization is the one most commonly found around the world today. In many respects, as already mentioned, such decentralization may usefully be characterized in terms of a "principal-agent" problem, with the principal being the central government and the local government (or local administrative agency, if – as, for instance, in Vietnam – there is no formal democratic system) as the agent.

From this perspective, the central design problem with delegated decentralization is to set up the rules (tax assignments, transfer programs, and so on) in such a way as to ensure that self-interested agents (local governments) will face incentives inducing them to act as closely as possible in accordance with the wishes of the principal (the central government). Alternatively, as in the traditional economic theory of fiscal federalism (Oates, 1972), both levels of government may be seen as acting as agents of different groups of citizens, with the central government of course encompassing all the subsets included within the purview of the local governments. In this approach, it is usually assumed that the central government should in the end dominate in any conflict (Tresch, 1981). Indeed, as Seabright (1996) shows, so long as local governments are strictly hierarchically subordinated to the central government, the fact that localities may be at least partly independent political entities does not alter the outcome: central-government preferences – whether viewed as representing the "sum" of the preferences of all citizens or simply those of the "higher" jurisdiction – dominate.

In contrast, *devolution* refers to a situation in which both implemen-

---

[3] For a formal example, see the discussion of Romania in Bird, Ebel, and Wallich (1995); for a more informal example, see the case of Vietnam (World Bank, 1996a).

tation authority and at least some say in what is to be done are in the hands of local governments.[4] There is no longer any presumption that local interests are, or should be, subordinated to central interests. At one extreme, a system of government in which more than one level or tier exists, with some functions shared through common institutions and others determined independently by regional units, is the classical case of a federation (Wheare, 1969). More broadly, a wide range of possible organizational forms exist that fall somewhere between a unitary state – one like New Zealand, in which the constituent territorial units act primarily (or exclusively) through the common organs of the general (central) government rather than through any tiered-government structure – and simple leagues or joint authorities set up by separate national states for specific purposes (such as NATO and ASEAN). As the case of the European Union perhaps suggests, such associations may evolve toward a more federal state – though, as I have argued elsewhere (Bird, 1989), it is important to understand that there is no necessary direct mapping between different degrees of economic union and different degrees of political integration.

The many varieties of what may loosely be termed "federal" arrangements found in the world today have recently been usefully characterized by Watts (1996) as "decentralized unions" on the one hand, and more formal "federations" on the other.[5] *Decentralized unions* are basically unitary states, in the sense that the ultimate authority rests both constitutionally and operationally with the central government. Nonetheless, regional units of government may have a greater or lesser degree of policy autonomy, which may or may not be constitutionally protected. Italy, Japan, the Netherlands, and the United Kingdom are well-known examples among developed countries. This is also the most common form of "federal" system found in developing and transitional countries. Examples include China, Colombia, Ghana, Indonesia, Tanzania, and Ukraine.[6] As Colombia and Indonesia show in one direction (toward decentralization – more devolutionary in character in the first example) and China in the other (toward recentralization), many of these countries are currently in a state of flux with respect to

---

[4] In the terms used by Breton, devolution thus relates to the assignment of "powers" over policy design and implementation. For a clear distinction between such assignment and what I have labeled delegation, see, for example, Breton, Cassone, and Fraschini (1998), p. 24, note 10.

[5] For discussion of still looser unions, such as leagues, federacies, and associated states, see Watts (1996).

[6] As the examples of Tanzania and Ukraine suggest, different regions within the same country (respectively, Zanzibar and the Republic of Crimea) may have quite different degrees of autonomy.

the degree and nature of decentralization.[7] Moreover, and importantly, it is this type of "federal" system that may sometimes be taken to apply to some degree to relations between local and higher-level governments even in countries in which there is no formal or effective decentralization of policy autonomy to regional governments (for example, Hungary), as well as in other countries in which there is some decentralization of varying degrees to both regional and local levels (such as Vietnam).[8] As suggested earlier, principal-agent models seem to provide a broadly appropriate analytical framework for such countries.

In sharp contrast to such decentralized unions, *formal federations* combine constitutionally strong subnational units with a strong central government, with each tier having its own powers and each dealing directly with citizens. Although there are relatively few such countries, and there may sometimes be considerable differences between constitutional form and operational reality, a number of important developed countries have long been federations in this sense – Australia, Austria, Canada, Germany, Switzerland, and of course the United States. More recently, Spain and Belgium have adopted interesting forms of federal government. Among less developed countries, Argentina, Brazil, Ethiopia, India, Malaysia, Mexico, Nigeria, Pakistan, and Venezuela are formal federations. Recently, South Africa and Russia have also adopted a federal structure of government. The degree of divergence between formal and operational federation may sometimes be great (as in Pakistan) and may sometimes change significantly, as is perhaps now occurring in Argentina.[9] Nonetheless, in contrast to the delegation (principal-agent) framework that I have suggested is generally appropriate when discussing intergovernmental relations in decentralized unions, the existence of a formal federal structure as a rule implies substantial devolution, as defined earlier. In such cases, a different analytical framework is needed, as will be discussed further. One way to illustrate this point may be to note that while the desired end result of delegation is presumably *uniformity* in service provision, the basic rationale for devolution is essentially to permit *variation* in service provision.[10]

---

[7] On Colombia, see Bird and Fiszbein (1998); on Indonesia, see Shah and Qureshi (1994). On China, see Bird and Chen (1998b).

[8] The Hungarian case is discussed in Bird, Wallich, and Peteri (1995) and the case of Vietnam in World Bank (1996a).

[9] On Pakistan, see Shah (1998); on Argentina, see World Bank (1996b).

[10] Of course, there may be wide divergences regarding such matters even among federations. Contrast, for example, the German constitutional provision with respect to "uniformity of living conditions" (Basic Law, Article 72 [2]; see Spahn, 1982) with the Canadian provision for "equalization" (Constitution Act, 1982, subsection 36.2). The former clearly directs attention to equality of *outcomes*; the latter, by contrast, simply makes (roughly) equal outcomes *feasible* – if provincial governments so desire.

Many factors may affect both the ideal and the actual form of decentralization in any country at any time: the nature of the subnational units (their number, their absolute and relative sizes, their absolute and relative wealth, and so on),[11] the formal distribution of functions (as related to the "span" of public goods, externalities and jurisdictional spillovers, transaction costs, and so on),[12] the nature of "common" institutions (with particular attention to their effects on governmental competition), and the role and status of the constitution (for example, with respect to the independence of the judiciary and collective and individual rights). Much discussion of decentralization presumes that it is a matter of choice or deliberate design. In the circumstances of many countries, however, some degree of decentralization may be either a political necessity – to hold together a fractious heterogeneous country, for instance – or, as it were, a default option, a way to carry out some of the necessary functions of the state in the face of fiscal crisis or political weakness at the center. Indeed, all of these rationales may be at work simultaneously to varying degrees in a country such as Russia (Wallich, 1994). "Decentralization" may thus encompass a very nuanced set of activities that can be understood and analyzed only on the basis of thorough local institutional knowledge.

Decentralization may also occur to varying degrees in different spheres. The technical characteristics and policy objectives with respect to specific public services may lead to very different forms and extents of decentralization. *Fiscal decentralization* – who collects what taxes, who makes what expenditures, and how any "vertical imbalance" is rectified – has been especially prominent in recent discussions around the world. This emphasis is understandable, since governmental reorganization has often been motivated in whole or in part by fiscal crisis. Nonetheless, the more fundamental questions clearly relate to what may be called political and administrative decentralization.

Political decentralization refers at one level to the extent to which political institutions map the multiplicity of citizen interests onto policy decisions (Inman and Rubinfeld, 1996). To put this another way, regardless of the extent to which any government's decisions may reflect citizen interests, policy decisions may be made on a common (shared/central/national) basis or on a self-rule (local autonomy) basis. The key factors determining outcomes in this sense hinge on what powers are assigned to what governments and how local interests are

---

[11] For an interesting formal analysis of some of these factors, see Crémer and Palfrey (1997).

[12] The best exploration of these matters remains Breton and Scott (1978).

represented in central decisions (Inman and Rubinfeld, 1996). The central question with respect to political decentralization is thus basically "who decides," and the relevant literature draws heavily on political science (Watts, 1996) as well as public choice economics (Inman and Rubinfeld, 1996, 1997). As noted earlier, such issues tend to be most important in formal federations.

In contrast, *administrative decentralization* – which obviously is closely related to delegation as already defined and hence applies most clearly in decentralized unions (and with respect to relations between various tiers of subnational government) – is concerned with how political institutions, once established, turn policy decisions into allocative (and distributive) outcomes through both fiscal and regulatory actions. The central question here obviously relates to the incentive constraints facing various decision makers. Unsurprisingly, the emerging literature on this theme, as mentioned earlier, draws heavily upon the principal-agent and transactions costs literature (Crémer, Estache, Seabright, 1995; Seabright, 1996).

Federal finance and fiscal federalism

Another way to view some of the issues touched on above is to note that in the traditional world of *fiscal federalism* in principle everything – boundaries, assignments of finances and functions, the level and nature of transfers, and so forth – is malleable. In contrast, in what may be called the world of *federal finance* (Bird and Chen, 1998a), jurisdictional boundaries and the assignment of functions and finances must be taken to be fixed at some earlier (for example, constitutional) stage and not open to further change under normal circumstances. As discussed previously, in the conventional economic approach to fiscal federalism that has shaped most of the policy literature on decentralization, central government preferences are clearly dominant in practice (if not so clearly in theory).[13] In federal finance, however, neither consensus nor preference imposition can or should be assumed with respect to such matters as the desirable degree of fiscal and regulatory harmonization, or the extent to which an internal common market is a policy goal. Instead, such matters can in principle be determined only jointly by

---

[13] Bird (1980) argues that the conventional literature on fiscal federalism is, so to speak, schizophrenic, in the sense that it derives its rationale for the existence of autonomous local governments as representatives of "local" interests but makes sense only if the central government in the end really determines outcomes. Of course, not everyone accepts this proposition.

both levels of government in an appropriate political (or constitutional) forum.[14]

In addition, in a federal finance setting both levels of government may properly pursue their own distributive and perhaps even stabilization policies, again with no presumption of central dominance. This does not mean, of course, that subnational distributive or stabilization policies will necessarily be *effective* – an outcome that may often be doubtful, given the openness of subnational economies. The mere likelihood of failure, however, has never deterred governments, central or local, from attempting to respond to perceived political demands. From a normative perspective, what is critical in this regard is to ensure to the extent possible that those who make the decisions bear the consequences – or, to reverse the proposition, that those who will bear the consequences give their informed consent. Accountability in this sense, difficult as it may sometimes be to achieve in practice, is a key characteristic of any analytically acceptable norm in analyzing federal finance.

These brief allusions to some deep and important matters may suffice to make clear why, as already mentioned, I have suggested that the appropriate analytical framework in a pure fiscal federalism setting is essentially a principal-agent framework in which the principal (the central government) may, in its attempt to overcome the familiar agency problems of information asymmetry and differing objectives between principal and agent, alter such basic factors as jurisdictional boundaries, local government revenue and expenditure responsibilities, and intergovernmental fiscal arrangements. By contrast, in the federal finance setting the appropriate analytical framework is one of bargaining between principals (who are not necessarily equal) – what one Canadian author, in a useful analogy to the world of international relations, has labeled "federal-provincial diplomacy" (Simeon, 1972). More formally, federal finance problems can probably be analyzed only in a complex game-theoretic framework – a task far too ambitious to attempt here.[15] In some countries, such as Canada, *both* of these models may simultaneously be applicable in different contexts – fiscal federalism with respect to provincial-municipal relations and federal finance with respect to federal-provincial relations (Bird and Chen, 1998a). The cohabitation of these two approaches helps explain the often-noted

---

[14] A classic analysis along these lines is Wiseman (1987); see also Dafflon (1977). For an application to tax harmonization and common markets, see Bird (1989); see also Bird (1999).

[15] For references to preliminary analyses along these lines, see Inman and Rubinfeld (1996); see also Crémer and Palfrey (1997).

phenomenon of "centralized decentralization" in Canada – increasing decentralization from the federal to the provincial level combined with increased centralization from the local to the provincial level.[16] The difference between fiscal federalism and federal finance is, admittedly, largely one of degree. When great enough, however, the difference in degree seems sufficient to warrant a difference in the appropriate analytical perspective.

Where the federal finance perspective is applicable, for example, not only must close attention be paid to the institutional analysis of reality, but interactions among equals must be taken as the basic framework. In the Canadian case, for example, Prince Edward Island is not equal to Ontario, let alone to the federal government, in most senses. But in the sense used here it *is*, or can be considered to be, equal.[17] In this framework, one cannot simply presume, as in the normal fiscal federalism approach of the economist, that the aim of policy design is to solve the problem of a benevolent federal planner seeking to maximize the utilities of representative citizens. Even should such an unlikely creature as either a representative citizen or a benevolent dictator exist, his or her interests would carry no more normative weight than anyone else's.

The traditional normative approach of the fiscal federalism literature deduces the nature of an ideal federal fiscal system on the dual assumption that all governments are benevolently concerned to maximize the economic well-being of their citizens *and* that the central government has the last word. This approach may provide a useful standard of reference for assessing intergovernmental fiscal arrangements in a particular setting, provided that one is willing to accept the underlying assumptions as ethically compelling, descriptive of reality, or perhaps both. Often, however, such analysis is of little assistance either in explaining why particular fiscal institutions exist in any federal country or in evaluating the likelihood, or the desirability, of changes in such institutions. Because there is no analytical short-cut, serious analysts of federal

[16] No precise definition or measurement of "centralization" is provided here: for a skeptical view of the usefulness of such measurements, see Bird (1986b). Breton (1996), p. 183, recognizes this criticism but nonetheless argues that such measures can still tell us something useful about the issues with which he is concerned. (I remain skeptical.)

[17] In the famous phrase of Wheare (1969, p. 10), in a federal system "each [government is], within a sphere, co-ordinate and independent." "Equality" in this sense should not be confused with the "uniformity" assumed by Oates (1972) (and by many other writers on fiscal federalism), as properly criticized by Breton (1996). Specifically, it is important not to assume, even in a federal country, that "equality" of the component jurisdictions either requires or implies uniform treatment.

finance must probe deeply into the historical and institutional reality of the country in question.[18]

Indeed, one reason economists have had difficulty in dealing with issues of federal finance is precisely because there is no one set of stylized facts that adequately fits all federations (Watts, 1996). Federations differ in many dimensions: How many provinces are there? What are their relative sizes in terms of population and economic activity? What are the disparities in per capita income and in natural resource wealth? What is the historical origin of the federation: bottom-up or top-down? peaceful or violent? What is its geography (compact or disperse)? How homogeneous is the federation in terms of language? ethnicity? cultural myths? To what extent do provincial boundaries overlap with heterogeneity in any of these dimensions? Are regional interests explicitly represented in the central political structure? How? Are all regional units treated uniformly? These and many more factors impact on the nature and working of federal institutions, and must be understood at least to some extent by analysts of federal finance in any particular country.

Nonetheless, two general lessons emerge from the study of comparative federal finance (Bird, 1986a, 1994). The first lesson is that, since every federal country is unique and in some sense constitutes an organic unity – or at least a transitorily stable equilibrium – the significance of any particular component of its federal finance system (such as the assignment of taxes or the design of intergovernmental transfers) can be understood only in the context of the system as a whole. One cannot pick an institution from a specific setting, plant it in the alien soil of another environment, and expect to obtain the same results. Policy recommendations in the area of federal finance must be firmly rooted in an understanding of the rationale for the existing intergovernmental system and its capacity for change if they are to be acceptable and, if accepted, successfully implemented. What is feasible and desirable in any particular setting depends upon what that setting is, and why it is the way it is.

Federal finance thus illustrates what has been called "path dependency" – where one will be tomorrow depends largely upon where one is today, and why one is there. Moreover, in federal finance, as in a clothing store, one size does not fit all. Simple general pronouncements – such as that unconditional transfers are better (or worse) than condi-

---

[18] Of course, this comment may be applied well beyond the field of federal finance. As Miller (1997) has recently noted, an interesting, and promising, effect on economists of their "imperialistic" advance into the realm of political science has been increasing awareness of the need to understand and analyze such institutional realities as social norms and conventions as well as political and bureaucratic processes.

tional ones, or that income taxes should always be assigned to central governments – may be worse than useless as a guide to federal finance policy: they may sometimes be positively dangerous. On the other hand, there may of course also be some very useful general lessons – for example, the desirability of transparency and "hard" budget constraints – that can be extracted from experience and applied to new instances.

The second lesson from comparative analysis of federal finance is rather different. In the end, the processes and procedures through which solutions are reached are likely to be more important than the precise nature of the technical solutions in any particular setting to such universal problems as vertical and horizontal imbalance. If each level of government has its own redistributive objective, for example, how should the inevitable conflicts be managed? The fiscal federalism answer essentially amounts to saying that the central government should determine the final outcome.[19] The federal finance answer, on the other hand, is that there can never be a final answer to such questions but only a continually evolving process of ongoing negotiation. In contrast to the "realist" (Machiavellian) style of argument that dominates social science discourse – for example, in agency theory – federalism is, as its original American designers such as Madison clearly realized, better understood in terms of the more process-oriented "civic republicanism" of Cicero (Hariman, 1995).

Theory and practice

"Federation" and "decentralization" are the terms used here to describe various types of governmental organization found in the world. As just indicated, however, "federalism" as the term is usually employed refers not to reality but rather to a normative position. From this perspective, different authors have distinguished among "economic" federalism (Oates, 1972), "cooperative" (unanimity) federalism, "majority-rule" (democratic) federalism (Inman and Rubinfeld, 1997), and, of course, "competitive" federalism (Breton, 1996).[20] Others have distinguished "executive" from "legislative" federalism with reference to the forum within which "federal" negotiation takes place (Watts, 1996), and "parliamentary" (in which there is no distinction between executive and legislature) from "non-parliamentary" federalism (Breton, 1996). Each

---

[19] As an example, see the discussion in Boadway and Hobson (1993), Chapter 3.

[20] For a useful discussion of some of these concepts, particularly cooperative and competitive federalism, see Kenyon and Kincaid (1991).

of these characterizations in turn subsumes a variety of differing combinations of features, with different implications for both political and administrative decentralization.

Federalism thus relates to *principles*, not to institutions (such as federations), let alone to outcomes. In contrast, as emphasized earlier, the decentralization that has occurred in many countries around the world in recent years has been motivated almost entirely by the desire to alter certain *outcomes*. To achieve any desired outcome one must of course understand a good deal about institutions. Fortunately, for the most part this can be done without reaching a final decision as to the applicability of particular "principled" arguments. For example, much of the existing literature on fiscal decentralization understandably reflects the fiscal federalism orientation of traditional public finance. While this approach, with its emphasis on expenditure and tax assignment and the design of intergovernmental transfers, is clearly important given the potential impacts of such matters on efficiency, equity, and macroeconomic stability, it is equally clearly inadequate. A broader institutional perspective is needed to encompass both the lessons of the past, the realities of the present, and the emerging new literatures bearing on decentralization issues. Such a perspective is especially needed for developing countries, given the characteristically stronger interaction of political relative to economic variables in such countries (Litvack, Ahmad, and Bird, 1998). Similarly, with respect to the transitional countries, the "systemic" nature of the process of institutional change means that an appropriate intergovernmental financial structure must take into account not only the usual concerns of fiscal federalism (tax assignment, expenditure assignment, transfer design) but also such important institutional factors as the severe downsizing of the public sector, the continuing importance of public ownership of enterprises, housing, and land, and the lasting effects of generations of authoritarian hierarchial political and administrative institutions (Bird and Wallich, 1994).

Different policy instruments related to decentralization may thus have very different effects in different circumstances, and very different approaches may be needed to achieve similar (or acceptable) results in different countries. At the local level, for example, some countries have "over-controlled" their local governments from the perspective of efficient and effective service provision, some have "under-controlled" them, and in still others the overall effect of central controls can only be considered "perverse" (World Bank, 1995a). Even within a single country, similar measures may have very different effects in different communities depending upon both their objective characteristics (size, heterogeneity, wealth) and the degree of local integration or "community" (World Bank, 1995b). To the extent that this is the case, asymmetrical central policies – differential treatment of different subnational jurisdictions – may be required to produce similar responses. Even in the traditional fiscal federalism literature, the need for such asymmetry is recognized to some extent in the case for equalization; but it extends much further than this.

As is increasingly recognized in the literature (Seabright, 1996; Breton, 1996), the conventional argument for fiscal federalism does not provide a very solid basis for establishing autonomous local governments. Local governments using exclusionary zoning (as is common in the United States, if not anywhere else to any great extent) may induce some preference revelation through market-driven locational choices (Tiebout, 1956). Additional arguments may be made for some degree of local autonomy in decision making on participation grounds (Inman and Rubinfeld, 1997). But it is not at all clear why similar advantages could not, if desired, be achieved by an appropriately deconcentrated central government. The most recent developments in the literature have attempted to provide a basis for local autonomy in part on information-theoretic grounds (Boadway, 1997), but as yet the major developments in this area simply attempt to set out incentive-compatible mechanism designs such as earmarking (Seabright, 1996) and "tagged" transfers (Boadway, 1997) that may, under certain conditions, lead self-directed local government agents to act in accordance with central government wishes.[21] Little serious research has yet been done to test such critical propositions as the presumed greater knowledge of local preferences by local rather than central governments, though there is some evidence that does point in this direction.[22]

What can and should be done in terms of decentralization thus depends very much upon where and when, and exactly how, it is done. Initial conditions – which in turn largely reflect past developments – are critical in terms of establishing the level of trust, the reputations of the various actors in the process, the existence (and rigidity) of various constraints to institutional change, and so on. The interests of the major stakeholders in the existing system must be understood in order to ascertain the degree of existing or potential political support for change and the resources available to make it happen, and to determine both the

---

[21] This literature usually assumes that both central and local governments are democratically elected and act to satisfy the preferences of their constituents, but this assumption – while necessary to put welfare content into the argument – is not strictly essential to the exercise.

[22] See, for example, Inman and Rubinfeld (1996), p. 77; a similar inference may perhaps be drawn from the survey evidence reported for Colombia in World Bank (1995b).

best strategy (objectives) and tactics (timing, sequence, duration) for change. Decentralization is inherently a political process, and considerable political and institutional analysis and understanding is needed to undertake it successfully or to analyze and appraise how successful it has been.

An interesting recent approach to this tangle of problems is offered by the competitive-government approach of Breton (1996), which argues that the principal efficiency rationale for decentralization is that it strengthens the "Wicksellian connection" between tax-prices paid and services received and hence restrains the Leviathan tendencies of government (Brennan and Buchanan, 1980) while fostering efficiency (and perhaps innovation) in the public sector. Some have argued on both theoretical (Salmon, 1987) and empirical (ACIR, 1991) grounds that intergovernmental competition may indeed be compatible with increased public sector efficiency.[23] Others have argued that such competition may lead to a "race to the bottom" in terms of taxes on mobile factors and hence to a smaller public sector than people "really" want – and again, there is some (weak) empirical evidence supporting this proposition (Inman and Rubinfeld, 1996). Most such discussion has focused on horizontal competition, that between jurisdictions at the same level. With respect to the vertical competition between central and local governments, which is the essence of the decentralization discussion, Breton (1996) seems so far to stand almost alone in asserting the potentially beneficial effects of increased governmental competition.[24]

However one interprets the small literature related to this issue that has so far appeared, it seems clear that the efficiency of any competition engendered by decentralization will depend to a considerable extent upon the "rules of the game," which are presumably set, and enforced, by the central government (or perhaps by an independent judiciary). As Inman and Rubinfeld (1996) show, electoral competition alone is unlikely to produce efficiency – although as Breton (1996) emphasizes, there are many other relevant forms that governmental competition may take in addition to counting votes. Only a very small amount of research has yet been done to analyze and understand the importance of alternative institutional forms in affecting outcomes (Mueller, 1997).[25] The issue is clearly important, but we equally clearly have much to learn about just what matters, and how much.

[23] See also Kenyon and Kincaid (1991) and Pommerehne, Kirchgässner, and Feld (1996).
[24] But see also Walsh (1992) and, from a somewhat different perspective, Frey and Eichenberger (1996).
[25] For additional references, see Frey and Eichenberger (1996); Pommerehne, Kirchgässner, and Feld (1996); and Kenyon and Kincaid (1991).

Policy implications

Despite the complexity of the issues, the lack of evidence, and the noise generated by the complexity of institutional structures in the real world, one conclusion that emerges clearly from the analysis in Breton (1996) is that one key to productive governmental competition – whether vertical or horizontal – lies in making the relevant decision makers accountable for their decisions. One condition for effective accountability is that relevant comparative information be made publicly available. At base, the ultimate mechanism driving good competition is, on one hand, the ability of citizens to compare governments in terms of the services they provide and the tax-prices they charge and, on the other, the ability of citizens to affect and alter the decisions of government, whether through "exit" (factor mobility) or "voice" (electoral action and other political means) or in some other way. To a considerable extent, the case for the beneficial effects of governmental competition rests on the ability of competition in certain circumstances to elicit information that would otherwise be hidden from citizens by bureaucratic monopolists seeking the famed "quiet life."

Democracy without the provision of good information to citizens is thus not enough.[26] Nor, of course, is information without democracy. Nonetheless, even in countries – like most in the world – which do not have well-established democratic institutions, so that decentralization is simply another instrument of the central government, good information is essential to ensuring enhanced service outcomes – though the information needed in this context relates primarily to the ability of agents (such as local governments) to hide actions from principals. One key lesson from experience that seems relevant everywhere is that the more that is known, and the more publicly it is known, the better the outcome of decentralization efforts is likely to be, whatever

---

[26] See Besley and Case (1995) for empirical examination of the "yardstick" argument at the U.S. state level. Mueller (1997) notes that Breton's argument suggests that only a federal country with a strong-party parliamentary system at both federal and provincial levels will produce even a roughly "efficient" outcome – and that most countries are not as fortunate as Canada in these respects! Loyal Canadian though I am, I find it a bit difficult to believe that Canadian political institutions are all that efficient or effective in establishing the Wicksellian connection. Indeed, Breton, Cassone, and Fraschini (1998, pp. 47–48) would seem to share my doubts, since they note that federal governments can resolve their inherent conflict of interest as both referees and players in the governmental competitive game only by "designing central governments so as to represent the interests and preoccupations of junior governments . . . in the institutional fabric of central governments," something that certainly has not been true in Canada (Bird, 1999); but this is not the place to attempt to elaborate this argument.

their rationale and whatever the circumstances in which they take place.[27] Providing information relevant to understanding and evaluating the impacts of decentralization thus plays a critical role in improving outcomes, almost regardless of the status of political democracy in the country.

The role of the central government in ensuring and monitoring effective decentralization, for example, is especially critical when, as is often the case in practice, a major concern is to enhance service delivery, for instance with respect to services such as health and education that are important not only for national development but for poverty alleviation and welfare in general. An unfortunate side effect of decentralization in some countries has been the virtual disappearance from the central government's cognitive horizon of reliable information on the provision of such services.[28] Decentralization of a function does not usually mean that the central government no longer has any responsibility in the area. What it means, rather, is that central responsibility has changed from direct service delivery to regulating and monitoring the efficiency and equity of services delivered by others – usually local governments. The essential tool needed for this task is an adequate and up-to-date information system – generated, for example, by requiring local governments to file uniform and informative budgets and financial and other reports. Unfortunately, this need for extended and reliable information has been sadly neglected in most decentralizing countries, in which those making the decisions – the politicians and bureaucrats – often understandably wish to hide the real reasons for, and results of, their actions and to live the quiet life of the unaccountable.

The needed incentive to comply with demands for information can be created for local governments to at least a limited extent by making timely submission of such reports a condition of receiving fiscal transfers.[29] This requirement may in turn imply significant initial set-up costs in the form of system design, training, and implementation. To spend money wisely in a decentralized system may often require some initial investment. While of course such concerns are less important when full responsibility for the efficiency and equity of services is devolved (as in a formal federal structure) rather than simply delegated to subnational

---

[27] Compare, for example, the well-known arguments of Amartya Sen on the incompatibility of famine and a "free press."

[28] For an example, see Bird and Fiszbein (1998). Further discussion may be found in Litvack, Ahmad, and Bird (1998).

[29] For an interesting discussion in a different context of the importance of incentives to elicit appropriate informational behavior from governments, see Bacchetta and Espinosa (1992).

governments, the need for an adequate information system remains critical to macroeconomic management even in this instance, given the importance of such services as education and health in total public expenditure. Regardless of the form of decentralization, an important institutional problem is thus how to ensure that the relevant central government agencies have adequate incentives to monitor subnational activity and that subnational governments have adequate incentives to report honestly. And, of course, as noted earlier, such information is at least equally necessary to achieve desired outcomes as efficiently as possible when democratic institutions are important.

Central governments in countries that have recently become more decentralized are learning through experience to carry out this essential information and monitoring activity more adequately in their own interests – for example, to avoid excessive subnational borrowing and hence potentially undesirable macroeconomic pressure. In no country of which I am aware, however, has any central government yet admitted that full disclosure (transparent accountability) should apply also to its own actions. Decentralization is a two-sided street, and the central role of central governments in determining the outcome of this complex process needs much more attention than it seems so far to have received. As Breton (1996) has clearly demonstrated, for the potential benefits of the resulting increased degree of governmental competition to be realized, governments at *all* levels must become more transparently comparable and hence accountable for their actions. Frey and Eichenberger (1996) note that such comparisons may be more feasible when confined to specific functional areas. A recent example in Canada, for example, is a federal proposal that an agency (not necessarily a public one) should be set up to monitor various dimensions of health care in various provinces and to make its findings public. While one might like to see a similar federal proposal for areas in which the federal as well as the provincial governments are engaged, at least such an agency would be a step in the right direction.[30]

Some years ago, in an analysis of public sector growth and efficiency in Canada, I noted that "without a public better informed of the real alternatives and choices facing them in their collective capacity as members of society, it is hard to believe that the outcome of the

---

[30] Unfortunately, in Canada as elsewhere, the record is fairly dismal when it comes to governments funding agencies that may criticize their actions: witness the abolition (in the name of "budget cuts") of such federal agencies as the Economic Council of Canada and the Tax Measures Evaluation Group of the Department of Finance. Similarly "enlightened" policies are, of course, not unknown at the provincial level, as in the case of abolition of the Ontario Economic Council.

political process . . . can become much 'better' than it now is."[31] Further experience over two decades with a wide variety of decentralized governmental systems around the world, combined with a reading of Albert Breton's systematic and seminal exploration of the dangers of governmental collusion and the potential virtues of governmental competition from the perspective of citizens, strongly reinforces my belief in the importance of improving information as perhaps the main role scholars have to play in the policy process.

As the world now turns, the decentralized governments existing or likely to be created in most countries seem unlikely to possess many of the efficiency properties so persuasively analyzed in Breton (1996). But they can, and should, take on some of these properties over time – or at least such must be the hope of all those concerned not just with improving scholarly understanding of the interaction of politics and economics but with utilizing such understanding, in the words of John Stuart Mill, for "the improvement of mankind" (Robson, 1978).

References

Advisory Commission on Intergovernmental Relations (ACIR) (1991) *Interjurisdictional Tax and Policy Competition: Good or Bad for the Federal System?* (Washington: ACIR).

Bacchetta, Philippe, and Maria Paz Espinosa (1995) "Information Sharing and Tax Competition among Governments," *Journal of International Economics*, 39: 103–21.

Besley, Timothy, and Anne Case (1995) "Incumbent Behavior: Vote-Seeking, Tax-Setting, and Yardstick Competition," *American Economic Review*, 85: 25–45.

Bird, Richard M. (1980) *Central-Local Fiscal Relations and the Provision of Urban Public Services* (Canberra: Australian National University Press for the Centre for Research on Federal Financial Relations).

Bird, Richard M. (1986a) *Federal Finance in Comparative Perspective* (Toronto: Canadian Tax Foundation).

Bird, Richard M. (1986b) "On Measuring Fiscal Centralization and Fiscal Balance in Federal States," *Environment and Planning C: Government and Policy*, 4: 389–404.

Bird, Richard M. (1989) "Tax Harmonization in Federations and Common Markets," in Manfred Neumann, ed., *Public Finance and Performance of Enterprises* (Detroit: Wayne State University Press).

---

[31] Bird, Bucovetsky, and Foot (1979), p. 170. In support of this view, I cited a close colleague of both Albert Breton and myself, the late Douglas Hartle (1976, 1977), who emphasized particularly the role of information in shaping public policy. This aspect of Hartle's thought has recently been interestingly developed in the Canadian context by another former colleague, Rodney Dobell (1999).

Bird, Richard M. (1993) "Threading the Fiscal Labyrinth: Some Issues in Fiscal Decentralization," *National Tax Journal*, 46: 207–27.

Bird, Richard M. (1994) "A Comparative Perspective on Federal Finance," in Keith G. Banting, Douglas M. Brown, and Thomas J. Courchene, eds., *The Future of Fiscal Federalism* (Kingston: School of Public Policy, Queen's University).

Bird, Richard M. (1995) "Fiscal Federalism and Federal Finance," in 28a *Jornadas de Finanzas Publicas* (Córdoba, Argentina: Facultad de Ciencias Económicas, Universidad Nacional de Córdoba).

Bird, Richard M. (1999) "The Federal Spending Power in International Perspective," paper prepared for the Ontario Ministry of Intergovernmental Affairs, Toronto, January.

Bird, Richard M., and Christine Wallich (1994) "Local Finance and Economic Reform in Eastern Europe," *Environment and Planning C: Government and Policy*, 12: 263–76.

Bird, Richard M., and Ariel Fiszbein (1998) "Colombia: The Central Role of the Central Government in Fiscal Decentralization," in Bird and Vaillancourt (1998).

Bird, Richard M., and Duanjie Chen (1998a) "Fiscal Federalism and Federal Finance: The Two Worlds of Canadian Public Finance," *Canadian Public Administration*, 48: 51–74.

Bird, Richard M., and Duanjie Chen (1998b) "Intergovernmental Finance in China in International Perspective," in Donald J. S. Brean, ed., *Taxation in Modern China* (London: Routledge).

Bird, Richard M., and Francois Vaillancourt, eds. (1998) *Fiscal Decentralisation in Developing Countries* (Cambridge: Cambridge University Press).

Bird, Richard M., Meyer W. Bucovetsky, and David K. Foot (1979) *The Growth of Public Employment in Canada* (Montreal: Institute for Research on Public Policy).

Bird, Richard M., Robert D. Ebel, and Christine I. Wallich, eds. (1995) *Decentralization of the Socialist State* (Washington: World Bank).

Bird, Richard M., Christine I. Wallich, and Gabor Peteri (1995) "Financing Local Government in Hungary," in Bird, Ebel, and Wallich (1995).

Boadway, Robin (1997) "Public Economics and the Theory of Public Policy," *Canadian Journal of Economics*, 30: 753–72.

Boadway, Robin W., and Paul A. R. Hobson (1993) *Intergovernmental Fiscal Relations in Canada* (Toronto: Canadian Tax Foundation).

Brennan, Geoffrey, and James M. Buchanan (1980) *The Power to Tax* (Cambridge: Cambridge University Press).

Breton, Albert (1996) *Competitive Governments* (Cambridge: Cambridge University Press).

Breton, Albert, and Anthony Scott (1978) *The Economic Constitution of Federal States* (Toronto: University of Toronto Press).

Breton, Albert, Alberto Cassone, and Angela Fraschini (1998) "Decentralization and Subsidiarity: Toward a Theoretical Reconciliation," *University of Pennsylvania Journal of International Economic Law*, 19: 21–51.

Crémer, Jacques, and Thomas R. Palfrey (1997) "Political Confederation," Institut d'Economie Industrielle, Toulouse.

Crémer, Jacques, Antonio Estache, and Paul Seabright (1995) "The Decentralization of Public Services: Lessons from the Theory of the Firm," in Antonio

Estache, ed., *Decentralizing Infrastructure: Advantages and Limitations* (Washington: World Bank).

Dafflon, Bernard (1977) *Federal Finance in Theory and Practice with Special Reference to Switzerland* (Bern: Paul Haupt).

Dobell, Rodney (1999) "Evaluation and Entitlements: Hartle's Search for Rationality in Government," in Richard M. Bird, Michael Trebilicock, and Thomas A. Wilson, eds., *Rationality in Public Policy* (Toronto: Canadian Tax Foundation).

Frey, Bruno S., and Reiner Eichenberger (1996) "FOCJ: Competitive Governments for Europe," *International Review of Law and Economics*, 16: 315–27.

Hariman, Robert (1995) *Political Style* (Chicago: University of Chicago Press).

Hartle, Douglas G. (1976) *A Theory of the Expenditure Budgetary Process* (Toronto: University of Toronto Press).

Hartle, Douglas G. (1977) *The Expenditure Budgetary Process in the Government of Canada* (Toronto: Canadian Tax Foundation).

Inman, Robert P., and Daniel L. Rubenfeld (1996) "The Political Economy of Federalism," in Dennis C. Mueller, ed., *Perspectives on Public Choice* (Cambridge: Cambridge University Press).

Inman, Robert P., and Daniel L. Rubenfeld (1997) "Rethinking Federalism," *Journal of Economic Perspectives*, 11: 43–64.

Kenyon, Daphne A., and John Kincaid, eds. (1991) *Competition among States and Local Governments* (Washington: Urban Institute).

Litvack, Jennie, Junaid Ahmad, and Richard Bird (1998) *Rethinking Decentralization in Developing Countries* (Washington: World Bank).

Miller, Gary J. (1997) "The Impact of Economics on Contemporary Political Science," *Journal of Economic Literature*, 35: 1173–1204.

Mueller, Dennis C. (1997) Review of Breton, *Competitive Governments*, in *Canadian Journal of Economics*, 30: 997–1003.

Oates, Wallace E. (1972) *Fiscal Federalism* (New York: Harcourt Brace Jovanovich).

Pommerehne, Werner W., Gebhard Kirchgässner, and Lars P. Feld, "Tax Harmonization and Tax Competition at State-Local Levels: Lessons from Switzerland," in Giancarlo Pola, George France, and Rosella Levaggi, eds., *Developments in Local Government Finance* (Cheltenham: Edward Elgar).

Robson, John (1978) *The Improvement of Mankind* (Toronto: University of Toronto Press).

Salmon, Pierre (1987) "Decentralisation as an Incentive Scheme," *Oxford Review of Economic Policy*, 3: 24–43.

Seabright, Paul (1996) "Accountability and Decentralization in Government: An Incomplete Contracts Model," *European Economic Review*, 40: 61–89.

Shah, Anwar (1998) "Indonesia and Pakistan: Fiscal Decentralization – An Elusive Goal?" in Bird and Vaillancourt (1998).

Shah, Anwar and Zia Qureshi (1994) *Intergovernmental Fiscal Relations in Indonesia* (Washington: World Bank, Discussion Paper No. 239).

Simeon, Richard (1972) *Federal-Provincial Diplomacy* (Toronto: University of Toronto Press).

Spahn, P. Bernd, ed. (1982) *Principles of Federal Policy Co-ordination in the Federal Republic of Germany: Basic Issues and Annotated Legislation* (Canberra: Centre for Research on Federal Financial Relations, The Australian National University).

Tiebout, Charles, "A Pure Theory of Local Governments," *Journal of Political Economy*, 65: 416–24.

Tresch, Richard (1981) *Public Finance* (Plano, Texas: Business Publications).

Wallich, Christine I. (1994) *Russia and the Challenge of Fiscal Federalism* (Washington: World Bank).

Walsh, Cliff (1992) "Fiscal Federalism: An Overview of Issues and a Discussion of Their Relevance to the European Community," Federalism Research Centre, Australian National University, Canberra.

Watts, Ronald (1996) *Comparing Federal Systems in the 1990s* (Kingston: Institute of Intergovernmental Relations, Queen's University).

Wheare, Kenneth C. (1969) *Federal Government*, 4th ed. (London: Oxford University Press).

Wiseman, Jack (1987) "The Political Economy of Federalism: A Critical Appraisal," *Environment and Planning C: Government and Policy*, 5: 383–410.

World Bank (1995a) *Better Urban Services* (Washington: World Bank).

World Bank (1995b) *Local Government Capacity in Colombia* (Washington: World Bank).

World Bank (1996a) *Vietnam: Fiscal Decentralization and the Delivery of Rural Services* (Washington: World Bank, Report No. 15745-VN).

World Bank (1996b) *Argentina: Provincial Finances Study* (Washington: World Bank, Report No. 15487-AR).

CHAPTER 7

On the reassignment of fiscal powers in a federal state

Stanley L. Winer

What we call the reassignment instruments are the ways and means, the techniques, the procedures, and the rules used. . . . to reassign functions, to redesign the jurisdictional map, or both.

One way of choosing a new assignment is to change the constitution . . . such as by a formal redrafting of the basic document, or by amending it on one or a number of selected issues, or by seeking a reinterpretation of a given clause by appeal to a court.

The delegation of a function. . . . from one jurisdictional level to another is a second reassignment instrument. Such a delegation can be upwards or downwards. . . . There has historically been enough delegation of powers from one jurisdiction to another that one need not underline the importance of this instrument.

Albert Breton and Anthony Scott, *The Economic Constitution of Federal States* (1978, 65)

Intergovernmental competition will drive governments to seek to improve their productive capacity through a division of functions among levels of government.

Albert Breton, *Competitive Governments: An Economic Theory of Politics and Public Finance* (1996, 203)

1   Introduction

Much of the economic analysis of the assignment of fiscal powers across jurisdictions in a federation is normative or prescriptive in character. The

Helpful comments were provided by an anonymous referee. Jim Feehan, Walter Hettich, Allan Maslove, Doug May and Frank Vermaeten, Dave McDowell, Roger Perchard, Munir Sheikh, Steve Tierney, Stewart Wells, Karen Wilson, and Robert Vardy were especially helpful with the harmonized sales tax case. Errors and omissions remain the responsibility of the author.

150

primary concern is with the conditions required for economic efficiency, although the regional distribution of welfare may also be considered. The allocation of expenditure functions is usually based on an assessment of the economies of scale in the supply of public services achievable by different jurisdictions, and on a geography of individual preferences. If economies of scale are not substantial, the decentralization theorem – that public expenditure patterns that cater closely to regional differences in preferences Pareto-dominate those that don't (see, for example, Wallace Oates 1972) – coupled with an appeal to the quality of information about individuals possessed by lower levels of governments, are relied upon to establish a presumption that the assignment of expenditure responsibilities should favor noncentral governments.

Optimal tax assignments are usually based on an assessment of how elasticities of each base with respect to its tax rate may change when each is assigned to a higher or a lower jurisdiction. Relatively mobile bases are assigned to the central government to minimize tax evasion and avoidance and the associated excess burdens. Intergovernmental grants of different kinds are introduced to deal with imbalances created by imperfect matching of expenditure responsibilities and tax assignments across jurisdictions, and to implement interregional redistribution. Finally, the assignment of expenditure responsibilities and taxing powers, and especially the nature and size of intergovernmental grants, is adjusted to allow for the fact that individuals as well as governments in any particular location may not appropriately take into account the consequences of their own actions for the citizens of other political jurisdictions. Over the past four or five decades, this social planning approach to the optimal assignment of fiscal powers in a federation has given rise to a substantial literature that includes many contributions that are both elegant and insightful.[1]

In contrast to the large body of work on the optimal assignment, there is only a small literature on the positive theory of the federal assignment, the sections on representative government in Albert Breton and Anthony Scott (1978) and Chapter 8 of Breton's (1996) recent book being perhaps the two most important contributions.[2] Most of the positive analysis of reassignment is a by-product of studies of federations that have a broader historical focus, and is a source of

---

[1] For an introduction to the normative literature on the optimal assignment of fiscal powers in a federation, see Oates (1972), Pauly (1973), Chapter 7 of Breton and Scott (1978), Gordon (1983), Wildasin (1986), Gramlich (1987), Dahlby (1996), Inman and Rubinfeld (1996), and Boadway, Marchand, and Vigneault (1998).

[2] One might be tempted to use the theory of the optimal assignment as a basis for predicting what will actually occur. However, as long as voters, politicians, and bureaucrats

stylized facts about reassignment only if the reader is interested in digging them out.[3]

While Breton and Scott (1978, 65) accept the existence and importance of reassignment in federal systems as established facts, the sparse nature of the literature explicitly concerned with the positive theory of reassignment suggests to me that this view is not widely held. It therefore seems worthwhile to draw attention once again to the substantial role that reassignment actually plays in shaping the evolution of the public sector. It is the modest purpose of this chapter to do so.

In sections two and three I review selected aspects of fiscal history in Australia and in Canada in order to demonstrate that reassignment has played a substantial role in the development of the public sectors of these countries. The power to tax of central and state or provincial governments is given particular attention in each case. In the fourth section, I discuss a reassignment of the power to tax that has just occurred in Canada to show that reassignment is of contemporary as well as historical relevance. Although consideration of these cases does not amount to a general argument, taxation is at the core of public life, and federalism in Australia and Canada is widely studied around the world. Knowledge that reassignment is essential to an understanding of the evolution of the power to tax in these particular countries should provide students of federalism with food for thought.

The chapter concludes with a discussion of the implications for positive and normative research of the stylized fact that reassignment is a normal state of affairs in a federal system of government. This fact must be a source of concern for anyone intent on using the existing theory of the optimal assignment as a basis for reform, since that theory is not formally cognizant of reassignment. In the absence of an understanding of how and why the effective assignment of fiscal and other policies evolves, and a way of coming to terms with this in the context of the theoretical framework that underlies policy advice, any proposal for reform of the federation is at risk of being swept aside. I suggest another approach that may be more robust.

As a prelude to the fiscal history presented later, it is useful to review

are not solely motivated by concern with Pareto-efficiency in the country as a whole, such a normative-as-positive theory will not supply an adequate account of how the assignment of functions is actually determined.

[3] For samples of this large and complex historical literature in the two countries that I shall be concerned with, see Smith (1993) on the history of taxation in Australia and Gillespie (1991) on the history of taxation in Canada. Additional references to the literature can be found in Bird (1986) and in Breton (1996).

the essentials of Albert Breton's (1996) recent contribution to the positive theory of reassignment.[4] Breton's framework highlights several important determinants of reassignment in federal systems, including technological economies of scale in the use of governing instruments, the nature of property rights to the various policy instruments that may be determined by the constitution, changes in such rights due to judicial interpretation, and intergovernmental bargaining and coordination costs. All of these elements can be identified in one or more of the cases I consider, though I hasten to add that no attempt is made here to fashion these case histories into a test of Breton's hypotheses.

Breton argues that the effective assignment of control over various policy instruments is driven by electoral competition that forces different governments to exploit technological economies of scale in the use of governing instruments. Capturing the benefits of these economies requires that the use of policy instruments be delegated or exchanged between governments or, in other words, that instrument use be appropriately (re)centralized or decentralized as economies of scale change. Property rights in instrument use, which is a precondition for intergovernmental exchange of fiscal and other powers, are established by the constitutional division of powers and altered from time to time by judicial interpretation. The giving up of a policy instrument and resulting payment to compensate for the loss of quasi-rents from its use, including intergovernmental grants of different kinds, occurs in a situation where contracts between governments are implicit and incomplete, and where postcontractual opportunism may therefore be a serious problem.

In this world, the costs of negotiating and of coordinating policies across jurisdictions play key roles in determining the types of intergovernmental contracts that are finally arrived at. Tax collection technologies sometimes exhibit significant economies of scale, for example, a fact that also plays an important role in the theory of the optimal assignment. However, in Breton's view, even if such economies are substantial, bargaining and coordination costs may prevent exploitation of them and lead to less centralization than technological considerations alone would dictate.

---

[4] Breton (1996, Chapter 8) discusses all governmental systems that have more than one level of government, including those states usually referred to as unitary but in which some powers are exercised by local governments. I deal here only with federal systems in which there are state or provincial jurisdictions that have powers granted to them by a written constitution.

2   The reassignment and balance of fiscal powers in the Australian federation[5]

At the end of the nineteenth century,[6] the framers of the Australian constitution of 1901 appear to have looked carefully at what had been done in the United States in the previous century as well as what had occurred in Canada about thirty years before, and decided that the Canadian approach to the division of powers in the British North America Act of 1867 was not what they wanted.[7] This was so despite the fact that Australia and Canada had inherited common political, legal, and administrative traditions from the British, and despite the fact that the two economies were similar in structure, with a strong natural resource base in a sparsely populated and geographically large land mass, both countries economically small and open in the world as a whole.

The rejection of the BNA Act as a model is not readily apparent in the treatment of the major revenue source at the time the constitution was enacted, namely the tariff. In Australia as in Canada, customs duties were reserved for the senior government. The rejection of the Canadian model by the Australian framers is more obvious in the manner in which the fiscal powers of the different governments are generally specified. The British North America Act explicitly assigns taxing powers and expenditure responsibilities to both federal and provincial governments in Canada, and there is a clause assigning any residual power to the federal government. However, the smaller states' delegates to the constitutional discussions in Australia were, it seems, wary of any proposition that could diminish the relative powers of the states, as James Warden (1992, 14) points out in his fascinating discussion of the framers' intentions; and they were especially suspicious of a clause that granted all residual rights to the center. Since delimiting state fiscal power appears to have been considered tantamount to limiting it, no explicit list of taxing or spending powers of the state governments is included in the Australian constitution – as noted in Table 7.1, which summarizes the original legal framework of the Australian fiscal assignment – and there is no statement about which level of government is to receive any residual power.[8] Moreover, the taxing and spending powers of the common-

---

[5] This section draws to some extent on Winer and Maslove (1996).
[6] In the debates of 1891 and 1897–98.
[7] The British North America Act is the original Canadian constitution. In 1982 the BNA Act was renamed the Constitution Act of 1867.
[8] The entries in Tables 7.1 and 7.2 are revised excerpts from Tables 4.1 and 4.2 in Winer and Maslove (1996). The figures in Table 7.2 are based on Searle (1996) and McMillan (1993).

Table 7.1. *The constitutional framework of fiscal federalism in Australia*

Taxation	
Direct	Commonwealth and states have similar access to direct tax bases.
Indirect	Customs duties assigned to the commonwealth. Access to other indirect tax bases shared by commonwealth and states.[a]
Taxation of one level of government by another	Prohibited
Public debt	Explicit allowance for state debt and borrowing to be taken over by the commonwealth
Public expenditure	
Distribution of spending powers	General rule: concurrent commonwealth/ state responsibility, with commonwealth paramount when powers conflict
	Commonwealth exclusivity in some areas (e.g., defense, immigration)
	Local government not mentioned in constitution
Special features	
Listing of fiscal powers	**Federal**: yes **State**: no[b] **Local**: no
Residual power	Not explicitly assigned
Ownership of natural resources	Shared by commonwealth and states
Customs union	Guarantee of free internal trade Commonwealth explicitly forbidden to discriminate between states

Footnotes in the table report significant reassignments of functions that occurred via judicial reinterpretation of the original constitution of 1901: (*a*) State access to indirect tax bases constrained relative to the commonwealth by subsequent judicial interpretation. (*b*) State powers limited by subsequent judicial interpretation to powers not assigned to the commonwealth.

wealth (as the federal government in Australia is called) and the states are constitutionally concurrent in most cases, with the notable exception of customs duties. There is an allowance for commonwealth paramountcy in cases where explicit conflicts of legislation arise. As a whole this setup is similar to the American constitutional framework, as Watts (1996) notes in his comparison of federal countries, a framework with which the Australian framers tended to be more comfortable.[9]

The threat to state sovereignty posed by concurrency of powers and a formal statement of commonwealth supremacy in case of conflict is not a problem for the states if the commonwealth legislature is designed in part to prevent the expansion of power beyond its intended sphere. Although the Supreme Court in Australia was not, it seems, intended to serve this purpose, the framers did expect that the elected Senate would serve as the needed protection of state rights against encroachment by the commonwealth (Warden 1995, 17). What a mistake that proved to be.[10]

The current state of the fiscal assignment in Australia is summarized in Table 7.2.[11] The picture is one of a highly centralized public sector, however centralization is measured. A high degree of fiscal centralization can be observed in the distribution of total spending and in the importance of central government grants as a source of state revenues. The commonwealth raises (1994–95 figures) about 72 percent of all government revenues from own sources, and commonwealth own-purpose expenditures *excluding* transfers to other governments are about 57 percent of the total for all governments in Australia.[12] State governments, which still have significant expenditure responsibilities, directly raise only about 63 percent of the tax revenue that they need, the balance being made up by commonwealth grants of various kinds.

Concerning the assignment of tax instruments, Table 7.2 records that only the commonwealth government in Australia levies taxation on income, the major tax of the post–World War II era, although the constitution allows for, and constitutional interpretation has not altered, the right of the states to tax income. Moreover, the states in Australia have been blocked in the courts when seeking broader access to general consumption taxation, although the constitution of 1901 did

---

[9] Warden (1995) convincingly states the case that many delegates to the constitutional conventions favored the American model, especially the version presented in the 1888 work of the American scholar James Bryce.

[10] It is not my intention to consider at length why the elected Senate in Australia failed to act as a house of the states. I simply note here, as does Watts (1996, 22), that the Senate has become more of a party house than a regional house. Watts attributes this to the impact of the parliamentary system as a whole on the functioning of the Senate. On this issue, see also Uhr (1989).

[11] A concise history of the evolution of fiscal federalism in Australia – that is, of the transition from Table 7.1 to Table 7.2 – can be found in Smith (1992). The details concerning the evolution of the power to tax are provided in Smith (1993).

[12] The figures in this paragraph are based on Searle (1998).

Table 7.2. *Actual assignment of fiscal powers in the Australian federation*

Taxation	
Tax sovereignty – general	States exercise much less tax sovereignty than does the commonwealth
	In 1994–95, commonwealth raises about 72% of all tax revenues, states raise about 24% and localities about 4%
Distribution of specific tax sources	
Income	Levied only by commonwealth
Consumption	Levied by commonwealth and states without coordination. State taxation narrowly based on selected excises and transactions
Natural resources	Levied by commonwealth and states
Payroll	Mostly (71%) at state level. Largest own-source revenue of states
Social Security	None
Formal tax collection and tax harmonization agreements	Very limited
Public debt	State borrowing constrained and coordinated to some extent by the commonwealth
Public expenditure	Commonwealth predominates
Relative size of central government sector	Direct spending by the commonwealth *excluding grants* to the states about 57% of total
Relative size of state sector	States' share of total spending about 38%
Relative size of local government sector	Local government sector small (direct spending about 5% of total)
Role of grants in state finances	Commonwealth transfers about 37% of total state spending
Distribution of specific functions	
Education	Primarily a state function (89%)
Health	Shared about equally by the Commonwealth and the states
Welfare	Primarily a commonwealth function
Transport and communications	Shared unequally by the states (64%), local governments (22%), and the commonwealth (14%)

Table 7.2. *(cont.)*

Intergovernmental Grants	
Equalization grants	Formula comprehensive:
	Both taxes and expenditures equalized
	States equalized down as well as up to national average
	Explicit allowance made for cost differentials
Conditional grants-in-aid	Commonwealth grants conditional on state expenditure patterns

Except for the distribution of specific functions, figures are from Searle (1998) and refer to fiscal year 1994–95.

not prohibit such taxes.[13] Consequently, in addition to payroll taxes and mining revenues, the states now levy only selective excises, fees, and narrowly defined transaction taxes.

The high degree of centralization is also apparent in the extent to which differences between states are offset by equalization payments provided to the states by the commonwealth. Poorer states in Australia are equalized up to a national average, and, in addition, richer states are equalized down to this average. Moreover, the equalization formula takes into account inequalities in expected expenditure needs as well as in potential revenue sources, and it also includes allowance for cost of living differences among the states. Thus the ability for any state to maintain a fiscal system that differs substantially from that of other states is limited.[14]

The roles of the central, state, and local governments in education, health, social services, and transport and communications, the major expenditure categories, are also briefly described in Table 7.2. These entries are of interest here because they apparently cannot be pre-

[13] For an interesting recent discussion of this constitutional issue, see Petchey and Shapiro (1997).

[14] Still further evidence of fiscal centralization in Australia is provided by the differential nature of the access that state and provincial governments have to capital markets. In Australia, state borrowing has been constrained to some extent by the commonwealth through the Loan Council, though this oversight may be somewhat less severe today that in the past. For further discussion of the Loan Council, see Saunders (1990).

dicted using the assignment outlined in Table 7.1, a point to which I shall return. In Australia, education is primarily a state function, while health costs are approximately equally shared between the commonwealth, which funds the Medicare system and private hospitals, and the states, which are responsible for public hospitals and other services. Social services, including pensions, are primarily delivered by the commonwealth. Transportation and communication expenditures are the joint responsibility of the commonwealth, the states, and local governments, with the states' expenditures constituting about two-thirds of the total.

To complete this discussion of the Australian case, I want to draw attention to two conclusions that are suggested by the comparison of the stylized facts recorded in Tables 7.1 and 7.2. Together, these conclusions indicate that an explanation of reassignment is essential to an understanding of Australian fiscal history. First, as I have already pointed out, knowledge of the formal legal framework for the assignment of fiscal powers summarized in Table 7.1 does not appear to be a useful basis for predicting the actual, contemporary assignment of either tax or expenditure responsibilities recorded in Table 7.2. Second, the effective reassignment of fiscal powers that has occurred since the constitution was adopted has subverted the original framers' intentions, especially with respect to the overall degree of centralization. Fiscal centralization is so pronounced in Australia that one is tempted to ask if an initial constitutional division of powers imposes any constraints at all on the actual effective assignment of policy instruments.

3   The evolution of the power to tax in the Canadian federation, 1867 to 1996

The Australian case study contrasts an assignment of fiscal powers at the time a constitution was adopted with the assignment of powers as it presently stands. The second case I present as a way of suggesting that the positive theory of reassignment is a topic worthy of further study concerns the historical evolution of the power to tax in Canada.

The British North America Act of 1867 grants the Government of Canada the power to tax "by any mode or system ...", while the provinces are granted the right to "direct taxation within the Province ...".[15] However, just as the original assignment of powers in the

---

[15] See Sections 91 and 92 of the Constitution Act of 1982.

Australian constitution does not provide a guide to what actually happened over the decades since the framers finished their work, the formal constitutional assignment of the power to tax in Canada is at best a starting point for an understanding of taxation since the Canadian constitution was first adopted.

Table 7.3 records most of the significant events concerning the federal dimension of the power to tax in Canada since the inception of the modern state in 1867.[16] The events recorded in the table may be separated into four periods, in each of which either the provincial or the federal power to tax is in ascendency. The first and relatively longest period, which I date from 1867 until just before the beginning of World War II, is one in which the provincial power to tax increased more or less without interruption. As can be seen from the table, the provinces began to establish their own personal income tax systems even before the federal government adopted an income tax in 1917 as part of its efforts to finance Canada's participation in the First World War. The autonomy of the provinces in the area of the income tax continued to develop relative to that of the federal government through the twenties, when provincial governments were busy electrifying the countryside and building highways, and continued into the Depression years.

The introduction of a retail sales tax in Saskatchewan in the late 1930s is a major event in the first period. Sales taxation at the provincial level required an extraordinary set of decisions by the courts to allow indirect taxation by a province even though this was not consistent with the intentions of the framers of the Canadian constitution.[17] Key steps in the judicial reinterpretation that opened the door for provincial sales taxation include the adoption of John Stuart Mill's flexible definition of a direct tax as one that is demanded of the person who is intended to pay it, and the view that retail merchants may be considered to be agents of the provincial government for the purpose of tax collection. As in Australia, it seems that the written constitution is not a barrier to reassignment in the right circumstances – in this case, the Great Depression and its consequences for the finances of the Canadian provinces – and in the face

---

[16] Further details concerning the reassignment of the power to tax in Canada can be found in Gillespie (1991), Perry (1955), and La Forest (1981). Table 7.3 is a revised and updated version of Table 10.1 in Winer (1992). The table leaves aside aspects of fiscal federalism in Canada besides the reassignment of the power to tax. In particular, it does not contain any information about the rich history of intergovernmental grants. An extensive discussion of the Canadian grant system is given by Boadway and Hobson (1993).

[17] See La Forest (1981) for further discussion.

Table 7.3. *Selected aspects of the evolution of the power to tax in the Canadian federation, 1876–1997*

1876	British Columbia establishes an early version of the personal income tax.
1894	Prince Edward Island establishes an early version of the personal income tax.
1917	The federal government establishes a personal income tax.
1920	The federal government establishes a sales tax.
1922	The Judicial Committee of the Privy Council confirms that the federal government has the right to levy a personal income tax.
1923	Manitoba establishes its own personal income tax.
1932	Saskatchewan and Alberta establish their own personal income taxes.
1932	Quebec and Ontario establish their own corporate income taxes.
1936	Ontario establishes its own personal income tax, which the federal government administers and collects. (Ontario removes the rights of municipalities to levy income taxes). Alberta establishes its own sales tax, to be repealed the next year.
1937	Saskatchewan establishes its own retail sales tax.
1938	Manitoba and Prince Edward Island arrange to have their personal income taxes administered and collected by the federal government.
1939	Quebec introduces a personal income tax based on the Ontario model.
1940	The Rowell-Sirois report recommends that the provinces transfer direct taxation to the federal government.
1940	Quebec establishes its own retail sales tax.
1940	A constitutional amendment allows the federal government to provide unemployment insurance.
1941	Wartime (Tax Rental) Agreements: Provinces repeal personal and corporate taxes in exchange for transfers from the federal government.
1947	Quebec reestablishes its own corporate income tax following the lapse of the wartime agreements.
1948	British Columbia establishes its own retail sales tax.
1950	New Brunswick and Newfoundland establish their own retail sales taxes.
1951	A constitutional amendment allows the federal government to offer old age pensions.
1954	Quebec reestablishes its own personal income tax.
1957	Ontario reestablishes its own corporate income tax.
1957	The tax-sharing agreements: Tax abatements to the provinces rise, and a formal equalization program is established.
1959	Nova Scotia establishes its own retail sales tax.

Table 7.3. *(cont.)*

1960	Prince Edward Island establishes its own retail sales tax.
1961	Ontario establishes its own retail sales tax.
1962	The tax collection agreements: The provinces resume a more direct role in the personal income tax field.
1967	Manitoba establishes its own retail sales tax.
1972	The federal government agrees to administer some tax credits for the provinces. Reforms stemming from the Royal Commission on Taxation come into force, including transfer of succession duties to the provinces.
1977	Additional federal personal and corporate tax (percentage) points granted to the provinces as part of the Established Program Financing reforms. Since this transfer is part of a reform under which conditional grants for health and education are transformed into block grants delivered via a combination of tax points and cash payments, the control of these tax points remains with the federal government.
1979	Only Quebec still levies succession duties (it abandons them in 1985).
1981	Alberta establishes its own corporate income tax.
1982	The Constitution Act: Equalization payments to the provinces are enshrined in the constitution without a specification of the scale and distribution of these payments; and indirect taxation of non-crown-owned natural resources is granted to the provinces.
1987	Meech Lake constitutional amendment (fails in 1990): Provinces would have been able to opt out of shared cost programs with compensation if national objectives were met.
1991	The federal government introduces a value-added tax – the Goods and Services Tax, or GST.
1991	Quebec reaches agreement with the federal government to harmonize its own retail sales tax with the new federal GST, and to collect both its own and the federal GST with substantial federal contributions to the province for tax administration. The base of the Quebec tax is more or less harmonized with the federal tax by 1996.
1991	Saskatchewan and Prince Edward Island reverse their recent decisions to harmonize with the GST, and continue to collect their own retail sales taxes.
1997	The federal government and the Atlantic provinces of Newfoundland and Labrador, New Brunswick, and Nova Scotia implement a harmonized value-added tax (HST) replacing provincial retail sales taxes and the GST. Administration of the HST is combined with that of the federal GST and provincial sales tax administration and collection is abolished in these provinces.

The table is not intended to present a complete history of taxation in the Canadian federation. For further details, see Gillespie (1991) and Perry (1955).

of determined assaults on the superior courts by one or the other level of government.[18]

The second period that can be identified in Table 7.3 begins with the onset of World War II, when the federal government abruptly and decisively assumed a dominant position in taxation that lasted until the mid 1950s.[19] Early in the war years, the provinces gave up their personal and corporate income tax systems in exchange for "tax rental payments" by the federal government. After the war, discussions about these rental payments gradually took the form of arguments over tax points or percentages of federal income tax collections that were to be given to the provinces. But from the onset of the tax-rental agreements until the middle of the 1950s, the federal authorities were widely assumed to be responsible for changes in personal and corporate income tax rates.

In a third distinct period, from the middle or late 1950s until the early 1990s, the provinces slowly but surely regained taxation powers ceded to the federal government during the war. This is in marked contrast to what happened in Australia, where the commonwealth government also took over state income taxation as a wartime measure, but where the Australian states never recovered the general use of the income tax.[20] The reestablishment of provincial income taxation in Canada began, not surprisingly, with Quebec, which has always carefully guarded its independence from Ottawa and the rest of the country. Moreover, at the same time that provincial income tax systems were being renewed, the provinces that had not yet implemented a retail sales tax began to do so, so that by 1967, every province except Alberta collected its own sales tax on a base it alone controlled.[21]

During this third period, the wartime tax rental agreements gradually evolved into the present tax-on-tax, or piggyback, system in which provincially determined provincial personal income tax rates are levied as a percent of the federal rate of tax, with the determination of the base of the personal income tax and income tax collection remaining in federal hands.[22] By the time the tax rental agreements had evolved into

---

[18] For a recent study of the process of constitutional reform via judicial reinterpretation of the constitution, see Voigt (1999).

[19] During the Great Depression, the federal government's superior revenue sources had already begun to reverse the trend toward provincial tax autonomy. Accordingly, one might date the start of the second period from the onset of the Depression.

[20] This fact is not recorded in Tables 7.1 and 7.2.

[21] The province of Alberta is still the only province that does not levy a provincial sales tax.

[22] Again, Quebec is the exception. Quebec levies and collects its own personal income tax on its own base.

the formal tax collection agreements of 1962, the provinces were, in my judgment, once again being held accountable by the electorate for increases in personal income tax rates.

It is during the third period that three provinces (Quebec, Ontario, and Alberta) began to collect their own corporate income tax, though the base and rate of the provincial taxes remained very similar to that of the federal government. This period of rising provincial power also includes the turning over to the provinces of succession duties in 1972, following the reforms initiated by the Royal Commission on Taxation, and the subsequent death of this tax as a result of interprovincial tax competition. It includes the reform of the Canadian constitution in 1982, as part of which the provinces gained the right to levy indirect taxation on natural resources taken from non-crown-owned land within their jurisdictions in return for agreeing to repatriation and amendment of the constitution. This important reassignment of the power to tax allowed the provinces to substitute indirect taxation of natural resource production for less reliable taxation of corporate profits.

In a fourth and most recent period that began in the late 1980s or early 1990s, the taxation pendulum begins to swing back toward the federal government. After successfully resisting most provincial requests to implement tax deductions, credits, and exemptions through the federally administered personal income tax, in 1991 the federal government dropped its manufacturers' sales tax that had been in place since the early 1920s and introduced a national credit-invoice type value-added tax on consumption at a rate of 7 percent, the Goods and Services Tax (GST).[23] This placed it in direct competition with the provinces for control over the consumption tax base, one that is becoming increasingly attractive relative to corporate, capital, and personal incomes as globalization accelerates.

Even before the GST was officially introduced, the federal government tried to entice the provinces to join with it in levying a national consumption tax on a base that would be jointly determined and controlled, but without much success. Despite the intentions of the framers of the constitution of 1867, the sales tax had become one of major revenue sources used by the provinces. No doubt they too were aware of the increasing value of access to this base in an era of high capital

---

[23] More recently (1998), after threats to introduce a separate provincial income tax, the province of Ontario has been somewhat successful in having the federal government administer provincial tax credits through the personal income tax. Whether the number of provincially determined special provisions of this sort will grow remains to be seen.

mobility. The larger provinces were especially unwilling to share their power to tax consumption, or (with the exception of Quebec, to be discussed) to trade their ability to manipulate the structure of the sales tax base.

In an interesting turn of events, in 1996 the federal government was successful in convincing three of the poorest provinces to give up their own retail sales taxes and allow the federal government to administer and collect a Harmonized Sales Tax on the same base as it own value-added tax. I explore this episode at some length in the next section in order to suggest that the reassignment of fiscal powers in a federal system is an ongoing process, of more than historical interest. Before turning to this third case, however, it is important to note that the discussion of the events recorded in Table 7.3 may be summarized in the following manner: the story of taxation in the Canadian federation is, to a considerable extent, a history of changes in access to, and control over, the major tax bases by federal and provincial governments.

4   The harmonized sales tax in Canada, 1997

As previously noted, even before the introduction in 1991 of its Goods and Services Tax, the federal government tried to interest the provinces in a national consumption tax that would be jointly administered. Before 1996, however, only Quebec had agreed to harmonize the base and rate of its own sales tax with that of the GST, and in this case, Quebec successfully insisted on the right to maintain its own tax collection system.[24]

Strong provincial opposition to a national consumption tax complicated an ongoing political problem faced by the federal government of the day. The Liberal Party's official pre-election platform – the "Redbook" of 1993 – had unwisely included a promise to reform the federal GST, and a national sales tax would have gone a long way toward meeting this commitment without the need to raise income tax rates to compensate for a loss of GST revenue. When the tax was not substantially amended or replaced after the landslide victory of the Liberals in the 1993 election, the credibility of the government and of the prime minister was sharply called into question in the media. The deputy prime

---

[24] Quebec presently collects both its own value-added tax *and* the GST. The federal government pays the province of Quebec to administer both the provincial and the federal value-added taxes on domestic trade, while it collects the Quebec tax owed on international imports along with its own GST.

minister, who had been closely associated with the election promise, was forced to resign from Parliament in 1996 as a direct result of the issue. But even though she successfully defended her seat in a by-election, the failure to replace the GST in the face of what was widely perceived to be an unambiguous pre-election promise kept the issue on the national political agenda.

It must therefore have been with a strong sense of relief that the Liberal government in Ottawa finally reached agreement with the Liberal provincial governments of New Brunswick, Nova Scotia, and Newfoundland and Labrador to adopt a Harmonized Sales Tax (HST) to take effect on April 1, 1997. (The fourth and by far the smallest of the Atlantic provinces, Prince Edward Island, was and at this writing still is not a party to the agreement.) The following paragraphs provide a brief overview of the terms of the Comprehensive and Integrated Tax Coordination Agreement (1996) signed by the three participating provinces and the federal government:[25]

- The base of the new HST is that of the GST. A limited number of rebates that effectively create distinct provincial tax treatments will be provided to residents of participating provinces with respect to purchases of housing and books and in the municipal, school, and hospital sectors. Separate registration by businesses for the GST and the HST is not required. Domestic firms selling into or operating in a participating province simply remit the HST on the same basis as the GST, while the HST on imports is collected by the federal government.[26]
- The rate of the tax is 15 percent, consisting of a federal component of 7 percent, and a provincial component of 8 percent that is levied on the base exclusive of GST. (A comparison of provincial tax rates before and after the HST is provided in Table 7.4.)
- The provincial component of the tax cannot increase for an initial period of four years, but may be reduced upon unanimous approval of the participating provinces. After this time, *increases* in the provincial rate are subject to approval by a majority of the participating provinces. Future provincial rate *reductions* are

---

[25] For comparison of the HST to other similar taxes around the world, see Bird and Gendron (1997).

[26] The tax on imported noncommercial goods is assessed based on the province of destination of the goods. For commercial importations, only the GST is collected because the final destination cannot always be determined. (An importer may subsequently distribute them throughout the country, including the participating provinces.)

Table 7.4. *Atlantic Provinces' sales tax rates before and after harmonization with the goods and services tax*

Province	PST rate before harmonization	Combined PST and GST rate before harmonization	HST rate (after harmonization on April 1, 1997)
Newfoundland	12	19.84	15
New Brunswick	11	18.77	15
Nova Scotia	11	18.77	15
Prince Edward Island	10	17.7	—

PST = provincial retail sales tax; GST = federal goods and services tax; HST = harmonized sales tax. The GST rate is 7%. Prior to harmonization with the GST on April 1, 1997, each PST was applied to the price *inclusive* of the GST, so that the effective combined rate in each province was greater than the simple sum of PST and GST rates.

to require the unanimous approval of all participating provinces (thus ensuring that interprovincial competition will not lead to unwanted tax reductions).

- HST revenues are divided among participants on the basis of each province's share of taxable consumption in Canada as a whole. Statistics Canada, a respected quasi-independent federal agency, is to be responsible for providing improved measures of taxable consumption on a provincial basis, and is given about $40 million to improve its provincial economic accounting. A joint federal-provincial committee is established to ensure the revenue allocation formula functions as intended.

- The tax is administered and collected by the federal government at no financial cost to the participating provinces, and provincial sales tax administration is eliminated.

Transition payments offered to the provinces by the federal government were obviously important in the negotiations leading up to the HST. No doubt this was a key factor in dealing with substantial opposition to the new tax in some of the participating provinces. The federal government agreed to pay the three provinces an amount that is estimated to be about one billion dollars (in total) over the first four years of the agreement to mitigate revenue losses due to the lowering of the overall sales tax rate applying in each province to 15 percent and the granting of input tax credits under the credit-invoice VAT system.[27] Moreover, provision is made for provincial tax administrators to be hired by the federal revenue collection agency, and employment in the participating provinces is to some extent to be maintained in the short term in regional offices.

A further benefit provided to the participating provinces that should also be noted is the following: In 1993 the federal government disallowed the use of future increases in provincial capital tax levies as a deduction for federal tax purposes. According to the Memorandum of Understanding (1996), the provinces participating in the HST are exempted from this restriction (subject to certain limits), so that firms in these provinces could partly offset any further increases in provincial capital taxes at the expense of the federal treasury.[28]

Despite the transition payments and other arrangements, the question remains why the three provinces agreed to give up their ability to adjust the definition of the sales tax base to meet specific provincial needs as well as their general control over the rate of sales taxation. The transition payments last for only four years, and reinstating a provincial sales tax after several years would be both administratively difficult as well as unwelcome in the business community. Moreover, other revenue sources such as provincial capital levies and payroll taxes are not good substitutes for a general sales tax in provinces that must be concerned with attracting investment and employment.

In suggesting some answers to this question, I speculate freely. The participating provinces may have anticipated cutting their own sales tax rates in a few years anyway, as the economic situation improved and as provincial deficits declined. The HST transitional payments, financed almost entirely by federal taxation levied on the rest of the country, allowed them to do this much sooner and at the expense of someone else's voters. In addition, the mail-order business had been eroding the sales tax base, and this problem could have been expected to continue and perhaps to worsen as internet commerce expanded. Under the HST, on the other hand, interprovincial and international trade is dealt with more effectively, and at the federal government's expense.

---

[27] The adjustment assistance offsets 100 percent of the revenue loss in excess of 5 percent of previous retail sales tax collections in years one and two, 50 percent of this amount in year three, and 25 percent in year four.

[28] Section 12(ii) of the MOU (April 23, 1996) states that Canada will, at the province's request, "allow the deductibility of incremental provincial payroll and capital taxes for federal corporate income tax purposes, not to exceed an amount equal to the retail sales tax that otherwise would have been collected from corporations had the province not harmonized with the value added tax . . ."

Finally, the provinces may have calculated that a national sales tax was on the way, sooner or later, and that by joining with the federal government early on, their position in future negotiations with the larger provinces would be enhanced.[29] Since its promise to replace the GST is easy to monitor, this is a rationale that the Liberal government in Ottawa would like to confirm before the next national election.

5   Concluding remarks

The fiscal history reviewed in this chapter indicates that the assignment of the power to tax in the Australian and Canadian federations is only loosely connected to the assignment specified in the original constitutions and is, at least in Canada, highly flexible.[30] In Australia, the framers wanted a decentralized federation and history bequeathed something that is decidedly the opposite. In Canada, despite the tightly drawn initial assignment of fiscal responsibilities, the power to tax has shifted back and forth between federal and provincial governments, while remaining more decentralized than in Australia.[31]

As a whole, the history suggests that reassignment of governing instruments should be regarded as a normal event in a federal system. If this

[29] Even more speculative is the possibility that for Newfoundland, participation in the HST was linked to a partial buyout of Term 29 of the Terms of Union of Newfoundland with Canada (1949) negotiated at about the same time that the HST agreement was finalized. Under Term 29, Newfoundland is to receive $8 million per year in perpetuity as compensation for joining Canada in 1949. In 1996 these payments were replaced for a term of twenty years by a one-time payment of $130 million. The discount rate implied by this deal is 2.3% ($8 million discounted at 2.3% for twenty years has a present value of $130 million). Such a low interest rate is favorable to Newfoundland. One may also note that the governing parties in the three provinces were nominally all Liberal ones, as was the government in Ottawa, although this too seems unlikely to have been an important factor in an agreement over a transfer of something as vital as the power to tax.

[30] The assignment in Canada continues to evolve. As this chapter was being completed, the province of Alberta announced (March 1999) that it intends to break away from the piggy-back system of personal income taxation, in which provincial taxes are levied as a percent of the federal tax and collected by the federal authorities, and institute its own tax on personal income. Recent work by Painter (1998) on cooperation between the commonwealth and the states suggests that the effective assignment in Australia will continue to evolve as well.

[31] It is interesting to ask why the federal assignment has developed so differently in the two countries despite similarities in economic structure and political heritage. An obvious guess, one that has often been made, points to the demands for autonomy by the French-speaking majority in Quebec, a situation that has no parallel in Australia. A convincing "proof" of this hypothesis remains to be given.

conclusion is accepted, it is reasonable to begin thinking of federalism, including the courts that interpret the constitution, as a mechanism for reallocating the effective use of governing instruments among various political jurisdictions in the face of unforseen events. Such a perspective concerning the nature of federalism carries with it interesting implications for economic theorizing about the federal assignment, and I conclude by briefly considering this matter.

If a federal system is a mechanism for reassigning policy instruments among competing governments, one ought to ask the questions of such a system that one usually asks of any allocation mechanism: Under what conditions does an equilibrium assignment of fiscal powers among jurisdictions exist? Is the equilibrium unique? Is it stable? And how is the assignment of powers among levels of government affected by initial or historical conditions, including the original constitutional assignment, and by shocks of various kinds?

In the normative context, treating federalism as a mechanism for continually centralizing or devolving policy instruments leads to the traditional questions posed by classical welfare economics: What is the nature of the standard of reference that should be used to judge an actual assignment in a democratic federal system?[32] Under what conditions will an equilibrium assignment coincide with this standard of reference? What factors lead to "failure" of the existing mechanism or federal system to result in a good outcome? One should note that the last two questions cannot be dealt with in the absence of a positive analysis of reassignment, just as the study of the conditions under which a private economy generates or fails to generate an efficient allocation cannot proceed without an understanding of how private markets actually work.

The study of federalism as a mechanism for reassigning policy instruments would provide a useful complement to the traditional, exclusively normative approach that is focused on the design of the optimal assignment by a social planner, and with reference to which I began this chapter. It is, more or less, the approach that Albert Breton takes in his recent book. In view of the role actually played by reassignment in federal systems of government, I suggest that this approach to federalism has much to offer.

---

[32] Perhaps the existing theory of the optimal assignment can serve as a standard of reference. For discussion of alternative standards that attempt to incorporate collective choice and transactions costs, see Breton (1996) and Hettich and Winer (1999, Chapter 6).

References

Bird, Richard (1986). *Federal Finance in Comparative Perspective.* Toronto: Canadian Tax Foundation.

Bird, Richard and Pierre-Pascal Gendron (1998). "Dual VATs and Cross-Border Trade: A Review of International Experience." Discussion Paper No. 13, International Center for Tax Studies, Rotman School of Management, University of Toronto, October.

Boadway, Robin and Paul A. R. Hobson (1993). *Intergovernmental Fiscal Relations in Canada.* Canadian Tax Paper No. 96. Toronto: Canadian Tax Foundation.

Boadway, Robin, Maurice Marchand, and Marianne Vigneault (1998). "The Consequences of Overlapping Tax Bases for Redistribution and Public Spending in a Federation." *Journal of Public Economics* 68(3), 421–452.

Brennan, Geoffrey, ed. (1987). *Constitutional Reform and Fiscal Federalism.* Federalism Research Centre, Discussion Paper No. 42, Australian National University, Canberra.

Breton, Albert (1996). *Competitive Governments: An Economic Theory of Politics and Public Finance.* New York: Cambridge University Press.

Breton, Albert and Anthony Scott (1978). *The Economic Constitution of Federal States.* Toronto: University of Toronto Press.

Dahlby, Beverly (1996). "Fiscal Externalities and the Design of Intergovernmental Grants." *International Tax and Public Finance* 3: 397–334.

Gillespie, W. Irwin (1991). *Tax, Borrow and Spend: Financing Federal Spending in Canada, 1867–1990.* Ottawa: Carleton University Press.

Gordon, Roger (1983). "An Optimal Taxation Approach to Fiscal Federalism." *Quarterly Journal of Economics* 48: 567–586.

Gramlich, Edward (1987). "Subnational Fiscal Policy." *Perspectives on Local Public Finance and Public Policy* 3: 3–27.

Hettich, Walter and Stanley L. Winer (1999). *Democratic Choice and Taxation: A Theoretical and Empirical Analysis.* New York: Cambridge University Press.

Hogg, Peter W. (1992). *Constitutional Law of Canada*, 3rd edition. Toronto: Carswell.

Inman, Robert and Daniel Rubinfeld (1996). "Designing Tax Policy in Federalist Economies: An Overview." *Journal of Public Economics* 60(3): 307–412.

Inman, Robert and Daniel Rubinfeld (1997). "The Political Economy of Federalism." In Dennis Mueller, ed. (1997). *Perspectives on Public Choice: A Handbook.* New York: Cambridge University Press, 73–105.

Inman, Robert and Daniel Rubinfeld (1997). "Rethinking Federalism." *Journal of Economic Perspectives* 11(4): 43–64.

James, D. W. (1992). *Intergovernmental Fiscal Relations In Australia.* Information Series No. 3. Sydney: Australian Tax Research Foundation.

La Forest, G. V. (1981). *The Allocation of Taxing Power Under the Canadian Constitution.* Canadian Tax Paper No. 65, 2nd edition. Toronto: Canadian Tax Foundation.

McMillan, Melville (1993). "A Local Perspective on Fiscal Federalism: Practices, Experiences and Lessons From Developed Countries. University of Alberta, unpublished manuscript, December.

Oates, Wallace (1972). *Fiscal Federalism*. New York: Harcourt, Brace, Jovanovich.

Painter, Martin (1998). *Collaborative Federalism: Economic Reform in Australia in the 1990's*. Cambridge: Cambridge University Press.

Pauly, Mark (1973). "Income Redistribution as a Local Public Good." *Journal of Pubic Economics* 2: 35–58.

Perry, J. Harvey (1955). *Taxes, Tariffs and Subsidies*. Vols. I and II. Toronto: University of Toronto Press.

Petchey, Jeffrey and Perry Shapiro (1997). "One People, One Destiny: Centralization and Conflicts of Interest in Australian Federalism," in David E. Wildasin (ed.), *Fiscal Aspects of Evolving Federations*. Cambridge: Cambridge University Press, 196–219.

Searle, R. J. (1998). "Fiscal Federalism in Australia," in H. Shibata and T. Ihori (eds.), *The Welfare State, Public Investment, and Growth*. Tokyo: Springer-Verlag, 295–331.

Smith, Julie P. (1992). *Fiscal Federalism in Australia: A Twentieth Century Chronology*. Federalism Research Centre, Australian National University, Canberra.

Smith, Julie P. (1993). *Taxing Popularity: The Story of Taxation in Australia*. Federalism Research Centre, Australian National University, Canberra.

Saunders, Cheryl (1990). "Government Borrowing in Australia." *Publius* 20(4): 35–52.

The Australian Constitution (as altered to 30 April 1991). Canberra: Parliamentary Education Office.

The Constitution of Canada (including the Constitution Act of 1982 and the Constitution Act of 1867). Ottawa, Supply and Services Canada, 1982.

The British North America Acts, 1867 to 1975. Ottawa, Department of Justice, 1976.

Uhr, John (1989). "The Canadian and Australian Senates: Comparing Federal Political Institutions," in B. Hodgins (ed.). *Federalism in Canada and Australia*. Peterborough, 130–146.

Vaillancourt, Francois (1992). "Subnational Tax Harmonization in Australia and Comparisons with Canada and the United States." Federalism Research Centre, Discussion Paper No. 17, Australian National University, Canberra.

Voigt, Stefan (1999). "Implicit Constitutional Change – Changing the Meaning of the Constitution without Changing the Text of the Document." *European Journal of Law and Economics* 7(3): 197–224.

Walsh, Cliff (1996). "Making a Mess of Tax Assignment: Australia as a Case Study," in Paul Boothe (ed.), *Reforming Fiscal Federalism for Global Competition: A Canada-Australia Comparison*. Western Studies in Economic Policy. Edmonton: The University of Alberta Press, 109–140.

Warden, James (1992). "Federalism and the Design of the Australian Constitution." Federalism Research Centre, Discussion Paper No. 19, Australian National University, Canberra.

Watts, Ronald (1996). Comparing Federal Systems in the 1990's. Institute of Intergovernmental Relations, Kingston: Queen's University and McGill-Queen's University Press.

Wildasin, David (1986). *Urban Public Finance* New York: Harwood Publishers.

Winer, Stanley L. (1992). "Taxation and Federalism in a Changing World," in Richard Bird and Jack Mintz (eds.), *Taxation to 2000 and Beyond*. Canadian

Tax Paper No. 93. Toronto: Canadian Tax Foundation, 343–368, with Comments by Albert Breton (369–371) and Anthony Scott (372–380).

Winer, Stanley L. and Allan M. Maslove (1996). "Fiscal Federalism in Canada and Australia: A Brief Comparison of Constitutional Frameworks, Structural Features of Existing Fiscal Systems and Fiscal Institutions," in Paul Boothe (ed.), *Reforming Fiscal Federalism for Global Competition: A Canada-Australia Comparison.* Western Studies in Economic Policy. Edmonton: The University of Alberta Press, 45–85.

Zines, Leslie (1990). "Federal Constitutional Control over the Economy, *Publius* 20(4): 19–34.

CHAPTER 8

Assigning powers over the Canadian environment

Anthony Scott

I   Introduction

Much of the literature on the assignment of powers in a federation concerns powers over very large "branches" of government, such as redistribution and welfare, or the regulation of industry. Albert Breton's writing, however, has for the last twenty years been concerned with the process of the assignment of specific, rather narrow, powers. Most economists have been slow to follow him, and it is to academic political scientists and constitutional lawyers that we must look for hard information about piecemeal assignment or amendment.[1]

The fact that several chapters of Breton's *Competitive Governments* (1996) are devoted to this question provides an opportunity to try a case study, relying chiefly on published sources. The extraordinary off-and-on cooperation, in Canada, between environmental agencies at two levels of government provides interesting illustrations and food for speculation. Why, in late 1997, did the federal government step out

I'm grateful for conversations with Kathryn Harrison, Albert Breton, Mike Harcourt, John Halstead, and Blair Seaborn.

[1] Among the resource- or environment-policy pioneers in political science I may mention Susan Rose-Ackerman and Elinor Ostrom, though federalism has not been the context they have studied most. In Canada, I mention M. H. Sproule-Jones, whose years of work is laid out in the text and bibliography of Sproule-Jones 1993, and O. P. Dwivedi, Robert Paehlke, N. A. Swainson, R. B. Woodrow, Bruce Doern, Don Munton, D. Tingley, and Mark Zacher. For the Canadian authors, federalism is a prime concern. A helpful source, but one dealing more with resources than with the environment, is Clark, Crommelin, and Saunders, eds., 1990. Since about 1990 the literature has seen contributions from people I regard as a new group. I have to thank Kathryn Harrison for introducing me to these studies, including her own recent book (Harrison 1996). As well, there are a number of law-school scholars and a few applied economists, some of whom are cited. Many of the noneconomists are aware of the contributions of economists such as Albert Breton, and refer to their work.

174

from the provinces to promise a reduced level of greenhouse-gas emissions that it cannot, and that the provinces will not, enforce? Alas, this paper does not present an answer. But it does show how powers over the environment are still being passed backward and forward among governmental levels, in a rather curious illustration of Albert Breton's "competition."

II   Economists, spillovers, and environmental powers

To most economists, the subject of the environment automatically conjures up the subject of interpersonal externalities. By analogy, for public-sector economists the subject of assigning powers over the environment ought to evoke the subject of interjurisdictional geographical externalities. (These are often referred to as spillouts, leakages, or cross-boundary spillovers. The water-quality problem of the Great Lakes is described as TFP: transfrontier pollution.) After all, these externalities can cause heavy costs: health hazards, flood damage, fires, siltation, soil erosion, crop and livestock disease, fisheries depletion; and navigation, irrigation, waterpower, and water-supply losses. These costs all provide reasons for predicting where provincial borders will be placed and/or what powers the provinces will be assigned.

In what follows, I record that some earlier economists did follow this kind of reasoning, and that resource and environmental economists, at least, did offer some analyses in which geographical externalities did play some part. But I will end the discussion by insisting that such externalities have not after all been central to the problem of the assignment of powers over the environment. On the whole, each jurisdiction's environment has been regulated as if there were no spillovers. The national involvement, if any, is in setting local standards, not in preventing local pollution from leaking out.

The water-resource and environmental economists who wrestled with the regulation and planning of whole river basins rarely related their recommendations to the concerns of the emerging field of public choice.[2] Such questions as whether the Ohio or the Columbia basin ought to be

---

[2] The U.S. federal government was originally assigned the power to regulate interstate commerce. In 1824 it was determined that this included power over navigation, and, eventually, all regulatory powers over navigable rivers. The states, however, retain the power to make laws concerning the appropriation and use of waters within their boundaries, subject to the federal power. In the 1920s the federal power became the basis of a boom in dam-building development projects, such as the Tennessee Valley Authority and the later Columbia basin projects. More recently, it has served as the basis for the federal Clean Water Act. However, in many water-policy fields Congress has left the states free

developed by the self-coordination of state agencies or by a comprehensive federal agency were not "economic" issues. Even the local and regional economists, who *did* consider urban geographical spillovers, in their work on public goods, were slow to turn to their implications for the structure of governments.[3] Eventually, Albert Breton (1965), in the company of a host of others, forced economists to consider the fact that by creating new jurisdictions, changing boundaries, making interjurisdictional payments, or coordinating the provision of public services, different structures of government could provide public goods and services at different costs. As these contributions were presented in the vocabulary of the "optimum" jurisdiction or spillover, they made sense to the environmental and resource economists whose theoretical work made similar use of welfare economics.

Nevertheless, it is difficult to point to any group of environmental economists that has contributed to the analysis of the assignment of powers over the environment.[4] Apparently, the instinct is still to take as given the structure of government with respect to pollution and land use.

Apart from their being locked into the paradigm that organizations and institutions are not the business of economists, I can think of three explanations for this. One is that the assignment of powers with respect to spillovers is generally OK and does not need investigation or analysis. This explanation is closely linked to a second, that the actual span of the results of provincial or state environmental management is so narrow

to act regarding their own rivers as long as they meet the rules or standards in various federal navigation, development, and pollution laws.

   The Canadian federal government was assigned specific powers over fisheries, navigation, and agriculture, in addition to its general or global powers over trade and commerce, criminal law, taxation, spending, and "peace, order and good government [POG]." Probably the highly specific fisheries power has been most effective in justifying federal activities on rivers and lakes. The others have been evoked, but the fact that the provinces *own* the rivers and lakes as property has meant that Ottawa's role is not as large as Washington's. For the Australian commonwealth's role see A. Kellow 1996, p. 143, and Clark, Crommelin, and Saunders, eds., 1990.

[3] Most of the influential authors were much influenced by papers by C. M. Tiebout in 1956 and 1961. A current bibliography can be found in Alan Williams 1966.

[4] In the middle 1960s RFF economists such as Kneese and Herfindahl, and Harvard water projects economists including Robert Dorfman, Otto Eckstein, and Stephen Marglin, began to write about the economies of water-resource and river-basin "systems." Dorfman later made upstream-downstream jurisdictional relations central to his river-basin analysis. But most others, from Dasgupta and Heal 1979 through Hartwick and Olewiler 1986 and more recent writers on pollution and the environment, have mentioned "externalities" but ignored the political aspects of geographical externalities.

that environmental spillovers are relatively rare.[5] A third explanation is that while the geographical assignment of powers is not OK, the costs of dealing with unwanted externalities, by coordination, is not high.[6] These explanations may all apply at once. They result in economists' indifference to the subject of interjurisdictional externalities and to their belief that, while there may be good reason for expecting that the assignment of environmental powers among governments will change, externalities are not one of them. In the following sections, therefore, I turn from geographical spillovers to apply economic reasoning to other possible causes of contention in the assignment of powers over the environment in a federation.

III   Powers, policies, and agencies

A   *Assigning powers, jurisdictions, functions, or what?*

Economists inherited the problem of explaining the assignment of "powers" from others: lawyers and politicians mostly. The word itself refers to the constitutional division of Parliament's original right to make laws regarding any subject. The share of these powers assigned to each government is to be found in the written constitution and in its complementary interpretative court decisions. As well, some governments and agencies may gain powers that are "delegated" to them by municipal law or the equivalent. On the other hand, a government may lose powers because of restrictions in the country's charter of liberties or in international law.

It is not surprising that economists have not shown much interest explaining the division of powers. The very concept of a "power" is not homogeneous enough to invite economic explanation. Sometimes it refers to authority over a sector of the economy, such as agriculture, but sometimes to means of enforcement (police or navy); sources of revenue (issuing bonds); a social problem (e.g., hospitals, criminal law); or an activity (running schools, qualifying doctors, controlling navigation, patching roads.) So substituting another word such as "functions," "field," "area," or "subject" cannot simplify analysis of the assignment of powers.

[5] This has been my own view: see Scott 1964. Legal writers, taking a more conservative view, assert that spillovers were rare or nonexistent at the time that the three federations constitutions were enacted. See the contributors to Holland et al., eds., 1996.

[6] In all three federations there are horizontal and vertical coordination agreements governing multi-jurisdictional river basins.

In the economics of public finance, early writers made a halfhearted attempt to prescribe what taxes and what spending powers should be decentralized to local governments or to provinces. The currently prevalent textbook approach owes much to Richard Musgrave (1959).[7] He met the challenge by aggregating the dozens of possible powers into three or four economic functions (or "budgets"), such as "regulation," "stabilization," and "redistribution."

This approach should be contrasted with an alternative: treating the allocation of "powers" like the allocation of an input to an industry (or a firm). Governments seek powers just as employers seek such rights as property over land or patents over products and processes. Their doing so is part of the process of introducing specialization among public and private units in the economy. Once holding a power, a government (like a firm) can choose the amount and quality to produce, or whether just to hold the power unexercised.[8]

It is wrong, however, to assume that governments at different levels, offered the power to, say, reduce river pollution, would utilize the power in the same way. Each would develop activities that were complementary to its activities under its other powers, and would also be influenced by its financial resources and by the geographical distribution of political party strengths within the polluted river basin. Examples were provided by early skirmishes over the power to deal with river pollution by organic wastes. Junior governments tended to improve sewage waste treatment. But senior governments preferred to extend big river projects so as to achieve river flow augmentation, river waste spreading, or river waste aeration.[9]

B   *The three subjects that environmental agencies deal with*

In spite of the ambiguity of "powers over the environment," environmental agencies do exist in most governments at all levels. Furthermore, laymen and politicians seem in no doubt about what activities should be allotted to these agencies.[10] The distinguishing features, apparently, have to do with *publicness* – the absence of exclusive property, inability to charge for services and easy access, by industry – and location in a *natural setting*. When problems arise, and when these conditions exist, politicians

---

[7] See Musgrave 1959; Oates 1972, p. 14, n. 2; Breton and Scott 1978; and Breton 1996, pp. 183–4.

[8] Breton and Scott 1978, p. 11.

[9] See Robert David in Kneese and Smith, eds., 1966, pp. 114–117.

[10] For informal definitions, see Holland et al. 1996, pp. 1–2, and Rose-Ackerman 1995, p. 18. Most writers do not attempt to define the field or the powers.

call in their environmental ministries. Usually, the problem requires one of three government activities: pollution abatement, ecosystem protection, or land use control.

Pollution abatement, called for by waste disposal into air or water, fits this definition very well. Polluting varies in a geographical dimension, ranging from the local disposal of degradable organic wastes (from very early times the subject of local "sanitary" regulation) through the dumping of more enduring and transportable substances (leading to regional smog and basin-wide water contamination), to the worldwide emission of greenhouse gases. Such classifications of pollution types by the extent of their geographical effect has suggested to many a rule for the assignment of environmental functions to governments classified by the area of their jurisdiction, and so by their level: the management of local pollutants should be assigned to local governments, of regional pollutants to states or provinces, and so on, until global pollutants ought to become the concern of an international government. Clearly this suggestion has had some influence in actual assignments.

There is another way of classifying types of pollutants, one that also suggests how environmental powers ought to be assigned. They can be classified by the extent of the damage they cause: some are "harmless" (such as turbidity in drinking water), some cause seriously unpopular effects (such as water eutrophication and smoke), and a few are toxic, deleterious, contaminating, or radioactive. This classification has also suggested a rule: harmless pollution should be entrusted to local governments, but dangerous pollutants should be the concern of the central government. The rule evidently makes sense to some people, but it does not appear to have become very influential.

Second, even when there is no pollution of air or water the absence of exclusive property rights in much of the "ecosystem" has recently led to the expansion of types of *protective action over nature*. These range from centuries-old policies of protecting certain animals and birds, setting aside forests, and regulating hunting and fishing, to the more modern creation of parks and other reserves for wildlife habitat and wilderness. Powers to deal with pollution usually lead to policies that prevent nuisances to people, but holding powers to protect nature leads to policies that are harder to classify. True, many such policies are responsive to demands from defined groups of user clients, such as commercial fishermen and trappers, recreational anglers and hunters, and the service firms that serve these "industries." But in addition to these actual users, there are groups who demand policies to protect the mere "existence" of endangered species, the conservation of their habitats and a related ecological diversity. Many of these policies make no distinction between wildlife, habitat, and aesthetics in open and in private lands. Perhaps because of this jumble of demands for protection there is no suggested general rule as to which kind of protected thing should be assigned to which level of government.[11]

Land-use control, a third type of government action, actually does not fit well into my "externality" definition. The subject lies in the overlap of "conservation" and "environment." It has always been hard to classify, and governments have long had difficulties explaining how certain of their land-use controls fitted into any justification of government intervention.[12] For example, the Roosevelt New Deal was criticized even by its supporters for its generous soil-conservation programs. What business had the state in preventing farmers from mismanaging their own land?[13] Today, soil erosion has become a target of land-use environmentalism. Similar programs also aim at tidying up (private and public) landscapes, watersheds, cityscapes, logging sites, and old industrial and mining properties, where the land use or misuse is offensive and possibly threatening. What have they all in common? To salvage my identifying definition, it can be argued that they are directed against offensive public bads; that is, against land misuse in which there is a kind of exclusivity failure.

I must recognize a fourth category, a ragbag of common-property resource regimes, for water and fisheries. Control over inland waters is usually allocated to individual users by a specialized branch of government, enforcing or administering a specialized water law. Levels and flows can come into conflict with other "common-property" uses such as recreation, fisheries, navigation, wildlife habitat, and waste disposal, and with private uses such as urban water supply, electric power generation, and irrigation. Government involvement in the distribution of these services has a long history, especially in the common law, and so antedates "environmental" concern. Typically, river basins come under fragmented control; there is rarely undivided authority over the whole thing, either within a political jurisdiction or in its relations with neighboring jurisdictions, nor is there much demand for it.

Like inland waters, the oceans, and wildlife, fisheries are technically a matter of environmental concern, but have been the concern of specialized ministries for at least a century. Inland and ocean fish stocks have

---

[11] Except that the owner of crown lands has a head start in protecting the environment on these lands.

[12] See Van Kooten 1993, Chapter 11, pp. 246–69, and Van Kooten and Scott 1995.

[13] There were of course various justifications. Unchecked erosion caused siltation and dust-bowl conditions beyond the farm. As well, it signaled the need for financial assistance by desperate drought-ridden farmers, and for a kind of belated education of farmers advancing into massive monoculture.

by location or migration typically been subject to more than one government,[14] and have suffered for it. Where the management of these common-property resources fits as between the private sector and government, and as between levels of government, has been debated in the courts for centuries. There is little understanding to be gained by squeezing them into a discussion of powers over the environment. Consequently, while understanding why dedicated environmental philosophers tend to include them in their worldview of "nature," I omit their control from my list of the functions of "environmental" agencies.[15]

To summarize, there are three (or four) kinds of environmental action for which levels of government need powers: pollution abatement, ecosystem protection, and land use control. There are few suggested rules about how powers to take these actions are, or should be, divided among levels of government. The present rule seems to be that whatever government was dealing with activities that decades later were found to "insult" the environment has become the policeman to control the insults: the level that regulates "navigation" also regulates the dumping of wastes by freighters; and the level that controls "railways" also controls the use of herbicides on the right-of-way.

C   *What environmental powers are governments given?*

No modern federation has given its governments explicit environmental powers. Lacking them, governments must stretch or adapt their other powers.

In Canada, the 1867 constitution assigned the central government general (or global) and specific (or sectoral) powers. Many of the former have been suggested to the courts at one time or another as providing niches for federal government environmental initiatives or policies. The wide, general (global) powers to legislate include those referred to as "Peace, Order and Good Government," criminal law, taxation, and trade and commerce (between provinces and between countries). The

---

[14] For a good comparison of Canadian and American federalism at work on drafting the fisheries' sections of the 1960 and 1970s law of the sea conventions, see Hollick 1974 and Johnson and Zacher 1977.

[15] It must be recognized, however, that these two resources provide excellent examples of the kind of geographical spillovers or externalities that may justify concern about local or provincial control of the environment. How to bring a transfrontier river, lake, or fish stock under control so that the "downstream victim" and the "upstream source" of injury are treated justly has sometimes been answered by leaving the matter to the bargaining of the neighboring governments, and sometimes by placing it under one higher legislature, or tribunal.

narrower specific (sectoral) powers that have so far been invoked include fisheries, agriculture, and navigation.

It often happens that a provincial government and the central government can both, by exploiting their general powers or by extending their specific powers, claim the right to make laws to, say, abate pollution in a province. Sometimes such "concurrency" is regarded as a good thing, allowing the two levels of government to work together. Sometimes, though, the overlap is regarded as conflict-ridden. In Australia and the U.S., the central governments were given fewer specific powers or functions than was the case in Canada, but received paramountcy or supremacy rules that enable them to intervene or to legislate on subjects that are otherwise subject to state powers. Indeed, their regulatory power over the environment is virtually unchallengeable. Only when the central governments attempt to control the behavior and activities of state officials does their dominance weaken. In the U.S., especially, once the central government has made laws about an issue, any state laws which interfere with Washington's purpose or procedure are unconstitutional. Even if Congress has not made laws, its dominance under the general interstate commerce power is so overwhelming as to nullify a state law.[16]

Much of what governments do for each other is to contribute inputs to a joint output. For example, instead of all powers to tax, we already have one government setting the tax base while another collects them. Instead of "protecting air quality," we find a scattering of agencies forecasting weather, choosing and drafting the rules (emission or ambient standards), licensing polluters and collecting fees, monitoring firm compliance, monitoring air quality, and enforcing. Some of these agencies are at different levels from the rest. When we observe them, each is performing its role in a complementary equilibrium with the others.

Theory suggests we shall observe that eventually each level has expanded until it finds itself in a competitive relationship with the others, all pursuing their comparative advantages and exploiting their returns to scale. We do not expect to find that competition has proceeded so far that a single agency performs all the functions needed for a government to protect air quality. In Canada, the constitutional distribution of such very general powers as "property and civil rights," "inter-jurisdiction commerce," "matters of national concern," "foreign affairs," and "taxation" all stand in the way of one level of government holding all the

---

[16] For useful short summaries see Stewart 1982, pp. 87–109; Fitzerald 1996, pp. 20–21; Findley and Farber 1988, Chapter 4. The Australian constitution summarizes itself well: "when a law of a State is inconsistent with a law of the Commonwealth, the latter shall prevail . . ." (Section 109, Australia, Constitution Act [U.K.] 1900.)

powers that would be needed. True, in its attempt to invade the environmental field, a governmental level is free to exploit its confirmed rights under other powers. One of the latter is its treasury's "spending power," which has unlocked many social policy fields that would otherwise be closed.[17] Another standby has proved to be the "commerce" power. A third, just rediscovered in Canada, is the "criminal law" power. (It seems that if an environmental rule is enforced by a criminal-law-like procedure, the power to make the rule goes to the level of government holding the power to legislate on criminal subjects.)[18] By the same token, an attempt to broaden jurisdiction in the environmental power is rarely successful if it is defended by invoking a narrow or specific power. Just as powers over "education" or "health" have not been sufficient to keep these subjects under the exclusive legislative authority of one level of government, so specific powers over "fisheries" or "local works" have not saved governments from being forced to share their environmental jurisdiction with another level of government.[19]

D *Are environmental ministries and powers really needed?*

In this section I pause to check whether a government bent on protecting the environment really needs constitutional powers to do so. I show that such a government has an alternative. In the normal course of enforcing price or quality regulations under its existing constitutional powers, it can insert regulations or standards that reflect its environmental concerns. For example, a local government can beef up its rules concerning litter, smoking in restaurants, separating degradable from nondegradable wastes, and using recycled paper products. A government

---

[17] For example, Ottawa's assistance to local sewage works in the name of the protection of receiving waters is, in most federations, an exercise of the spending power.

[18] On the basis primarily of the Peace Order and Good Government power (POGG), the courts approved Ottawa's initiating procedures under the Canadian Environmental Assessment Act (CEAA) to have a panel check provincial projects in Alberta, Saskatchewan, and Quebec. The extent to which this procedure inconveniences the province depends both on the finding of the assessment panel and on what the Ottawa government decides to do about the panel report. Presumably it could use any of its many powers to force the project to be abandoned or modified. See Skogstad 1996, pp. 115, 123. Recently, the criminal law power has been used by the courts, effectively transforming an agency's carelessness or neglect in handling toxic materials into a criminal offense and so subject to federal regulation, enforcement or penalty. That the agency was Quebec Hydro, a government body, made no difference to the Supreme Court (September 1997).

[19] This has been observed in several countries by Smith 1997 and Van Nijnatten 1997.

at the highest senior level can follow suit, at least with regard to airports, fishing boats, lighthouses, armories, and government offices.

The reasons that few explicit environmental powers exist are of course that the environment is a new subject, and that it lacks the tangibility of the "schools," "hospitals," and "fisheries" that characterized the original assignment of powers. As already noted, powers to deal with pollution are most like those over property, civil rights or industrial relations, and perhaps taxation and finance in the sense that their exercise is characterized by regulation and enforcement (using a wide range of penalties and instruments, including subsidies, charges, fines, loss of licences and permits.) Because they rarely call for spending on public works, their domain often seems unbounded, and their emphases arbitrary and unpredictable.

Some order is brought to each government's assumption of powers over the environment by the appointment of a specialized environmental bureaucracy organized into a department or agency (such as the American Environmental Protection Agency). These groupings are descended from governments' nineteenth-century sanitary bureaucracies, some of whose methods they still use. Like the early health officers, the environmental leaders have a professional ethic and a cultlike mission. In one respect, though, their present mode of action is changing from that of public health agencies to that adopted by finance departments. To ensure control over money and spending, governments allow finance officers to penetrate into both the long-range decision making and the daily operations of every other department. (Other kinds of specialists, also, monitor the various departments.) Environmental bureaucrats believe that they too should be able not only to monitor the behavior of other departments, but also to piggyback on their inspectors' and field officers' dealings with the public. So far, however, they are mostly specialized and isolated, their absence from line departments permitting other politicians and bureaucrats to neglect the environmental aspects of their activities and plans.

Governments continue to rely on environmental departments to define their own missions. I believe that even those elected politicians who are environmentally minded have little idea of the range of an environmental ministry's powers and policies. Business groups are much better informed, for they are frequently in technical liaison with the bureaucrats. Thus they may "capture" their particular regulators, as Stigler said was common in regulated utilities. However, each industrial grouping has its own technology, and so its own waste disposal system, and so its own specific pollution regulatory regime. So "business" cannot become the chief source of the department's information, methods, or ideals.[20] Instead, the ethic prevailing in an environmental ministry or agency is likely to be derived from the same sources that inspire the environmental movement. To the bureaucrats will fall the role of seeking constitutional powers and of recommending the extent of cooperation with other governments or agencies.

The environmentalists, in and out of government, transmit the successive waves of popular environmental enthusiasm and inattention,[21] evident in every aspect of ministry activities. Of course, all departments undergo reconceptualizing fluctuations, but these leave many of their subdepartments and bureaus untouched. In the short history of the environmental movement, there have already been at least three major waves. First, the departments picked up the old mission of regulating pollution emissions, with a main aim of clean air and water, and a subsidiary aim of nabbing the businesses who disposed of wastes into them. A green wave fifteen years later then swept the departments, carrying with it an intense interest, almost philosophical, in "deep ecology" and in restoring natural systems. The recent third wave was more technocratic, centering on the economy and waste of energy, and on a general conservation of scarce materials for future generations. It has blended into an upsurge of political concerns about global "sustainable development." Each wave, redirecting the slow broadening of environmental goals, has shaken everyone's ideas about the powers that a government must obtain for an environmental ministry. A single ministry may not be enough.

Environmental constraints and incentives must be funneled through all ministries to the clients with whom they deal. As already mentioned, bureaucrats think by analogy with the treasury's influence. Each activity in every department is planned to be consistent with treasury plans and goals, and is controlled by treasury representatives, and is audited for conformity with treasury directives. Another analogy is the government's human-resource establishment. It too pervades every agency, keeping an eye on labor practices, safety, minority employment, and so on.

Constitutional law and public administration experts may look to powers over the environment to cover the creation and strengthening of specialized environmental bureaus and agencies. These analogies, however, suggest another process. A government may not merely attach its new environmental activities to its other activities, as is implied by supplementing "fisheries" with "clear water" regulation. It may actually embed environmental rules and incentives in the instruments and

---

[20] Stigler 1975, p. 166.
[21] Harrison 1996 calls these "waves" and makes their timing central to her book.

controls with which it regularly deals with its clients.[22] It may respond to demands for clean air, protected species, or multiple land-use *without* special legislation or special environmental powers. Instead, the provision of a greener environment may simply be a joint product with its bureaucracies' usual provision of other goods and services. To the extent that the spectrum of all the powers actually assigned to any level of government includes the source of all the insults to the environment that a government wishes to address, special powers over the environment may be redundant.

This condition, that environmental regulation is jointly produced and enforced with other regulation, is already often typical of local government. But provincial and central governments get called on to prevent environmental abuses arising from actions or persons they have otherwise no occasion or power to regulate or serve. It is these that must handle new demands by setting up special environmental agencies, and by supporting them with acquired powers.

IV   Piecemeal vertical competition for environmental powers

A   *The theory of how vertical competition works in assigning powers*

In this section I examine the working of interlevel relations in a multi-tiered government. The examination assumes that the governments are rivals, that they "compete," and that this competition is sufficiently like that in the private sector that we can make predictions about comparative advantage, specialization, and a tendency to achieve efficient production of goods and services.

Albert Breton's 1996 explanation of this is relatively brief, relying on his earlier full description of competition within a single-tiered government structure. He considers an upper-tier government and several at a lower level.

The model starts with some initial distribution of activities between levels. The activities result in policies and programs. These have been produced by combining the outputs at various stages of completeness of private firms and of government agencies at both levels. When there is competition between all these units, production migrates in and out

---

[22] For a discussion of the problem of getting the bureaucracies and tribunals in non-environmental departments to respect the whole range of "sustainable development" goals, see the essays in Scott, Robinson, and Cohen 1995, especially Chapter 7, pp. 165–202.

(among private firms and government agencies) or up and down (between levels of government).[23]

Albert Breton focuses attention on this latter case. Many outcomes are possible: In one, a good with a service span covering several lower-level jurisdictions migrates to be produced by a consortium of such jurisdictions; in another, it migrates to the upper governmental level; in a third, parts of it are produced at different levels; and in a fourth parts of it are transferred to the private sector and/or to volunteer agencies.

The necessary processes will entail many kinds of information, transaction, and organization costs. Albert Breton focuses on one: the "coordination costs" arising when policies, programs, or products are divided between levels. He points out that this division requires something like *contractual* relations, and argues that contracts and agreements can be so difficult to enforce as between governments that it is necessary either to draft them to be "self-enforcing" or to have recourse to an external enforcer or monitor.[24]

B   *What "advantages" will help a competitive government to capture powers over the environment?*

In a competitive race or contention such as just outlined, what "advantages" must a government possess in order to win the environmental power? Of course, much depends on special circumstances, such as leadership by an attractive politician. But, beyond these special circumstances, one can list more humdrum properties that, in combination, will enable the government to take, or hold, jurisdiction over pollution, nature, and land-use policies and programs.

My list is presented here. It is different from the list of "organization costs" that Breton and Scott argued would determine the assignment of a power. That is because Breton and Scott, like many before them, assumed that in the long run the production costs of the two levels of government would be much the same. Alternatively, they argued that

---

[23] It is assumed, for simplicity, that there are no long-run legal barriers to the reassignment of legal powers to implement the new competitive equilibrium. This assumption creates a theoretical difficulty. In the real world, a government faces the prospect of a constitutional change cautiously, whereas it may consider its gains and losses in day-to-day competition in a more strategic, even insouciant, fashion. In the competition theory, however, these are two views of the same activity. Governments are never lighthearted about day-to-day competition because they know it leads, in the long-run, to reassignment. See Kathryn Harrison 1996, p. 18.

[24] The migration of policy making (or production) between governments will change the budgetary balance at each level, eventually requiring offsetting migration of taxing powers or the payment of new grants.

jurisdictions without production advantages (high-cost producers) would be able to farm out their orders for products to a jurisdiction with low costs. It would be the level of its organization costs that determined if this would be feasible, not its production costs. Either way, the authors concluded, it is low organization costs, not low production costs, that determine whether a power is won by, and so assigned to, a level of government.

In my list, I present government cost and quality characteristics that will be advantageous in the *short run*. In the long run these may disappear, but competition between governments seeks electoral or pressure-group support in the current period. For example, a government may win jurisdiction over a pollution problem because it already regulates sanitation and provides sewage services. No matter that in the long run another level of government could manage all three functions less expensively. The shift of jurisdiction is caused by short-run perception of ability, capacity, or cost.[25] For example, Alberta may find its long-run comparative advantage to be in providing flood control services for jurisdictions far downstream. But who knows this today? In the short run, Saskatchewan, with its Diefenbaker Dam, seems to have been the low-cost contender.

I believe, therefore, that the elements that give a government a short-run competitive advantage are of interest. But the reader should be warned again that just as private-sector competition in the short run must take account of personalities, collusion, mergers, and the strategic acquisition of rights to technology and land, so intergovernment competition in the environmental field includes public-sector versions of the same things. These are not what the international trade theorist thinks of as the determinants of comparative advantage. Nevertheless, they are included in the listing that follows.

1. Low costs: We can think of a government's competitive advantage in terms of the *costs* of providing environmental services. A government must reckon with three kinds of cost: that of *producing* the service, that of removing harmful environmental uses and restoring natural conditions, and that of adapting to or circumventing the existing division of powers.

---

[25] This is known as "piggybacking" pollution services on sewage and sanitation services. It is interesting that in most countries government *did* progress from urban sanitary laws to sewage and garbage services to pollution laws and infrastructure. Economists' analyses, on the other hand, tended to evolve from work on rural water supply policies to water-pollution projects to environmental regulation.

a. Production costs: Some governments' costs of providing environmental services of a given quality will be lower than others'. This may be because they have a "head start" and so are better set up to measure, monitor, and police the actors, victims, and "media" (water, air, or soil). For example, the federal fisheries service and the federal meteorological service had, from the beginning, more experience and capacity for dealing with aspects of water and air pollution than other agencies and governments. By the same token, the various provincial forestry and fish-and-game bureaus already had experience and capacity in dealing with both the planning and the implementation of what was to become ecosystem preservation. At both levels of government, the "piggyback" advantages include not only the expenses of actually providing the necessary inputs, but also "organization" of citizens and governments.[26] Note again that a government's initial cost advantage may not be permanent. For example, Ottawa had a head start in looking after endangered species of wild fowl, thanks in part to its roles under the Migratory Birds Treaty convention of 1910. This experience is no longer considered to be an advantage, however, and the provinces are now eager, under any new endangered species accord or law, to remove Ottawa altogether from the care of species crossing the international border.[27] The provinces' head start in environmental protection is also thought to have lost its value. At first Ottawa left monitoring and enforcement to them. Then in the 1970s it launched its own Environmental Protection Service, an agency that followed the provinces' lead and also learned something from the federal fisheries, meteorological, and northern territories services. Although Ottawa has subsequently scaled down this initiative, it was not because it turned out to be more costly than the provinces' services.

b. Finance and opportunity costs: Governments that set out to remove harmful activities and restore degraded environments impose costs on polluters and land users, or, if they expropriate their land and compensate them, they incur heavy financial costs themselves. It is sometimes said, therefore, that a government that seeks powers over the environment must have deep pockets to the extent that it proposes to buy out those whose property rights stand in the way of restoration.[28]

---

[26] Breton and Scott 1978 classified organization costs as those of citizen signalling, mobility, and government administration and search. For "piggyback" advantages, see Breton 1996, following a 1991 study by Cliff Walsh.

[27] M. Valpy, *Toronto Globe and Mail*, 7 October.

[28] If it proposes not to compensate them, it usually must introduce its new regime very slowly. This slowness may be facilitated by delays while outraged owners opposed polit-

Does this mean that by being itself the owner of crown lands, a provincial government can provide environmental restoration more cheaply than the central government or than a municipality? It would seem so, but the circumstances of the disposal of rights over crown lands can make their ownership a doubtful, or mixed, blessing for environmental policy. On the one hand, owning extensive lands does give a government an advantage in the sense that it may, at low expense, create reserves or dedicated tracts for environmental/recreational/conservation purposes. But on the other hand, its developmental policies may have led it, in the past, to dispose of many forest/mineral/farm/water/subdivision rights that then must be expropriated with compensation. There is no doubt that financial aspects of powers over the ecosystem and land use have been a shock to politicians, especially in the less wealthy provinces.[29]

Deep pockets are also needed to pay for such public works as sewage disposal systems, and for such land tidying-up projects as cleaning contaminated soil, planting trees in cut-over and burned lands, restoring fish and wildlife habitats, and establishing landfills. Local governments often cannot afford such outlays; indeed, some provinces have balked at them.

Of course, although having access to cash or to revenue can never be a disadvantage, some reading about the environmental policies and programs of Canadian governments suggests to me that Canadian governments have not given it much weight in deciding whether to act competitively. One reason is that, to the public and to environmental groups, regulation and management of air and water quality seem to be more important than land use and habitat. A second reason is that environ-

---

ically in the courts. A famous example is in the upgrading of Strathcona Park, Vancouver I, B.C., where the provincial government dispossessed a claim-holder without compensation.

[29] Note that I am discussing provincial governments' cash costs. It is not evident that they give much heed to their opportunity costs in disposing of the public lands. Whether persons should be compensated for the loss of their claims, licences, or permits to use public lands is not a settled question. The quality of their entitlement certainly falls short of a common-law fee simple ownership. Governments have struggled to make clear that the entitlements they dispose of are *not* "property." On the other hand, many users, who have observed or experienced governments' automatic renewals of old licences and leases, are justified in believing an expectation of continued possession will harden into expected rights of use and disposal. Robert H. Nelson 1982 and 1986 has pointed out that both Charles Reich and George Stigler have described the appropriation or capture of some privilege made available by the American government's policy by the beneficiaries. There are many Canadian examples, such as the "capital" of particular paragraphs of the Charter of Rights claimed by natives, women, ethnic groups, Francophones, etc., described by Alan Cairns.

mental outlays, either for land acquisition or for public works, need not be made all at once. In many of its aspects, the environment is durable, flexible, and forgiving. As with the highway program, spending that cannot be fully "afforded" one year can be phased in or delayed. For example, the costly federal department of fisheries program of spawning-enhancement works on salmon streams in British Columbia was spread out over a dozen years.[30] No doubt, had the responsibility for this program been handed to the province, it would have been spread out over an even longer period.

3. Constitutional adaptability: Another set of advantages includes the holding of the helpful *general* constitutional powers mentioned in the opening section. One of these is the treaty power (see the following discussion).[31] Another is responsibility for the criminal law: today there seems to be a tide of environmental decisions in which the Supreme Court has declared that Canada is entitled to take certain environmental actions as an exercise of its criminal law power.[32] There are others. Another way of putting this is that Canada's legislation to deal with criminals, like that for foreign trade and navigation, has spare capacity, which gives it an advantage over the provinces in dealing with regulation of the environment.

But Canada's constitutional powers leave it weak when it comes to creating new regulatory systems based on the markets or property. Here the provinces come into their own. They have not only the strength that comes from their ownership of the crown lands, but also that which comes from their exclusive powers to make laws for property and civil rights. Holding these powers, the provinces have scope not only to change the laws so as to introduce control techniques that rely on marketlike fees and subsidies, but also, especially, to have institutions that

---

[30] Note that this program is not described by the federal government or most Canadian authors as "environmental." The works are carried out by offshoots of the fishery department. Their construction is connected with Canada's international salmon-management obligations.

[31] Of course, as discussed here, it has the disadvantage of lacking the special bureaucracies needed to implement treaties.

[32] Quebec's James Bay project was halted by the environmental assessment process that the federal government had begun to conduct in the 1970s. In the 1980s an order made this procedure (EARP) more formal and more uniform. A court ruling in 1990 made the process mandatory. In 1991 a new EARP law confirmed that where there was any involvement of federal lands or financing, there *must* be a federal environmental assessment, and licence, even on a provincial government project. The courts have reinforced the mandatory nature of federal involvement in Alberta, Saskatchewan, and Quebec.

already deal in tradable and transferable cutting rights, emission rights, water rights, and so on.[33]

Note that this advantage of having a constitutional niche can be considered an opportunity-cost advantage: a government that has such a niche is spared the organizational expense of negotiation or litigation to acquire a new one. Albert Breton makes a similar point about the advantage of not having to harmonize tax collection arrangements with another government; and it could also be made about the cost advantage of not having to negotiate environmental standards with other governments.[34]

4. Coordination and foreign relations: geographical spillovers: Any government that plans to exercise powers over environmental policies will be aware that it will need to coordinate its activities with other governments. It will have a considerable advantage if it can do this easily and cheaply. The elements of "environmental diplomacy" is a huge subject, part to be summarized here, part to be postponed.

Today neighboring jurisdictions attempt to "coordinate" a host of regional water pollution, smog, river-flow, lake-level, and animal-habitat problems regionally and globally.

In theory there is no reason, the written constitution aside, why even the smallest jurisdiction should not participate in global bargaining and planning. They already do so at the private end of the public sector, marketing their bonds, arranging cultural exchanges, luring industrial development, and so on. But in dealing with externalities they have a disadvantage, which might be classified as a kind of diseconomy of scale. A government at a national level already has an assignment of powers and an adaptable bureaucracy for dealing with foreign political and economic affairs of all kinds with all countries. Up to a point, it can cheaply facilitate most of a lower-level government's environmental relations with neighbors.

And, in addition, it has a bargaining advantage. Because it deals with other countries on many subjects, it has more implicit credits to use as bargaining chips when seeking an environmental agreement. These can be especially useful when a downstream province wants to induce an upstream jurisdiction to reduce harmful emissions. (As against this it must be recorded that Canadian diplomats have a horror of "relating"

---

[33] Undoubtedly the dominance of the provinces in adaptation and innovation in local property concepts has slowed the federal government's drive to introduce tradable individual fish quotas and emission rights.

[34] On tax harmonization costs, see Breton 1996, p. 211. Environmental-standard negotiation costs are rarely mentioned by the standard writers on environmental federalism.

or "linking" issues. Perhaps this is because Canada, a small country with little to offer its large neighbor, has learned that some cross-border disputes over externalities had best be settled on their merits. Or perhaps federalism has taught it that Canada cannot and should not trade a loss borne in one province for a benefit gained in another.)

5. Preferences and quality: A government's advantage in providing environmental services may lie, not in low costs, but in better-quality services. To say this at once raises the problem of how "better quality" is to be identified. The problem is particularly difficult when it is realized that we are looking for a quality advantage in *all* environmental programs a government might launch. I will avoid this problem by considering a substitute. Since quality must be in the mind of the beholder, I ask whether we can identify consumers who consistently act as though one government provided better-quality environmental goods and services. Put otherwise, are there identifiable groups that consistently prefer that environmental powers be assigned to a particular level of government? While the answer is yes, it must be admitted that the groups differ widely in the reasons for their preferences. Some oppose action by a particular level of government, under any power. Some oppose any environmental interference, especially by a particular government. None of them makes a clear distinction between a power and a program, a habit that of course does not square with the assumed or asserted separation of power from policy in the kind of theory mentioned earlier in section III. It does, however, fit well with the idea of assignment by competition.

a. Right-wing environmentalism: This approach is rare in Canada. In the U.S. its tenets are reported in Anderson and Hill's *Environmental Federalism* (meaning devolving central environmental powers to state and local governments.) The editors admit that elevating natural resource and environmental regulation to the national level may have some benefits in dealing with geographical spillovers. But the one-size-fits-all character of central policy has left too many problems unsolved, especially a large federal bureaucracy that is unaccountable to resource users and environmentalists. For most natural resource and environmental problems, devolution (to the states) is an alternative that can reduce costs and align results with the demands of (local) citizens. Devolution of most environmental problems to private ownership is impractical, but devolution to local and state levels would allow their governments to decide the boundary between public and private. The authors go on to show where devolution could be expected to produce better (or less public) management of public lands,[35] parks, wildlife, pesticides, and western rivers, or to produce higher revenues from resource rents and environmental charges.

It is doubtful that Canada has a significant equivalent group with the same aversion to the environmental programs of the federal government. There are of course hostile groups. One of these is the government of Quebec; its Bourassa predecessor was guided by the Allaire report, which called for the provinces (or at least Quebec) to acquire all environmental responsibilities. A second is in Alberta, where, since the days of the National Oil Policy, any federal resource and environmental initiative meets strong opposition. The Supreme Court's *Hydro Quebec* decision (1997) and the *Oldman Dam* decision (1992), both involving the applicability of federal environmental assessment procedures, worsened this hostility. But these attitudes are less those of Canadian citizens who prefer provincial environmental powers and policies, than of Canadian provincial governments that are already in conflict with Ottawa. They are, in other words, manifestations of the very intergovernmental competition we are examining.

b. Canadian environmental organizations: Environmental organizations in Canada appear to prefer the top level. They have been envious of their parent and counterpart organizations in the United States, who have had easy entrée to the Washington decision makers who contribute to American environmental policy.[36] For Canadian organizations to duplicate such access, Ottawa must become, and remain, the center of Canadian environmental decision making. This reason for their preference leads to another. Canadian environmentalists understand well that under

---

[35] Anderson and Hill exaggerate a little their authors' beliefs that the states could perform much better than the federal government. In one well-balanced chapter, Robert H. Nelson investigates the various financial impacts to be expected if the vast western Bureau of Land Management lands were to be transferred to state ownership and management. These lands amount to about half the area of western lands owned by the U.S. government run by all agencies. He shows that most states would lose in the short run because they would lose the local impact on employment and jobs of federal government spending on land management. In the long run these lost transfers may diminish. He argues that in the long run the states could earn more than Washington does from operating and leasing the lands. Analogous arguments are advanced with respect to wildlife management (some private state-licensed game farms can take over from senior government agencies) and the control of pesticides (present responsibility is shared between Washington and the states, but Washington's statute is far beyond its capacity to enforce and so is increasingly dependent on state farm services, for example, for enforcement).

[36] This could be described as an instance of the Salmon external benchmark mechanism. See Breton 1996, p. 233.

federalism environmental protection needs a partnership of the two levels of government. So they press for a *major* role for Ottawa, to prevent it from becoming merely a subcontractor below the provinces. They know that Ottawa's public service and politicians listen to them more sympathetically than do the province's. As Kathryn Harrison reports of the major actors in the late 1980s: ". . . many environmentalists simply trusted the provinces less than the federal government, . . . One environmentalist explained, 'the provincial attitude is that "the resources are ours and it is up to us to decide whether to protect them or despoil them."'" In addition to their suspicions of the provinces as resource owners, many environmentalists perceived provincial governments to be more vulnerable to threats of job losses and reductions in the tax base. One offered that "the feds are just farther away from the cash register, so hopefully they're less motivated by economic gains and more able to take into account costs to the environment." As for interprovincial agreements to harmonize standards, they feel that Ottawa's presence is needed to enforce the agreements.[37]

c. Canadian industries: Environmental groups set themselves up as representatives of the victims of abuses of the natural environment. Opposite them, on most issues, are ranged individuals and groups representing the industries that benefit from using the natural environment for industrial purposes, resource extraction, and waste disposal. On some issues the industries find themselves in alliance with municipalities and other nonprofit agencies, such as universities, who also have waste disposal "problems."

In present circumstances (1997), industries generally prefer to deal with provincial governments. This preference is particularly strong in the natural resource industries. Firms are often tenants of the provinces, holding crown mineral claims, for example, and in constant contact with crown regulators in the field, with whom they have come to understandings. If new environmental standards are to be introduced the firms would prefer to be able to "negotiate" the amounts, times, and prices of enforcement with the same bureaus. To a lesser extent, this familiarity

---

[37] Harrison 1999. Among the many environmental groups there are various attitudes toward the provinces. Some, concerned with wildlife, habitat, and endangered species, feel it is useless to expect Ottawa to take the lead in regulating the use of provincial public lands. Monte Hummel, head of World Wildlife Fund in Canada, told the *Globe & Mail*, "I don't mind having provinces control things, but I want to see binding commitments that the provinces are going to do those things. . . . I don't want to see the words 'may', 'could', or 'if we feel like it' in their agreement." ("Ottawa's Environmental Joyride," 4 October 1997, *Globe & Mail*, p. D2).

also explains the preference for provincial jurisdiction displayed by non-resource firms, municipalities, and the nonprofit sector.

The best-known exception is the large multijurisdiction firm, which typically expresses a preference for one environmental regulation regime that extends to everywhere the firm and its rivals are located.

Indeed, industry complaints are divided between those who are mostly exercised about being subject to a level of government they can't get along with, and those who say they are exercised about the costs of compliance in terms of time devoted to liaising with enforcement agencies, coping with a multiplicity of uncoordinated rules, adjusting to changed regulations, and negotiating for new laws, settlements, rules, and procedures. They ask for clarity, speed, and simplicity. It appears that most of them believe they are more likely to get these from the provinces than from Ottawa, applauding various provinces' efforts to provide "one-window" offices and procedures where all government requirements can be met and settled at once.

The attitudes of many of those who have access to provincial ministers and politicians are easily understandable when one examines recent Supreme Court of Canada cases. The federal government was seeking to strengthen its environmental assessment activities in various provinces. More often than not, the litigation worked out so that Ottawa was attacking a development, with the provinces positioning themselves alongside, or intervening on behalf of, the firm using or proposing to have some impact on the environment.[38]

This interdependence between the resource industries and the provinces is not nearly so evident in the United States. The difference must be due, in part, to the fact that there the main resource industries' landlord is in Washington, not in the state capitals. Consequently, the petroleum, logging, mining, and even tourist industries spend more of their government-relations time with federal politicians and appointees, and are less keen that environmental powers be assigned to the states than are Canadian industries.[39]

---

[38] Typical examples: *Rex vs. Crown Zellerbach* 1988; *Canadian Wildlife Federation vs. Canada* ("Rafferty-Alameda") (federal court 1990); *Cree Regional Authority vs. Quebec* (federal court 1991); *Friends of the Oldman River vs. Canada* 1992.

[39] This reasoning might be tested by comparing marine salmon fishing to logging. In Canada the legislative or land-ownership powers over the first are state, over the second federal. Consequently, we might predict that in Canada the industry would prefer that river environmental protection be in Ottawa hands, while in the United States it would prefer that it be under state controls. The trouble with this "test" is that in both countries the fishing industry looks on environmental protection as beneficial, while the logging industry regards it as costly.

Of course, while provincial governments are particularly anxious to ease the burden of environmental regulation on employment and investment by the firms to which they lease the crown lands and resources, they are almost as anxious to do the same for their nonresource firms. They do not wish to drive away *any* important sources of fiscal and job benefits. But this generous feeling does not give the provinces any special advantage in winning the support of industry.

5. Information and science advantages: In my original piecemeal paper I mentioned that modern pollution regulation, toxic-substances control, and even ecosystem protection are science-intensive, so that a government having easy access to "science" has an advantage. There is something to this, but not much. It helps a government to have scientific support when it is setting standards or negotiating over standards with other jurisdictions or countries. But it appears that provinces, states, and countries without their own scientific establishment do not suffer much. For one thing, it is always possible to rent, share, or buy some scientific capacity of information.[40] For another, it is always possible to divide environmental management between the governmental level with science facilities and that with an administrative establishment. It is difficult to find examples where the extent to which a government sharing responsibility in this way has suffered depending on the extent of its in-house scientific advice. There are also many ways a government can place the burden of science – or of information generally – on the polluter or on the general public. One well-known example is in the American policy with respect to automobile emissions. After much uncertainty, the federal government simply left to the major manufacturers the problem of finding, by a certain date, a technology for reducing the emissions of the nationwide fleet of cars sold by each firm. The state of California went even further, setting very general dated targets and demanding that each firm meet them. California's "advantage" did not stem from access to information but from having enormous economies of scale in detecting a firm's failure to meet its standard.

6. Concluding notes on advantages: By way of relating this list of advantages to the economics of federalism, I must point out their novelty. In my previous paper on piecemeal assignment I generally followed the rea-

---

[40] This might as well have been headed "economies of scale" or "the advantages of a head start." It is certainly true that some jurisdictions have advantages of size or head start in many aspects of providing environmental services. What is true of science and information is also true of collecting a pollution change or maintaining a wildlife habitat: it can be farmed out to a supplier with the requisite advantages.

soning of Breton and Scott (1988) about the variables that would be important. That is, I laid most emphasis on information and organization costs. This was because following an implicit tradition in this field, I could assume that governments' production costs would in the long run become uniform across all levels, and that because transaction costs could prevent a government without such economies from obtaining supplies from one that had them, transaction costs mattered most.

This attitude arose from the fact that Breton and Scott and previous writers had been considering a government's advantage in a comparative-static or long-run framework, where nearly everything was eventually feasible. But if we now join political scientists and other observers in asking about a government's "capacity," "ability," "preparedness," or "suitability" for winning powers over the environment, we must switch to the short run, to the nearness of the horizon within which decision makers and those lobbying them decide whether to compete for an environmental function.

When we do this we find that a government's expected short-run advantages in the cost of producing services, the government's popularity, the quality of its services, and the ease with which constitutional and partnership arrangements can be overcome are just as important as its expected long-run advantage in organization costs.

This conclusion brings me back to the theory of intergovernmental competition. The contest will be fought out by the governments as they are, not as they will be in the long run. In Canada, for example, Ottawa has entered and abandoned environmental aggressiveness twice in twenty-five years or so, obviously on the basis of fairly immediate political advantage (demand) and its currently available bureaucracy and infrastructure (supply). In the long run, this capacity to supply may change, but so may the demand (once again). Such a government will, I think, keep its eyes on opportunities within a short-run horizon. It will therefore not be governed by the eventual gain in "efficiency" from taking over the field, even if, in a ceteris paribus sense, the more efficient level of government can be predicted to prevail.[41]

V   Is the distribution of powers over the environment explained by the theory of competition?

A   Introduction

Although in the previous section I illustrated some aspects of competition by referring to environmental policy and powers, I did not

[41] Breton 1996, p. 200.

show that the actual assignment of environmental powers had come about through intergovernmental competition. This is the more difficult of two questions that now arise. The first, the easier one, is whether the assumptions of competitive *theory* are matched by the circumstances in which environmental powers, in Canada, are obtained or transferred. The second is whether, disregarding whether or not competitive assumptions are matched in the real world, the competitive process of assignment actually predicts the present distribution of powers. The first question is the subject of this section. The second would throw some light on the theory itself, but requires a more finely specified theory, and more knowledge of actual environmental rivalry, than is now available.

In section B, I deal with the assumptions. There are three features of the existing powers over the environment that do not seem to match the assumptions underlying a simple statement of the theory. The first is that while the theory pictures governments vying with one another to acquire powers over the environment, the reality has been that governments have been competing to get rid of these powers. The second is that while the theory is based on the assumption that the given tastes and preferences of citizens lead to demands for services that the governments compete to supply, the reality has been that tastes, preferences, and demands are not fixed, but fluctuate widely: furthermore, tastes may have been created by governments. The third is that while in theory governments seeking electoral support by obtaining powers over the environment do so by competing with each other, the apparent reality is that they do not compete so much as they cooperate, collaborate, collude, bargain, and contract with one another. Subsections 1, 2, and 3 deal with these mismatches.

In subsection 4, I discuss whether the answers to these three questions constitute a challenge to the theory itself. Then, in section C, I carry the examination of the theory a step further by considering horizontal competition – or at least one aspect of it. It is said that when provinces compete they may get locked into a race to the bottom. Is this correct? If so, how do the governments adjust? Does their adjustment constitute another challenge to the theory?

B   *The assumptions of competitive theory: vertical competition*

In this section I examine three implicit assumptions of competitive theory, to see whether they are visible in the record of actual intergovernmental dealings in powers over the environment. For the most part the examination is limited to vertical competition between levels of government.

1. Competition to get out: passing the buck: The theory likens the relationship between the levels of government to that between competitive firms, at least to the extent that the reassignment of powers is likened to the transfer of market share. Albert Breton, for example, illustrates the theory by considering competition to provide the services of a "labor" ministry and a "revenue" ministry. The assumption is that voters know what they want and that levels of government are contending to provide it. This assumption does not square with the observation that levels of government have seemed to be contending *to escape* from providing the three types of environmental functions listed earlier. In at least two periods of receding public demand since the 1960s, successive administrations in Ottawa have tried to "pass the buck."[42] Even in the alternating green periods, Ottawa's show of determination was unconvincing.

A governmental level's endeavor to climb out of using, or even holding, certain powers is not inconsistent with what goes on in the private sector. Alfred Marshall insisted that long-run stationary equilibrium of supply and demand in a market is consistent with the rise and decline of particular firms.[43] In their quests for profits, one firm may pass another when both are expanding, are moving in opposite directions, or are contracting. So it may be with governmental levels: both may be contracting, perhaps intending to get out. The outcome may be a *vertical* "race to the bottom." With neither government seeking the power to, say, manage the extent of a certain kind of pollution, the final equilibrium may be where both governments disown the power, and so wind up giving their voters less than the amount of management they would choose under some other social or political arrangement. For example, if groups of voters were free to choose, they might privately contract with groups of polluters to limit themselves to agreed amounts of pollution. This might make everyone better off. By "withholding consent from their governments" they would have opted for a nonfederal, even nongovernmental, regime for pollution.[44] Of course, high transaction and information costs of various kinds could prevent citizens from successfully implementing the contractual alternative.

---

[42] So conspicuous has this been that Kathryn Harrison's 1996 book was given this simple title.

[43] For example, in his eighth edition he wrote (V. XII. 2): ". . . the rise and fall of individual firms may be frequent, while a great industry is going through one long oscillation, or even moving steadily forwards; as the leaves of a tree . . . grow to maturity, reach equilibrium, and decay many times, while the tree is steadily growing upwards year by year."

[44] See Breton 1996, p. 246, for illustrations of when voter revolt, withholding consent, leads to an equilibrium assignment, and when it fails to do so.

Why would both governmental levels want to back out? It reminds us that the theory is useful only if there is a positive demand for the good or service the two levels of government would be able to produce at a cost voters would agree to pay. One reason for the attempted exit could be that after a shock, demand has decreased. Competition would serve to choose the level that can provide the small amount of good or service – pollution regulation – at a price voters are willing to cover. A second reason could have to do with economies of scale in regulation. In either of these circumstances, however, the postulated desire of *both* levels to contract would not arise.

The flight to the very bottom would arise if majorities of voters at both levels induced their governments to contract, each intending to leave the function to the other government. If both succeeded in exiting, the situation would be unstable, and one of them, even chosen at random, could economically recommence production of environmental services. Of course, if both blindly recommenced, the race to the bottom would repeat itself.

The importance of passing the environmental buck is that it suggests that vertical intergovernmental "competition" is far from the pure competition of price theory textbooks, or even from the more informal competition relied on by Chicago economists. There are only two levels, and entry is limited. The planning that goes on at each level is not governed by expectations of competitive prices but by expectations regarding the actions of the rival level. The situation is like that once described by Chamberlin, in which each party had some loyal customers, yet sought to capture others who were not so committed. Models of repeated games might serve the analyst as well as the theory of competition. In any case, it seems that the idea that the governmental levels' rivalrous behavior tends to capture of a power by the most efficient level of government needs reexamination.

2. Preferences not fixed: A second explanation is suggested by observation of "passing the buck." This is that the competing governments find that voters' preferences or demands are not fixed. In the Canadian case, "cycles of inattention" cause the trend in demands for environmental protection to rise and fall like the tides. Why the periodic inattention? Those involved confuse several possible causes. It may be that people get fed up with the policies' costs: the increased private and tax costs of enforcement, garbage disposal, recycling, avoiding products with toxic residuals, and so on. Or it may be that the concern about the environment is fairly constant but that the business cycle alternately presses and releases problems such as jobs and deficits.

What is clear is that it is the governments, in alliance with the environmentalists, who are informing and educating. To the extent that preferences cannot reasonably be said to be fixed, the conventional analyses of demand and of market competition cannot apply to assigning environmental powers as they do to powers over "hospitals" or "highways." True, the intensity of demand for government activity in the latter fields also is changeable. But the changeability is trivial compared to that for environmental activities.

The contention we observe, therefore, is not competition but rivalry in which demand and supply are far from being independent. The voter and the governments are both learning from the same outside sources about new dangers from abuse of the environment; at the same time, the voters' fears and preferences are being changed by hot-and-cold information from governments; and, at different intervals, voters are learning that some earlier abuses or dangers have abated, have been controlled, have been exaggerated, or can be handled in the private sector or by voluntary organizations.[45]

3. Collusion: A third phenomenon observable among governments that offer environmental policies is that they work together rather than competing. This is particularly true in Canada, where there is a surprising amount of cooperation, both vertical and horizontal. The provinces and Ottawa interact *indirectly* through a Council of Environmental Ministers, arguably the oldest and most effective of the many institutions sandwiched between the two levels of government. Meetings of this body serve for "harmonizing" the members' pollution and toxic-substance policies, and for planning joint strategies for Canada in international relations and treaty making. There are also many *direct* agreements in which a particular province and Ottawa arrange to divide the administration, regulation, monitoring, and financing of a specific policy between them. There are many of these, so many that political scientists find that individualistic and competitive arrangements are in a minority compared to various kinds of cooperative, collusive, coordinated, harmonized, and shared arrangements.[46]

4. Competition through collusion: I have drawn attention to two respects in which the Canadian provinces and Ottawa are not behaving

---

[45] See Breton 1996, pp. 286–309. Even when environmental activities are dominated by free-riding and externalities, there are alternative sources of response: the family, the cooperative, the environmental pressure group, local governments, or/and privatization under property law. It is probable that no government need deal with *all* aspects of an environmental problem.

[46] See Fafard and Harrison 1999.

as they would if there were orthodox, open competition to offer environmental policies. First, both levels sometimes seem to withdraw from rather than expand into a field; and second, the two levels seek to collude rather than to contend. Furthermore, I have shown that the "market" for environmental policies is characterized by ever-changing and unpredictable demand.

However, whether these special conditions combine to refute the theory that marketlike competition can explain the vertical assignment of powers over the environment can be doubted. They do show that intergovernmental relations are not usually characterized by open competition. Accordingly, a corollary to the theory might be proposed: when there is no competition, the assignment of powers is not changed.

Can we find an *essential* reason for the absence of competition? Perhaps one can be found in Albert Breton's propensity to differentiate a federal structure of government from ones that are confederal or unitary by saying that in a federation the governments at both levels "own" their powers. They cannot peaceably lose them by open competition (or by transfer) any more than a landowner can lose his title by competing with his neighbor. Instead, transfers of powers must be accomplished by formal amendment of the constitution, or by implicit amendment by interpretation of the courts. If proposing amendments and/or bringing suits are regarded as outlets for "competition," then there is some support for the competitive theory of assignment of powers. While formal amendment has not been tried, environmental power lawsuits have been initiated and have found their way to the Supreme Court. These cases have shown what an unreliable weapon appeal to the courts can be. The provinces have found that they must relinquish or share their powers, and Ottawa, disconcerted, has found that it must assume new ones.

The situation then is that the provinces provide environmental services under the powers that they own. These powers supplement their other constitutional powers. But the provinces, like Ottawa, find that the demand for environmental policies fluctuates a good deal. So they tend to alternate between attempting to avoid the exercise of some of their powers, and acquiring more powers. They have found that "competing," in the market sense, to expend or contract their powers has not been effective. Instead, they have embraced collusion and cooperation, carrying on competition in the process of coordination. As a result, they achieve roles for themselves, and desired qualities or standards of performance, by trading, bargaining, and threatening. Their claims to exercise powers can be reinforced by occasional recourse to the courts or to formal amendment procedures, but these can easily backfire.

C   *Horizontal competition: racing to the bottom*

Probably the outstanding special topic in any discussion of competition in the provision of environmental management is a complaint about assigning environmental powers to lower-level governments.[47] It has been given a name of its own: environmental federalism. It borrows from the literature on cutthroat price competition among firms, and on tax-rate competition among regions (and nations).[48] It is typically aimed at showing that, when environmental power has been assigned to localities, competition among them forces each government's standards down, not just to other governments' preferred levels, but to standards below what even the most anti-environmental government would have accepted. This would be a horizontal "race to the bottom," a more important version of the vertical-competition race mentioned above.

1. Competition maintained: It must be said that there is almost no evidence that, under competition, the feared race to the bottom is more than theoretical.[49] In what follows I develop the theory, hoping to explain why the race is feared and why it may be rare.

We imagine an initial condition in which isolated[50] provinces have powers to choose pollution standards.[51] The higher the standard, the less the polluters can pay to the provinces' workers, capitalists, landlords, and tax collectors to spend on other things. Each province makes its choice.

---

[47] Provincial disputes about spillovers do not get resolved by a horizontal competitive process. The role for aggressive provincial governments seeking to exercise authority over spillovers is to be found in bargaining or seeking support from the central government, not in competing. There can of course be vertical competition, with the two levels of government jockeying over the taking over the upstream-downstream relationship.

[48] Obviously governments can compete in the standards of any good or service. An earlier version was referred to as beggar-my-neighbor tariff protection. In the U.S. the race to the bottom was thoroughly studied in connection with local governments' services and revenues, especially their levels of property taxes. Albert Breton 1996 cites William Carey's investigation of a "diffusion" to other states of one state's policy of watered-down legal requirements for shareholder protection.

[49] For references to the known empirical studies see Rose-Ackerman 1995, p. 163, n. 15; Cropper and Oates 1992, pp. 694–5; and Wilson 1996.

[50] "Isolated" means that the provinces are not connected in any way – by trade, factor movements, or federal grants.

[51] Pollution abatement is the first of the three pollution activity classifications. Either of the other two would have suited this sketch of the theory. Abatement policy could depend on equipment requirements, emission taxes or permits, or transferable quotas. Most of the literature refers to emission taxes, but these do not exist in North America and are anyway easily confused with other taxes to be mentioned later.

The resulting variety of provincial pollution standards depends on local preferences as between the cleanness of the environment and consumption of goods and services, and on the local costliness of pollution abatement. Under these assumptions, "competition" takes the form of the kind of emulation between jurisdictions described by Pierre Salmon.

The first step in developing the theory of the race to the bottom under competition is to remove part of the isolation condition. Imagine then that the industrial firms that emit pollutants become mobile as between provinces.[52] Imagine also that governments can compete only in terms of pollution standards. To follow firms' relocations would be complicated, but it would certainly reveal a tendency for the firms that emit the most pollutants to move from provinces with high standards.

The ideas of those who predict that in these conditions there will be a race to the bottom can be summarized as a prisoners' dilemma. At one extreme, the provinces could join in setting high standards and holding them. But if some are dissatisfied with the amount of industry that has located in their province, they can cut the standards they demand. This arrangement is unsatisfactory to the others, and so unstable. In the prisoners' dilemma, all of them cut their standards.[53] Avoiding this result is what motivates arguments that environmental standards ought not be assigned to competing governments.

Most economists' discussions of horizontal competition admit the possibility of this disastrous result, but point out that it comes from a drastically oversimplified model of interjurisdictional competition.[54] When the simplifications are removed, the fall is moderated. It is conceivable, even, that competition could raise standards, as governments compete to exclude polluting industries. Here I mention two circumstances that must be recognized.

First, industrialization is costly to a province. Even where industry is popular, few governments will continue to seek industry to the extent that the benefits of an additional plant will cost it more in infrastructure, health services, and so forth, than it contributes in benefits. This calculation can set a fairly high limit to the competitive cut in standards.

Second, some capitalists and their workers prefer clean environments.

---

[52] Recall that in my previous description of theory, everything was mobile: population, labour, information, and industry. Here provinces compete only with respect to industry.

[53] For explicit prisoners' dilemma treatments see the sources cited earlier (note 50) by Rose-Ackerman 1995.

[54] One of the best surveys is Wilson 1996. He deals with the circumstances mentioned here under which the provinces could compete or race to raise standards and exclude industries. He calls this a NIMBY outcome (i.e., Not In My Back Yard).

Even where governments do not cut standards, few firms may leave, for abatement costs are not a major element in many firms' location decisions. (Furthermore, the owners of some polluting firms may be willing to use their profits to clean up their operations, in order to work and reside in an attractive, clean environment.) Of course, both clean and dirty firms can *threaten* to leave.

The specter of a prisoners' dilemma–like race to the bottom is adduced by those who oppose assigning environmental powers to provinces. These two points were introduced to suggest that the prisoners' dilemma exaggerates the likelihood that the provinces will compete their way down to permissive pollution standards. When complexity is added to the competitive model, no outcome is assured. In my opinion the most that can be said about the effect of industrial location choices is that if, without firm competition and mobility, a few provinces were to maintain very high environmental standards, then, with competition and mobility, they would be under increased pressure to lower, not to raise, them.

2. Competition removed: In this section on the theory we examine the prevention of a competitive fall in standards, either by the provinces or by the central government.

a. The provinces, singly and together: I have observed that firms and capitalists may not migrate so as to bring about a prisoners' dilemma race to the bottom. Here I point out that some governments, even though competitive, may have their own ideas about dealing with industry and pollution.

Some provinces are not economically dependent on their polluting industries, and do little to retain them or to attract more. A likely result of this changed assumption is similar to that in urban-tax studies: some provinces cut their standards and become pollution havens, but others choose to become clean-environment havens. Their politicians' reward for doing this would be even greater had I not made the simplifying assumption that firms, rather than people, are migratory.[55]

Most provinces that want to hold polluting industries will consider ways other than cutting pollution standards. The alternatives are mostly forms of subsidy, such as paying the firms' abatement costs, tax reductions (exemptions, cuts, or holidays), provision of infrastructure, low-

---

[55] Scott and Bloss 1988, pp. 180–201, follow the migratory persons and capital to their new provinces and speculate about their effect on their new provinces' tastes and decisions.

interest loans, and cash subsidies.[56] When governments also compete in terms of these alternatives, their environmental "bottom" is not so far down.

Provinces may recognize the dangers of acting the way the prisoners' dilemma suggests. They may perceive that they and the others will face incentives to cut again. Indeed, under some circumstances (if numbers are small, or if for some other reason all provinces perceive their mutual dependence) they will weigh the probability that by not taking the first steps, they can help prevent the others from doing so.

These three points suggest that independent provincial governments, even though they are free to compete, may not race to the bottom. They may attempt to collude, restricting themselves from cutting standards. For example, they could cooperate to set standards.[57] For them to do this, I suggest three necessary conditions. First, the governments and electorates of the provinces with the lowest standards must be convinced that they must start denying licences for polluters (or whatever is the process for raising standards). This is not easy for people already accustomed to a damaged environment. It seems they would be most easily induced to "head off firm mobility" if they believed that the total stock of mobile firms was fixed. In that case continued competition could be opposed as a mere game sponsored by the polluters, a game that only feebly leads to actual relocation of industry, but that enriches the owners of the polluting firms.

Second, the provinces must be able to "harmonize" – to come to an agreement. They can work on a level of pollution, or emission quotas, or abatement equipment standards (one for each pollutant), seeking "cross-provincial" rather than "federal" standards. Midlevel jurisdictions have done this, but the bargaining process can easily fail or run into excessive coordination costs. Some holdout provinces will not share the goals of the rest, and even among the latter, provinces will become free-riders or demand compensation for not free-riding.

A third condition is that the provinces must be able to enforce

---

[56] This paragraph merely nods at a most important element in economists' writings about tax and environmental competition. Economists can't escape the fact that governments can call on more than one instrument to steer private behavior. If governments call on taxes, they can then select among many variants, from general revenue raisers to charges for emissions. Each has a different effect on pollution and on capital migration. This range of alternatives is particularly well brought out in the paper by Wilson 1996. See also Cropper and Oates 1992, pp. 694–95, and Markusen, Morey, and Olewiler 1995.

[57] For the function of "heading off citizen mobility" see Breton and Scott 1978, p. 126; Breton 1996, p. 254, and elsewhere.

whatever agreement (quasi-contract) they can reach. They may be helped to do this by electorates pressing their own governments to hold fast. And some provincial governments may hold bargaining chips or weapons for getting their neighbors to conform. But nothing in the recent history of environmental harmonization, agreement, or cooperation suggests that Canadian governments, long accustomed to defending their constitutional powers against outsiders, will live up to their pollution agreements as faithfully as private citizens would live up to a contract.

b. The central government enters: When the provinces fail either to compete or to collude, politicians at the national level may sense a vote-gathering opportunity for themselves. Vertical competition may take the place of horizontal competition. They may choose among three possible roles for the central government.

First, it can act as an external referee or rulemaker presiding over interprovincial competition. There is an excellent example in the U.S., where in its environmental legislation Congress has provided procedures whereby the central government, after consultation, sets standards, while the states are called on to add details to the basic rules and to look after enforcement.[58] These federal guidelines or minimum standards often leave scope for the states to set their own higher standards. At the time of writing, there is reason to believe that Ottawa wishes to copy this American model.[59] This first choice can be almost indistinguishable from the second.

Second, it can set up as an enforcer of interprovincial contracts. Albert Breton has pointed to the desirability of its assuming this function, and has indicated roles for the courts and for the legislature.[60] Third, the central government can itself capture the power over pollution policy making and enforcement.

Any one of these can bring to an end the provincial horizontal competition that has been the subject of section C, although they may leave scope for rivalrous provincial consultation and for less visible provincial lobbying. These do not guarantee either a high standard or a uniform standard. But both results may be more likely than under continuing interprovincial competition.

---

[58] For a brisk textbook summary see Findley and Farber 1988 with respect to pollution and toxic-substances laws. For a view by an experienced public-administration expert see John Kincaid's contribution to Holland et al. 1996, pp. 79–101. For a more economic approach, see Rose-Ackerman's comparison of German and American procedures.

[59] Green 1997.

[60] Breton 1996, pp. 248–58.

D   *Reconciling vertical and horizontal competition*

Do these features of interaction in the provision of environmental services suggest any revision of the idea of assignment through competition? The simple theory regarding vertical competition seems intact. But it clearly does not take into account the special features (that to a greater or lesser extent are found in connection with environmental federalism also in Australia and in the United States.) We may also ask why citizens' preferences change so frequently, and why governments want to get out. An examination of a model of interprovincial rivalry may suggest how the nature of vertical competition depends on the nature of horizontal competition, and incidentally lead us on to answer our earlier questions.

If in the model there were no trade or factor movements across provincial boundaries, and if the voters in each province somehow were oblivious of other provinces' policies and performances, the voters could compare their government only with the central government. Such a comparison would confirm the voters of some provinces in their preference for the environmental policies of their provincial governments. But it would lead the voters of other provinces to prefer the policies or performance of the central government. Vertical competition might technically exist, but with this division among the provinces, it could hardly lead to a transfer of powers. That is, in a country where people did have preferences regarding environmental policy, vertical competition might be too weak an engine to lead to reassignment of powers.

Vertical competition takes on more meaning if we change the model's assumption about unawareness of policy in other provinces. Salmon-process emulation would, I think, tend to make provincial environmental policies more uniform. If so, one can imagine voters comparing the typical (uniform) provincial policy with one that would be offered by the central government. If the central policy were for some reason of a preferred quality or was available at a lower tax-price, competition could lead to a demand for a transfer of power to the central government. (However, there is a problem here. It is possible that with interprovincial emulation the provinces' policies would drift in two directions, so that eventually two groups of provinces would be divided on the basis of their pollution standards. If so, the division among the provinces would, again, work against vertical competition leading to the reassignment of powers.)

Vertical competition becomes even more certain if we now relax both restrictive assumptions and introduce voter awareness of policies in other provinces *and* trade and factor movements among provinces. Competition for industrial location presses all the provinces' policies to converge. Furthermore, the policies almost certainly converge by moving toward those of the provinces with the lowest standards. (They may even converge by racing these provinces to the bottom.) Admittedly, as noted earlier, these are all just possibilities. But they suggest that the provinces as a group could, by the force of horizontal competition, be driven to policies from which they could not easily extricate themselves.

If this is so, we find answers to the three questions posed at the outset.

First, vertical competition depends on there being a typical (uniform) provincial policy, against which the central government can compete. The provinces are moved to acquire such a typical policy by horizontal competition among themselves. If this horizontal competition takes place in circumstances that could produce a race to the bottom, a typical low-standard policy is likely to emerge, inviting the emergence of a central-government alternative. Thus extreme horizontal competition increases the opportunities for vertical competition, and vertical competition can be the basis for a reassignment of powers.

Note that in this model there is no need for the constitution to assign a policing or enforcing function to the central government. True, the competition arising among the provinces when they exercise their powers can lead to an equilibrium environmental-quality standard that is irreversible or unstable. According to Albert Breton, such instability is generally not observable because there are institutions in place that secure stability. He suggests that stability can be secured by the actions of a central government acting as a monitor. However, the model here, based on intergovernmental competition over the environment powers, suggests that there is no need for the concept of a special stabilizing institution. The central government need only pursue its own political interest. This will guide it in deciding whether to allow the horizontal competition to proceed unchecked, or to encourage and enforce harmonization agreements, or to venture via vertical competition to produce environmental services itself. It need not be guided by any conscious tidy-minded duty to prevent an unstable level of environmental standards. To vary Adam Smith, a hidden hand induces it to act like a guiding hand.[61]

This point is also made by Albert Breton. Although in one place he has the central government "acting as" a monitor, he goes on immediately afterward to say that the government's behavior is "consistent" with its "effectively" (that is, "in effect") monitoring horizontal and vertical competition. What has just been said supports this implicit mon-

---

[61] See Breton 1996, pp. 262–3.

itoring idea.[62] Albert Breton's follow-up has to do with efficiency. He writes that, to the extent that central governments do act as though they were monitors, they contribute to tightening what he has called the Wicksellian connection. This means that they are contributing to the efficient allocation of resources to the production of social goods and services in the amounts and to the standards that citizen-taxpayers are willing to pay for. In one sense, this is a truism: to the extent the government's monitoring ensures that the rules governing efficiency are respected, efficiency will emerge. In another sense it may not work. What incentives have real-life politicians to ensure that such rules be respected? If they "in effect" act like monitors of the competition between governments at both levels, they do so only in their own interest. For example, a deadlock among the provinces may provoke federal intervention, with popular support. But the intervention need not lead to a "more robust" public-good version of marginal-cost pricing. Recall that Stigler, in his work on regulation, showed that industrial watchdogs do not promote efficiency, yet they continue in office. Similarly, in the theory of federal government, we may find that central governments, aware of and perhaps monitoring instability, do not promote efficiency, and yet do not get ousted by competition.

Second, passing the buck arises from the extremes of unstable and irreversible equilibria said to arise in interprovincial horizontal competition. In these circumstances, the provinces, paralyzed by competition, try collusion. Failing in this, they try to saddle the central government with "monitoring" competition, or with enforcing a collusive agreement to harmonize standards, or with taking on implicit powers to make and carry out an environmental policy. But their governments see no political need to support the central government, however it sets about these functions. Instead, they can blame the national government for the policies that emerge from its actions, whether too weak or too strong. In these circumstances, the central government's politicians, perhaps after experimenting with an environmental takeover, may see no advantage in taking on the environment. Consequently, the environmental policy at each level may seem to abandon the field to the other.

Third, while the waxing and waning of the voter preference for antipollution policies cannot be explained entirely by interprovincial competition, it is helpful. Admittedly, fluctuations in "green-ness" are also to be found in countries where there are no provinces. They are presumably due to the almost-random emergence of new information about environmental dangers, and to macroeconomic events producing cycles

---

[62] I believe experienced observers of the environmental wars would also support it.

in the opportunity cost of pollution abatement. But beyond what can be explained by these influences, some governments experience sharply changing popular demands for green policies. That these are governments of federal countries suggests that the federal structure itself is a source of off-and-on enthusiasm.

I suggested earlier that it is the advertising and propaganda typical of vertical competition that intensifies changes in demand. Casual observation reinforces the professional literature on this. In a period of low income and employment, horizontal competition for industry heats up. The provincial governments, seeking to abandon high standards, play down the urgency of environmental action. When business conditions improve this direction of government propaganda will be relaxed and possibly reversed. Investment will increase in response to external changes. The need to discredit the publicity of environmental groups will decrease, and may vanish. Indeed, the provinces may be willing to sell their voters on paying the costs of strengthened environmental enforcement and standards.

In this cycle of policy and explanation, the provincial governments will seek to attribute the depressions to federal policies, including federal environmental actions. To distance themselves from such environmental obstacles to new investment, they will seek to blame them on Ottawa. On the business-cycle upswing, they will seek to recapture control over and credit for environmental policies.

If Ottawa wishes to expand, it may accept the responsibility. But in a depressed state of the economy, it has nothing to gain by proclaiming an immediate intention to expand its clean-up activities. If on the other hand, as has been the case, Ottawa does not wish to expand in the environmental field, it can claim the environment is a provincial matter, and that anyway environmental problems are not serious enough to justify an intervention by the central government. Thus, the depression tendency of provincial governments to reassure citizens and taxpayers that they have no incentive to erect environmental obstacles to industrial investment, is actually reinforced by the general thrust of central-government advertising and propaganda. To put in different words the explanations of the observed unsteadiness of demand for environmental policy: the root cause is the business cycle, reinforced by "government" that blows hot then cold. In a federal system with competition between provinces and between levels of government, there are two governmental apparatuses to blow hot and cold together. This super-reinforcement intensifies the swings in citizen awareness and demand for action against pollution and other environmental abuse.

V   Concluding notes

In these final paragraphs, I point to other special features of jurisdiction over the environment in Canada that would figure in a fuller treatment: the unusual Council for Resources and the Environment; the "responsiveness" of the parliamentary system; the changing role of the courts; and the minor place of environmental policies in Canadian government.

First, special coordinating institutions. If provinces were isolated and labor and capital immobile, there would be little need for a special organization to coordinate the environmental activities of the provinces. As these two conditions are not met, coordination is perceived as an urgent activity, the costs of which could be prohibitive. Canadian governments met this problem in 1961 by creating the Canadian Council of Resource Ministers, which later changed its name and took on more responsibility for the environment. It is the oldest such body in Canada, having a small secretariat. In its meetings, Ottawa has the same weight as each province. There is no doubt that their continued willingness to set up and support such a body reflects the provinces' uneasiness with horizontal competition and confirms many people's suspicions that in the absence of the collusion it makes possible, a race to the bottom would be likely. The council therefore helps to create a common provincial stance, and by doing this facilitates vertical competition, blended with vertical negotiation. It deserves to be regarded as a permanent institution in Canadian federalism, one that certainly warrants study in terms of the competitive approach to the assignment of powers. In my opinion it reduces the pressure that competition would otherwise exert to assign powers over the environment more formally.

Second: a subject which *has* attracted study is the differences found in the influence of the ENGO, the voluntary environmental organization, in the U.S. and in parliamentary countries. These are interesting to political scientists as a phenomenon in themselves. In terms of the economic theory of the allocation of powers, they are interesting because they throw light on "responsiveness." Study reveals that there are at least three places where differences in responsiveness can crop up. The first is in the contrast between parliamentary and congressional governments. The second is in the comparison of unitary and federal governments. And the third, encountered within federal structures, is in the comparison of provincial and central governments. Environmentalists and other lobbyists often remark on the different receptions they receive on one side or the other of one of these three pairs. Understanding these three comparisons may help to distinguish characteristics of competition in federalism from those of competition in other structures.

Third, the courts. In studies of the recent history of the environment in various countries, the changing decisions of the courts are treated largely as external events. The authors note the "greening of the courts": the new willingness of judges to reconsider recent interpretations of the assignment of powers in the light of their application to environmental questions. A good example, in Canada, is the courts' increasingly firm insistence that the federal government's own laws require it to conduct an environmental impact assessment of what had been regarded publicly as provincial projects. According to Harrison, this change happened because the judiciary was becoming more comfortable in the post-Charter era with its role as a guardian of public rights (p. 154). This is probable, but it is an external explanation that makes little use of the fact that as an institution the court system is a forum where competitive strategies are played out. The courts' recent interventions have made a difference in vertical competition. But they have not yet played a similar role in horizontal relations: in the drafting and enforcement of interprovincial agreements, in refereeing competitive tactics, or in ruling on either air or water externalities or on the agreements that surround them. Changes in needs for these roles may draw the courts, not the central government, into playing the umpire, enforcer, or monitor.

Fourth and finally: piecemeal studies. These many special features of environmental relations in a federation leave one wondering which of them are typical of the whole field of intergovernment relations, and which are so special that they merely confuse the student. The Breton competitive theory is illustrated by examples taken from special fields. But the reader correctly, I think, understands the theory as applying to intergovernmental competition as a whole, which must be quite different from its parts. It must be that if I had commenced the piecemeal examination of other special fields such as transport, criminal law, education, health, and welfare, I would have found new sets of special features: different roles for the municipalities and foreign interests, different kinds of special interests and environmental groups, and different amounts of rent or profit at stake. And, on the supply side, I would have found that the public-ness, economies of scale, and organization costs in these other fields were quite different.

That realization makes me suspect that piecemeal studies are important in themselves but are not very helpful for firming up the competitive theory of the assignment of functions. Public-choice economists and their friends may be developing a kind of macroeconomics of government structure, in which assignment is affected by aggressive expansion of one government, or level, in all the fields in which there are political incentives. Obviously, that government cannot succeed in capturing all the fields, or not all at once. The written constitution prevents it from simply appropriating powers "owned" by others. Nevertheless, its behavior in borrowing or buying powers as elements of its policy in all fields may be of greater interest to students of the assignment of powers than is its behavior in one minor field. There may be more competitive behavior in aggregate than in any particular field, or competitive behavior in a particular field may be obscured by the clutter of the field's special features.

References

Anderson, Terry L. and P. J. Hill, eds. [1997], *Environmental Federalism*, Lanham: Rowman and Littlefield.

Bastable, C. F. [1892], *Public Finance*, London: Macmillan.

Baumol, William J. [1952], *Welfare Economics and the Theory of the State* (2nd edition 1969), Cambridge Mass.: Harvard University Press.

Bennett, R. J. [1980], *The Geography of Public Finance: Welfare under Fiscal Federalism and Local Government Finance*, London: Methuen.

Boardman, Robert, ed. [1992], *Canadian Environmental Policy*, Toronto: Oxford University Press.

Borts, G. H. and Jerome L. Stein [1964], *Economic Growth in a Free Market*, New York: Columbia University Press.

Bowen, James [1994], "The Great Barrier Reef: Towards Conservation and Management," in Dovers, ed. [1994], pp. 234–256.

Brennan, G. H., Bhajan S. Grewal, and Peter Groenewegen, eds. [1988], *Taxation and Fiscal Federalism: Essays in Honour of Russell Mathews*, Sydney: Australian National University Press.

Breton, Albert [1965], "A Theory of Government Grants," *CJEPS* 31, pp. 175–187.

Breton, Albert [1996], *Competitive Governments: An Economic Theory of Politics and Public Finance*, Cambridge: Cambridge University Press.

Breton, Albert and Anthony Scott [1978], *The Economic Constitution of Federal States*, Toronto: University of Toronto Press.

Carroll, John E. [1983], *Environmental Diplomacy*, Ann Arbor: University of Michigan Press.

Clark S., Michael Crommelin, and Cheryl Saunders, eds. [1990], *The Constitution and the Environment*, Melbourne: Centre for Comparative Constitutional Studies.

Courchene, Thomas J. ed. [1978], "Avenues of Adjustment: The Transfer System and Regional Disparities," in *Canadian Confederation at the Crossroad*, Vancouver: Fraser Institute, pp. 145–184.

Cropper, Maureen L. and Wallace E. Oates [1992], "Environmental Economics: A Survey", *Journal of Economic Literature* 30, pp. 675–740.

Crosson, Pierre R. and Ruth B. Haas [1982], "Agricultural Land," in Portney, pp. 253–282.

Cumberland, John H. [1979], "Interregional Pollution Spillovers and Consistency of Environmental Policy," in Siebert et al., eds., 1979, pp. 255–283.

Dafflon, Bernard [1977], *Federal Finance in Theory and Practice with Special Reference to Switzerland*, Bern: Paul Haupt.

Dalton, Hugh [1922], *Principles of Public Finance*, London: Routledge.

Dasgupta, P. S. and G. M. Heal [1979], *Economic Theory and Exhaustible Resources*, Cambridge: Nisbet and Cambridge University Press.

De Viti de Marco, Antonio [1934], *First Principles of Public Finance*, Turin, 1936 translation by Edith Pavlo Marget; 1950 edition, London: Cape.

Doern, G. Bruce, ed. [1990], *Getting it Green: Case Studies in Canadian Environmental Regulation*, Policy Study No. 12, Toronto: C.D. Howe Institute.

Doern, G. Bruce and Thomas Conway [1994], *The Greening of Canada: Federal Institutions and Decisions*, Toronto: University of Toronto Press.

Dorfman, Robert and Nancy [1978], *Economics of the Environment: Selected Readings*, 2nd edition, New York: Norton.

Dovers, Stephen, ed. [1994], *Australian Environmental History: Essays and Cases*, Melbourne: Oxford University Press.

Doyle, Timothy and Aynsely Kellow [1995], *Environmental Politics and Policy Making in Australia*, Melbourne: Macmillan.

Dwivedi, O. P., ed. [1980], *Resources and the Environment: Policy Perspectives for Canada*, Toronto: McClelland and Stewart.

Fafard, Patrick C. [1976], "Canada-United States Environmental Relations," *Proceedings of the Academy of Political Science* 32, pp. 152–163.

Fafard, Patrick C. [1997], "Groups, Governments and the Environment: Some Evidence from the Harmonization Initiative," preliminary draft, School of Policy Studies, Queen's University.

Fafard, Patrick and Kathryn Harrison [1999], *The Environment and Intergovernmental Relations*, forthcoming, Institute for Intergovernmental Relations, Kingston: Queen's University.

Findley, Roger W. and Daniel A. Farber [1988], *Environmental Law in a Nutshell*, 2nd ed., St. Paul: West Publishing.

Fitzgerald, Edward A. [1996], "The Constitutional Division of Powers with Respect to the Environment in the United States," in Holland et al. [1996], pp. 19–36.

Fox, Annette B., A. O. Hero, and J. S. Nye, eds. [1974], *Canada and the United States: Transnational and Transgovernment Relations*, New York: Columbia University Press.

Green, Andrew J. [1997], "Institutional Structures and Policy Outcomes: The 'Americanization' of Environmental Regulation in Canada" (CSSM WPS #26-1997), Conference paper, Toronto: University of Toronto Faculty of Law.

Grewal, Bhajan S., Geoffrey Brennan, and Russell L. Mathews, eds. [1980], *The Economics of Federalism*, Canberra: Australian National University Press.

Harrington, Winston and Anthony C. Fisher [1982], "Endogenous Species", in Paul Portney, ed., *Current Issues in Natural Resource Policy*, Washington, DC: Resources for the Future, pp. 117–148.

Harris, Seymour E. [1952], *The Economics of New England*, Cambridge, MA: Harvard University Press.

Harrison, Kathryn [1996], "The Regulator's Dilemma: Regulation of Pulp Mill Effluents in the Canadian Federal State," *Canadian Journal of Political Science* 29, pp. 469–496.

Harrison, Kathryn [1996], *Passing the Buck: Federalism and Canadian Environmental Policy*, Vancouver: University of British Columbia Press.

Harrison, Kathryn [1999], "The Origins of National Standards: Comparing Federal Government Involvement in Environmental Policy in Canada and the United States," in Fafard and Harrison.

Hartwick, John M. and Nancy D. Olewiler [1986], *The Economics of Natural Resource Use*, New York: Harper.

Hogg, Peter W. [1977 (1982)], *Constitutional Law of Canada [including Canada Act 1982 Annotated]*, Toronto: Carswell.

Holland, Kenneth M., F. L. Morton, and Brian Galligan [1996], *Federalism and the Environment: Environment Policy Making in Australia, Canada and the United States*, Westport, CT: Greenwood Press.

Hollick, Ann [1974], "Canadian-American Relations: Law of the Sea," *International Organization* 28, pp. 755–800.

Isard, Walter [1975], *Introduction to Regional Science*, New Jersey: Prentice-Hall.

Johnson, Barbara and Mark W. Zacher [1977], "An Overview of Canadian Ocean Policy," in Johnson and Zacher, eds., *Canadian Foreign Policy and the Law of the Sea*, Vancouver: University of British Columbia Press.

Kellow, Aynsley [1996], "Thinking Globally and Acting Federally. . . . in Australia," in Holland et al., eds., pp. 135–156.

Kennett, Steven A. [1996], "Environmental Assessment and Intergovernmental Relations," draft paper, Calgary: CIRL, University of Calgary.

Kneese, Allen V. and Stephen Smith, eds. [1966], *Water Research*, Baltimore: Johns Hopkins.

Krugman, Paul [1997], "Review" (of Bhagwati and Hudec, eds., *Fair Trade and Harmonization*, vol. 1), *Journal of Economic Literature* 35, pp. 113–121.

LeMarquand, David G. and Anthony Scott [1980], "Canada's International Environmental Relations," in Dwivedi, ed., pp. 77–107.

Lucas, Alistair R. [1997], "Underlying Constraints on Intergovernmental Cooperation in Setting and Enforcing Environmental Standards," University of Calgary School of Law.

Macdonald, Doug [1991], *Politics of Pollution*, Toronto: McClelland and Stewart.

Markusen, J. R., E. R. Morey, and N. Olewiler [1995], "Competition in Regional Environmental Policies When Plant Locations Are Endogenous," *Journal of Public Economics* 56, pp. 55–78.

Meiners, Roger E. and Bruce Yandle, eds. [1993], *Taking the Environment Seriously*, Lanham, Maryland: Rowman and Littlefield.

Musgrave, Richard A. and Alan T. Peacock, eds. [1958], *Classics in the Theory of Public Finance*, London: Macmillan.

Musgrave, Richard [1959], *The Theory of Public Finance*, New York: McGraw-Hill.

Musgrave, Richard [1961], "Approaches to a Theory of Political Federalism," *Public Finances: Needs, Sources and Utilization*, Princeton: National Bureau of Economic Research.

Musgrave, Richard [1969], "Expenditure Coordination," in his *Fiscal Systems*, New Haven: Yale University Press, Chapter 12, pp. 292–320.

Nelson, Robert [1982], "The Public Lands," in P. R. Portney, ed., pp. 14–73.

Nelson, Robert [1986], "Private Rights to Government Actions," *University of Illinois Law Review* 1986, pp. 361–386.

Oates, Wallace [1972], *Fiscal Federalism*, London: Harcourt Brace.

Portney, Paul R. [1982], *Current Issues in Natural Resource Policy*, Washington, DC: Resources for the Future.

Powell, J. M. [1976], *Environmental Management in Australia 1788–1914*, Melbourne: Oxford University Press.

Price, Kent A., ed. [1982], *Regional Conflict and National Policy*, Washington, DC: Resources for the Future.

Oates, W. E. [1972], *Fiscal Federalism*, New York: Harcourt.

Rose-Ackerman, Susan [1995], *Controlling Environmental Policy: The Limits of Public Law in Germany and the United States*, New Haven: Yale University Press.

Russell, Clifford S. [1982], "Externality, Conflict and Decision," in Price, ed., pp. 110–124.

Saunders, Cheryl [1996], "The Constitutional Division of Powers with Respect to the Environment in Australia," in Holland et al., eds., pp. 55–76.

Sawer, Geoffrey [1975], *The Australian Constitution*, Canberra: Government Publishing Service.

Scott, Anthony [1964], "The Economic Goals of Federal Finance," *Public Finance* 19, pp. 241–288.

Scott, Anthony [1976], "Transfrontier Pollution and Institutional Choice," Chapter 13 in Walter, ed., 1976, pp. 303–318.

Scott, Anthony [1976], "Fisheries, Pollution, and Canadian-American Transnational Relations," in Fox et al., eds., pp. 234–257.

Scott, Anthony and G. Bloss [1988], "Inter-Provincial Competition," in Brennan, Grewal, and Groenewegen, eds., *Taxation and Fiscal Federalism*, Sydney: Australian National University Press, pp. 180–201.

Scott, Anthony [1992], "Piecemeal Decentralization: The Environment," in R. W. Boadway et al., eds., *Economic Dimensions of Constitutional Change*, Kingston: Queen's University, John Deutsch Institute, pp. 274–297.

Scott, Anthony, John Robinson, and David Cohen [1995], *Natural Resources in British Columbia: Markets, Regulation and Sustainable Development*, Vancouver: University of British Columbia Press.

Siebert, Horst, Ingo Walter, and Klaus Zimmermann, eds. [1979], *Regional Environmental Policy: The Economic Issues*, New York: New York University Press.

Skogstad, Grace [1996], "Politics of Environmental Protection in Canada," in Holland et al., eds., pp. 103–132.

Smith, Heather [1997], "International Environmental Policy-making and Intergovernmental Relations," preliminary draft.

Smith, R. T. and Henry van Egteren [1996], "Harmonization and Racing for the Bottom in Environmental Standards," Edmonton: Department of Economics, University of Alberta.

Sproule-Jones, M. H. [1993], *Governments at Work*, Toronto: University of Toronto Press.

Stewart, Richard B. [1982], "The Legal Structure of Interstate Resource Conflicts," in Price, ed., pp. 87–109.

Stigler, George [1975], *The Citizen and the State: Essays on Regulation*, Chicago: University of Chicago Press.

Tanguay, G. A. and Nicolas Marceau [1996], "Fiscal Competition and Polluting Firms Location under Incomplete Information," preliminary draft, 27 September, Université Laval.

Tiebout, C. M. [1956], "A Pure Theory of Local Expenditures," *Journal of Political Economy* 64, pp. 416–424.

Tullock, Gordon [1969], "Federalism: Problems of Scale," *Public Choice* 6, pp. 19–29.

van Kooten, G. Cornelis [1993], *Land Resource Economics and Sustainable Development*, Vancouver: University of British Columbia Press.

van Kooten, G. Cornelis and Anthony Scott [1995], "Constitutional Crises, the Economics of Environment, and Resource Development in Western Canada," *Canadian Public Policy* 21, pp. 233–249.

VanNijnatten, Debora L. [1997], "Intergovernmental Relations and Environmental Policy-Making: A Cross-National Perspective," Kingston: Environmental Policy Unit, Queen's University.

Walker, K. J. [1994], *The Political Economy of Environmental Policy: An Australian Introduction*, Adelaide: University of New South Wales Press.

Walter, Ingo [1975], *International Economics of Pollution*, New York: Wiley.

Walter, Ingo [1976], *Studies in International Environmental Economics*, New York: Wiley.

Williams, Alan [1966], "The Optimal Provision of Public Goods in a System of Local Government," *Journal of Political Economy* 74, pp. 18–33.

Wilson, John Douglas [1996], "Capital Mobility and Environmental Standards: Is There a Theoretical Basis for a Race to the Bottom?", in J. Bhagwati and R. E. H. Hudec, eds., *Fair Trade and Harmonization*, Cambridge, Mass: MIT Press.

CHAPTER 9

Art and culture goods and fiscal federalism

Francesco Forte

1

In their book on fiscal federalism,[1] Albert Breton and Anthony Scott give several seminal contributions that provide useful insights for the present chapter's argument in favor of the assignment of the main part of controls and of public services of art and culture goods (henceforth AC goods) to the intermediate and lower levels of government (henceforth IL governments and IL levels) rather than to the central one (henceforth C governments and C levels), as in most European countries now.[2]

A first contribution by Breton and Scott relevant for the present chapter is the explicit consideration of public services consisting of regulation (henceforth R services or functions) in the discussion on the assignment of the various public functions to the different levels of government (Breton and Scott, 1978, Chapter 9). Public services in the

---

[1] Breton and Scott (1978).

[2] However, in Germany, according to the federal constitution (the "Grund Gesetz"), the arts, like education, are administered by the Laendern, not the central government. In the U.S., where a more liberal model for the art goods applies, the central government has only a limited role, mainly through its (controversial) National Endowment for the Arts, created in 1966 as a part of the Great Society program of President Johnson. The money administered by this fund is devoted to cofinancing of initiatives at lower government levels and by private nonprofit institutions, and is modest – on average, 38 cents per U.S. citizen, i.e., $100 million per year. Obviously, the dollar value has changed. And the nominal amount has gradually expanded. But still, in 1992 the appropriation to this fund, in the federal budget, was $176 million. And the total allocated to arts in the federal budget, including the financing of the Smithsonian Institution and of the National Gallery in Washington, was about $300 million. The states arts agencies got, in the states' budgets, an appropriation of $258 million, while the local governments' budgetary appropriation for arts was estimated at $328 millions. So the lower-level governments' aggregate budgetary appropriation was nearly $600 millions: twice the central government's arts budget. See Heilbrun and Gray (1993), Chapter 13, Table 13.1, p. 252.

220

proper sense, consisting in the delivery of goods and services or in financial support for the activities of private and nonprofit units (henceforth G services or functions), traditionally, in the literature on the assignment of functions, receive more attention than R services, because they entail much more spending than regulation. But it is wrong to judge the importance of a (potentially) public function merely by its costs for the government, because there are also costs for the market economy units and because the impact on civil and social life of the various public activities may go beyond their measurement in cost terms (as is typically the case for the functions in the AC goods area).

Public bureaucracies and groups of interests (which may be intellectual, as in the case of AC goods' "experts") related to central governments often cover their vested interests (which may be cultural influence giving cultural power) in keeping the R functions originally assigned to them, with the taboo of superior noneconomic reasons that economists should not dare to discuss. This may be, more generally, an additional explanation of the fact that economic analysis of the attitudes of the different levels of government to the regulatory functions is less developed than that relating to public goods *stricto sensu*. This appears to be the case with AC goods for countries heavily regulated, like those of continental Europe.[3] But, as I shall try to demonstrate, for relatively large countries like Italy, endowed of a large heritage of AC goods,[4] this leads to highly unsatisfactory results for their preservation and promotion.

On the other hand, the very fact that R functions, with a modest public expenditure content, may exert a great impact on social life in areas

---

[3] As for Italy, see Degiarde et al. (1995). In France, Jacques Walter, owner of Van Gogh's *Jardin à Auvers*, which he had purchased in New York in 1955 and brought to France in 1957, eventually decided to sell it at a French auction in December 1992 for $9.6 million. After having being repeatedly denied by the Ministry of Culture permission to export the painting, considered to belong to the "French art treasury," he sued the French ministry, because unjustly damaged in his property rights. A first-degree French court decided in his favor, fixing at the amount of $72.2 million the indemnity due to Mr. Walter. Actually Van Gogh's *Portait of Dr. Gachet* had been sold for $82.5 million in 1990. The government appealed the sentence, defining it as "extravagant"! Whatever the final result shall be, the example shows how heavy may be the burden of the regulation of the circulation of art goods in Europe. Italian regulation is at least as severe as the French, because the state may expropriate "Italian art treasures" from owners who try to sell them at prices different from the market prices, set unilaterally by the government's experts.

[4] Italy, according to UNESCO valuation, owns 60 percent of the entire world AC goods heritage. Two-thirds of the Italian arts heritage, however, is abandoned in the underground. In 1989 more than 12,000 items of this patrimony have been stolen. See Degiarde et al. (1995).

where important noneconomic values are at stake, that is, are *financially high-powered,* makes them particularly interesting for devolution to IL governments in centralized countries trying to adopt significant elements of federalism but committed to reduce deficits and to contain public expenditures. This appears to be the case for European countries like Italy having a big demand for "federalism" but constrained to fiscal soundness by the Maastricht rules. In these cases, *financially high-powered* public functions seem particularly apt for devolution to IL governments (Forte 1997a), provided that, in the assignment table, they get a good ranking for devolution. On the other hand, it is no accident that most of the financially high-powered functions belong to the central governments, given their original objectives of maximizing their power in the country. However, federalism aims to distribute the numerous public powers not necessary to keep national unity, to enhance freedom of choice.

2

Indeed, a second seminal contribution by Breton and Scott consisted in a shift of attention, in the assignment discussion, from the mere cost-benefit point of view, under the assumption of homogeneous social preference functions, to the need for reconciling majoritarian electoral rules with the variety of individual preferences: the assignment of a public function characterized by pronounced heterogeneity of individual preferences to the multiplicity of IL governments may reduce the frustration of preferences (Breton and Scott 1978, Chapter 9).

In the AC area, both for R functions and for G services, preferences of citizens and intellectual élites who exert influence on artistic tastes typically differ. Even if there is a broad agreement on the need for protecting and promoting these goods by public means, the question remains of how to perform these activities without authoritarian interference in individual preferences. Centralized systems may end with a set of "preferences on preferences" paternalistically and monopolistically dominating both R and G services, while appearing to be zealous in preserving, protecting, and promoting the arts and artists.

Recently Pierre Salmon[5] has put emphasis on another aspect in which, in a federal structure, the multiplicity of governments may improve citizens' satisfaction: competition *by comparison.* This competition, relevant to promoting efficiency, is also important to broadening the variety

---

[5] See particularly Salmon (1987). For a positive valuation of federalism applied to art goods see Dimaggio, in Benedict (1991), and Netzer, in Towse and Khakee (1992).

of choices. In the area of AC goods it may break cultural monopolies and spur innovations. One may combine Salmon's "competition by comparison" with Breton and Scott's "reduction of frustration" of individual preferences, as potential benefits of federalism for AC goods. Here competition among a multiplicity of governments, at the various levels (inclusive of the central government) may be decisive to avoid paternalistic and monopolistic inprintings by a central political and bureaucratic power.

An objection that may be raised, in general, against the paradigms of competitive supplies of public services, is that mobility of electors-taxpayers-consumers of public goods may be expensive and difficult. Even if Salmon's "competition by comparison " offers a way to respond to this argument, one may still maintain that lack of mobility hinders the most effective means to make comparisons, that is, direct experience. Now, in the area of AC goods, ad hoc mobility is much easier than for other public goods, such as, say, schools services: to enjoy AC goods located in a given place, a citizen coming from the outside does not need a prolonged stay; and he can decide when it his convenient for him to do this optional "consumption." Experience here may also be obtained through reproductions, even if not in a perfect way. And, generally, information is much less costly and less tedious than that needed to compare other services of the various governments. Thus, here competition by mobility and by comparison may easily interact.

3

But why may one consider AC goods as a matter of public intervention, with both R and G services? Most of these goods do not appear to be Samuelsonian goods, to which the exclusion principle cannot be (absolutely) applied. Monuments – including sculptures and mosaics – may be enclosed, even if some of them are not so because the reason that they were built and remain in place is their open exhibition to the public. Paintings, drawings, old books, and antiques "need" to be enclosed to be preserved. Ancient constructions – even the largest, such as the Coliseum – are normally enclosed, to protect them and their premises from disturbance and reckless behavior. Archeological remainings and relics are protected in several ways to preserve them from decay. Thus for most of these goods not only the exclusion principle may be applicable; it has to be applied for reasons prior to the question of whether or not to exclude free-riding. Truly, buildings endowed of architectonic and/or historical value, currently utilized, may normally be admired freely from the outside: but it is their use, as public or private and religious edifices, which provides the services for which they are meant. And if "exclusion" here is not applied (as in the case of most churches and of public offices open to the public), it is because it would damage their very functions. AC goods, to conclude, are *often* suitable to " exclusion."[6] Pricing may be applied and it is frequently applied here, in one form or another.[7]

Yet there is no assurance that they shall be spontaneously preserved and managed by those who happen to own them in ways that provide satisfaction to the "collective preferences" of the community.[8] In other words, for the supply of AC goods often there are divergences between the private returns and social returns.

The standard causes of divergence given by the literature here consist of three factors: externalities of economic and "moral" value (i.e., a value not measurable in economic terms); intrinsic "merit goods" characteristics; future generations' interests (which, in turn, consist in "private-not-discounted-to-the-present" economic values and in social returns not reflected in private future returns, for the reasons considered above).[9]

4

An appropriate examination of these factors of divergence between private and collective returns, as we shall see, should lead to assigning these functions *chiefly* to IL governments rather than to the C govern-

---

[6] On the limits of the public nature of art goods see Peacock (1969). That art goods are *never* pure public goods is sometimes taken for granted. This, for instance, seems to be the implicit assumption in the discussion of the normative aspects of subsidization of the arts by Throsby (1994). One should, however, distinguish *Samuelsonian pure public goods* from public goods that are not Samuelsonian but still are unsuitable to the exclusion principle, for practical or legal and ethical reasons. Sometimes there are congestion problems that make the good impure, à la Dupuit (on Dupuit public goods see Forte 1993). However, pricing may not be applicable for ethical or legal reasons, even in these cases.

[7] Admission fees to museums, according to 1988 U.S. data, provided only 4.6 percent of their operating income, with earned income in the range of 30 percent. See Heilbrun and Gray (1993), p. 188, Table 10.4. In Italy, however, there are cases where earned income, including admission fees, covers a much higher percentage of the costs. Vatican Museums cover 80 percent of their costs with earned income. See Forte (1997), p. 113 note 5. Galleria degli Uffizi of Florence seems to earn a similar percentage. And it seems that Pompeii museums have an earned income exceeding their costs. Data on the earned incomes of Italian main museums are not easily available because, belonging to the C government public administration, they are not endowed with financial autonomy and their revenues go directly to the ministry of cultural goods.

[8] On this issue, see in general Hamlin, in Brennan and Walsh (1990).

[9] See, for instance, the analysis by Heilbrun and Gray (1993), Chapter 11, "Should The Government Subsidize the Arts?"

ment. But before entering this discussion, it seems necessary to show that even if externalities (economic and moral), the (dubious) merit good argument, and the concern for future generations, in a strict individualistic view, were irrelevant (this last appears an heroic assumption), there may still be a strong argument for putting AC goods in the (semi)public goods area, in spite of the fact that they are not Samuelsonian goods. It is an argument that, in essence, traces back to the Dupuit-Hotelling theorem, relating to the impossibility of the suppliers getting the full consumer surplus when fixed costs and therefore increasing returns, inherent to that supply, are particularly important.[10]

In Figure 9.1 we assume that the only cost facing the private individual to preserve (or to acquire) a given AC good A consists in the fixed opportunity cost aa of the money foregone by not transforming that good (for instance, a building or a piece of land protected because of the presence of archeological relics); or by not selling to a purchaser who would not keep it available to the public. Because aa consists only of fixed costs, marginal costs are zero, and average costs, represented by aa, take the form of a rectangular hyperbole. The direct benefit which I may draw from A, for sake of simplicity, is assumed to be zero or to be already subtracted, as a stock of capitalized utility, from the fixed opportunity cost curve aa. The actual demand curve facing the individual owner I, reflecting the various degrees of supply and hence "preservation" of the good, may be as DD, which encounters aa at point P. "Preservation," as reflected in the demand curve DD of Figure 9.1, shall not mean simply to keep the good, but to allow the consumers to enjoy it. I offering a supply greater than OQ, would incur a loss. Thus I delivers only a supply of OQ, and the "consumers' surplus" in the area $PQ'Q$ up to Q' where

---

[10] On the "educational" externalities see, in particular, Heilbrun and Gray (1993), Chapter 11; on the "moral" externalities as a "collective endowment," see Forte (1997) and, more generally, Taylor in Brennan and Walsh (1990): his "irreducibly social goods" are actually goods whose *want* is collective, in the sense that the individual want for them consists in wanting that a given community own them. Obvious examples of collective or indivisible wants of this kind are the desire for the territorial integrity of our country; the desire that a given idea of justice should be satisfied in general in our community or country; the desire for prestige and reputation for our hometown, region, state, nation. This last want is particularly relevant to the AC goods endowment. Throsby and Withers (1986) have found that individuals (in Australia) perceive the benefits of "national identity" and cultural values relating to art goods at a level higher than that corresponding to the existing amount of government subsidies. On art goods as merit goods in a strictly individualistic approach, see Forte (1993b) and Heilbrun and Gray (1993), pp. 214–15, who consider this aspect under the category of "lack of information." More generally, see Becker and Murphy (1988). For the argument regarding the protection of future generations' interests see Peacock (1969, 1994) and Netzer (1978).

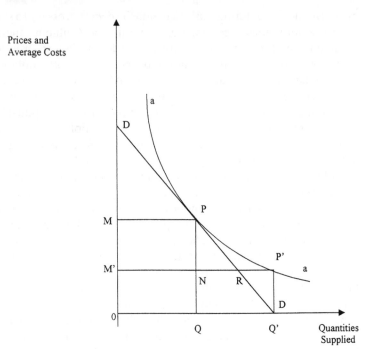

Figure 9.1.

the demand curve becomes zero, is lost. Thus, even if potentially there is enough private consumers'surplus to cover the costs for the entire supply of OQ', I is not able to capture it, and therefore is spurred by self-interest to behave, for his AC property A, in ways which cause an unnecessary loss of community welfare. A subsidy as $P'Q'OM'$ in Figure 9.1, with a deadweight loss of $RP'D$, may be justified because the social loss $RP'D$ is smaller than the additional consumer surplus PNR.

Obviously, however, to keep A and to allow consumers to enjoy it, I is likely to undergo variable costs to maintain A in a proper status and to accommodate consumers and collect from them prices to see A. In Figure 9.2, thus, we introduce a variable marginal costs curve Cma. The average cost curve is Ca, which crosses Cma in T'. In Figure 9.2, I is not interested in supplying *any amount* of A, since his average cost curve is above any point of the demand curve. Yet for the community, if the supply were set in Q' where marginal costs cut average revenues, and the

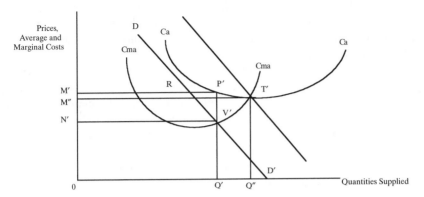

Figure 9.2.

price was V', a consumer surplus of $DN'V'R$ would be captured by a hypothetical subsidy of $M'N'V'P'$: and, clearly, in the not-unrealistic case of Figure 9.2, the deadweight loss of $RP'V'$ would be more than counterbalanced by the net benefit $DM'P'$.

Now, if the government wants to preserve A, allowing free use, to deliver to the consumer the entire consumer surplus, it must either transform it into a G good or subsidize I adequately or oblige him to preserve it. If A is a historical building or an archeological site, and if the only measure adopted by the government is a constraint on I, the result shall likely be gradual degradation if not destruction in disguised ways of A. And if A is a piece of visual art, I may not report his property to the government in order not to be constrained by a veto of its sale or by its expropriation at a price lower than the market price. In any case, I shall not have reasons to offer free visits to the artistic property unless enticed to do so by economic benefits or other kinds of recognition.

5

Let us go back to Figure 9.2. Here we may consider a "social" demand curve DD' on the right of DD because inclusive of the external effects and other components not captured by the private demand curve. The "social" demand curve DD', in Figure 9.2, meets Ca in T'. But because I, personally, is not interested in offering such a supply, R and G means might be adopted to supply OQ''. But, strictly reasoning, here there is no need to call in a social demand curve higher than the private one to justify public intervention. This demand curve, however, is relevant to deciding the supply equilibrium point. But to which level of government should these interventions for AC goods and the choices of related equilibrium points be assigned?

An argument that is currently used to urge keeping at the C government level both R and G functions is that national (and European and worldwide) externalities here are very important.[11] The simplistic reasoning derived from this undeniable consideration is that if the AC goods are assigned to the care of IL governments those overlooking the nationwide externalities shall not preserve and promote these goods up to the equilibrium point at which social benefits equal the costs. For two reasons, this is a rough way of reasoning.

The first is that it implies that C government will take into proper consideration the regional and local externalities. A brief examination of the kind of externalities that matter, in the area of AC goods at the C level and at the IL level, shows that this is an untenable assumption. A first important group of economic externalities of AC goods is given by the touristic and residential attraction of the area in which these goods are situated. Certainly, some consideration of these externalities may take place at the C level, particularly for the biggest and most influential cities, but the IL governments are *directly* concerned with the touristic attractions and amenities of their communities: and because these benefits are locally concentrated, IL governments will be more motivated than the C government to take care of the protection and proportion of the AC goods that generate these externalities.

A second important group of externalities of AC goods may consist in "moral values": even citizens who never expect to visit a museum or derive scarce artistic and cultural benefit from observing historical edifices and monuments in their community, often are proud of them, feel a sense of collective ownership of them, and have a commitment to leave them to the future citizens of *their community*. To be sure this is not a universal sentiment, in every generation and place, and one should not expect that without the commitment of the more responsible citizens, who care for the cultural and artistic heritage, these "moral values" will be at the forefront in local and regional communities. However, both because there are informational problems and because there are limits to the individual capacity to take commitments, it is more likely that the "moral values" of preservation and enhancement of the dispersed cultural and artistic patrimony of the several communities composing a big

---

[11] See Hotelling (1938). On museums as a decreasing cost industry see Heilbrun and Gray (1993), pp. 175–179 and Figure 10.1, p. 176.

country will be taken into account, at regional and local levels, by non-profit organizations and individuals, rather than at the C level, except for some very important cases. And, if some of the issues relating to AC goods are perceived more strongly by nonprofit and intellectual groups not residing in the community where they are situated, it will be easier for them to put pressure on the IL governments of these communities than on the more complex and distant C government.

6

The second fallacy is that, when one overlooks some of the externalities, there will necessarily be undersupply. This may not be the most frequent case with the preservation and acquisition of AC goods, because of the lumpiness *of their benefits*. Many externalities, when this lumpiness is important, do not matter for the equilibrium point of I because they do not operate as marginal externalities (Buchanan and Stubblebine, 1962). This may be the case also for the regional and local communities interested in their AC goods. The fact that their actions provide important external effects for the national and international community as well may not be relevant for the equilibrium point of the supply, even when they act from the mere point of view of the benefits "internal" to their regional or local community. Figure 9.3 represents a situation like this: cc is the fixed and variable total costs curve for the preservation or the purchase and maintenance of a given artistic good A. OPL is the gross total benefits curve of the community L consisting of its benefits (it may also represent the gross total "internal" benefits of an individual sponsor of arts or of a nonprofit group in that community). $OP'N$ represents the gross total benefits of the entire nation N, consisting both of the subset of the gross benefits OPL and of the additional subset of benefits arising for N. Both curves, OPL and OPN, become flat at supply OQ corresponding to points P and P', because there is no more addition to the gross benefit going either to L or to N. Suppose, for instance, that A is an old fresco that has been completely restored or a painting that has been acquired with the aid of a sponsor (or not sold), and that it is maintained in the best way. The equilibrium point for L is at OQ, the last point of increase of the gross benefits curve OPL, and this is also the optimum equilibrium point for N. The reasons that this result takes place are that after Q the benefits for L and for N become zero, and the cost curve, after having crossed for the first time the benefits curve of L, rises more gently than both benefits curves, because of its important component of fixed and semifixed costs. In P, for the supply OQ, the difference between costs and benefits, for L, is a maximum because after it bene-

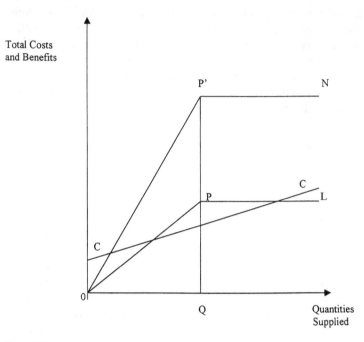

Figure 9.3.

fits do not increase, while costs increase. A similar behavior may be observed in Figure 9.3 for the aggregate benefits curve of N, which, as noted, before P' is steeper than the costs curve and after P' is flat. Here too the supply OQ gives the maximum net benefit.

Admittedly, this is not the only possible case generated by lumpiness. In the previous example relating to Figure 9.3 we have considered a *lumpiness of benefits*, which causes the equilibrium for L and N to be the same and implies that "externalities" of L, flowing to N, are irrelevant for the "social aggregate" optimum. But an important assumption was that CC lay below P. *Lump sum costs* goods might be such that CC in any of its points lies above P. Then L would not be able to undertake that activity, unless subsidized by N or in cooperation with N. This may be the case for very important pieces of art, as for local museums. Indeed I am not maintaining that all AC supplies should be given to the IL governments, but that this should be the preferred solution and that the *national* benefits argument is very often not decisive.

7

Let us now consider the merit *goods* argument for the supply of art goods free or at prices lower than the costs for the benefit of individuals who cannot afford them. These choices imply a sort of empathic behavior, consisting both of pure altruistic motivation and of a desire of reputation, which induces selection of the consumption of the citizens to be "aided" by the donors, according to *the preferences of these last*. Now these kinds of redistributional empathies are likely to be stronger at a local or regional, rather than a national level, as affection for others diminishes with increasing distance while information costs to build a reputation increase. A bequest of AC goods to a regional or local museum implies that the nation too gets an increase of its collective AC heritage, but the opposite is not true: giving that bequest to a national government museum means that the good shall not be a "treasury" of the regional-local community.

8

It is argued that economies of scale render more efficient the supplies of AC goods and services by the C government. The argument is not decisive, because one must also consider the economies of scope and the transaction costs and, among them, the information costs. Beginning with R services, the economies of scale, which may consist in the specialized knowledge required to inspect and supervise AC goods preservation and control their trade, may be relevant to assign these functions to the intermediate levels of government. They, as for many tasks, may be assisted by local governments where there are important economies of scope in connection with urban planning and related licensing of new construction, maintenance, and renewal of real estate. The information costs criterion too points to the IL level: particularly in countries, such as the European ones, with a long history of civilization and an enormous amount of AC value deserving care and dispersed in all parts of the territory. But I would argue that also in the (relatively) new countries, such as the American ones, information costs may make it difficult for the C government to perform well-informed and prompt supervision.

This much from the governments' point of view. But one should consider also the costs of the private owners subject to these regulations. Clearly it is much easier, for them, to get information and to deal with the public controls when they are done at the IL level than when they are done at the C level: even if there are regional offices of the C government, as may happen in the case of R services for AC goods, they still depend upon rules given at the central level. Admittedly there are R functions where autonomy of choices cannot be given to the IL government, because of their "indivisibility" (which may be considered a sub-case of the *lumpiness of supply*): as in the case of controls on exports of "art treasuries" or of the recovery of AC goods lost or stolen. But if the basic tasks of R services are assigned to the IL government, they may cooperate in the above-mentioned C government functions, at low cost, by virtue of their economies of scope and by the asset of information related to their decentralized localization.[12]

9

Considering now the supply of G services in the AC area, such as museums, here the economies of scale criterion may at first glance appear particularly relevant, together with the *lumpiness of supply* argument considered at the end of section 6: indeed, the purchase of important art goods to improve some collections may be very expensive.[13] However, one has to consider the gifts in money and in kind by nonprofit institutions and private "*mecenates*" and the fact that a great many of the old pieces to be preserved in museums, in countries rich in "art treasuries" and in "valuable antiques" and archeological items, are already public property;[14] and C governments often run decentralized museums, in the places where these pieces and items were originally situated.[15] Furthermore, if it is true that the assembling of new items to make significant collections in given sectors of AC goods, such as the modern or contemporary arts, may exceed the financial capabilities of many ordinary L governments, this does not appear true for the L

[12] Until the early 1960s in the U.S., the federal government and the states offered virtually no direct permanent support to arts. Public opinion was hostile to central government interference in such areas. See Heilbrun and Gray (1993), p. 227. The nationwide "external benefits," in other words, did not appear to overcome the damage caused by central government interference with art and culture. The French and Italian tradition is the opposite. For Germany, see note 2.

[13] On the high costs of art goods belonging to the stars' category see note 3 above and Forte and Mantovani (1998b).

[14] An effective public control of the preservation of the AC heritage implies an accurate cataloguing of the AC goods deserving public protection. This task can hardly be accomplished accurately and comprehensively without field recognition.

[15] Actually a relevant share of the items belonging to the Italian museums originally were a property of ancient minor states, absorbed into the Italian state with the national unification, so that their devolution to the IL governments would represent a mere restitution to the communities that originally owned them.

governments of big cities such as Paris, Berlin, and London, or Milan or Rome, or of art cities such as Venice or Florence, which benefit from international attention. These easily get support from international sponsors and gifts from "*mecenates*" and might also finance new purchases by selling some of their artworks.[16] The argument of inadequate funding a fortiori does not appear valid for most intermediate governments, given their size, provided that they are prepared to spend and invest in the arts.[17] On the other hand, I am not arguing that C governments should keep museums and run art activities in sectors where lumpiness and economies of scale are very important. I am arguing that they should perform these functions in competition with lower-level governments of communities "specialized in the arts" and cities and intermediate governments big enough to be able to exploit the relevant economies of scale.

10

A standard objection, at this point, would be that poorer regions may be at a disadvantage vis-à-vis the rich ones. But two replies are available here. Federal models do not imply overlooking the horizontal distributional issues arising among rich and poor regions. And many poor regions are rich in history and culture and have monuments of the past and art resources that they, with their local forces assisted by transfers from other governments and private sponsors and donors, might exploit with a deeper interest than a distant central government. In the vast areas of local history, tradition, and cultural movements, IL governments may have much lower information costs than the C government. Furthermore, preservation services for AC goods, as already noted, should not end in merely protecting them from theft and damage; they should be easily available to the public and knowledge of them should be promoted. And at the IL level the costs of these activities may be reduced by the fact that they may be connected with other IL public functions, such as those in the areas of promotion of tourism, provision of leisure time facilities, and education.

For the local nonprofit institutions and for individuals active in the AC goods areas, obviously, transaction and information costs are much lower at the IL levels than at the C level. And the same is true for the

---

[16] Or they might rent or lease or give in multiproperty or in other "nonfinal" ways their artworks, to avoid the entire transfer of the property. See Forte (1997b).

[17] One may mention the great initiative of the Bilbao Modern Arts Museums, financed by the autonomous government of the Pays Basque and by the local authorities together with the Guggenheim Foundation.

transaction and information costs of the governments vis-à-vis these entities and persons.

Last but not least, the final consumers' demand for G services cannot be satisfactorily met by highly centralized supplies of them, because this implies a great disparity of access to these services favoring those who live in the city chosen as the site of these centralized institutions or nearby. This outcome, considering the public expenditures borne by the general taxpayer as those of the C government, runs counter to the benefit principle. One may then reply that G services of C government should be largely decentralized: and this is what happens, in countries like Italy. But then, why not let the IL governments become owners of these AC public goods and undertake the related activities?

11

Let us now consider an argument which might be put forward to keep the R functions at the C level while accepting an extensive devolution of the G functions to the IL governments.[18] The argument is that IL governments are under strong pressure form powerful local and regional interests involved in urban development and real estate "speculation" to destroy AC heritage values, in order to create new *economic* wealth: the loss, it is argued, may be important for the nation and the international community at large, while the benefits are concentrated at the local level, as in the case of possession of "art treasuries" by persons and entities who do not assure their (proper) availability in the country. IL governments, it is argued, under the pressure of local interests, may adopt a relaxed attitude with these properties, thus damaging important nationwide interests with irresponsible, hardly reversible choices.

There are two replies to this argument. A preliminary one it is that in this reasoning there is a confusion between the power of enacting general regulatory principles and that of making, under given principles, specific interventions. The purposes of general interest may be fixed in C-level rules to which the specific IL-level interventions should conform. But this argument is wrong at its very root. Why should private individuals bear, without compensation, a cost for the benefit of the national community, if the collective goods that they keep are so important? It

---

[18] This is the line of policy of devolution that, *at most*, seems likely to be enacted in the frame of a federalistic reform of the Italian constitution. The most recent (Bassanini) laws on decentralization allow the devolution of the *management* and *restoration* of C government's AC goods to IL governments' institutions, while the property and chief decisions shall remain with the state. Not many IL governments appear willing to accept this sort of partial devolution.

is only logical to expect that many of these persons and entities, because they either cannot afford to bear this cost for the benefit of others or do not care about these external effects, should try to evade these restrictions on their property. Rather than *compel* owners of valuable AC goods to keep them, at any cost, public regulations and administrations should provide *incentives* to do so. Regulations hindering changes in the existing real estate to preserve the past, without any incentive to proper maintenance, may lead to gradual decay of the AC goods thus "protected." Severe constraints on the free circulation and marketing of AC goods, such as those set forth by the European continental countries and particularly by Italy, have a negative effect on the availability of the domestic "art treasures" and on their international appreciation, while depressing the domestic art market.[19]

12

The experience of countries like Italy, where R services relating to AC goods are assigned to the C level, with severe and extensive controls, and where the entire network of museums, whether belonging to the C governments or to the IL ones or to private institutions, is kept, *in principle*, under strict control by the C government, certainly is not positive. Most of these goods are not yet catalogued. An enormous heritage of "protected" AC goods remains in the basements of the museums and, sometimes, in different locations.[20] Because of the severe burdens imposed by

[19] See a comparison between the modest market values of paintings of Italian masters of the nineteenth century and the early twentieth century, scarcely present in the international museums, and the high values of French impressionist paintings, widely present in these museums and particularly in those of the U.S., in Forte and Mantovani (1998a). Generally speaking, the art markets of continental Europe whose regimes are dirigistic show lower average prices and less activity than the British free-trade art market, not to speak of the U.S. During the 1996–97 year sales in the British official art market totaled £348,780,000, in France the equivalent of £68,000,000, in Germany the equivalent of £39,980,000, and in Italy the equivalent of £24,330,000. In U.S. they totaled the equivalent of £578,970. Average prices have been respectively £10,789, £5,260, £3,813, £5,724, and £27,806 or equivalent values in the domestic currencies at the current average rate of exchange. See the data in *Il Giornale dell'Arte*, October 1997.

[20] Of the Italian state museums (44% of the total, but with a larger share of valuable AC goods), according to official statistics (see ISTAT, 1992), only 60.6% in 1992 were open regularly to the public. Another 20% could be opened by request, and the remaining 10% were under restoration or new projects. The percentage of regional museums open regularly to the public was slightly lower (59.3%), but these were only 2% of the total. The percentage of provincial museums (another 2% of the total) open regularly was 81%, while that of the municipalities open regularly was only 56.2%. This last figure must be interpreted: in municipal museums were 21,806,119 items, nearly three times

the regulations, private owners of a large share of artworks do not report them, so that the locations of a large portion of the production of important Italian masters are unknown. And it has been proved that it is relatively easy to illegally export art goods from Italy to free art-market countries, even if these goods had been recently purchased at well-known auctions houses and were recorded in their official catalogues, provided that the artists are not so famous as to attract the attention of the authorities supposedly supervising these trades.[21]

References

Becker G. and Murphy K. M. (1988), "A Theory of Rational Addiction," *Journal of Political Economy* 96(4), 675–700.

Benedict S. (ed.) (1991), *Public Money and the Muse: Essays on Government Funding of the Arts*, New York: Norton.

Brennan G. and Walsh C. (eds.) (1990), *Rationality, Individualism and Public Policy*, Camberra: Centre for Research on Federal Financial Relations, Australian National University.

Breton A. (1996), *Competitive Governments: An Economic Theory of Politics and Public Finance*, Cambridge and New York: Cambridge University Press.

Breton A. and Scott A. (1978), *The Economic Constitution of Federal States*, Toronto: University of Toronto Press.

Buchanan J. M. and Stubblebine W. M. (1962), "Externality," *Economica* 29, 371–384.

the number in the state museums, most of them of minor importance. Private museums regularly open to the public were 45.6% (their number being 15% of the total of Italian museums), while the ecclesiastic museums regularly opened to the public were 42.6% (these museums were 14% of the total). Only 22% of the items owned by the state museums were available to the public. The percentage rose to 25% for the municipal museums, 28% for the regional museums, 34% for the provincial, 35% for the private, and 66% for the ecclesiastic. Of the items owned by the state museums, only 15% were catalogued and another 55% were merely inventoried, while the items photographed were no more than 9% of the total; 30% of the items were neither catalogued nor inventoried! The percentage of items catalogued rose to 19% for the provincial museums and to 37% for both the regional and the municipal museums, while in the ecclesiastic museums the items catalogued were 24% and in the private institutions 30%. The percentage of items merely inventoried was 34% for the municipal museums and 39% and 52% for the provincial and regional museums, and rose to 54% for the ecclesiastic.

21 A British amateur of Italian arts, to prove that the severe Italian regulations, while damaging free circulation of Italian art goods, may be easily evaded, bought in 1997, in a well-known international art house of Milan, at a public auction, for an average price, a "woman's portrait" of a not famous but not unknown Italian painter of the nineteenth century, and then exported the work "illegally," without any difficulty, to London, from which he reexported it "legally" back to Italy, disclosing the episode to the international press, which has reported it with due emphasis. See Forte and Mantovani (1998a).

Chiancone P. and Osculati F. (eds.) (1993), *Il merito della spesa pubblica*, Milan: Franco Angeli.

Clark D. E. and Khan J. R. (1988), "The Social Benefits of Urban Amenities," *Journal of Regional Sciences* 28(3), 363–377.

Clotfelter C. T. (1991), "Government Policy toward Art Museums in the United States," in Feldstein (1991).

Chummings M. C., Schuster J. Jr. and Davidson M. (1988), *Who's to Pay for the Arts? The International Search for Models of Art Support*, New York: American Council for the Arts.

Degiarde E., Gregorio D., Brosio G., Frigo M. and Santagata W. (1995), *Il mercato delle opere d'arte e i problemi della circolazione a livello europeo*, Milan: Franco Angeli.

Dimaggio P. J. (1991), "Decentralization of Art Founding from the Federal Government to the States," in Benedict S. (1991).

Feldstein M. (ed.) (1991), *The Economics of Art Museums*, Chicago: University of Chicago Press.

Forte F. (1993a), *Principi di economia pubblica*, Milan: Giuffrè.

Forte F. (1993b), "I beni meritori: scelte razionali e superazionali, esternalità, paternalismo e preferenze sulle preferenze," in Chiancone and Osculati (1993).

Forte F. (1997a), "Devoluzione federalista e beni artistici/culturali," *Il Risparmio* 45(1) (January–February), 108–145.

Forte F. (1997b), "Toward a European Market for Arts and Culture Goods: Some Proposals," in Hutter and Rizzo (1997).

Forte F. and Mantovani M. (1998a), "L'investimento nell'arte sul mercato internazionale libero e in quello italiano regolamentato," *Il Risparmio* 46(1) (January–February), 47–69.

Forte F. and Mantovani M. (1998b), "Patrimonio culturale pubblico: alcune riflessioni sulla sua valutazione e sul ruolo dell'informazione," *Moneta e Credito* 203 (September), 331–362.

Hamlin A. P. (1990), "The Normative Status of Consumer Sovereignty," in Brennan and Walsh (1990).

Heilbrun J. and Gray C. M. (1993), *The Economics of Art and Culture*, Cambridge: Cambridge University Press.

Hendon W. S., Shanahn I. L. and Macdonald A. J. (eds.) (1980), *Economic Policy for the Arts*, Cambridge, Mass.: Art Books.

Hendon W. S. and Shanahn I. L. (eds.) (1983), *Economics of Cultural Decisions*, Cambridge. Mass.: Art Books.

Hotelling H. (1938), "The General Welfare in Relation to Problems of Taxation and of Railway and Utility Rates," *Econometrica* 242–269.

Hutter M. and Rizzo I. (eds.) (1997), *Economic Perspectives on Cultural Heritage*, Macmillan: London.

ISTAT (1992), *Indagine statistica sui musei e le istituzioni similari*, Rome: ISTAT.

Macdonald G. M. (1988), "The Economics of Rising Stars," *American Economic Review* 78(1), 155–166.

McCain R. A. (1980), "Market for Works of Art and Market for Lemons," in Hendon, Shanahn and Macdonald (1980).

Netzer D. (1992), "Cultural Policy in an Era of Budgetary Stringency," in Towse and Khakee (1992).

Padoa Schioppa Kostoris F. (1996), *La valorizzazione del patrimonio storico-artistico-culturale*, Working Document No. 51/96, Roma: ISPE.

Peacock A. T. (1969), "Welfare Economics and the Public Subsidy to Arts," *Manchester School of Economic and Social Studies* 37(4), 323–335.

Peacock A. T. (1994), *A Future for the Past: The Political Economy of Heritage*, Hume Occasional Paper No. 44, Edinburgh: David Hume Institute.

Salmon P. (1987). "Decentralisation as an Incentive Scheme," *Oxford Review of Economic Policy* 3(2), 24–43.

Schneider F. W. and Pommerehne W. (1983), "Private Demand for Public Subsidies to the Arts: A Study in Voting and Expenditure Theory," in Hendon and Shanhan (1983).

Schuster J. and Davidson M. (1988), "The Search for International Models: Results from Recent Comparative Research in Arts Policy," in Cummings, Schuster and Davidson (1988).

Singer L. P. (1981), "Rivalry and Externalities in the Secondary Art Markets," *Journal of Cultural Economics* 5(2) (December), 39–57.

Singer L. P. (1990), " The Utility of Art versus Fair Bets in the Investment Market," *Journal of Cultural Economics* 14(2) (December), 1–13.

Taylor C. (1990), "Irreducibly Social Goods," in Brennan and Walsh (1990).

Throsby D. (1994), "The Production and Consumption of the Arts: A View of Cultural Economics," *Journal of Economic Literature* 33(1) (March), 1–29.

Throsby D. and Withers G. A. (1986), "Strategic Bias and Demand for Public Goods: Theory and an Application to the Arts," *Journal of Public Economics* 31(3) (December), 307–327.

Towse R. and Khakee A. (eds.) (1992), *Cultural Economics*, Heidelberg: Springer-Verlag.

CHAPTER 10

Vertical competition in a unitary state

Pierre Salmon

1   Introduction[1]

An important component of Albert Breton's analysis of competitive government (1987, 1996) is his theory of competition among governments located at different levels of jurisdiction. This type of competition, called vertical competition, is to be distinguished from the horizontal competition that takes place among governments situated at the same level. The latter is based on the well-known "voting with the feet" mechanism (extended to firms and factors) as well as on a less well-known "tournament" or "yardstick competition" mechanism in which (some) voters compare the performance of their own government with that of other jurisdictions situated on the same level and, when satisfied with the relative performance of the former, are more likely to vote for the incumbents in the next election (Salmon, 1987). Vertical competition is based on the second mechanism only. If A is a country and B a region of that country, and if the two governments provide at least some services that are comparable, voters in B compare the performance of B's government with that of A's.[2] If they are pleased with the performance of B's government more than with that of A's, this makes them somewhat more likely to vote for the incumbents in the next regional election, and at the same time somewhat less likely to vote for the in-

---

[1] A first version of several sections of this chapter was presented in October 1997 at a seminar on federalism organized by the University of Turin and Torino Incontra (and published in *Amministrare*; see Salmon, 1998). I am grateful for the comments made on that occasion.
[2] As argued convincingly in Breton (1996), governments situated at different levels of jurisdiction always provide at least some goods and services that are identical or close substitutes, and thus comparable.

cumbents at the national level.[3] Incentives are thus provided to office-holders at both levels.

There is no reason to doubt that horizontal competition based on comparative performance – for instance, performance competition between municipalities – is a mechanism that is at work in all kinds of governmental systems. By contrast, one might be inclined to perceive the scope or relevance of vertical competition as being limited to the relationship between, say, the central government of Canada, the United States, or Germany and the governments of the provinces, states, or *Länder*, respectively – that is, to vertical relations within systems that have the two characteristics of being federal and being structured around two tiers of government. Breton, however, insists that his theory of vertical competition is quite general. He clearly means it to be relevant also in the case of countries with regard to which neither assumption can be upheld, that is, countries whose governmental systems are unitary and structured around more than two tiers. The analysis that follows is focused on one such country, France. The theoretical objective is both to verify that vertical competition is not meaningless outside its more obviously appropriate federal habitat and to contribute to the exploration of the variety of forms that it can take depending on the institutional context.

Vertical competition raises a problem which is more serious in unitary systems than in federal ones. A major characteristic of unitary states is that there is no significant constitutional protection of the powers used by subcentral governments.[4] This raises the following problem. Suppose that A, the central government of a country, is entitled to define what B, a subcentral government, is allowed to do, including the amount of resources B can get. Government A may favor vertical competition between itself and government B for various reasons, for instance, because that will enhance the efficiency of the country as a whole and hence A's relative position in the horizontal – yardstick or tournament – competition in which it is engaged with the governments of other countries (Salmon, 1987). However, there are necessarily limits to this benevolence. In particular, if competition between A and B turns too clearly to the advantage of B, A will be tempted to nullify this advantage by limiting the powers and resources available to B. The federal solution – that is, some protection of B entrenched in a constitution that A alone cannot

[3] From now on, A, B, and C will refer indistinctly to jurisdictions, governments of these jurisdictions, or officeholders in these governments.
[4] Whether there is such protection in all federal systems is not completely clear (Ordeshook, 1992, p. 167), but I will assume that, as a rule, there is.

change – mitigates the problem where it applies but is unavailable here by assumption. The question, then, is whether other mechanisms, in general or in the case of unitary systems, protect the autonomy of junior governments and, with them, the stability of vertical competition.[5]

An apparently completely different (although in fact related) problem is created by the existence of more than two tiers of government, which entails a more complex set of interlevel relationships. Suppose that there are three tiers of government: central government (A), provincial governments (Bs), and municipal governments (Cs). To decide whether the system is federal or not, only the nature of the relationship between the first and the second levels, that is, between As and Bs, is normally considered to be relevant. When that relation is federal, the relationship between Bs and Cs in turn can be of either a federal or a unitary-state kind, but in most accounts of federalism, it is implicitly assumed to be of the latter kind.[6] Taken together, the two problems suggest that even when federal solutions protect vertical competition between the first two levels, they are unlikely to protect vertical competition all the way down to the lowest interlevel relationship. Whether this limitation is important depends on whether there are other means available to protect competition, and whether vertical competition is more relevant or intense when taking place toward the top or toward the bottom.

France is interesting in these respects because it experienced in the early eighties a significant process of decentralization in favor of three levels of subnational government, followed at a short distance – as a consequence of the European Single Act, that is, in the late eighties and early nineties – by the acceleration of a process of federalization common to all the member countries of the European Community/Union. Contrary to other decentralizing processes, in particular those that have taken place or are contemplated in other European countries, decentralization in France, it must be stressed, remains strictly circumscribed within the limits of unitary systems. With respect to the internal structure of government, there is no significant tendency toward federalism. At the higher, European, level, this is in my opinion different. Thus we have a case of a multitier unitary state, albeit potentially one whose sovereignty is limited in some areas, as is the case of provinces or states in federations.

---

[5] For Barry Weingast (1993, p. 290), "the essence of federalism is that it provides a viable system of political decentralization" – a formulation suggesting that the viability of decentralization without federalism is to say the least doubtful.

[6] In his oft-quoted definition of federalism, William Riker (1964, p. 11) refers to "*two* levels of governments [that] rule the same land" (my emphasis).

In section 2, I describe a number of characteristics of the French case, in particular where they depart significantly from those observed in other countries engaged in a process of decentralization or devolution. This will allow me, in section 3, to return with augmented institutional and factual baggage to the systemic problems of vertical competition in unitary states already mentioned. It will turn out that intergovernmental competition at the subnational level is important in this case. Section 4 is concerned with the interpretation of this kind of competition, in particular with the question of whether it should still be considered vertical. Concluding remarks are formulated in section 5.

2   Institutional characteristics of the French case

The process of decentralization and regionalization which has taken place in France since 1982 may be considered impressive relative to that country's tradition of centralism, but certainly not compared to the transformations accomplished in Belgium and Spain, the devolution recently enacted in Britain (at least that concerning Scotland), or the changes contemplated in Italy. Let me note some of the characteristics of the French experience which should be kept in mind when attempting an interpretation.

Motivation

Two important motives often underlie transformations towards federalism, regionalization, or simply a more decentralized system. One is the existence of strong demands and traditions of an ethnic or linguistic kind. They are clearly essential in Spain and in Belgium, and to a lesser degree in Britain. Another important motive in many countries is related to a phenomenon that can be labeled the "frustration of the rich" (that is, of the inhabitants of the most prosperous parts of the country). Such frustration seems very important in Italy and far from negligible in Belgium and Spain. From the perspective of the prosperous regions, there is a tendency to consider that the unitary state both hides their exploitation by the poorer regions – which are more or less consciously viewed as responsible for their fate – and follows a mode of governance that is ill-adapted to the most dynamic parts of the country. These feelings clearly underlie the attitudes of many in northern Italy, and, in combination with the linguistic or ethnic motivation, also in Flanders and in Catalonia. To both problems (ethnic demands and frustration of the rich), federalism (or, as a first step, increased regionalization) may be the only peaceful solution short of separatism and secession.

With the unimportant exception of Corsica, there has been no serious ethnic or linguistic pressure towards federalism or decentralization in France for some time. As to the frustration of the rich, this phenomenon is not relevant in France because the only significantly richer part of the country, the area around Paris, has always been and still is favored rather than disfavored by the allocation of public funds.[7]

Thus the explanation of the decentralization that took place in 1982 must be sought elsewhere. It is particularly noteworthy in the context of a discussion of vertical competition like this one that the main motivation of the reform was of a purely systemic kind, involving the concepts of democracy or participation and of efficiency. In 1981, when the Socialists came into power, some decentralization had already taken place (Schmidt, 1990; Ohnet, 1996) but France was still very centralized.[8] Two groups of people wanted that to be changed substantially. Some of the proponents of decentralization wanted first of all more democracy in the form of increased "participation" and self-management. Their position was to a large extent the outcome of the extended discussions, involving many intellectuals and members of political parties, that had taken place over the previous decades. Other proponents were more concerned with the inefficiencies of excessively centralized governance. Within the Socialist Party, in which many were still unfavorable to any form of decentralization, Michel Rocard and Gaston Deferre, two prominent but unorthodox party members, personified the two decentralizing tendencies. In the common platform of the Socialist and Communist Parties and then in the agenda of the new majority, decentralization was also a kind of compensation conceded to Rocard and his friends, and perhaps to public opinion in general, for tolerating the major increase in state power that was then expected from the nationalization of many additional firms and sectors. The actual framing and implementation of decentralization, however, was in the hands not of Rocardians but of Deferre, whose main concern was one of efficiency.[9] The main thing in his view

---

[7] Alsace is slightly better off, notably in terms of unemployment, than the rest of France and thus there may be in that small part of France some scope for feelings of frustration and of course of ethnic specificity. So far though, ironically, frustration has found an outlet in the relatively high level of the vote in favor of the Front National, an extreme right-wing French nationalistic party, rather than in support for movements advocating more autonomy.

[8] In the sixties and seventies, several sociologists and political scientists argued that local elected officials, especially those in charge of large cities, had much more power in reality than was suggested by their rhetoric (see an excellent discussion and many references in Schmidt, 1990).

[9] Deferre was *Ministre de l'Intérieur et de la Décentralisation* (i.e., home affairs and decentralization) and at the same time mayor of Marseille (the second-largest city in France), while the prime minister, Pierre Mauroy, was the mayor of another large city, Lille.

was to liberate local policy making from the tutorship and intrusions of the state bureaucracy – both the bureaucracy located in the ministries in Paris and, led by the prefects and other representatives of the central state, the state bureaucracy located in the provinces. As he said retrospectively, what really mattered to "citizens at the base" was that "now ... the files that were formerly sent to Paris for a decision and came back one, two or three years later, can be dealt with on the spot within normal delays."[10]

The extent of decentralization

The 1982 reform, completed by various laws and decrees enacted in the following years, made significant progress in the directions both of increased democracy at the subcentral level and of a reduction in the powers of the central state bureaucracy. The regions (about twenty) already existed (they had been created by the Vichy regime) but as entities of a purely administrative kind. The reform created a new tier of elected governments at their level, endowed with proper legislative (the "regional council") and executive branches (led by the president of that council). The *départements* (about 100) already had a legislative branch in the form of a "general council," but the executive branch was in the hands of a prefect appointed by the central government. The reform substituted the president of the general council for the prefect as the head of the executive branch. It also transferred blocks of powers and the corresponding financial and human resources to the regions and the *départements*, and abolished a priori administrative and financial control by the central government or its representatives over all three levels of subcentral government.

To give a few figures, central government now employs about three million people (if we include public hospitals but not the post), most of them located in the provinces. Subcentral government employs about half that number (Kerouanton, 1999). If we look into subcentral government, we observe that most people are employed by the communes, many less by the *départements*, and very few by the regions. Overall spending by subcentral government is about 10 percent of GDP; regions account for about 10 percent of that, *départements* for about 30 percent, and communes for about 60 percent. The regions' strength is capital formation (see, e.g., Crédit Local de France – Dexia, 1998). Capital formation by subcentral government represents more than 2 percent of GDP and more than 70 percent of capital formation by government in general,

---

[10] *Le Monde*, 16 August 1985, quoted by Preteceille (1991, p. 145).

and regions are responsible, either directly or through cofinancing and grants, for a large part of that.

Unitary state characteristics

Despite the creation of democratic government at the level of regions and of a democratic executive branch at the level of *départements*, as well as the granting of increased autonomy at the level of municipalities, the French experience remains strictly within the limits of a unitary system of government. It has, in particular, little to do with regionalization in the sense given that term in the context of Spain or of Italy.

Three characteristics make the French system of government strictly unitary. First, subnational government is only weakly "embedded" in the French constitution. Article 72, which refers both to "free administration" of the *collectivités territoriales* by elected councils, and to the law as the means of specifying this principle, has been interpreted by the Constitutional Council as precluding any encroachment on the autonomy of these jurisdictions by acts of the executive branch of the central government, but not, to a significant degree, by laws voted by Parliament (Roux, 1993).[11] In any case, the constitution itself can be amended without consultation of the subcentral levels.

Second, regions have no legislative power.[12] Only the Parliament in Paris can make laws. This is different not only from what is the case in federations such as Germany but also in so-called "regional states" such as Italy and Spain. The dividing line here is between strictly unitary states and all others, including regional states. With regard to constitutional power, however, the dividing line fluctuates somewhere between the unitary and the federal, with some "regional states" leaning this time toward the unitary state solution. Thus, in Italy the political organization and electoral rules pertaining to each level of government are set by central government laws. In Germany, the *Länder* have their own constitutions and shape relatively freely their relationships with lower levels of government. Spain is increasingly federal in this respect as in others, moving from competence of the central government alone to joint competence with increasing weight at the regional level. In France, all the rules governing the organization of the three subcentral levels of government, including notably electoral rules, are fixed by the national

---

[11] I am simplifying a bit. Whether the regional level is constitutionally on a par with the other two subnational levels is a moot point (see Roux, 1993).

[12] Nor have *départements*, except in some very specific fields (hunting, etc.). Municipalities have authority over urban planning and zoning in particular.

Parliament exclusively. This characteristic will play a role in the argument developed in the next section.

Third, there is no hierarchy among the three levels of subcentral government.[13] Of course, in spatial terms or with regard to voting constituencies, communes are parts of *départements* and *départements* are parts of regions. But in terms of authority, regions are not above *départements*, and *départements* are not above communes. Each level has some powers specified in the decentralization laws voted by the Parliament in Paris, as well as a general competence (as already noted) with regard to its own affairs.

The European dimension

That one should already treat Europe as the highest level of government in some areas seems clear to me from the following facts. First, from a purely legal point of view, there are the twin principles of supremacy of European law over national law and of "direct effect" (that is, of the direct effect of many European legal acts in purely national proceedings). As stressed by legal scholars such as Stephen Wheatherill (1995, Chapter 6), this creates a hierarchy of law of a kind not unlike that found in strictly federal systems. Second, since the implementation (in 1987) of the Single Act, the standard decision-making procedure in the European Council of Ministers is qualified majority voting instead of unanimity. As a consequence, European directives or regulations can now be imposed on one or several unwilling member state governments. This deprives the widely shared interpretation of the EU mode of governance as a form of intergovernmental decision making of one of its main justifications and makes it, in my opinion, a rather inappropriate characterization of the current state of affairs. Third, also as a consequence of qualified majority voting, the annual flow of EU directives and regulations has increased enormously. As a matter of fact, European-made directives and regulations now typically outnumber the laws and regulations enacted by the governments of individual member countries. Thus "in 1991, the European authorities in Brussels issued 1,564 directives and regulations as against 1,417 pieces of legislation (laws, ordinances, decrees) issued by Paris, so that by now the Community introduces into the corpus of French Law more rules than the national authorities themselves" (Majone, 1996, p. 57).

---

[13] A law of January 1983 is particularly explicit in this respect (see Mabileau, 1997, p. 363).

3   How the systemic problem is mitigated

As noted in the introduction, a link may be established between the two systemic questions of how decentralization is protected in a unitary state and of what happens when more than two levels of government are assumed. To display that link, let me consider in turn a two-tier and a three-tier system.

The two-tier case

In addition to constitutional entrenchment, two mechanisms may operate in a two-tier system to prevent the central government from eroding the powers that it itself assigns to subcentral governments. One mechanism is the representation of the lower level within the decision-making apparatus of the higher level. An example of that is the Bundesrat in Germany. If one is willing to admit, as I propose, that Europe is already partly federal, another illustration of the representation mechanism is the Council of Ministers in Brussels.[14] In both cases, even a minority of second-tier governments is generally enough to block an attempted encroachment of their powers. In France, the Senate considers itself to be the representative and protector of local government. Given the way senators are elected, this claim is justified to some extent. The problem is the French Senate's lack of legal powers. As a formal institution, the Senate can play a protective role only weakly because, in most cases, a simple or qualified majority in the lower house (National Assembly) can overrule its decisions. This does not imply, however, that, as individuals, members of both houses (i.e., senators included) and of the executive branch (ministers) do not represent and protect subcentral governments in an informal but highly effective way. This capacity and willingness to protect decentralized government are consequences of a practice known in France as *cumul des mandats*, to which I will return.

A second mechanism protecting decentralization or vertical competition in a unitary state is monitoring by the electorate itself. If people are satisfied with or attached to the current state of affairs, it may well prove highly perilous to the incumbent politicians in the national government

---

[14] It may not seem literally true, of course, that the European authorities in Brussels assign powers to the member state governments. One may even feel that it is the other way around. However, it is a fact that in all the policy areas that have something to do with the internal market, the main issue is what regulatory powers should be left to national governments (see Breton and Salmon, 1999).

to try to change that state of affairs substantially. In other words, in this quasi-constitutional matter as well as in others of the same nature, voters, by the way of ordinary elections, exercise a power of monitoring or influence which is much more important than constitutional legal or economic scholarship typically acknowledges (Salmon, 1999).

The three-tier case

If there are three tiers of government, however, a third additional mechanism may become available – more easily so, though, in a unitary state than in a federal one. Assume again that A is the central government of a country, B a provincial or regional government, and C a municipality. I consider first the federal case. There is a federal constitution, B is protected from A, and A does not interfere in the relationship between B and C (that it should not interfere is a claim made in most accounts of federalism; see Brosio, 1994).[15] As a rule, the relationship between B and C will not be federal. As a consequence, the fairness of the competition between B and C will depend only on the "two additional mechanisms" mentioned previously. This will tend to make it less protected than is, thanks to the federal constitution, the fairness of vertical competition between A and B. An illustration of the powerlessness that may ensue at the C level is the way the city of Toronto has been treated, recently, by the provincial government of Ontario. I think that the fear of such developments explains the reluctant attitude often displayed by large cities toward the prospect of regionalization or federalization (for Italy, see Piperno, 1996).

Now, suppose that the relationship between A and B is of a unitary state nature. Then, A will be concerned with the relationship between B and C, and if A decides that this relationship should be competitive, it can make sure that it remains so.[16] Thus, in addition to the two supplementary mechanisms mentioned above we now have, with regard to

---

[15] Increased regionalization in Italy, something rather close to federalism, would imply logically, in the view of several authors, that regions would become more or less responsible for organizing the funding of local government (see Giarda, 1995; Brosio, 1996; Piperno, 1996). Although Spain is more advanced than Italy toward quasi-federalism, in Spain "regional government has no exclusive power over local government," which has "a double dependence on both central and regional governments in terms of expenditure responsibilities and financial assistance" (Solé-Vilanova, 1990, p. 333). Suarez-Pandiello (1996, p. 428), however, argues that this contradicts the logic of the system and should be changed.

[16] Indeed, because competition between B and C prevents any one of the two subcentral governments from becoming too strong a rival to itself, A may well have a direct, selfish interest in maintaining the competition.

what happens between the two subcentral levels, a third mechanism, which is the monitoring of subcentral competition by the central government.

In the case of France, as already noted, each level of subcentral government is completely independent from the other two, whereas none of the three is independent from the central government in Paris. Given the decision by the central government to decentralize, this mutual independence will allow competition to be very active between the three levels of subcentral government and relatively limited between the central level and subcentral government as a whole.[17] With sufficient decentralization, the net effect could even be more competition than if the system were federal. More intense competition at the bottom would compensate for weaker competition at the top. This discussion raises the question of whether, in such settings, both the distinction between subcentral levels and the one between horizontal and vertical competition remain relevant. Before addressing that question, let me elaborate on the way subcentral government as a whole has so far been protected in a unitary country like France.

The "cumul des mandats"

As already indicated, a major protective mechanism is the one stemming from the *cumul des mandats*, a practice that has been a major characteristic of the French institutional system for a long time, even though it might be currently on the point of disappearing. The mechanism is simple. Most decision makers who count at the national level are also important decision makers at the subnational levels, and vice versa. Thus mayors of large cities and presidents of regional or general councils are typically also members of one or the other of the two houses of Parliament in Paris, whereas about half the members of Parliament also have important functions in local, departmental, or regional government. In 1997, the new prime minister asked his ministers to cease being mayors or presidents of regional or general councils. The offices of minister and of member of Parliament being in general less secure than that, say, of mayor, the ministers complied but made sure to keep an eye on, or some relations with, the collaborators or friends who replaced

---

[17] That interlevel competition at the subcentral level was a conscious objective of Deferre seems clear from his presentation of the reform to the Parliament: "Les municipalités, les conseils généraux et les conseils régionaux . . . créeront par leur action concurrente et stimulante les conditions d'un nouveau développement économique, social et culturel de la France" (cited by Mabileau, 1997, p. 363).

them, for an indeterminate but possibly short time, in the subcentral governments.

It cannot be denied that the "*cumul des mandats*" is a peculiar habit, which has many ill effects, some of them clearly anticompetitive.[18] But it also has the effect of providing constitutionally unprotected subcentral governments a means to resist attempts by the central government, including its powerful bureaucracy, to erode their autonomy. A prohibition of the "*cumul des mandats*" is currently on the legislative agenda. But if the "*cumul des mandats*" is not replaced by some other form of protection of subcentral government, this well-meaning, apparently pro-competitive reform could well prove counterproductive.

4   The nature of subnational competition

In addition to being completely mutually independent, the governments of French communes, *départements*, and regions have four characteristics that are important from a systemic perspective. First, their major source of finances is made up of taxes whose rates they can fix almost completely freely (see Gilbert and Guengant, 1991). To give some figures, subcentral taxation represented about 4.5 percent of GDP in 1994 – roughly the same as in Spain, but much more than in Italy (2 percent) and Britain (1.5 percent).[19] This is complemented, mainly on a nondiscretionary basis, by global grants from the central government, and also by borrowing.[20] Second, as noted, subcentral governments have no legislative power and very little rule-making power in general. Third, in many basic sectors (health, education, justice, police, tax collection, etc.) the central government directly implements its policies, with the help of its own employees and not through the employees of subcentral government. This means that in France the central government can afford to be much more relaxed about the behavior of subcentral government than it is in systems such as the British or German ones, in which the central government depends on subcentral government for the implementation of its own decisions. It means also that the equalization issue is much less important. Fourth, the distribution of powers among the three levels is extremely flexible. Powers specific to each level are allocated by the decentralization laws, but they are not binding because any

---

[18] See, e.g., Schmidt (1990), Mény (1992, Chapter 2). Some evidence that voters themselves have mixed feelings about the *cumul* is provided by Olivier (1998).

[19] I.N.S.E.E., *Tableaux de l'économie française 1997–1998*, p. 123.

[20] Earmarked and targeted grants represent only about 10 percent of grants (Marcou, 1994, p. 71).

subcentral government can also invoke the general principle of free administration or general competence already mentioned. To borrow a commentator's (somewhat excessive) words, "the unwritten rule of French local government" is "that each level of government may intervene in any domain it wishes, irrespective of specific powers accorded to it" (Le Galès, 1995, p. 86). To these characteristics, one must add an observation concerning the general setting in which governments at all levels operate: over the last decade, this setting has been drastically changed by deregulation, internationalization, and transfers of responsibilities from state to market.

Taken together, these characteristics have two consequences. First, subcentral governments now act not only by collecting taxes and producing goods and services but also, most significantly, by engaging in all kinds of contracting and financing. In doing this they increasingly behave like private institutions (with which, incidentally, they often compete). Subcentral governments contract with each other at the same level of jurisdiction to create new institutions: various forms of intercommunal entities at the level of metropolitan areas to deliver services, interregional groupings (often transnational) to lobby Brussels or canvass China, and so forth. They contract with governments at other levels of jurisdiction, including the central government in Paris and the Commission in Brussels, to cofinance all sorts of projects. They contract with firms to improve rail or air transportation, to create industrial or science parks, to promote tourism and attract residents and firms, to borrow and invest funds, and of course to construct and repair buildings and roads and to provide many goods and services. They provide subsidies to induce other jurisdictions, associations, private firms, and individuals to engage in actions that they consider useful, from the creation of new firms and the employment of young people to participation in costly nautical contests.

The second consequence of this quasi-market setting is that competition often involves indistinctly governments located at different levels of jurisdiction. For instance, because unemployment and deprivation are major concerns of many voters, new schemes addressing these problems are tried out at all levels of government. People can then compare what is being done by the city of Paris with what is being done by the regional council of Auvergne or the *département* of the Hauts-de-Seine: three levels of government, but no hierarchical relationship.[21] Thus, at the limit, whether we should keep referring to vertical competition with regard

---

[21] And, incidentally, as presidents of the respective councils, three prominent politicians, Jacques Chirac (until recently), Valéry Giscard d'Estaing, and Charles Pasqua.

to intergovernmental competition at the subcentral level is not entirely clear.

In fact, we should distinguish two cases. In the foregoing example, the city is not included in the *département*, and the *département* is not included in the region. In this case, competition should probably be assimilated to horizontal rather than to vertical competition. For obvious reasons, however, comparisons between governments situated at different levels of jurisdiction are likely to be more frequent and significant when there is a relationship of inclusion between the governments concerned. If this is so, the fact that, in spatial and electoral terms, a jurisdiction C is included or encompassed in a jurisdiction B is not without effect on the nature of the relationship between the two governments, and this is true even when B has no authority over C. In other words, competition between B and C will be different from horizontal competition between C and another government situated at the same level of jurisdiction – or, more generally, any government C' not involved in an inclusive relationship with C. In the case of horizontal competition, the voters of jurisdiction C have nothing to do with government C'. In particular, they cannot increase or reduce support to C'. The only political markets are the ones between the incumbents and the opposition in each of the two jurisdictions. The tournament or yardstick competition between governments C and C' is of a purely informational kind. However, in the case of competition between governments B and C (jurisdiction C being included in jurisdiction B), in addition to being informational, competition is for electoral support. The voters of C are also the voters of B and change the distribution of their support to the two governments as a consequence of changes in their relative assessment. Competition, beyond rank order, is also for the patronage of the same constituency. This becomes particularly clear in the case of an open conflict between C and B. Then, voters can play the role of arbiters and their votes (or expected votes) can compel one of the two governments to give in.

Whether that first difference caused by the existence of an inclusive relationship is really significant, only further research could tell. In any case, a second difference is probably more important. It concerns interjurisdictional spillovers. Voters and officeholders of C are not directly concerned with the opinions or feelings of voters or officeholders in the other jurisdictions included in B. This gives these officeholders an inducement to neglect the effects of their policies on these other jurisdictions. Politicians in office in B are in a different position. Their chances of winning the next election depend on assessments made by voters in all the lower-level jurisdictions included in B. Consequently, if policies adopted in C have spillover effects on the welfare of citizens in other parts of B, politicians in B will not disregard them in the same way that politicians in C may be inclined to do (but may not – see Breton and Salmon, 1999). This again changes the nature of competition between B and C and makes it different from horizontal competition.

5   Concluding remarks

Because most commentators on decentralization in France have not read Breton, they are taken aback by what they perceive as the untidiness of decision making at the level of subcentral government.[22] Once one has read Breton, instead of disorder one might be inclined to see competition and consider a large part of the discussion of the matter in France as mistaken. What is typically perceived as a set of problems (duplication of responsibilities, blurring of the distinctions between levels, spatial variation in priorities and in levels of taxation and borrowing; excessively innovative or unorthodox schemes, etc.) often illustrates instead essential aspects of what Breton calls intergovernmental competition. Thus, if one believes in the virtues of competition of that kind, there may be reasons to find something satisfactory in the present situation, in which a lively competition at the bottom is combined with monitoring rather than competition at the top.[23] A question then arises: what are the prospects for decentralization to be pushed further? To conclude this very tentative essay, let me consider three points.

First, although the process of decentralization that has taken place in France in the eighties is really impressive (Schmidt, 1990), one may find it still too limited or circumscribed. Another substantial transfer of responsibilities to regions, for instance in the areas of education, culture, and health, would not necessarily change the type of intergovernmental competition analyzed here. Of course, it would require that two important issues be tackled. One is how to combine the need to increase the resources available to regions and the need to safeguard their autonomy in matters of taxation (see Gilbert and Guengant, 1991, 2nd ed. 1998). The other is how to get more resource equalization at each level.[24]

---

[22] For some collective volumes dedicated to an assessment and discussion of decentralization in France, see Conseil Régional de Picardie (1992), Gilbert and Delcamp (1993), and Institut de la Décentralisation (1996).

[23] Among current problems whose seriousness cannot be denied, however, the two most prominent, perhaps, are the growth of expenditures at some of the levels, and corruption. I venture the view that both problems will prove to be transitory.

[24] Some equalization (more than generally thought), integrated into the general grant given by the central government, already exists at the level of communes, and a law of

Second, should not decentralization be more strongly protected, perhaps constitutionally? The question is topical because the practice of "*cumul des mandats*" is endangered.[25] Third, the two preceding points might suggest a move toward something like regionalism, federalism, or quasi-federalism. The question that is the most debatable in my opinion is whether regions should be given authority over lower-level jurisdictions. Here, one must distinguish between *départements* and communes. There are reasons to think that, inasmuch as it is generally believed that there are too many levels of jurisdiction, the level of *départements* is the one the most likely to be sacrificed.[26] To give regions authority over communes or over their intercommunal creatures is another matter. Large cities are currently very powerful, prestigious, and autonomous entities. Subordinating them to regional governments would completely change the system and bring it close to a form of federalism. In France, as in most other European countries, municipal government is the one that citizens like best. Would it be sufficiently protected, notably with regard to its finances, if its well-being were entrusted to the regions? Another consideration to keep in mind is the build-up, already referred to, of the European level as the quasi-federal highest level. When, or if, simultaneously, the regions of a country are becoming more or less like the states of a federation, the question arises of the conditions that must be satisfied for multilevel federalism to work, a question that in the current debates is not given the attention that it deserves.[27]

References

Breton, A. 1987. Towards a theory of competitive federalism, *European Journal of Political Economy*, **3** (1–2), 263–329.

1995 initiated its extension to the other levels. But more equalization would become indispensable if decentralization were extended to basic services such as education and health.

[25] I have already noted the possibility that voters themselves could monitor competition between levels. An encouraging indication is some evidence from surveys that voters trust more willingly subcentral than central governments (see, e.g., Lancelot, 1992).

[26] As argued elsewhere (Salmon, 1993), a slow process of transfer of powers from the *départements* to the other levels, leading ultimately to the *département* level becoming insignificant, is probably in the order of things. Among various reasons, *départements* are increasingly challenged by the contractual building up of intercommunal institutions. To give regions some authority over *départements*, although politically very difficult, might be justified in this context.

[27] Except, under the concept of the "*Europe des régions*," when the level whose waning is announced is that of the national governments, a perspective which I do not find plausible.

1996. *Competitive Governments: An Economic Theory of Politics and Public Finance.* Cambridge University Press, Cambridge and New York.

Breton, A., and P. Salmon. 1999. A comparison of international and internal barriers to trade. Mimeo.

Brosio, G. 1994. *Equilibri instabili: Politica ed economia nell'evoluzione dei sistemi federali.* Bollati Boringhieri, Turin.

1996. Introduzione alla ricerca, in *Federalismo fiscale: Proposta per un modello italiano*, G. Brosio, ed., pp. 13–40, IRER and Franco Angeli, Milan.

Conseil Régional de Picardie, eds. 1992. *1972–1982–1992: Deux décennies de régionalisation, Colloque Amiens-Picardie des 17 et 18 octobre 1991.*

Crédit Local de France – Dexia. 1998. *Dix ans de finances locales 1896–1996: Statistiques commentées.* Librairie Générale de Droit et de Jurisprudence, Paris.

Giarda, P. 1995. *Regioni e federalismo fiscale.* Il Mulino, Bologna.

Gilbert, G., and A. Delcamp (eds). 1993. *La décentralisation dix ans après: Actes du colloque organisé au Palais du Luxembourg les 5 et 6 février 1992.* Librairie Générale de Droit et de Jurisprudence, Paris.

Gilbert, G., and A. Guengant. 1991. *La fiscalité locale en question.* 2nd ed., 1998. Montchrestien, Paris.

Institut de la Décentralisation. 1996. *La décentralisation en France: L'état des politiques publiques, la dynamique des réformes locales, la dimension européenne.* La Découverte, Paris.

Kerouanton, M.-H. 1999. L'emploi dans les collectivités locales, *INSEE-Première*, **637**.

Lancelot, A. 1992. Deux décennies de régionalisation, in Conseil Régional de Picardie (1992), pp. 164–177.

Le Galès, P. 1995. Regional economic policies: An alternative to French economic Dirigisme?, in *The End of the French Unitary State? Ten Years of Regionalization in France (1982–1992)*, J. Loughlin and S. Mazey, eds., pp. 72–91, Frank Cass, London.

Mabileau, A. 1997. Les génies invisibles du local: Faux-semblants et dynamique de la décentralisation, *Revue Française de Science Politique*, **47** (3–4), 340–376.

Majone, G. 1996. *Regulating Europe.* Routledge, London and New York.

Marcou, G. (ed.). 1994. *State Budget Support to Local Governments: A Report for the SIGMA Programme.* OECD, Paris.

Mény, Y. 1992. *La corruption de la République.* Fayard, Paris.

Ohnet, J.-M. 1996. *Histoire de la décentralisation française.* Le Livre de Poche, Paris.

Olivier, L. 1998. La perception du cumul des mandats: Restrictions contextuelles et politiques à un apparent consensus, *Revue Française de Science Politique*, **48** (6), 756–771.

Ordeshook, P. C. 1992. Constitutional stability, *Constitutional Political Economy*, **3** (2), 136–175.

Piperno, S. 1996. I rapporti finanzari e funzionali tra Regioni ed Enti locali, in *Federalismo fiscale: Proposta per un modello italiano*, G. Brosio, ed., pp. 231–258, IRER and Franco Angeli, Milan.

Preteceille, E. 1991. From centralization to decentralization: Social restructuring and French local government, in *State Restructuring and Local Power: A*

Comparative Perspective, C. Pickvance and E. Preteceille, eds., pp. 123–149, Pinter, London and New York.

Riker, W. H. 1964. *Federalism: Origins, Operation, Significance*. Little, Brown & Co, Boston.

Roux, A. 1993. Le Conseil Constitutionnel et la décentralisation, in Guy Gilbert and Alain Delcamp (eds), pp. 51–88.

Salmon, P. 1987. Decentralisation as an incentive scheme, *Oxford Review of Economic Policy*, **3** (2), 24–43.

1993. Transferts de compétences et réallocation du capital social à la disposition des collectivités territoriales, *Revue Economique*, **44** (4), 821–834.

1998. La regionalizzazione nei sistemi unitari: il caso francese. *Amministrare* **28** (1), 26–38.

1999. Ordinary elections and constitutional arrangements. Mimeo. Forthcoming in *Rules and Reason: Perspectives on Constitutional Political Economy*, R. Mudambi, P. Navarra, and G. Sobbrio, eds., Cambridge University Press, Cambridge and New York.

Schmidt, V. A. 1990. *Democratizing France: The Political and Administrative History of Decentralization*. Cambridge University Press, Cambridge and New York.

Solé-Vilanova, J. 1990. Regional and local finance in Spain: Is fiscal responsibility the missing element?, in *Decentralization, Local Governments, and Markets: Towards a Post-welfare Agenda*, R. J. Bennett, ed., pp. 331–354, Clarendon Press, Oxford.

Suárez-Pandiello, J. 1996. Financing local government in Spain: New solutions to old problems, *Environment and Planning C: Government and Policy*, **14**, 411–430.

Weatherhill, S. 1995. *Law and Integration in the European Union*. Oxford University Press, Oxford and New York.

Weingast, B. R. 1993. Constitutions as governance structures: The political foundations of secure markets, *Journal of Institutional and Theoretical Economics*, **149** (1), 286–311.

PART IV

Ethnicity and nationalism

CHAPTER 11

Nationalism and federalism: The political constitution of peace

Geoffrey Brennan and Alan Hamlin

> Care must be taken ... to ensure that devolution of political authority does not ... allow for retrogression toward the "natural" chaos of tribal anarchy in which groups are classified along racial, ethnic or religious lines. Competition among units within an integrated [federal] polity with a strong but limited central authority, this is a pattern to be desired. But as among the separate units themselves, the membership should ideally be classified orthogonally to tribal boundaries.
>
> J. M. Buchanan, "Three Research Programs in Constitutional Political Economy"

I Federalism, Europe, and the legacy of war

Albert Breton's name is associated with three major themes in the economic theory of politics: bureaucracy, nationalism, and federalism. And he has done important and highly original work in all three areas. In this chapter, we shall be concerned with two of these areas – nationalism and federalism and, more particularly, with the intersection between the two. More specifically, we shall seek to engage the question, What are the implications for the optimal design of a federal structure of a political process in which nationalism is a highly significant feature?

This is not a question that has received much serious attention in the public choice literature.[1] There are several reasons for this state of affairs. For one thing, the political model typically used in the "rational actor" tradition makes an assumption about agent motivation that does not leave much scope for nationalism as a primary phenomenon: agents may

---

[1] There are some pregnant suggestions in some of Buchanan's recent work, however. See his review of Jean Hampton's *Political Philosophy* and his "Transcending Genetic Limits."

exploit distinctions of various kinds between nations to promote their individual interests, but neither the existence nor the promotion of nationalist sentiment itself seems to be particularly plausible within that model. In the same way, the principles of politico-fiscal decentralization developed in the standard economic analysis of federalism are derived in the context of a model in which the spatial features of public goods and taxes, and the mobility of resources, play the central roles, and where nationalist or local affections and loyalties play at most an implicit role or, more commonly, no role at all.

Yet, as a matter of fact, many (perhaps most) federal systems are constructed *because* loyalties and rivalries render a potential or actual unitary political organization problematic. In other words, the driving force in federal partitions is more often the desire to minimize the likelihood of conflict by satisfying the demand for more local autonomy/identity, than to exploit possible efficiencies in the provision of local public goods. Quebec is a separate province in Canada, for example, more by virtue of its localized cultural and political identity than because of any spatial efficiencies in the provision of traditional public goods. Within the Spanish federation, the special treatment of the "autonomous regions" and the impulse toward separatism in the Basque and Catalan communities is also best explained in terms of their particularly strong localized identities. Other cases – the partitioning of India, Pakistan, and ultimately Bangladesh after the demise of imperial rule; the federal structure of Nigeria along tribal lines; the issue of Scottish devolution in the United Kingdom, to mention a few – may also be seen as cases in which localized identities and loyalties are fundamental. To seek to explain or even inform such cases by appeal to interjurisdictional public goods or tax spillovers involves either a radical reconstruction of the idea of what a "public good" is (so that "political identity" becomes the main public good that states provide) or an obstinate placing of the blind eye to the telescope. In short, to attempt to explain and/or proffer advice on the most obvious and vibrant aspects of real-world federalism by reference to the standard analysis of "the economics of federalism" is to invite making oneself look ridiculous.

Perhaps the most interesting contemporary example of a federal experiment is the "European project." Clearly, what is at stake in this project is exactly the kind of recasting of political/jurisdictional boundaries and reallocation of collective-decision responsibilities with which the "economics of federalism" deals. In an interesting, and ultimately highly instructive, commentary on the European project, Dennis Mueller (1996) applies the expanded efficiency tests of the economic federalism literature and poses the central normative question within that framework – namely, what precisely *are* the interjurisdictional spillovers that the creation of a supranational European polity is supposed to internalize? Mueller's answer to this question is guardedly negative: "One might argue that there are *no* market failures whose geographic impact matches the boundaries of today's EU" (p. 298). And, one might add, none that seems to match the boundaries of any plausible *future* EU either. Mueller is probably right here – but one could as easily conclude that this fact reveals a narrowness in the analytic categories that Mueller employs, as conclude that it identifies a significant inadequacy in the case for the European Union.[2] After all, to take the European project on its own terms, it has always been clear that a *primary* impulse of the exercise has been to reduce the likelihood of the kinds of conflicts that characterized Europe in the first half of the twentieth century. European peace was an explicit theme in Jean Monnet's foundational rhetoric – and remains a vibrant element in the speeches of the EU's most vigorous and influential supporters (Helmut Kohl and Jacques Chirac, for example). Even accepting Mueller's claim about the geographic scope of *market* failures, one surely cannot deny the legitimacy of anxiety about the geographic scope of possible *political* failures. Seen through the lens of twentieth-century European experience, it seems self-evident that political failures associated with nationalism have exerted huge "negative externalities" throughout Europe and beyond. Perhaps it is the case that closer political union would not solve such "political externality" problems. Perhaps *European* Union specifically is a ward against an angel of death that has long since passed over – perhaps. But whether these particular criticisms of the European project are valid or not is in no real way informed by the analysis offered by the traditional "economics of federalism." And it is therefore natural to question whether the conventional economic theory of federalism engages with the central issues.

It should be noted here that, if there is a failure in the conventional economic theory, the failure is *not* that the theory takes no account of political processes: in fact, the economics of federalism is much more explicitly informed by public-choice insights than almost any other area of economic analysis. The problem lies, we believe, in the nature of the model of politics that public-choice theory promotes, and in the kinds of issues that the theory highlights as normatively relevant. As recognized long ago by Thomas Hobbes, the chief good that stable political order

---

[2] A discussion of the European project that is rather closer to our own, and stresses the idea of individual attachments to political entities, is provided by Salmon (1995).

seeks to deliver is *peace*. Kant famously argued[3] that peace depends on the more detailed nature of the political regime, and that the only prospect for providing "perpetual peace" was republican democracy. In this chapter, we aim to recapture the normative preoccupation with peace, and to ask what role federalism specifically might play in promoting peace in the face of nationalist tensions. The central issue here is therefore captured by the question: What is the optimal size and structure of political units? This question is exactly the one that the conventional political economy of federalism engages. The distinctive features here lie in the focus on peace as a primary value, and the underlying model of politics that we shall employ.

Our discussion of this question begins, in section II, with a brief description of the main aspects of the standard economic approach to federalism. We then proceed to sketch the model of political process we shall employ, and use it to explain the possibility of "democratic" wars, and the particular impulses to which that possibility attaches (section III). Section IV offers an outline of a model of the optimal *size* of "nations," based on underlying assumptions about key parameters – the capacity to wage war; the vibrancy of community feeling; and the rationality of collective decision processes. Section V adds a discussion of the optimal *structure* of nations – including specifically the 'divided sovereignty' aspect of federalism, as well as the implications of jurisdictional specialization in particular policy areas, and specialization in military matters in particular. Section VI offers a brief conclusion.

Throughout, the style of the discussion is abstract and conceptual. We wish to set out an outline of an account that recognizes the political significance of nationalism, and links that recognition to a potential role for federalism in restraining nationalist excess. We will not offer any evidence to support the particular claims about federal structures that we derive, nor will we engage with the application of this account to the details of the European case. At one level, our argument can be viewed as merely *illustrative* of the kinds of considerations that might weigh if political institutions were to be designed with the ambitions of internal and external peace uppermost in mind. But such considerations are ones that the European project highlights. And, alongside them, the considerations that are central in the more conventional economic account of federalism rather pale in significance.

II   The economic analysis of federalism

The standard economic analysis of federalism has two major strands – one focusing on the spatial properties of public goods (in the Samuel-

---

[3] In 1795, reprinted as Kant (1939).

sonian sense), the other focusing on mobility among jurisdictions. We consider these strands briefly in turn.[4]

1   The spatial dimension

The central considerations here revolve around three sets of individuals: the set of persons who benefit from a particular public good, denoted B_J, where J designates the particular public good in question; the set of persons who are effective taxpayers under a particular tax used to finance the public good, T_I, where I designates the tax in question; and the set of persons who vote on the level of J provision – the set of citizens C_J. Essentially, the object of federal design is to bring these three sets into tolerable alignment. If one or other set is ill-matched with the others, then problems of various kinds emerge; and indeed, it is possible to categorize the possible problems that may emerge by reference to this schema. So, for example:

(i) $B_J > C_J = T_I$ implies rational free-riding in the provision of J, analogous to that occurring in the marketplace, and predicts the undersupply of J;

(ii) $B_J = C_J < T_I$ predicts an overexpansion of J provision, as citizens rationally vote for expenditures to be paid for, in part, by others;

(iii) $B_J = C_J > T_I$ implies scope for either underexpansion or overexpansion of J provision, depending on whether the taxpaying group is a majority or minority of the citizenry, C.

And so on.

Accordingly, if the political structure is already given, the analysis indicates which expenditure responsibilities and which tax instruments should be assigned to which levels of government. To the extent that the size of B_J is a decision variable – that is, to the extent that there are various technologies for providing the public good that vary in their degree of "publicness" – then the choice of technology must weigh purely productive efficiencies against those "public choice" efficiencies associated with closer alignment of the benefiting population with the relevant tax base and political jurisdictions. In some treatments, the choice of publicness-technology is detached from questions of taxing and voting: government decision making is taken to be driven by a benevolent despot who applies utilitarian "efficiency" considerations directly to all expenditure policy questions. In that framework, "fiscal federalism" becomes

---

[4] A more detailed sketch of the economic analysis of federalism, and further references, are provided in Brennan and Hamlin (1998b).

a matter of purely administrative decentralization, depending solely on the spatial properties of various public goods. The public-choice-informed account of spatial *alignments* between benefiting, taxpaying, and voting groups seems, however, more complete, more plausible, and more attentive to the essentially *political* dimensions of federalism.

If, at the most general level, the political structure is itself a decision variable, it is possible to devise an "optimal constitution" in which the size of political jurisdictions can be adjusted to match benefit and taxation areas, as well as vice versa. It is this broader analytical agenda that is particularly relevant to the issues at stake in the European project, and hence to the matters we seek to focus on here. In that connection, two related aspects of the framework are worth noting. First, although in principle demand for local/regional/national identity *could* be factored into this analysis, it generally is not. What matters, for example, is the *size* of jurisdictions, not the way those jurisdictions are constituted across salient historical, cultural, ethnic, or linguistic divides. Once these latter aspects are admitted, however, matters become more complicated. If a particular religious or ethnic group is regionally concentrated, then that group may form a "natural" political jurisdiction; considerations of the spatial properties of public goods and taxes may be entirely secondary. Note, however, the use of the conditional "may" here. Whether political jurisdictions *ought* to be designed along these religious or ethnic lines is a matter to be scrutinized. The very "naturalness" of such divides should not exempt them from interrogation.

The second (somewhat related) point about the standard framework is that the model of politics used is essentially "interest-based": the crucial parameters refer exclusively to the effect of jurisdictional structure on citizens' *interests*. Voting is presumed to be driven by "fiscal residuals" – the excess of (marginal) benefits over (marginal) taxes paid for voters within each jurisdiction. This emphasis is entirely consistent with public-choice orthodoxy, but seems to us to be misplaced. It hinges on an instrumental view of the individual vote – on the idea that each voter votes as if her vote *brings about* the outcome to which the vote is attached. But this is, we believe, a mistaken view. Each individual, if she is rational, recognizes that the probability of her vote actually deciding the issue is very small – that if she voted in some way other than the calculus of private interest indicates, the political outcome would almost certainly not be affected. Accordingly, if there are any considerations at all that might induce a voter to express support for one or another electoral option *for the sake of the expression itself*, such considerations will predictably be much more significant in electoral politics than in analogous market settings (where the choosing agent does get what he or she chooses). Voting is an opportunity to pass comment on the electoral alternatives – to applaud. And in predicting electoral behavior and the nature of political competition, we need to focus much more on those attributes of political options that induce voters to applaud, rather than on those aspects that might serve voters' interests. Voting is "associational" or "symbolic" or "identificational," in short, voting is "expressive," rather than instrumental. And things like the voter's ideological position and moral values, and the candidates' personal attributes (exemplary character, for example, but also tribal, ethnic, and linguistic associations) are predictably more important than the voter's expected net gain from policies pursued.[5]

Now, one can perhaps overstate the conflict between expressive and instrumental considerations: we do not need to claim that individual interests are totally irrelevant, or that the issues that will excite expressive concern are completely distinct from those that arouse instrumental interest. Our more modest claim is that expressive considerations – whatever they are – will be systematically more important in political, voting contexts than they will be in market, choosing contexts more familiar to most economists. If I am a Croat voting in a national Yugoslav election, I may vote for a Croat candidate rather than for a Serb candidate who offers a more beneficial policy package because I can express my ethnic and religious identity by my vote at very low expected (instrumental) cost. By contrast, when choosing to hire a plumber, I am more likely to choose the best or cheapest plumber available regardless of whether he is a Serb or a Croat – the instrumental considerations are foregrounded by the strictly consequential nature of the choice. Serbs and Croats may live easily together in the market context, but the nature of the political process may divide them.

At the same time, electoral competition among rational candidates will tend to focus on "expressive" elements. Rhetoric (political advertising) will be a significant element in democratic processes and will tend to focus on expressive considerations. There is, then, under the "expressive" account of politics both a static and a dynamic aspect: the static aspect has voters identifying themselves across salient divides; the dynamic aspect has rhetorical competition among candidates underlining and reinforcing these divides, and political-rhetorical entrepreneurs occasionally inventing new identities (or reinventing old ones). Thus, the

---

[5] The expressive account of voting is discussed in detail in Brennan and Lomasky (1993) and in Brennan and Hamlin (1998a). In Brennan and Hamlin (2000) we attempt a much more wide-ranging account of an expressive approach to constitutional design.

communities and causes that voters identify with become, in the expressive theory of voting, both a significant "demand-side" fact *and* a significant "supply-side" resource. These two observations are central to the model of politics we shall develop in a little more detail in section III. Before we do this, however, we need to say a little about the mobility dimension of the standard economic analysis of federalism.

2   *The mobility dimension*

Mobility is important because it offers citizens an exit option relative to the government they face. Such an exit option is important both in itself and in relation to the incentives it creates for the behavior of political "managers." The mere fact that citizens of a jurisdiction can exit will, under plausible circumstances, set limits on the extent to which these citizens can be exploited. If jurisdictional governors choose *random* policy combinations, for example, residents faced with particularly bad outcomes can exercise their right of moving to another jurisdiction where the policy outcome is preferable – and the exercising of such mobility rights will be of lower cost by virtue of a federal structure.

This lower cost exit option will be valuable even if its existence induces no supply-side responses. But if residents are bearers of net taxable capacity and if jurisdictional governors derive any share of total rents (or if esteem of office is positively related to jurisdictional size), then jurisdictions may actively compete for residents and be led, like genuinely competitive firms, as if by an invisible hand, to offer policy packages that are attractive to their residents. Or at least this would be so if all residents were equally mobile. Opponents of interjurisdictional competition tend to point out that residents/factors-of-production are *not* equally mobile, and that competition of this type tends to redistribute from the less mobile to the more mobile. Thus, interjurisdictional tax competition will often involve lower (even negative) rates of taxation on mobile capital and higher rates of taxation on relatively immobile labor than would prevail if the same aggregate expenditure and tax revenue were to obtain in the absence of mobility and competition. It is, however, by no means clear that interjurisdictional competition would leave aggregate spending and taxing unchanged: It could be argued that the very point of interjurisdictional competition is to influence these aggregates.[6]

It is a feature of the standard argument for federal structures that such structures tend to reduce mobility costs and encourage interjurisdic-

---

[6] See, for example, Brennan and Buchanan (1980), Chapter 9.

tional competition. This is so whether the federal structure involves creating a larger, more inclusive polity out of existing ones (federalism from below), where the emphasis is normally on the reduction of mobility costs through the elimination of artificial barriers; or political devolution to smaller jurisdictions from larger (federalism from above), where the emphasis is normally on the stimulation of interregional competition. At this level of generality, smaller jurisdictions are normally to be preferred on mobility grounds, since mobility is physically easier and the number of alternative options larger. In this sense, the argument for federalism based on mobility interacts with the spatial considerations outlined above to create a presumption in favor of a largest feasible number of jurisdictions at every level in any jurisdictional hierarchy. Equally, it is worth noting that jurisdictional boundaries based on salient linguistic, cultural, ethnic, or religious divides tend to inhibit mobility and hence reduce the benefits that the mobility dimension of the economic account of federalism offers.

III   Nationalism and the politics of war

Voting is undeniably a cause of electoral outcomes, but this does not mean that electoral outcomes are the reason for voting. Within the expressive account of politics, voting is essentially a consumption activity – something done for its own sake, by virtue of its direct expressive benefits. One such direct expressive benefit involves the voter's "identification" with one or another of the options offered. It will often be a particular party – or perhaps a particular candidate – who is seen to instantiate particular values or beliefs with which the voter identifies. The capacity of parties or candidates to associate themselves in voters' minds with the values/beliefs with which an appropriately large numbers of voters will identify is an important element in electoral competition. This process of party association is, however, necessarily self-effacing, in the sense that to the extent that parties/candidates are seen to identify with prevailing values merely as a means of getting additional votes, their efforts will be less effective. Indeed, it will pay parties to establish well-grounded reputations for embodying particular values: the cost of pursuing newly emergent, more fashionable values will be the appearance of integrity forgone.[7] This fact in turn encourages parties to attach them-

---

[7] An essentially expressive argument that uses these ideas to develop an argument for popular voting over candidates rather than popular voting over alternative policies – that is, for representative democracy rather than direct democracy – is offered in Brennan and Hamlin (1999).

selves to and develop strong associations with values that are less ephemeral and more widely shared.

We want to argue that among such values will be a concern for the "national interest" rather than the "public interest" – for "nationalism" rather than "social welfare." Although parties will want to differentiate themselves to some extent from their opposition, it will typically be profitable electorally to present their distinctiveness in terms of a particular view of what the national interest consists in, rather than to oppose the national interest. The rhetoric of electoral competition will tend to concentrate around telling articulations of "motherhood" values, and hence serve to reinforce those values. One such "motherhood" value is the "national interest," and since this value depends on the existence of a radical disjunction between those who are members of the "nation" and those who are "outsiders," the promotion of this value will often promote, in turn, a heightened sense of nationalist awareness and a heightened xenophobia.

Breton's writings on nationalism tend to focus on the private interests of particular groups as the primary stimulus for promotion of nationalist sentiment. Breton argues that, because nationalism characteristically redistributes wealth between "nationals" and "foreigners," and in particular favors "the middle classes" (see Breton, 1964 and Breton and Breton, 1995), this consequence must *explain* the promotion of nationalist sentiment.[8] We consider explanations of this type to be at best partial, because they fail to take sufficiently seriously the "free-rider" problem in rationalizing individual action (including individual voting) in support of nationalism. It may be that the middle classes will be led by class identification to support differentially policies that increase the wealth of the middle classes. But the direct link between *my* interests as a member of the middle classes and my particular vote is mediated by the "veil of insignificance" – the fact, that is, that my vote will in all probability not cause the outcome for which it expresses support.

Moreover, many nationalist policies do not so much redistribute between nationals and foreigners as they do between different groups of nationals – and it is not always the middle classes specifically that benefit. Restrictions on the sale of domestic assets to foreigners, for example, may protect *some* middle-class individuals from the threat of foreign takeover but are not obviously in the interests of domestic wealth-holders as a whole. Restrictions on international capital flows more generally may serve to keep domestic rates of return higher for net

---

[8] The private interest basis of group identity is also explored by Hardin (1995).

capital-importing countries but keep them lower for capital-exporting countries and probably render all domestic capital owners more susceptible to higher tax rates than they would face in a world of free capital movement.

Given that citizens can be expected to vote expressively, and that nationalist sentiments loom large among their expressive concerns, political parties can be expected systematically to promote nationalist sentiment. Similarly, special interest groups will wherever possible use "national interest" arguments to clothe their special pleading. What Canadian political party will make a public assault on "the Canadian way of life" (whatever exactly that may mean)? That way of life, along with "truth," "beauty," "justice," "integrity" (the list can be extended, though not indefinitely) is something that everyone (at least, every Canadian) supports, and with which all political parties of whatever persuasion will seek to create powerful associations.

Notice that we do not claim that nationalist sentiment is in any way irrational – we are content to see nationalist sentiment and urges as desires alongside other desires in the basic motivational makeup of rational individuals. Our claim is, rather, that the particular institutional arrangements associated with democratic politics tend to highlight some desires while backgrounding others. In particular, the institution of voting tends to highlight expressive considerations and background instrumental considerations – highlighting nationalism and backgrounding interests. And this fact will have considerable implications for both the predictions one would wish to make concerning political decision making, and for the normative evaluation of those decisions.

Not all nationalist sentiment is necessarily "xenophobic." But as Breton and Breton (1995, p. 211) recognize, much of it often is. That is, nationalism takes the form not just of promoting a nation, but also of deprecating "competitive" nations and harboring suspicion of "foreigners" and/or of foreign influence. As Schumpeter (1991, p. 211) writes, "Nationalism is affirmative awareness of national character, together with an aggressive spirit of superiority." It is this xenophobic aspect that transmutes an affection for the "Canadian," "Australian," or "British" way of life into anxiety and mistrust concerning other "ways of life." Such xenophobia is the primary resource of the bellicose and creates the link between nationalism and war that is so crucial to the implicit theorizing of the new Europhiles. It may not be entirely true that "nationalism is war," as Helmut Kohl is reported to have declared; but this is an understandable view of one who contemplates twentieth-century European history. And it can hardly be denied that nationalism is a necessary condition for the modern conception of war between nations: one needs a "core of national sentiment" to be mobilized in the face of perceived aggression from foreign powers. And what is such a striking feature of the European experience (and more generally) is how readily that nationalist sentiment *can* be aroused and transformed into an enthusiasm for conflict.

As Hayek puts it (1976, vol. 2, p. 134): "Most people are still unwilling to face the most alarming lesson of modern history: that the greatest crimes of our time have been committed by governments that had the enthusiastic support of millions of people who were guided by moral impulses." Moreover, he observes soberingly, "It is simply not true that Hitler or Mussolini, Lenin or Stalin, appealed only to the worst instincts of their people: they also appealed to some of the feelings which also dominate contemporary democracies." Hayek may present a rather different diagnosis than the one offered here – but his general point bears.

The puzzle in the pursuit of war is how it can be the case that an activity that yields very substantial net expected costs (even to the so-called "victors") can be consistent with generally rational behavior. This may seem to be less of a puzzle in the case of a dictatorial regime. In this case, since the dictator does not bear the full cost of his own actions, it is perhaps plausible to suppose that the dictator may find that bellicose policies increase the expected wealth *of the dictator*, even though the expected costs to the dictator's subjects may be huge. But this possibility makes inadequate allowance for the enthusiasm with which large numbers of the dictator's subjects embrace the reckless warlike course – and indeed for the necessity of their doing so if the war is to be pursued faithfully and successfully. After all, opportunities of various kinds to "free-ride" arise – even for combatants.[9] In any event, our own discussion here deals with democracies, and two recent examples are worth recounting.

On the eve of the Falklands War, Margaret Thatcher was in serious electoral trouble. An election was not far away, and the Tories were expected to lose: The public opinion polls indicated a solid Labour victory. But the Falklands War changed all that. Summoning up a nationalist unity in the face of the Argentinean threat and enthused by the *success* of Britain's defiant stand, the citizenry backed their government, displayed their national loyalty, and Mrs. Thatcher was duly returned to office in the subsequent election. We are aware that other interpretations of these events are possible, including the possibility that the Tory success can be explained by the improvement in economic condi-

---

[9] See Brennan and Tullock (1982) and Ardant du Picq (1991).

tions. But the interpretation we offer here undoubtedly represents a popular view.

Equally, when "Stormin" Norman Schwartztopf was roaring around in the Arabian desert, teaching Saddam Hussein a lesson he would allegedly never forget, President George Bush was, by the testimony of the opinion polls, the most popular U.S. president among his own citizens since the polls have been in operation. It is doubtful whether George Washington or James Madison or Thomas Jefferson (during their incumbencies, at least) ever enjoyed such vibrant and widespread support. Yet a mere year later, when the shouting and tumult had died away and the captains and kings had departed, George Bush was still there – looking increasingly like an "ancient sacrifice" – but now the most *un*popular president in modern U.S. history. In this case the half-life of the public approval associated with a military adventure was short, but there can be no denying that the military adventure was popular and that this popularity attached to political leaders.

We do not claim, in either case, that the electoral or popularity advantages were the sole or even the major motive for the military involvement. Our point is simply to note the apparent positive relationship between expressions of political support (whether in the opinion polls or at the voting booth) and at least certain types of military activity. Within the public-choice tradition, in which electoral competition is supposed to be the chief discipline on political conduct, this positive relation is a source of concern. Far from constraining nationalist and xenophobic tendencies, democratic politics may actually promote them: If it is true that a "good" war increases the political popularity and likely electoral success of incumbents, this is a rather alarming fact.

In recent papers, Hess and Orphanides (1995, 1997) develop a rational-actor model of democracy in which war is a characteristic feature. Their model makes no use of the idea of expressive voting, but rather operates via a mechanism involving the signaling of an electorally desirable capacity to be a competent wartime leader – so that voters have an instrumental interest in electing a good military leader, and incumbents can signal this quality only by demonstrating it. The authors use this model to amend the Kantian hypothesis concerning the relationship between democracy and "perpetual peace" such that, although the Kantian possibility is still available, there will be other equilibria in which wars between democracies will occur.

Our own model is rather different. While we do not challenge the idea that wars might act as signals in an instrumentally rational world, we do challenge the more basic idea that democratic electoral politics is best conceived in terms of instrumental rationality. Our model, therefore,

		(Majority of) All		
		Upholding national dignity	Wimpish pusillanimity	Tie (probability h)
Each	Upholding national dignity	5	105	5
	Wimpish pusillanimity	0	100	100

Figure 11.1. The voter's dilemma.

depends on the failure of collective action that can arise from (individually rational) expressive voting. The argument is developed in Brennan and Lomasky (1993, especially pp. 49–51). Here, the basic idea can simply be illustrated, as in Figure 11.1. The illustration is one instance of the "expressive voter's dilemma" – a predicament that can (though it need not) arise in ordinary electoral politics. In this illustration, each voter within a particular nation is faced with a choice between voting for a course that expresses "national dignity" but also serves to make war more probable, on the one hand, and voting for a course that expresses appeasement or "wimpish pusillanimity" even though it also serves to reduce the probability of war, on the other hand. We make no apology for the use of such emotive labels, since it is a part of our thesis that such affective labeling will play a key role in electoral politics.

The vote raises both expressive and instrumental issues for each voter. In expressive terms, the choice is perceived as being between upholding national dignity and demonstrating a wimpish pusillanimity (a contemptible timidity); and, on a purely expressive calculus, the former is preferred by, say, 5 units, as shown in Figure 11.1.[10] In instrumental terms,

---

[10] For the sake of this illustration we will simply assume that both expressive and instrumental concerns can be measured in terms of a common, cardinal (but not necessarily interpersonally comparable) utility, so that the payoffs in Figure 11.1 can be read as utilities. Nothing in our argument depends upon this. We also assume, for simplicity, that all individuals vote simultaneously, and that each individual knows only the payoff matrix shown and some estimate of h.

however, the increased probability of war associated with the nationalist stance involves expected costs that are considerably greater, say, 100
units for our typical voter, as shown in Figure 11.1. That is, our typical
voter has a strict instrumental preference that war not be invoked; and
this is reflected in the fact that, if a majority votes for "wimpish pusillanimity," so that the probability of war is low, each will actually be better
off. Equally, if each believes that she would be decisive (h = 1), then
"wimpish pusillanimity" is the dominant strategy. But our typical voter
also has a strict expressive preference for the expression of nationalism
over wimpishness; and this is reflected in the fact that if each believes
that she would not be decisive – that is, if h = 0 and the final "tie" column
can be ignored – then voting to uphold national dignity is the dominant
strategy.

Of course, the "tie" column is not totally irrelevant to each person's
calculus: she *might* turn out to be decisive, although the probability of
that contingency in a large-scale election is very small. And as the probability of her vote actually *determining* the outcome reduces, so the relative price of expressing her nationalism falls. In our simple illustration,
she will, for example (if she is risk-neutral and acts to maximize expected
payoffs), vote for upholding national dignity, under the conjectured
payoffs, provided that *h*, the probability of an exact tie, is less than .05
(which it surely is in any large-scale election). In other words, where
expressive considerations enter, they will be rendered disproportionately
influential by the nature of the political process, and will be likely to over-
whelm even substantial instrumental costs and benefits.

Now, we should emphasize that the "dilemma" aspects of the payoff
structure illustrated in Figure 11.1 are a matter of construction, not of
logic. Pure logic cannot rule out the possibility that instrumental and
expressive considerations might point in the same direction, or that
expressive considerations might be so small as to be irrelevant. But
equally, pure logic cannot reject the dilemma possibility either. And in
the case of war, the particular values illustrated certainly seem plausible.[11] The moral to be drawn from this discussion is that the electoral
process serves to create the possibility of a kind of collective "irrationality" or political failure, and that this possibility is most likely when
expressive considerations are significant and likely to indicate action in
opposition to that indicated by instrumental considerations. The military

---

[11] It should also be noted, however, that an extremely pacific citizenry, deeply imbued
with the symbolic values of peaceableness, may be led to adopt policies of appeasement
even when a little serious saber rattling might discourage the bellicose tendencies of
others.

case seems a natural instance: Nationalistic passions are significant and so are the instrumental costs associated with them when they are too vigorously expressed.

IV   The optimal size and composition of nations

We now turn to the central issues at stake in the design of "optimal constitutions" (to use a Bretonesque phrase) – namely, the size, structure, and scope of political jurisdictions. We shall pursue the analysis in two steps. First, we consider the optimal *size* of political jurisdictions, assuming that jurisdictions are nonoverlapping. That is, we seek to partition a given territory into "nations," which are mutually exclusive and each of which has the full range of expenditure and taxing powers. Then in section V we shall examine the structural aspect – the issue, that is, of whether a federal structure is desirable and, if so, the appropriate allocation of expenditure responsibilities that goes with that structure.

In neither case will the "design" of political jurisdictions be independent of patterns of communal sentiment. However, as we have already indicated, there is both a static and a dynamic element here. The static element takes communal identities as prior to, and independent of, political jurisdiction, so that political jurisdictions must accommodate, or work within the constraints imposed by, preexisting communal identities. The dynamic element, by contrast, recognizes that the establishment of a particular political jurisdiction creates a resource base for the creation of new communal loyalties along political jurisdictional lines, and that these new loyalties may cut across the original communal identities. Both static and dynamic elements are relevant to our presumed overall normative objective – which is to minimize the expected cost of war within the given territory.

It is helpful initially to take an extremely simple case. Suppose that agents are spread uniformly across a large, featureless plain. Suppose further that the basis for communal loyalty is simply physical proximity – each agent feeling an identity with and loyalty toward another according to the physical distance between them, with the strength of feeling declining with increasing distance. Then, as the size of the political jurisdiction increases, the loyalty each member feels toward the average member of her jurisdiction declines. This decline reduces ceteris paribus the probability that the jurisdiction will make war on its neighbors. Nationalism – in this simple model and ceteris paribus – is a weaker force in larger nations.

However, we may point to two countervailing effects. One is that as the numbers included in the polity increase, the problems of collective irrationality also increase: The probability of a voter being decisive falls systematically with the number of citizens. The other is that the damage caused by any interjurisdictional squabble increases with the size of "nations": At least over some range, there are economies of scale in inflicting damage. Hobbes's war of all against all may be nasty and brutish, but each can inflict harm on others only on a face-to-face basis: In the world of wars between nations and weapons of mass destruction, things are otherwise.

To be able to determine the optimal size of political jurisdictions as the resolution of these forces would, of course, require a detailed specification of the various functional relationships, which could in any event only be illustrative. But ultimately there are only three possibilities: one where the optimal size is a corner solution identifying a single polity exhausting the whole territory; one where the solution lies in the opposite "corner," identifying anarchy, with each person constituting his or her own state; and an interior solution where the given territory would accommodate multiple political jurisdictions. Each of these possibilities doubtless has its protagonists – world government on the one hand, *no* government on the other, and the many possibilities in between.

This simple example is essentially static. To add a dynamic element, note that the creation of political jurisdictions will tend to rigidify the pattern of community loyalties (which now become nationalist) and, perhaps, to strengthen their force. This suggests that nationalist tensions will tend to grow over time, and that an appropriate "optimal design" should allow for this fact. One possibility here, we would suggest, concerns the importance of the structure of relations between jurisdictions, and we shall return to that theme below.

Physical proximity is clearly not the only basis for communal sentiment and loyalty. Where there exist cultural, ethnic, lingual, or other communities to which individuals attach loyalty and at least some antipathy directed toward nonmembers, then the picture is more complicated. How exactly one might map these communal identities onto spatial dimensions is itself unclear, since the identities in question are often nongeographic. But if there is a possibility of war among them, then the creation of political jurisdictions that cut across the preexisting communities may play a role – in both static and dynamic frameworks. The static role might simply be to diffuse communal sentiment and thereby defuse potential conflict between nations. The more dynamic role might be to add alternative structures of national commitment and loyalty that might serve to counterbalance the preexisting community ties. Note that this is not an issue of community/polity size as such, but of the mapping from communities onto political jurisdictions. However, neither the static nor the dynamic benefit is guaranteed. There are risks associated with the creation of political jurisdictions that cut across existing communities. Both the potential benefits and the associated risks can be displayed in a simple model.

Suppose, for example, that the population of a featureless, square plain divides itself into two ethnic, religious, or other communities of equal size, with their attendant sentiments of loyalty and mutual antipathy. Assume that these two communities are geographically compact, and are illustrated by the shaded and clear areas labelled U and D in Figure 11.2. Suppose further that the optimal war-minimizing jurisdictional size (as discussed earlier) is exactly the size of each of our communities. Obviously, there are any number of feasible partitions of the whole territory that will divide the plain into two optimally sized jurisdictions, of which two seem particularly salient. One is to locate the political divide along the community divide *between* U and D, the line ab in Figure 11.2. On our reasoning, this would invoke the dynamic of political rhetoric in favor of an even more clearly articulated emotional divide between U and D, and thereby increase the probability of war, ceteris paribus (and optimal size notwithstanding). The other salient divide is exactly orthogonal to the divide between communities, the line xy at right angles to ab. This arrangement creates political entities, and a dynamic of political rhetoric and political identity, that cut across the preexisting communal loyalties. Any citizen of either polity so created has twin identities, twin loyalties, and within each polity the number who identify with community U is exactly the same as the number who identify with community D.

It would, of course, also be possible to create "mixed" polities with different numbers of Us and Ds. The line x^1y^1 would achieve such a position, consistent with the optimal jurisdictional size constraint. But the unequal numbers of Us and Ds in the two polities invokes the possibility of minority repression in both jurisdictions along community lines – and potential majority support in each jurisdiction for a military adventure against the other. This is the more likely because the U majority in one jurisdiction may naturally want to "liberate" their "exploited" U brothers/sisters in the other jurisdiction – and symmetrically for the D majority in the other jurisdiction. Indeed, this possibility is sufficiently plausible that a political division along communal lines (partition ab) may prove less war-conducive than one along *quasi*-communal lines (such as x^1y^1). When, in the epigraph to this chapter, Buchanan refers to the *orthogonality* of political and tribal boundaries, he is to be taken literally.

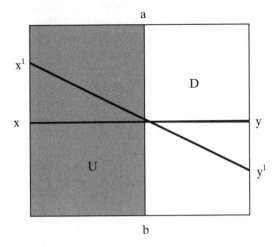

Figure 11.2. Federal partitions.

V   The optimal structure of nations

We come, at last, to the central idea of federalism as such – the idea, that is, of overlapping jurisdictions and explicitly divided political sovereignty. There are two issues here that are worth isolating. The first involves the pure theory of constitutional design – that is, whether a federal structure can provide additional institutional checks against the threat of war, even after all size and composition aspects of jurisdictional design are optimally solved. The second revolves around feasibility issues – that is, whether any additional checks associated with federalism are likely to be relevant in practical circumstances. After all, we have greatly simplified the problems outlined in the previous section in at least two important senses. First, the numbers of *U*s and *D*s were taken to be equal and conveniently distributed across the relevant territory so that it was always *possible* to create political jurisdictions of the right size and composition characteristics. But what are we to do if the numbers of *U*s and *D*s are not equal? Or if they are distributed across territory in such a way that the creation of political jurisdictions cannot meet ordinary territorial constraints – if, for example, there is an isolated pocket of *U*s surrounded by *D*s? Call this the issue of physical feasibility. The second simplification is even more important. It addresses the *political* feasibility of jurisdictional divides other than those that fall along community lines. The reason for thinking that war between *U*s and *D*s is a likely outcome is precisely a reason for thinking that orthogonality between community and jurisdictional divides may be politically infeasible. Such orthogonality seems to involve a suppression of electoral sovereignty, for on our assumptions all the natural forces of community identity would seem to dictate national boundaries along communal lines. At an appropriate constitutional level of analysis, individuals may recognize the instrumental benefits of designing polities to be orthogonal to communities; each may recognize, that is, that a political division of the world along natural communal divides is conducive to war. But at the level of the popular referendum or of any electoral contest, all voters will tend to vote on their expressive rather than their instrumental concerns, and this will encourage them to seek political community with their own kind. In this way our argument threatens to be too successful. If political action is dominated by expressive concerns, then constitutional action may also be essentially expressive in nature, so that there may be little possibility of the constitutional process selecting institutions that bind in-period politics in appropriate ways.

Our answers to both the theoretical and the feasibility problems can, of course, only be partial, and highly speculative. But, on the more theoretical point, it seems to us clear that federalism offers an important additional resource to the constitutional designer. Consider first the simple case. Suppose we have communities of the appropriate size, geography, and composition. What would a federal structure offer us here? First, it would offer intrinsically divided *political* loyalty. The citizen's political loyalties are split by virtue of the divided sovereignty that federalism involves. At each level of government, political rhetoric will have the effect of reinforcing existing communal ties and/or creating new ones; but across levels of government, political identity would be irreducibly plural. It is worth emphasizing that *political* decentralization is crucial here: mere administrative decentralization is often offered within the traditional economic theory of federalism as a way of handling the issues posed by the spatial properties of public goods, but the critical aspect of political expression is absent unless there is genuine *political* decentralization.

On our reasoning, divided political loyalty is desirable in itself: the more plural is political identity, the more ambiguous any particular military expression of it is likely to be. The very complexity of federal structures, with their lack of a clear overall sovereignty, is revealed as their chief merit. The image of an optimal constitution that is suggested is one in which at least some individual subnational political units are designed with preexisting communities in mind, so that the dynamic effects of seeing community loyalty as a political asset will tend to reinforce existing loyalties. But the fact that these various communities are a part of a larger federal nation adds both the element of divided loyalty and the possibility of allocating those functions that are most prone to nationalist excess to those levels of government that are least prone to such excess. For example, if defense and related issues are allocated to the most inclusive level of government, which is, by construction, answerable to an electorate that spans a number of distinct communities, it is relatively unlikely that voting on defense issues will be driven by any simple sense of nationalism. The expressive concerns of the electorate will be more varied than they would be if defense powers were granted to each individual community. And this is so whatever the facts about the geographic range of the public goods involved.[12]

There are, however, countervailing arguments that deserve some attention. The first concerns the rhetorical specialization that tends to be associated with functional specialization. If defense is allocated to the most inclusive political level, and most other policy functions are allocated to the more decentralized level(s), then political debate and rhetorical competition at the inclusive national level will naturally be focused on international questions and the pursuit of national interest via defense-related means. This suggests that the dynamic effect of such a constitutional arrangement might be to foster a sort of supernationalism that attaches precisely to military matters at the most inclusive level of politics. There is no doubt that such a prospect exists – that we might, in attempting to avoid the destructive power of nationalism, end up with the still more destructive power of supernationalism. But we doubt that the prospect is in any way inevitable. Two arguments support our view. First, there is the argument that the larger polity faces essentially divided loyalties for each citizen. Even if there is a degree of dynamic creation of nationalist sentiment at the more inclusive level, it will still be offset by the various loyalties at the subnational level. Of course, this implies that the retention of these regional or subnational loyalties is itself an important part of the overall structure. And this suggests that the functions allocated to these units of government should be nontrivial, in the sense that they are the sort of activities that reinforce a sense of community distinctiveness and identity (again, whatever the facts about the geographic extent of the underlying public goods). The second argument

[12] One might suggest that NATO provides an example relevant to the case of Europe. Of course, the membership of NATO is different from that of the European Union; individual EU states retain independent military forces to some extent; and there is still an active debate on the issue of a more genuinely European Defence Force. The political economy of NATO and its relationship to the federal project in Europe is of considerable interest, but beyond the scope of this essay.

is that the possibility for the dynamic creation of a military nationalism at the most inclusive level can be offset by allocating functions other than defense to that level of government, so as to avoid the most extreme form of rhetorical specialization.

The second countervailing argument concerns the vexed question of secession. It is clear that our discussion requires a degree of commitment, in the sense that the allocation of functions as between levels of government is seen as irrevocable, or at least difficult to revoke. If it is the case that each subnational community has a real exit option in the sense that it can (re)claim full nationhood and its share of military power, then the effect we claim of federalism will be reduced and, in the limit, destroyed. Indeed, we would think of such an arrangement not as federalism but as an alliance of nation-states. This point is particularly relevant to cases of federalism from below of the type epitomized by the European project. It should be recognized that the secession power very considerably weakens the force of any federal constitution: a critical aspect of the constitution's role (on our analysis) is to render the rhetoric of military action at the "tribal" level of politics illegitimate, and perhaps even unthinkable. Whatever its other benefits, a lively secession option undermines that role.

Let us now turn to the physical and political feasibility issues already mentioned. These issues are connected, because what is a physical or arithmetic necessity in one case may be a political necessity in another. Consider the case in which the population of the territory is, unobligingly, 60 percent Us and 40 percent Ds. Clearly, one possibility is to create five subnational jurisdictions, one consisting of all Us, the other four consisting of half Us and half Ds. We can then create from these jurisdictions two military "nations": one, say, composed of the all-U jurisdiction and two of the mixed jurisdictions, the other composed simply of two mixed jurisdictions. It is true that the all-U jurisdiction may be inclined to express its special communal sense militarily – but the fact that military questions are handled at a higher (more distant) level of politics offers some hope that any such tribal inclinations will be rendered ineffective.

Homogeneous, "tribal" subnational communities may be consistent with a tolerably pacific "national" polity, if those subnational communities can have their specifically military powers reassigned. The subnational communities may, in this sense, be allowed to retain their quasi-tribal identities, and their modicum of xenophobia, without these things receiving explicitly military expression. Precisely because a federal structure with jurisdictions set along tribal boundaries does not threaten existing loyalties too much, such a structure may be feasible where other more idealized structures may not. The critical feature of such a structure is its detachment of tribal loyalty from war-making capacity. Of course, constitutional design cannot provide any guarantees here and cannot hope to achieve anything without some recognition on the part of ordinary citizens of the moral ambiguity of their most fiercely held loyalties. But constituting a more inclusive state with specific and exclusive responsibility for military matters, rather than a mere alliance, can do *something*, and when there is much at stake that "something" is worthwhile. In this sense, and against the spirit of the Buchanan epigraph, a federal structure classified along tribal boundaries may still be desirable (because the "ideal" structure is infeasible), although a *national* structure along tribal lines is not.

We turn, finally, to the issue of political or electoral feasibility – the question of whether a constitution involving an appropriate federal structure that served to divide political loyalties and separate nationalist sentiment from military decision making could itself ever pass the electoral test, given our analysis of electoral behavior. The basic point to reiterate here is that the expressive approach to voting behavior points to the importance of the setting of any particular vote, and the perceptions of the alternatives offered, rather than to the instrumental implications of the alternative outcomes of the vote. We have argued that in at least some relevant settings, nationalist sentiment may be the expressive concern that is called into play, and that this may result in political failure and war. But nationalism is not the only expressive concern, and not all votes will be interpreted as an opportunity to express nationalist sentiment. There can be no presumption that just because a particular class of in-period political decisions is subject to the voters' dilemma outlined in Figure 11.1, all political decisions will have this structure. Of course, if we hold an essentially expressive view of voting behavior, we cannot argue that individuals will vote for an appropriate federal constitution on the instrumental grounds that such a constitution offers the best chance for peace; but we can believe that it is at least possible that the constitutional vote will be such that whatever expressive factors are relevant will tend to point in the same direction as those instrumental considerations, so that there is no social dilemma. This possibility will be greater to the extent that the constitutional issue is debated in the abstract – removed from any particular issue regarding which nationalist passions might run high – and to the extent that the debate is conducted across communities rather than within communities – so that there is no direct link from a nationalist sentiment to voting either for or against the proposed constitution (not least because any individual will see the proposed constitution as restricting the nationalism of others as well as restricting her own nationalism). The details here are by no means clear. All we can say is that the constitutional route offers at least the possibility of achieving the theoretically available benefits of federalism, even though that route is, of necessity, indirect. On our account, optimal constitutions (whether federal or not) cannot be democratically chosen *because* they are optimal, but may nevertheless emerge from the democratic process if they embody appropriate expressively relevant characteristics.

VI   Conclusion

The object of this chapter has been to expose what seem to us to be the general theoretical presumptions involved in the defense of the European project as a guard against war. As we see it, the questions posed by that project are precisely the same questions as are posed in the economic theory of federalism – the optimal size, scope, and structure of political jurisdictions. But the *considerations* invoked to deal with those questions and the underlying normative objectives are very different from those with which the economic theory of federalism normally deals. This may reveal either that this argument for the European project is flawed, or that the standard economist's account of federalism is inadequate. It is certainly no response to argue that the European project is about politics, while the economic theory of federalism is about economics, because the "economic theory of federalism" is into politics up to its ears. Federalism is essentially a *political* structure, and the economist's take on it, explicitly or otherwise, makes critical assumptions about how the political process works.

Here we have argued that the assumptions typically associated with the economic analysis of politics are inadequate, that they offer too instrumental and interest-based an account of the political process, and that "nationalism" (and more generally "community identity" in its various guises) is a much more potent force in in-period electoral processes than public-choice orthodoxy allows. Putting a political account of nationalism squarely into the theory of federalism makes, we think, for both a more complete account of actual federal structures and their particular problems, and a more sympathetic view of the European project. The analysis is speculative and requires both theoretical elaboration and empirical exploration. But we think it represents a viable alternative point of departure for the study of federal systems, while retaining the basic tools and essential perspective of the "economic approach."

References

C. Ardant du Picq (1991) *Battle Studies* (translated by J. N. Greely and R. C. Cotton), New York: AMS.

G. Brennan and J. M. Buchanan (1980) *The Power to Tax*, Cambridge: Cambridge University Press.

G. Brennan and L. Lomasky (1993) *Democracy and Decision*, Cambridge: Cambridge University Press.

G. Brennan and A. Hamlin (1998a) "Expressive Voting and Electoral Equilibrium," *Public Choice*, 95, 149–175.

G. Brennan and A. Hamlin (1998b) "Fiscal Federalism," in P. Newman (ed.), *The New Palgrave Dictionary of Economics and the Law*, London: Macmillan.

G. Brennan and A. Hamlin (1999) "On Political Representation," *British Journal of Political Science*, 29, 109–127.

G. Brennan and A. Hamlin (2000) *Democratic Devices and Desires*, Cambridge: Cambridge University Press.

G. Brennan and G. Tullock (1982) "An Economic Theory of Military Tactics: Methodological Individualism at War," *Journal of Economic Behavior and Organization*, 3, no. 2–3, 225–242.

A. Breton (1964) "The Economics of Nationalism," *Journal of Political Economy*, 72, no. 4, 376–386.

A. Breton and M. Breton (1995) "Nationalism Revisited," in A. Breton, G. Galeotti, P. Salmon, and R. Wintrobe (eds.), *Nationalism and Rationality*, Cambridge: Cambridge University Press.

J. M. Buchanan (1998) "Review" of *Political Philosophy* by J. Hampton, *Economics & Philosophy*, 14, no. 1, 131–135.

J. M. Buchanan (1997) "Transcending Genetic Limits," Center for Study of Public Choice Working Paper, Fairfax, Virginia.

R. Hardin (1995) "Self-Interest, Group Identity," in A. Breton, G. Galeotti, P. Salmon, and R. Wintrobe (eds.), *Nationalism and Rationality*, Cambridge: Cambridge University Press.

F. Hayek (1976) *Law, Legislation and Liberty, Vol. 2, The Mirage of Social Justice*, Chicago: University of Chicago Press.

G. Hess and A. Orphanides (1995) "War Politics: An Economic Rational-Voter Framework," *American Economic Review*, 85, no. 4, 828–846.

G. Hess and A. Orphanides (1997) "War and Democracy," University of Cambridge, mimeo.

I. Kant [1795] (1939) *Perpetual Peace*, New York: Columbia University Press.

D. Mueller (1996) "Constitutional Quandaries in Europe," *Constitutional Political Economy*, 7, no. 4, 293–302.

P. Salmon (1995) "Nations Conspiring against Themselves: An Interpretation of European Integration," in A. Breton, G. Galeotti, P. Salmon, and R. Wintrobe (eds.), *Nationalism and Rationality*, Cambridge: Cambridge University Press.

J. Schumpeter (1991) "The Sociology of Imperialisms," in *The Economics and Sociology of Capitalism*, Princeton: Princeton University Press.

CHAPTER 12

A political efficiency case for federalism in multinational states: Controlling ethnic rent seeking

Roger D. Congleton

I Introduction: Constitutional choice, rationality, and ethnic clubs

The last two decades have witnessed the most remarkable period of constitutional development since the early nineteenth century. A great wave of constitution-based democratization has swept through South America, Africa, Europe, and Asia. In most of these cases, the constitution writers confronted a population that was far from ethnically homogeneous. In most parts of the former Soviet Union the new nations included large numbers of Russians immigrants and one or more indigenous peoples. In Africa the regions to be organized and governed included many tribes with conflicting interests. In South America persons of European, Asian, and native Indian descent were to jointly govern under reformed constitutions. Constitutional reforms to accommodate differing national and ethnic interests continue to be debated in Canada and within the European Union.

Multinational countries confront a number of political and social problems that may not arise in more homogeneous countries. Perhaps the most difficult of these are political, as noted by Breton (1964). Political and social problems arise when ethno-nationalist groups use governmental powers to create and/or enforce public policies that advance ethno-nationalist aims. Such policies undermine the rule of law insofar as laws are neither enforced nor drafted with equal protection in mind. These unequal policies often undermine the legitimacy of governments in the eyes of the repressed, reducing the extent to which informal norms can be relied upon to buttress the formal rules of the state. Moreover, the mere possibility of such political power encourages ethno-nationalist groups to seek or resist that political power in a manner which unproductively consumes considerable time, energy, and other resources.

284

This chapter demonstrates that the institutions of federalism and competitive bureaucracy can diminish these undesirable affects of ethnic nationalism.

The analysis is based on a theory of what might be called "rational" nationalism (Congleton, 1995). Rational-choice models assume that individuals participate in all their activities with the aim of advancing personal goals in a setting of scarcity. Scarcity implies that all activities have a price. The trade-offs that must be considered are often complex, even in choosing among the mundane tasks of ordinary life. Persons "hire themselves out for wages" when the advantages of salary and other benefits more than suffice to compensate for inconvenience, lost leisure, and reduced personal autonomy. There are similar tradeoffs for persons who consider engaging in ethno-nationalist activities. Using more ethnic food, clothing, and/or expressions limits one's potential range of friends, hobbies, and business relationships. Voting exclusively for candidates from one's own group often reduces the range of potential public policies that may be considered. Providing favors for members of one's ethnic group risks offending people outside the group in a manner that reduces potential gains from exchange and fellowship. In the end, rational individuals participate in ethnic activities and work for ethno-nationalist organizations when the personal advantages of ethno-nationalist based activities appear to be greater than their costs.

The rational choice approach used in the present analysis is not meant to rule out other possible motivations, such as special altruistic bonds within ethnic groups. Insofar as ethnic nationalist groups are fundamentally based on long-term historic relations within and between various families, it is clear that bonds between group members may exist beyond those accounted for by narrow self-interest. Such bonds would increase the likelihood that those groups, as such, would survive through time. From a rational-choice perspective, these same bonds may be interpreted as increasing the benefits of continued membership in ethnic groups. A more durable group is able to provide a longer-term flow of benefits than a transitory group, and continued membership in such groups would warrant a greater personal sacrifice.

The claim that underlies the present analysis is that self-interest accounts for a significant portion of the behavior that we observe within and among ethnic interest groups. In Congleton (1995), I demonstrated that a good deal of the ebb and flow of ethnic nationalism can be explained within a rational-choice model. Ethnic "clubs" become more important in time periods when some sources of collective services decline and become less important while other sources of collective services flourish. In this chapter, I argue that self-interested behavior is sufficient to account for the general pattern of ethno-nationalist politics in a broad range of cases. Discriminatory social and political actions need not be based on supraindividual or monolithic notions of ethno-nationalist groups.

Political problems arise in multinational states because of several distinct "national" interests that may be said to exist in such states. National group distinctions may include such characteristics as geographic origin (Scandinavian), language (Francophone), religion (Jewish), culture (European), ethnicity (Chinese), or race (Iniuit). Often persons share several of these characteristics, which gives them a sense of being related to and belonging to a community of similar persons. That is to say, many or most persons in a multinational state have at least one national identity that is distinct from that generated by the civic and cultural life of the particular country in which they live (Breton, 1964; Hardin, 1995; Breton et al., 1995).

Organizations can be more easily formed by such "natural groups" than by most other collections of unaffiliated persons because a common national identity reduces organizational costs. A common language and culture provides a basis for communication. Common interests and aspirations provide the basis for mutually beneficial group services. Common norms and religion provide a basis for more accurately predicting the behavior of fellow group members in a wide variety of settings where trust or contracts might be at issue. Readily observable manifestations of a national identity – surname, language, accent, and appearance – make it relatively easy to distinguish members from nonmembers, which allows services to be better targeted at fellow "club" members and facilitates the punishment of free-riders.

The ethno-nationalist groups that emerge may be rather tenuous organizations that arise spontaneously, without any effort by a leadership to coordinate or encourage ethnic-based activities. Services in such a minimal "club" may be limited to preferential exchange of information about quality of services, the availability of discounts, and social and employment opportunities – that is, an ethnic "grapevine." In larger and more formal ethno-nationalist organizations, various forms of social insurance may be provided by the group: "We take care of our own." In still grander enterprises, direct job opportunities, political favors, and indeed political power may be provided to members. Formal ethnonationalist clubs or associations are carefully organized enterprises with a permanent staff of fund raisers, lobbyists, and coordinators.

All clubs provide differential services to members and nonmembers, but in most private clubs the distinction between members and nonmembers is more or less voluntary. Persons choose to join or not join most ordinary bridge clubs, health clubs, churches, and civic service organizations (Wintrobe, 1995). However, it is not generally possible to change one's memberships in ethno-nationalist "clubs" because membership is based largely on family history and its associated implications for race, language, religion, and heredity. Rewards and costs can lead one to be a *more or less active* member of an ethnic group, but not to change clubs.[1]

Since only persons who belong to "a people" are eligible for services provided by ethno-nationalist clubs, differential treatment of persons based on what loosely may be regarded as ethnicity is a natural consequence of such clubs. Moreover, because group membership is based on unchanging family membership and history, there will be essentially *permanent distinctions* between club and nonclub members that imply significant discrimination among groups in the production and distribution of all ethno-nationalist club services.

What potentially makes nationalist or ethnic-based clubs of greater interest to political scientists and economists than other hereditary clubs, such as the extended family or clan, is that an ethnic group's relatively large size potentially gives it the ability to significantly influence the distribution of wealth between members and nonmembers. Such wealth effects may be a consequence of favoritism in private activities alone, or more likely, they may be a consequence of the direct use of the coercive power of the state to further ethno-nationalist group ends; see Breton (1964) and Roback (1989). The stability of national identity also implies that political power may be wielded by a single group over a significant period of time with the consequence that discriminatory policies may remain in place for many generations. The hereditary basis of membership increases coalitional stability and makes electoral cycles less unlikely.

II   Two illustrations of favoritism under a unified government: Accidental natural monopoly and conscious rent seeking

The observation that the powers of government may be used to provide ethnic services does not necessarily imply that an organized self-

---

[1] In "melting pot" countries like the United States, Canada, and Australia, persons may belong to several ethno-nationalist groups simultaneously as products of intragroup marriages. In this case, it may well be possible to effectively change groups insofar as persons may emphasize only a small subset of their potential national identities. On the other hand, even in such cases, membership choices tend to be very limited. That is to say, either just a handful of options exist, or none at all. Options do not really proliferate in a "melting pot" state because the "melting" process attenuates links to specific ethno-nationalist groups. In the long run, a multinational state becomes effectively a homogeneous state of people with *clear* links only to their current place in the world – e.g., they become Canadians, Australians, or Americans.

conscious effort to influence policy will be forthcoming from all ethnic groups, nor are such efforts necessarily required. The first case examined below demonstrates that the private rewards available to members are often sufficient for favoritism to emerge even when ethnic clubs do not aspire to political power per se. The second case examined demonstrates that active political efforts by ethno-nationalist clubs may generate significant political costs whether legislated favoritism is obtained or not.

The analysis is based on the reciprocity that plays a role in every club. To maintain good standing within a club, every member of the club must "pay" his or her dues. These dues may be relatively modest for inactive members who receive relatively few services from the club. Indeed, insofar as ethnic club services are imperfectly excludable or targeted at club members, inactive members of an ethnic group may free-ride to some extent on the political and economic activities of fellow group members. However, as noted by Olson (1965) in his analysis of general features of collective action, most successful ethnic clubs will have at their disposal some selective incentives that can be used to provide larger rewards for those who provide greater contributions to club activities.[2]

In informal ethnic clubs, both club dues and club services consist of favors. An exchange of services takes place, but generally not illegal bribes in cash or kind. The terms of trade remain implicit rather than explicit. In such organizations, outstanding producers of ethnic services may be provided with more complete information about business, social, or political opportunities, may receive more or greater discounted services from other members, or may be singled out for significant approbation and respect from fellow club members. In formally organized groups, outstanding coordinators, managers, and producers may be directly rewarded with salary and bonuses, and with promotions to positions of greater authority and honor.

A   *Natural monopoly: A model of accidental favoritism*

Any member of an organized group that is employed by government is in a position to use the powers of his government office to secure club rewards. Consider the position of an isolated low-level government clerk,

---

[2] Although, as noted earlier, there is a broad range of criteria upon which nationalist groups may be based, this chapter will hereafter refer to all groups composed on the basis of nationalist aspirations, culture, or heritage as ethnic groups. The term "ethnic club" is used for expository convenience as a short form of the more cumbersome, and more accurate, ethno-nationalist club.

Al, perhaps an immigration official, building inspector, or tax collector. Al earns a salary from his job, Y, and has some prospect for advancement which will increase the present value of his salary by B. Suppose further that Al works in an ethnically neutral state, and is more likely to be promoted if he is unfailingly neutral in the discharge of his duties. In an ethnically neutral state, the probability of promotion, P, to a better paying position falls when Al provides ethnic services (favoritism, F) to members of an ethnic group, $P = p(F)$, with $P_F < 0$.

In compensation for any risk that Al runs for providing favors to fellow group members, Al receives indirect income from his ethnic club in the form of lower prices, better information, or approbation. The more favors that Al provides to his ethnic group, the greater is his ethnic-club-based income, $E(F)$ with $E_F > 0$. Al's total expected income is the sum of ordinary salary, expected promotion, and ethnic-club-based income:

$$Y^e = Y + PB + E$$

The income-maximizing ethnic clerk provides favoritism at the level that optimally trades off diminished prospects for promotion with the rewards of providing services to his group. Differentiating with respect to F and setting the result equal to zero allows the income-maximizing level of favoritism for Al to be characterized as:

$$P_F B + E_F = 0 \tag{1}$$

Al will produce favors for his own group up to the point where the expected marginal loss from reduced prospects for future promotion equals the marginal increase in ethnic income produced from those favors.[3] It is clear that as favoritism becomes less costly *at the margin* (P_F becomes less negative) and as the marginal rewards from the ethnic group increase (E_F increases).

In a competitive labor market where all ethnic groups are equally well organized and effective at rewarding favoritism, there will be many such clerks, from many different ethnic groups, and the overall effect is that on average the tax code, building code, or immigration rules are implemented in a manner that is somewhat more permissive than originally intended by those drafting the relevant rules and regulations. Each group gets treated more favorably by its "own" clerks, which in

---

[3] Of course, rather than receiving a bonus for good performance, the clerk might be subjected to penalties for poor performance. This difference is unimportant for the purposes of this chapter.

turn leads to an ethnic-based sorting of clients among clerks. But there is not any systematic bias in the resulting pattern of regulation and enforcement.

However, in cases where a few ethnic groups are better able to reward (or punish) their members than others, members of those better-organized groups will be most interested in positions where discretion allows valued favors to be produced at a relatively low cost. Moreover, since members of those more rewarding groups receive a higher total income from such positions, more talented members from such groups will be willing to accept employment at a given government wage level than will be willing to accept employment from less remunerative groups, other things being equal.

To the extent that the government's personnel office has an incentive to minimize the cost of qualified personnel, or to hire the most highly qualified person for each position at a given salary, members of the ethnic group that rewards government service most will tend to secure *all* such jobs. This kind of separating equilibrium in the market for clerks tends to occur even in cases where those making the hiring decisions are entirely neutral in evaluating the relative merits of prospective clerks. Discriminatory hiring is not necessary for this result to hold. Self-selection is sufficient.

One troubling consequence of such an "ethnic natural monopoly" is that only a single ethnic group benefits from the favoritism generated by the discretionary authority of government employees. Only the "insider" group benefits from the clerk's ability to confer favors, because it is only through serving fellow group members that clerks earn additional ethnic-club-based income. Persons outside that group are all treated equally, and persons within the group are all treated equally. However, even uniform regulations will be applied unequally across groups.

Favoritism at the level of individual clerks remains limited by the same personal tradeoffs as in the previous case – ethnic services versus reduced prospects for promotion – as long as the ethnic natural monopoly occurs only at lower levels of the bureaucracy. However, as the dominant ethnic group is gradually promoted in the organizational hierarchy, favoritism may be introduced into the hiring process, and into the drafting of rules and regulations developed to implement legislation. Indeed, even nonethnic clerks who report to members of a dominant ethnic group would be well-advised to continue providing favors to relevant ethnic group members.

In any case, it is clear that the existence of a dominant organized ethnic group can undermine the rule of law in areas under their members' authority. Clearly, equal protection of the law will not apply in such an ethnically captured bureaucracy, as the immigration regulations, the tax code, and so forth are applied in a differential manner across groups. As the drafted regulations themselves become discriminatory, equal protection of the law disappears even as a policy goal.

It is also clear that transfers from the population as a whole to the preferred group may be significant even in cases where the method of securing transfers is limited to a biased exercise of unavoidable bureaucratic discretion. For example, suppose that the bureaucratic service that is monopolized is on-site building inspection. Building inspectors have considerable discretion to decide whether a particular building practice does or does not meet the local building code. If it were known that builders from a particular ethnic group routinely received speedy approval for their work, demand for the services of such builders would clearly increase. Unless favoritism were extreme, it would be of little concern to consumers whether speedy approval of work done by a favored ethnic group was a consequence of favoritism or of high-quality workmanship. Nor would the standards applied to other builders have to be excessively high or arbitrary for favoritism to affect personal incomes. Time is money in the building trades. Income would increase for contractors from favored ethnic groups insofar as the supply of such builders is not perfectly elastic, and it would decline for other builders.

The wealth effects of ethnic-based favoritism are affected by a variety of demographic and cultural aspects of particular ethnic communities. For example, there may be taste or occupational differences that lead some ethnic groups to reward favoritism (and thereby government jobs) in some policy areas more than in others. One ethnic group might come to dominate building inspection, another immigration, and still another taxation. Specialization in particular government agencies or activities may be unintentionally reinforced by other informal rewards provided by ethnic groups that encourage investment in various forms of human capital – such as language instruction, military service, or higher education – which causes particular groups to have a comparative advantage at specific positions within the bureaucracy. Such factors may reinforce or limit net transfers from the community at large to members of a particular ethnic group.

The prospect of bureaucratic capture by an ethnic group may be reduced in a variety of ways. For example, legislation that requires a proportional ethnic quota system in hiring clerks, would, in a manner analogous to antitrust activities, artificially move the distribution of bureaucratic personnel back toward the diffuse competitive setting first explored. The quality of personnel would be diminished by such quotas, but favoritism in the implementation of policy would also diminish.[4] Alternatively, institutional structures may encourage competition between bureaus that reduces the possibilities for ethnic capture of particular government service areas without necessarily reducing the level of talent of the government work force. Bureaucratic transfers may also be limited by imposing stronger sanctions on those found engaging in favoritism.

However, the ethnic-based sorting characterized here does not have to be complete to be of interest, or to have significant consequences for the citizens of the country of interest. As long as some groups are able to secure preferential treatment, *on average*, both the effective legal system under which individuals operate and the consequent distribution of personal income will be affected by membership in ethnic groups that more or less successfully exploit the discretion associated with government office.

B   *Political competition and ethnic rent-seeking losses*

These "legal" effects of ethnic activities point to another potential source of ethnic favoritism. Rather than simply rewarding those individual members who secure useful political power, ethnic clubs may organize for direct participation in state politics. Within a democracy, a politically active ethnic group may attempt to influence legislation by directly lobbying policy makers for specific policies or by selecting particular parties or politicians to support with group resources. Within an authoritarian regime, a politically active ethnic group may promote or resist the rule of a particular dictator or ruling council. In either case, some policy is adopted or a particular candidate is elected, and favoritism becomes a matter of legislation rather than an accidental consequence of ethnic comparative advantage under neutral hiring practices.

In cases where two or more groups take opposing stands or back opposing candidates or policies, the resulting political contest has the general features of a rent-seeking game. That is to say, resources are invested in a contest which is itself largely nonproductive in the sense that decisions at the political margin redistribute existing wealth rather

---

[4] Such legislated solutions are less likely when the benefiting group constitutes the political majority, and are effectively ruled out under authoritarian regimes in cases where those groups benefiting are important supporters of the current regime. Within such authoritarian regimes, the end of preferential treatment may require a political revolution.

than create new wealth.[5] Resources invested in political conflict largely offset each other. Thus, in many cases a similar policy result could have been obtained at a lower cost if each group had proportionately reduced its investment in the political contest. The resources unnecessarily invested in ethnic conflict constitute a political and economic deadweight loss. In the case of open warfare between ethnic groups for political power, the deadweight loss of political conflict is often enormous as lives, labor, and capital are consumed by violent conflict. Peaceful forms of political conflict are often difficult to observe directly, but may also consume considerable resources.

The potential magnitude of the deadweight loss of both sorts of political conflict can be analyzed with a model of rent seeking drawn from elementary game theory. Suppose that ethnic group A's probability of securing a transfer, T, via the contest of interest is approximately equal to the ratio of their efforts, E^A, to all others, E^O, $P^A = E^A/(E^A + E^O)$. Suppose further that the cost of each unit of political effort is simply C. In this case, A's expected net benefit, N^e, from engaging in political activity is simply the expected transfer less the cost of the effort undertaken.

$$N^e = P^A T - E^A C \tag{2}$$

Differentiating with respect to E^A and setting the result equal to zero allows ethnic group A's political profit maximizing investment in rent seeking to be characterized as:

$$\left[-E^O \big/ (E^A + E^O)^2 \right] T - C = 0$$

or

$$E^A = -E^O + [T E^O / C]^{\frac{1}{2}} \tag{3}$$

Clearly the amount that any single ethnic interest group wishes to invest in the political contest depends upon the extent to which those investments increase the probability that it will be successful, which in turn depends on the efforts of all other ethnic groups. Equation 3 characterizes this relationship for a typical interest group. All the ethnic groups that seek this prize face a similar decision problem and would reach similar conclusions.

---

[5] The rent-seeking game has been applied to analyze interest-group activities in a wide variety of settings. For an overview of the literature and several applications, see Tollison and Congleton (1995).

A political equilibrium occurs when no group has reason to change its behavior given the choices of all other groups. This occurs at the Nash equilibrium of the political influence game where all the groups are simultaneously on their best reply functions (similar to those characterized by equation 3). Consider the very tractable equilibrium that emerges if there are $K - 1$ other equally well-organized and effective groups participating in the political influence game of interest. At the symmetric equilibrium all groups make the same investment in rent-seeking activities, so $E^O = (K - 1)E^A$. Substituting into equation 3 and solving for E allows the Nash equilibrium political effort of each group to be determined:

$$E = (1 - 1/K)T/KC \tag{4.1}$$

and total rent-seeking cost, R, across all K groups is:

$$R = KEC = (1 - 1/K)T \tag{4.2}$$

Note that both single group investments (equation 4.1) and the total amount invested among all groups (4.2) increase as the political prize (T) increases. In the illustrating example, the investments are proportional to the prize sought. In a two-ethnic-group contest, each group invests an amount equal to one-fourth of the prize sought, here $EC = (1 - \frac{1}{2})T/2 = \frac{1}{4}T$.

Perhaps of greater interest for the purposes of this chapter is the relationship between the total expenditure, R, and the number of ethnic groups involved in the political allocation contest. Note that as K becomes large, the total amount invested approaches T, the total value of the transfer sought. That is to say, a multinational state in which ethnic or nationalist groups seek transfers or favorable regulations from government tends to waste more and more scarce economic resources in political conflict as the number of politically active ethnic groups increases. In a state with two roughly equal-sized politically active ethnic groups, resources equaling about half of the desired transfers are consumed by the process of political conflict. In a state with four such groups, three-fourths of the transfers sought are consumed by political conflict.[6]

---

[6] These losses may be moderated to some extent if the groups form coalitions and agree to share any political prize obtained. Losses may also be limited in cases where there are fixed organization costs to participating in the political process. Here, a point would be reached where entering the political game becomes unprofitable. That is to say, fixed costs may limit the number of groups that would ever find it worthwhile to compete in such games.

Of course, these specific results follow from the model of ethnic conflict explored here and are not meant to be quantitative predictions. The model is meant to illustrate the fundamental structure of conflict between ethno-nationalist groups rather than to provide a totally faithful representation of actual conflict that we might observe.

Clearly, the model, as such, has several weaknesses. (1) The probability function used can only roughly approximate the complex web of personalities and ties within a nation's political process that give rise to influence. (2) There may be significant asymmetries among the various groups' abilities to devote resources to the political contest. (3) Moreover, as the number of groups increase within a given national population, group membership and resources may fall. Only the diminished probability of winning is accounted for in the multinational group setting by the model. To the extent that additional numbers of politically active groups are created by some reawakening of national identity induced by changing circumstances, it is possible that the decline in investment by members of now smaller ethnic groups would be more rapid than modeled here and that the analysis of total resources devoted to political conflict would not be directly relevant.

On the other hand, although particular features of every abstract model are necessarily unrealistic, the use of models remains a useful device for analyzing the world, because many "unrealistic" features of models are "sufficiently" close to reality in a large number of interesting cases. For example, many specific objections to using this particular model as an engine of analysis are less relevant than one might initially believe. The concerns just noted may be addressed at least partly as follows: (1) Many other probabilistic representations of the process of political influence would yield *qualitatively* similar results. (2) In the absence of long-standing discrimination, there is no particular reason to expect one group to be better organized or more politically effective than another. (3) There is no necessary decline in group membership as the number of groups included in the multinational state increases. Multinational states tend to be agglomerations of many peoples with separate national identities. To the extent that nationalist politics is based on long-standing differences in identity, changes in the number of groups does not take place within a given society but only across different countries or via merger or conquest.

Given these acknowledged limitations of the model developed, the game-theoretic representation of decisions to invest resources in political conflict indicates that multinational unified states will tend to consume considerable resources in political conflict among ethnic interest groups to the extent that institutional arrangements make such efforts potentially profitable. Not only are the political prizes in multi-national states relatively large, but the more numerous the politically active ethnic groups are, the greater the resulting rent-seeking employment of resources tends to be.

III   Federalism as an institutional solution: Advantages of local political competition and monopoly

The magnitude of the losses associated with political conflict and the extent to which polices are systematically biased to favor specific ethnic groups are affected by legal and political institutions in at least two ways. Institutions may explicitly restrict opportunities for discrimination by limiting the scope for government action and the extent to which the government may discriminate among persons or groups within the domain over which it retains jurisdiction. For example, rules requiring just compensation and due process limit the ability of governments to make direct transfers between individuals and groups. Secure general property rights and civil rights explicitly bound the domain of government policy in a manner that rules out some methods of government favoritism. Rules that assure equal protection of the law similarly make discriminatory legal practices more difficult to draft and implement.

Alternatively, laws may indirectly control the extent to which governments may discriminate by specifying procedures or organizational features that make discriminatory outcomes unlikely. For example, majority-rule elections limit large-scale transfers from mainstream groups to levels that can be readily tolerated by a majority. Reliance on a redundant, but competitive, bureaucracy also reduces the risk of ethnic capture, as noted earlier.

Another organizational feature of government that can limit the scope of ethnic favoritism and ethnic conflict of particular interest here is federalism. Federalism is a somewhat ambiguous "form" of government, inasmuch as nearly all governments are "federal" to some degree, although the degree of decentralization varies significantly across countries. The polar "nonfederal" case is that where all political authority resides in a single countrywide government, a unitary state. Local authority in such unitary governments is a consequence of revocable decisions by the central authority to delegate authority to local agents who are themselves appointed by the central government. Unitary government is implicitly the form of government analyzed earlier.

At the other end of the spectrum of "federal" governments are highly decentralized organizations in which the national government has very limited authority. Autonomous and independently elected local governments determine and provide most government services financed from local tax resources. The national government of a decentralized federal system guarantees the *free mobility* of people and products among local governments, and helps to *coordinate* the provision of nationwide public goods and the regulation of national externalities. In a broad range of intermediate cases, fiscal responsibilities may overlap or be shared by several levels of government, and significant services may be provided by the central government. In cases where considerable autonomy to make public policy remains in the hands of local governments, local government policy decisions depend in part on policy decisions made by other local governments.

The previous analysis of ethnic favoritism applies in a general way to the situation faced by each government within a federal system. Opportunities for ethnic favoritism exist at every level of governmental autonomy, and accidental and intentional ethnic preferences may emerge within all those areas of policy making, implementation, and enforcement. However, the analysis of this section of the chapter indicates that the degree of preferential treatment that specific ethno-national groups may *realize* is significantly more limited within federal governments than within unitary governments.

The relevance of federal systems of governance for addressing the political problems of multinational states has largely been neglected, although some hints of solutions are present in Wärneryd (1998), Congleton (1994), and Hoyt and Toma (1989). Most of the work that assesses relative advantages of competition within federal systems and within the bureaucracy has implicitly been done within fairly homogeneous communities. In such a setting, it has often been argued – Tiebout (1956), Henderson (1985), Breton (1987), and Wintrobe (1987) – that competition can improve the performance of government by constraining its ability to raise taxes without providing desired services, and by encouraging innovation. In extreme cases, local governments behave as if they were simply competitive firms, and local government services are provided to residents at marginal cost. Similarly, bureaucracies that provide services to the central government that are available from other government (or private) suppliers are constrained to provide high-quality services at least cost. In these cases, the costly redundancies of local governments and of parallel and overlapping agencies are more than offset by the productive competition engendered by multiple service providers.

Other conclusions about the relative merits of federalism in a multinational state differ from those of analyses conducted in homogeneous states. For example, Oates (1972) notes that fiscal federalism can be defended on the basis that uniform services provided by a central government do not properly account for variation in tastes among regions. The standard economic analyses of competition within federal governments tend to emphasize equilibria where local governments serve different local needs at least cost. By contrast, in a multinational state, the political problem may be the opposite of that which the fiscal federalism literature focuses on. The central government of a multinational state might provide service variation even in cases where uniform services would have been appropriate. That is to say, the central government of a multinational state may distribute services in a manner that discriminates *too well* among ethnic national groups. A well-functioning federalism in this case would produce *more uniform* service levels than a central state dominated by a subset of national groups would have.

To the extent that ethnic favoritism subjects nonfavored groups to higher taxes, more stringent regulation, or fewer government services, mobility will tend to reduce the impact of favoritism on *both* the favored and unfavored segments of society. Any local government that engages in relatively greater favoritism will tend to lose unfavored residents (and tax base) to other communities that provide services in a more neutral manner. At the same time that exit of the unfavored occurs, communities that favor one group over another will attract "favored" residents from other communities where they receive fewer advantages. These two effects imply that favoritism in the face of mobility tends to cause jurisdictional sorting by ethnic groups and relatively less actual favoritism than would exist in a society with more limited mobility.

A   *Competition between local governments*

Consider first the extreme perfectly competitive case in which the cost of moving, M, between local governmental jurisdictions is zero. That is to say, suppose people can relocate without cost from one political jurisdiction to another, $M = 0$. In order for moving costs to be so low, there must be a large number of perfect substitute communities for each person in the country as a whole. (In the absence of a large number of substitute communities, sacrifices and tradeoffs would necessarily be involved in every move, which would imply positive moving costs.) Under perfect jurisdictional competition, every person can choose to locate in a community that produces his desired services at least cost. In this case, it is clear that prospects for ethnic favoritism and exploitation are necessarily very limited.

In the case where every person can choose among several (efficiently sized) communities providing similar services, the existence of ethnic favoritism in any single community implies that that community will, in equilibrium, be perfectly homogeneous in its ethnic composition. Anyone who finds himself a member of an unfavored group will simply relocate to another community where his own ethnic group is favored or at least not relatively disadvantaged. Members of favored groups that are not equally favored in their current locations will migrate to the locality where they might best profit from local discrimination. Thus, Tiebout-type competitive equilibrium in a federal multinational state with local favoritism is characterized by many essentially *ethnically pure* local governments producing various local government services at least cost.[7]

Obviously, favoritism can have only very limited effects on the distribution of wealth within such an equilibrium. Complete sorting implies that *all* bureaucratic services will be monopolized by a dominant ethnic group. However, complete sorting also implies that *all* those seeking services will be members of the same ethnic group. Thus, a building inspector who provided preferential services to every member of his own group would in this case treat every builder under his authority in exactly the same way. Favoritism causes sorting, but in the end, sorting eliminates the effects and effectiveness of favoritism.

Favoritism is a relative notion. One cannot truly grant preferential treatment to everyone in a community. After sorting takes place, every resident receives the same treatment, because in the end the residents of each community are all the same in their ethnicity and in their demands for public services. What favoritism remains, discourages further emigration (or invasion) of other ethnic groups. This remaining element of favoritism eliminates the "ethnic mixing" that immigrant-based societies claim to benefit from, and may, thereby, somewhat impoverish the cultures of each community and the country as a whole. Nonetheless, equal protection of the law exists within every community, and incentives for ethnic-based rent seeking are eliminated. Perfectly competitive federalism thus avoids the principal political and legal disadvantages of politically active ethnic nationalist groups.

---

[7] Note that to the extent that multicultural communities are indeed financially or culturally wealthier, and therefore more desirable, communities, federalism also allows institutions that encourage the equal treatment of all citizens to be independently adopted. In long-run equilibria, one might find a mixture of homogeneous communities of individuals who receive substantial (nongovernmental) services from ethnic clubs and other heterogeneous communities where the principle sources of personal income and services are based on nonethnic affiliations.

B   *Ethnic favoritism within local governments with*
       monopoly power

That a perfectly competitive federal system can eliminate the two principal political costs of intrastate nationalistic conflict is at least of passing interest in large states where numerous opportunities for locational choice exit. On the other hand, moving costs are rarely so low that persons will relocate from one community to another for trivial reasons. In this respect, the advantages of federalism are exaggerated within perfectly competitive models of jurisdictional choice because of the extreme assumptions about individual mobility and about the range of local governments that services may be chosen from. Anyone who has moved knows that moving costs can be significant even when the distances involved are small. Moreover, the range of communities available to be chosen from is clearly more limited than is assumed in perfectly competitive models. Thus the complete sorting and efficient provision of government services implied by the perfectly competitive model are unlikely to fully obtain.

Fortunately, federalism has political advantages over unitary government in a multinational state even without extreme Tiebout-type assumptions. These political advantages arise largely because the cost of moving between local governments within a country is necessarily smaller than that of moving between countries. Far more moves take place between neighborhoods within a city, than between cities or between countries.

Consider, for purposes of illustration, the level of resources that will be invested in political conflict within a country with L equal-sized autonomous local governments. Suppose that there are N^L residents in each district and that moving between districts costs M^L, while moving between countries costs M^C, with $M^C > M^L$. By moving costs, it is again meant the total sacrifice involved in changing locations. These costs include such things as greater distance from friends and family, reductions in income, loss of location-specific information and amenities, as well as the physical cost of relocating one's possessions to the next-best community. The relative sizes of these tangible and intangible moving costs allow us to bound the maximal transfers that can be financed locally and nationally.

The greatest transfer that can be financed from a single local or national citizen is the opportunity cost of moving: M^L for local governments and M^C for national governments. The mechanism of the transfer is fundamentally unimportant to persons adversely affected. Regardless of whether losses from government services are an innocent consequence of accidental monopolization of relevant government services, or the result of intentionally discriminatory legislation generated by organized rent-seeking efforts and adopted by local legislatures, residents who expect to lose more than their moving costs can leave the community and avoid being the source of such transfers. Consequently, the maximal transfer that can be undertaken by a local government is $M^L N^L$.

Suppose that K local ethno-nationalist interest groups participate in a maximal local rent-seeking game for this transfer, which has the same format as the national game previously analyzed. From equation 4.2 above, we know that local ethnic political conflict will consume

$$R^L = (1 - 1/K)M^L N^L \tag{5}$$

resources at the Nash equilibrium. In the perfectly competitive federal environment, each community is homogeneous, so $K = 1$, and no ethnic rent seeking takes place. In the case of interest here, the number of ethnic rivals in a local jurisdiction, K^L, is greater than 1, but tends to be smaller than the number of groups in the country as a whole, K^C, to the extent that any sorting of groups has taken place under federalism. Given $K^L < K^C$, it is clear that fewer resources will be invested in political conflict locally than nationally whenever the same political prize is at issue.

On the other hand, national transfers can be much greater than that of any single local jurisdiction because national population is greater than local population, and perhaps most significantly, because moving costs are greater. Maximal national transfers can be represented as $LN^L M^C$. Resources devoted to political conflict to receive such a maximal national transfer would be:

$$R^C = (1 - 1/K^C)LN^L M^C \tag{6}$$

This is clearly much greater than the resources devoted to political conflict in any single local jurisdiction and, of greater relevance for the present analysis, exceeds those of all L jurisdictions combined. The latter can be written as:

$$LR^L = (1 - 1/K^L)LN^L M^L \tag{7}$$

Comparing equations 6 and 7, it is clearly the case that the amount of ethnic-based political conflict is smaller in a decentralized federal system for two reasons. First, greater mobility implies a smaller local political prize to be competed for, $M^C > M^L$. Second, greater ethnic homogeneity implies the presence of fewer competitors in the political game, $K^C \geq K^L$. Together these imply that maximal rent-seeking costs fall unambiguously as programs are moved from the central government to local governments.

Of course, both local and national jurisdictions can reduce the extent of conflict that actually occurs to levels below these maximal levels by adopting rules and procedures that make potential transfers smaller and more difficult to achieve. (It is not always sufficient to increase the cost of ethnic conflict itself, since changes in cost may not affect expenditure levels. In the examples cited previously, cost was an initial parameter of the game, C, but did not influence total expenditure levels.) Rules that reduce ethnic-based transfers – such as adherence to a generality principle, equal protection of the law, uniform service constraints, strongly punishing those engaging in favoritism, and the use of competitive bureaucracy – can reduce expected payoffs from rent seeking and thereby the extent to which a person or ethnic group would be willing to pursue political influence.

To the extent that both the national and local governments adopt institutions that reduce potential transfers, analysis of the relative costs of ethnic conflict in federal and unitary states would have to be modified to take account of the new maximal transfer levels. The methods used by national and federal governments would naturally tend to be similar, and potential transfers would be more or less proportionately reduced by measures taken at both levels of government. In this case, the relative size of the losses from ethnic conflict would be approximately the same as in our examination of the maximal case.

Federalism and parallel bureaucracy in a multinational state may actually *reduce overall political competition*, but increase welfare insofar as the forms of political competition in a unified multinational state tend to be unproductive ones.[8]

IV Ambiguous federalism?

The case for federalism as a method for reducing political costs in a multinational state is weakened somewhat in settings where services overlap or are shared among many levels of government. In this case,

---

[8] One would expect competition between local governments within a multinational state to encourage local innovation in institutions that reduce political conflict to the extent that there are obvious advantages to multicultural communities and insofar as institutional innovation is politically less difficult at local levels of government than at the federal level. Thus, it is likely that reductions in ethnic-based rent seeking will, on average, be proportionately greater within local governments than within the central government.

federalism creates another arena of political conflict over the appropriate level of government at which specific authority for particular policy decisions should reside, conflict that does not exist in a unitary state. Insofar as policy-making authority remains at least partly decentralized in such governments, the political advantages of federalism developed earlier still apply in areas of local control. However, the extent to which ongoing disputes over the division of power between local and federal governments tend to affect the relative merits of federal and unitary systems of governance is a matter of concern for the case of what might be called "ambiguous" federalism.

An ethnic group that expects to dominate a unified government would clearly benefit from efforts to shift control from local governments to the central government. Those who expect to be relatively disfavored in a unified state would lobby against greater centralization of authority and for greater decentralized control.

Some insight about the magnitude of the resources that would be invested in resulting political conflict over the appropriate level of decentralization can be obtained through a modest extension of the previous results. Recall that additional transfers can potentially be made by the central government because international moving costs exceed intranational moving costs, which allows central governments to engage in greater exploitation of groups out of power. In a country where relatively little sorting of ethnic groups takes place among local jurisdictions, so that each local jurisdiction resembles the nation as a whole, the increased "political prize" is proportional to the difference between international and intranational moving costs.

From equations 6 and 7, this additional potential transfer, T^C, avoided in a federal state, can be written as $T^C = LN^L(M^C - M^L)$. The resources used to seek and resist such a transfer would be:

$$R^F = (1 - 1/K^C)T^C = (1 - 1/K^C)LN^L(M^C - M^L) \qquad (8)$$

Equation 8 indicates that the net savings of federalism are partly dissipated in conflict over the "proper" locus of power in the model developed here. Thus, ambiguous federal systems have smaller political advantages over unitary government than federalisms with more rigid dispositions of authority between central and local governments. Nonetheless, ambiguous federalism still has a political advantage over a unitary state insofar as total political conflict remains smaller than it would have been within a unitary state.

The previous analysis also indicated that the extent of the conflict over the level of authority varies with the number of groups involved.

Equation 8 indicates this as well. However, it bears noting that decisions to locate policy authority at one or another level of government generally do not favor *specific* groups, as was the case examined in the previous analysis, but rather *all* groups that prefer a federal or centralized disposition of authority. Consequently, conflict over the proper extent of decentralization causes two natural coalitions of ethnic groups to form – those favoring and those opposing increased centralization – which reduces deadweight losses from political conflict. [Recall that as the number of parties to the conflict diminishes, rent-seeking losses diminish from $(1 - 1/K^C)LN^L(M^C - M^L)$ to $(1 - 1/2)LN^L(M^C - M^L)$.] Although half or more of the expected increase in the central government's power to make transfers may be consumed in political conflict within an ambiguous federal state, conflict as a whole diminishes within an ambiguous federal state relative to a centralized state.

V   Conclusion: Federalism's appeal in a multinational state

In any state not rigorously bound by what Buchanan and Congleton (1998) have referred to as a *generality principle*, governments are free to create policies which differentially benefit persons and groups. In such a setting, ethno-nationalist groups, like other interest groups, may regard the government as simply another possible means of producing "club services." Group members may desire new or increased regulations favoring particular industries in which they are owners or employees. They may also desire and secure relatively narrow services and targeted income transfers financed by taxpayers at large.

This chapter has shown that federalism can reduce two important political and legal problems associated with the political activities of ethno-nationalist groups. The argument can be summarized as follows: Political favoritism encourages persons to migrate between communities insofar as the costs and benefits of government services for specific peoples vary among communites. The cost of migration is smaller for movements between local governments than for movements between national governments. Consequently, communities will be more ethnically homogeneous than nation-states whenever ethnic groups are directly or indirectly politically active. Increasingly homogeneous communities reduce the scope for potential favoritism and imply that a smaller number of ethnic groups will compete for preferential treatment. Fewer *effective* discriminatory laws will be forthcoming in federal governments than under unitary governments, which reduces the interest and thereby the waste generated by ethno-nationalist rent seeking. Together these imply that investments in political conflict, rent-seeking losses, will be smaller in federal systems than in a unitary state. (In the limiting case with complete sorting of groups among local jurisdictions, ethnic conflict and most effects of favoritism disappear within the homogeneous jurisdictions that emerge.)

An implication of the analysis is that transferring program responsibilities to local governments reduces potential political conflict by reducing moving costs and increasing the degree of governmental competition. Consequently, more decentralized systems of federalism have smaller political overhead costs than more concentrated ones insofar as conflict over central government policies is replaced by somewhat smaller aggregate conflict over the policies of local governments.

On the other hand, the political efficiency advantage of decentralization of policy-making authority does not imply that central governments should be eliminated. Dividing a multinational state into separate independent countries fails to secure the benefits of decentralization within a federal state because moving costs, no matter how small, are nearly always greater, and therefore jurisdictional competition less, between countries than between jurisdictions within a single country. Conflict within a large number of independent countries would exceed that within even a fairly centralized federal system if the independent countries are ethnically heterogeneous. Both small and large unitary governments have incentives to make moving costs large in order to increase their power to make transfers. Moreover, advantages of scale in economic markets, in national defense, and in internalizing regional externalities suggest that a central government may be an important mechanism for producing genuine national public services.[9]

Around the world, we do observe a rough correlation between the degree of decentralization, discriminatory policies, and political conflict in multinational states. The highly centralized multinational governments of Africa often are dominated by a subset of ethnic groups that secure a variety of transfers from the groups excluded from government using the coercive regulatory and taxation powers of the state. Political conflict, and indeed internecine warfare, are often intense within these

---

[9] Many of the advantages of federalism can be secured via self-enforcing international treaties. Treaties that guarantee the free movement of persons and property, together with ones that provide for regional defense and regulation of externalities, provide the only method by which advantages of competitive governance may be secured by economically interdependent, but politically independent, unitary states. Such multilateral treaties create, in effect, a type of confederation where the power of participation, and at least a local veto, remains in the hands of "local" governments. Unfortunately, self-enforcing treaties become increasingly problematic to draft the larger the number of countries involved becomes; see Congleton (1995).

countries. By contrast, conflict within the multinational federal states in North America and Europe is relatively modest. Although other institutions and traditions also contribute to diminished conflict in these wealthier nations, the predicted consequences of federalism for national welfare seem to be observable, substantial, and obvious.

Overall, the analysis has illuminated some neglected advantages of federalism over unitary governments in the context of multinational states. Federalism does not end ethnic conflict, but it does diminish the political costs of political conflict and favoritism relative to unitary states. The analysis has developed several reason why fewer *effective* discriminatory laws tend to be forthcoming in federal systems, and why less ethnic political conflict tends to occur in federal systems of governance. Reduced political conflict allows scarce human resources to be shifted from divisive ethno-nationalist conflict to more productive activities. Federalism, thereby, increases the wealth and welfare of most citizens, and thereby the legitimacy of the state itself.

References

Akerlof, G. A. (1985) "Discriminatory, Status-Based Wages among Tradition-Oriented Stochastically Trading Coconut Producers," *Journal of Political Economy* 93: 265–276.

Becker, G. S. (1983) "A Theory of Competition among Pressure Groups for Political Influence," *Quarterly Journal of Economics* 98: 371–399.

Boucher, J., Landis, D., and Clark, K. A., Eds. (1987) *Ethnic Conflict: International Perspectives.* London: Sage Publications.

Breton, A., and Wintrobe, R. (1975) "The Equilibrium Size of a Budget Maximizing Bureau," *Journal of Political Economy* 83: 195–207.

Breton, A. (1964) "The Economics of Nationalism," *Journal of Political Economy* 72: 376–386.

Breton, A. (1987) "Towards a Theory of Competitive Federalism," *European Journal of Political Economy* 3: 263–329.

Breton, A., and Breton, M. (1995) "Nationalism Revisited," in Breton et al., Eds. (1995).

Breton, A., Galeotti, G., Salmon, P., and Wintrobe, R., Eds. (1995) *Nationalism and Rationality.* Cambridge: Cambridge University Press.

Breton, A., and Wintrobe, R. "Bureaucracies of Murder Revisited," *Journal of Political Economy* 94: 905–926.

Buchanan, J. M. (1965) "An Economic Theory of Clubs," *Economica* 32: 371–384.

Buchanan, J. M. (1987) "The Constitutions of Economic Policy," *American Economic Review* 77: 243–250.

Buchanan, J. M., and Congleton, R. D. (1998) *Politics by Principle Not Interest.* Cambridge: Cambridge University Press.

Buchanan, J. M., Tullock, G., and Tollison, R. D., Eds. (1980) *Toward a Theory of the Rent-Seeking Society.* College Station: Texas A&M Press.

Congleton, R. D. (1980) "Competitive Process, Competitive Waste, and Institutions," in Buchanan, J. M., Tullock, G., and Tollison, R. D., Eds. *Toward a Theory of the Rent-Seeking Society*. College Station: Texas A&M Press.

Congleton, R. D. (1989) "Efficient Status Seeking: Externalities and the Evolution of Status Games," *Journal of Economic Behavior and Organization* 11: 175–190.

Congleton, R. D. (1994) "Constitutional Federalism and Decentralization: A Second Best Solution," *Economia delle Scelte Pubbliche*, 15–29.

Congleton, R. D. (1995) "Ethnic Clubs, Ethnic Conflict, and the Rise of Ethnic Nationalism," in Breton et al., Eds. (1995).

Cornes, R., and Sandler, T. (1986) *The Theory of Externalities, Public Goods and Club Goods*. Cambridge: Cambridge University Press.

Ehrlich, I. (1975) "The Deterrent Effect of Capital Punishment: A Question of Life and Death," *American Economic Review* 65: 397–417.

Hardin, R. (1995) "Self Interest, Group Identity," in Breton et al., Eds. (1995).

Henderson, J. V. (1985) "The Tiebout Model: Bring Back the Entrepreneurs," *Journal of Political Economy* 89: 1197–1217.

Hirschman, A. O. (1970) *Exit, Voice, and Loyalty – Responses to Decline in Firms, Organizations and States*. Cambridge, Mass: Harvard University Press.

Hoyt, W., and Toma, E. (1989) "State Mandates and Interest Group Lobbying," *Journal of Public Economics* 38: 199–213.

Kuran, T. (1987) "Preference Falsification, Policy Continuity and Collective Conservatism," *Economic Journal* 97: 642–665.

Landa, J. (1981) "A Theory of the Ethnically Homogeneous Middleman Group: An Institutional Alternative to Contract Law," *Journal of Legal Studies* 10: 349–362.

Mcguire, M. (1974) "Group Segregation and Optimal Jurisdictions," *Journal of Political Economy* 82: 112–132.

Mueller, D. C. (1989) *Public Choice II*. Cambridge: Cambridge University Press.

North, D. C. (1991) *Institutions, Institutional Change, and Economic Performance*. Cambridge: Cambridge University Press.

Oates, W. E. (1972) *Fiscal Federalism*. New York: Harcourt, Brace, Jovanovich.

Olson, M. (1965) *The Logic of Collective Action*. Cambridge: Harvard University Press.

Olson, M. (1982) *The Rise and Decline of Nations*. New Haven: Yale University Press.

Ra'anan, U., Mesner, M., Armes, K., and Martin, K., Eds. (1991) *State and Nation in Multiethnic Societies: The Breakup of Multinational States*. New York: Manchester University Press.

Riker, W. H. (1964) *Federalism*. Toronto: Little, Brown.

Roback, J. R. (1989) "Racism as Rent-Seeking," *Economic Inquiry* 27: 661–682.

Tiebout, C. (1956) "A Pure Theory of Local Expenditures," *Journal of Political Economy* 64: 416–424.

Tollison, R. D., and Congleton, R. D. (1995) *The Economic Analysis of Rent Seeking*. Brookfield, VT: Edgar Elgar Publishing Company.

Tullock, G. (1974) *The Social Dilemma: The Economics of War and Revolution*. Blacksburg, VA: University Publications.

Tullock, G. (1992) "Federalism." University of Arizona, Tucson, AZ, mimeograph.

Wärneryd, K. (1998) "Distributive Conflict and Jurisdictional Organization," *Journal of Public Economics* 69: 435–450.

Wildasin, D. E. (1988) "Nash Equilibria in Models of Fiscal Competition," *Journal of Public Economics* 35: 241–249.

Wintrobe, R. (1987) "Competitive Federalism and Bureaucratic Power," *European Journal of Political Economy* 3: 9–31.

Wintrobe, R. (1995) "Some Economics of Ethnic Capital Formation and Conflict," in Breton et al., Eds. (1995).

Witte, A. D. (1980) "Estimating the Economics of Crime with Individual Data," *Quarterly Review of Economics* 94: 57–84.

CHAPTER 13

Quebec 1995: The rhetoric of the referendum

Robert Young

This chapter is about competition in political discourse. To the best of my knowledge Albert Breton has never analyzed rhetoric (in print), so this effort might appear disrespectful to those who do not know that Albert is a compelling speaker, much concerned with the place in Canada of its Francophone population, politically well connected, and preoccupied with the possibility of Quebec separating – as he would put it – from the rest of Canada. Because of this, and because he taught me much of what I understand about competition, it seems appropriate to honor him here, however inadequately, by pressing the paradigm into the realm of discourse, and focusing on the Quebec referendum campaign that culminated in a narrow No vote against secession on October 30, 1995.

The next section of the chapter gives a brief sketch of the campaign and its principal protagonists. The surprise of the campaign was the rise in support for sovereignty, to such an extent that a prosperous, peaceful country, a member of the G-7 and the United States' most important trading partner, avoided certain economic disaster and possible political chaos by a margin of fewer than 60,000 votes. To explain the shift towards sovereignty, I proceed to analyze the debate between the No (federalist) and the Yes (sovereigntist) forces. Rhetorically, the two sides confronted one another along four basic dimensions – the Canadian constitutional order, national identification, the economic ramifications of a Yes vote, and democracy. The last was the critical dimension, though it was largely subterranean in public discourse. Because the No forces could not present a firm position on this dimension, the sovereigntists were able to

A preliminary version of this chapter was presented at the Seventh Villa Colombella Seminar, Rome, September 4–7, 1996. I am grateful to participants there – and especially to Albert Breton – for useful comments and discussion.

make headway on the economic front by arguing that secession (or at least a Yes vote) would be costless, and so almost won the contest.

The campaign

The two sides were competing for the votes of "soft nationalists" in Quebec. These are the 30 to 40 percent of the electorate, overwhelmingly Francophone, who are neither committed federalists nor hard-core sovereigntists, and whose volatility was demonstrated both in the mid-1980s when support for Quebec independence sagged to around 35 percent, and in the early 1990s when the Meech Lake accord – which involved constitutional recognition of Quebec as a "distinct society" – failed to pass, propelling support for sovereignty up to about 60 percent (Cloutier, Guay, and Latouche). These swing voters have considerable attachment to Canada but a strong identification as Quebecers, seek linguistic security, and have a taste for sovereignty that is tempered by fear of its economic consequences (Bernier).

The Yes forces were to be led by Jacques Parizeau, head of the nationalistic *Parti québécois* (PQ), a relatively hard-line intellectual who had long been committed to sovereignty. He had become premier of the province in September 1994, when the PQ took power from the Quebec Liberal Party (QLP). The latter was led by Daniel Johnson, an unflamboyant but honest campaigner who was the nominal head of the No forces under the province's referendum legislation (which requires all participants to campaign within one of two umbrella organizations, whose spending is tightly controlled). Other No leaders were federal politicians from Quebec – Jean Charest, leader of the Progressive Conservative Party, and Jean Chrétien, the highly experienced leader of the federal Liberal Party and, since 1993, prime minister of Canada. The last important figure was Lucien Bouchard, who had quit the federal cabinet over the Meech Lake accord to form the *Bloc québécois*, a party that represented the sovereignty option in Ottawa and that took the majority of Quebec seats in the 1993 federal election, forming the official opposition in Parliament. Mr. Bouchard is a charismatic figure, the most popular and trusted person in Quebec politics.

Relations between Lucien Bouchard and the PQ government were not without friction. In April of 1995, after polls showed that Mr. Parizeau's drive toward a June referendum would produce failure, Mr. Bouchard made a momentous *"virage,"* calling for sovereignty to be accompanied by an economic and even political partnership with the rest of Canada. This move was cemented when the PQ, the *Bloc*, and a minor party made a formal agreement in June, one that was reflected in the legislation that triggered the referendum.[1]

In late August, the federalists and the sovereigntists were almost tied in public support, according to a poll that asked "if the referendum were being held today, would you vote for or against the sovereignty of Quebec with an offer of economic and political partnership with Canada?" Respondents answering No totalled 45.3%, those answering Yes were 44.4%, 6.5% were undecided, and 3.8% refused to answer. However, the No voters were firmer in their intentions than were those inclined to vote Yes. As well, on harder questions that asked about Quebec becoming an independent country, or that failed to mention association, Yes support sank to around 40% or even lower. On the other hand, large majorities of voters favored federal offers of constitutional change, and the credibility of the three principal sovereigntist leaders was significantly higher than that of any of the prominent federalists. Mr. Bouchard was by far the leader perceived as most competent (32% among Francophones, versus 9% for Mr. Chrétien and 6% for Mr. Johnson), even though a clear majority of the electorate (52%) identified the economy as their main priority, while few (6%) chose sovereignty (25.8, 16.8, 26.8, and 8.8).[2]

In this context, the federalist side stuck to its basic strategy, confident that the sovereigntists would lose ground over the campaign, and that the undecided voters would split predominantly toward the status quo in the end. The strategy involved placing upon the sovereigntists the burden of showing that their option was superior, appealing to Quebecers' sense of attachment to Canada, stressing the disruption that "separation" would cause, and showing that the federal system could provide good government, while flexibly accommodating the desire for change of many voters, without constitutional amendments. For their part, the sovereigntists aimed to appeal to Quebecers' sense of national identification, to portray the existing order as inflexible and even threatening, and to show that sovereignty would bring gains on several fronts, while the partnership would protect voters from short-term economic losses and eventual isolation from Canada.

In September, the PQ government introduced Bill 1, An Act Respecting the Future of Quebec. This declared, notably, that "we the people of Quebec, through our National Assembly, proclaim: Quebec is a sovereign country." But the bill was not to be passed before the referendum

---

[1] All this is treated in much more detail in Young, 1998.
[2] Such numeric references are to reports in the *Globe and Mail*, and refer to the year 1995, unless otherwise specified: 25.8, for example, means August 25, 1995.

sanctioned it. Moreover, the bill stipulated that the proclamation had to be preceded by an offer to Canada of an economic and political partnership. Following the June interparty agreement (which was distributed along with the bill to every Quebec household), this offer would involve a general framework treaty with provisions concerning a customs union, factor mobility, monetary policy, and many other matters, to be governed by joint institutions resembling those of the European Union. Negotiations with Canada could take a year or more, but the bill clearly provided that sovereignty could be proclaimed either after the partnership treaty was approved or else when negotiations had "proved fruitless." Bill 1, in short, could provide for a unilateral declaration of independence by Quebec. The bill also set the referendum question: "Do you agree that Québec should become sovereign, after having made a formal offer to Canada for a new Economic and Political Partnership, within the scope of the Bill respecting the future of Québec and of the agreement signed on June 12, 1995? YES or NO?"

At the outset of the campaign, the No side was confident, almost to the point of complacency. In his first address on the issue, Mr. Chrétien argued that the sovereigntists' question was duplicitous, because a Yes vote was really "a one-way ticket to separation," but he was certain that Quebecers would choose Canada: "[I]t's the best country in the world, and you all know that Canada will win." (12.9) Indeed, the sovereigntists appeared to be making little headway, despite the publicity surrounding the launch of the campaign. While some early polls showed the voters evenly divided, with the Yes support softer, others placed the No side clearly ahead, a trend that seemed to grow slightly – although the difference was often within the polls' margin of error, and much depended on how the undecided and nonrespondents were allocated (9.9, 11.9, 16.9, 26.9, and 30.9; *Le Devoir*, 23–4.9). By the end of September, there were rumors that the vote might be delayed, and Mr. Bouchard admitted, "I'm not saying the campaign is going marvellously well. I say that we are in a tight spot, that we will have to brace ourselves for a tough fight." (26.9)

The Yes side failed to make headway when its studies of the economic effects of sovereignty were ambiguous and contested. Attacks on business – natural for the social-democratic PQ – seemed to pay few dividends in a society proud of its economic leaders. Aboriginal peoples' declarations that they would resist secession did not succeed in polarizing opinion, though remarks by a federalist businessman to the effect that "we can't just win on October 30: we have to crush them" provoked outrage in a society where sovereignty was a legitimate option, along with appeals for moderation from Mr. Johnson himself (*Maclean's*, 9.10). With limited exceptions (the premier of Ontario and Preston Manning, leader of the federal Reform Party), non-Quebecers stayed out of the fray, assured by Mr. Chrétien that the No side would win.

With four weeks left in the campaign, a prominent Quebec columnist declared that the odds were in favor of a decisive federalist victory, with the only obstacles being arrogance on the No side and the possibility of strategic voting for the Yes in order to preserve Quebec's bargaining power within the federation.[3] A leading columnist in the rest of Canada wrote that the chances of a Yes victory were "exceedingly slim," and realizable only if the sovereigntists put Mr. Bouchard at the head of the campaign, increased appeals to ethnicity, and hinted at a second referendum on the outcome of the partnership negotiations; as well, the No side would have to make egregious mistakes.[4] Not all of these things occurred, but momentum did swing to the sovereigntist side in midcampaign.

First, Mr. Parizeau named five members of the committee that would oversee negotiations with Canada about the partnership treaty. Much more significantly, he announced that Lucien Bouchard would be the chief negotiator for Quebec. In effect, this passed the Yes campaign into the hands of a trusted leader who could attract moderate nationalists to the sovereigntist side, while reassuring them that the promised partnership was viable. This move undoubtedly injected new life into the Yes forces on the ground (12.10). And polls were showing some weaknesses in the federalist message. A very extensive survey conducted in late September placed the No forces firmly in the lead, but it also found that 62% of Quebecers believed they would still use the Canadian dollar after sovereignty, 45% thought they would retain Canadian passports, 69% anticipated an economic union, and almost 60% believed there would be an economic and political partnership after a Yes result (3.10). A later survey found that one-third of Yes voters were aiming "to give Lucien Bouchard a strong mandate to negotiate a new deal for Quebec within Canada": the other two-thirds wanted Quebec to become an independent country (*Montreal Gazette*, 20.10).

Such results were intensely frustrating to the federalist side. The No leaders stepped up their attacks on the economic front, warning that a Yes could bring trade disruption, heavy job losses, increased government deficits, and a sharp drop in the value of the dollar (11.10; *Montreal Gazette*, 20.10). In the context of a simmering debate about whether a sovereign Quebec would accede to the North American Free Trade

[3] Chantal Hébert in the *London Free Press*, 5 October 1995.
[4] Jeffrey Simpson in the *Globe and Mail*, 4 October 1995.

Agreement, federal finance minister Paul Martin warned that admission would not be automatic; hence, 90% of Quebec exports would be at risk, involving almost one million jobs. While he undoubtedly meant only that jobs in these export sectors would have some probability of being subject to protectionist measures, Mr. Martin's remarks were scorned by the Yes side as desperate hyperbole. Mr. Parizeau had an immediate riposte – "Last week for [Mr.] Johnson, it was slightly below 100,000. Next week I suppose we're aiming at ten million. . . . There are only 3,200,000 jobs in Quebec – and past that point they'll have to import the unemployed." (18.10) As will be seen, this was a typical counter to the federalists' dire predictions about the economic consequences of a Yes vote.

On October 20, in the wake of an Angus Reid poll showing the Yes side in the lead, financial uncertainty began to hit Canadian stock markets, and the dollar traded sharply lower. Internal polls confirmed the decline in No support, and near-panic struck the federalist camp. As a well-informed Montreal columnist put it on October 21, "if something doesn't start to happen very soon, probably by the end of this weekend, Canada is one done turkey." (Webster) Emergency changes were made to the basic No strategy: the prime minister increased his presence in the campaign well beyond his planned three major speeches, organizers desperately threw together a giant pro-Canada rally in Montreal, and there was a major shift in the federalists' constitutional position.

Constitutional movement was pressed by Mr. Johnson, who saw the Yes forces as successfully attracting all those Quebecers disaffected from the status quo and seeking change. So a No side document promised increased control over provincial jurisdictions (18.10). Then, after Mr. Chrétien stated in a Quebec City speech that the province formed a "distinct society," Mr. Johnson urged all Canadian federalists to "echo our view of what the future holds for Quebec as part of Canada." (23.10) This last was a clear appeal to Ottawa and perhaps to the other provincial governments to put some positive constitutional proposals on the table before the referendum, a stance that both responded to shifting public opinion and reflected the strong majority opinion in Quebec that the province's distinctiveness should be constitutionally recognized (19.10, 20.10). Initially rebuffed by Mr. Chrétien, who stated "there is no desire at this time to debate the constitution," the Quebec federalists were enthusiastically and effectively derided by the Yes forces for believing that Canada could deliver constitutional renewal (23.10). Mr. Johnson, however, managed to prod the prime minister to issue a joint declaration: "We state unequivocally that Quebec is a distinct society. We remind you that we have both supported the inclusion of this principle in the Canadian Constitution every time Quebec has demanded it."

(23.10) Pressed hard by the Quebec wing, the No forces went much further than this in promising constitutional change (24.10).

At a huge federalist rally in Verdun on October 24, Mr. Chrétien embraced the distinct-society concept, and held out the promise of a Quebec constitutional veto. His government would keep open all the paths for change, "including the administrative and constitutional paths." (25.10) The next day, in an extraordinary televised address to the whole country, the prime minister repeated this position: "We must recognize that Quebec's language, its culture and institutions make it a distinct society. And no constitutional change that affects the powers of Quebec should ever be made without the consent of Quebecers. And that all governments – federal and provincial – must respond to the desire of Canadians – everywhere – for greater decentralization." (26.10) Of course these promises were denounced by the sovereigntists as insincere, desperate, and too little – as only "vague allusions" to change (26.10). But they represented a major strategic shift by the No forces.

Meanwhile, citizens were mobilized. In many Canadian cities, unity rallies were held. Pro-Quebec resolutions were passed by several municipalities and some provincial legislatures. But organizers concentrated on a massive pro-Canada demonstration in Montreal on the Friday before the referendum. Members of Parliament and many businesses arranged transportation to the city, while the two major airlines and the railway offered drastically reduced fares. These preparations provoked scathingly sarcastic attacks from the Yes side, and outrage that they violated the strict regulations on referendum campaign expenditures (*La Presse*, 27.10, 28.10). But the rally drew well over 100,000 people to Place du Canada in downtown Montreal. There, as well as sounding the familiar themes about the uncertainties of a Yes result and the glories of Canada, Mr. Chrétien promised to bring about all the changes necessary to maintain unity, and Jean Charest pledged that he would be a steady force pressing for constitutional renewal (27.10, 28.10). Despite all this, the final published opinion polls were showing the Yes side clearly ahead among decided voters (*Le Journal de Montréal*, 28.10). In the end, however, the referendum result was 2,362,648 votes for the No option and 2,308,360 votes for the Yes, on a remarkable 93.52 percent turnout. If fewer than 30,000 people had voted differently, the No victory would have been reversed.

The logic of the referendum campaign

Major campaigns are fought with many tools, but in modern democracies they are fundamentally about language and argument. Given the structure of public opinion in Quebec, it was clear long before the referendum that there would be only a few key dimensions along which the sovereigntist and federalist forces would fight for support. They were Quebecers' sense of national identification (including perceptions of rejection and confidence), their economic expectations, and their views of the Canadian constitutional system. Our purpose here is to analyze the competing arguments that were deployed by the Yes and No sides throughout the course of the referendum campaign, in order to explain why the sovereigntists gained support and came so close to victory.

In some accounts of the campaign, it was national identification that produced the rise in support for the Yes side, especially after Mr. Bouchard took center stage when named as chief negotiator. As one commentator wrote, "He, more than the other secessionist leaders, can reach ordinary francophone Quebecers, summoning their *Volksgeist* in a supreme collective act of 'national affirmation' that will, once and for all, enable Quebec to meet the rest of Canada equal to equal, face to face, people to people." (Simpson) Far more cautiously, some political scientists have agreed. Vincent Lemieux, for example, has argued that the replacement of Mr. Parizeau by Mr. Bouchard heightened the importance of the national-identification dimension, and made it much less possible for voters to maintain a dual Canadian-Quebecer sense of identity.

But this explanation encounters two problems. First, it is not evident that support for the Yes side showed a sharp increase coincident with Mr. Bouchard's assuming the leadership of the campaign. A straightforward reading of the published polls suggests that support for the No side began to decline toward the end of September, well before the *Bloc* leader was named chief negotiator (*Montreal Gazette*, 28.10). On the other hand, Maurice Pinard (1997a) insists that there was a noticeable "Bouchard effect," with the proportion of voters intending to vote Yes increasing by four or five percent after the shift in leadership. This is a moot point. The various polls posed different questions to respondents, there is no universally accepted way of allocating the nonrespondents (who ranged from 8 percent to 31 percent of the samples), some polls were outliers (in each direction), and in many cases the difference between Yes and No support was within the polls' margins of error. But even if there was a "Bouchard effect," the important question is why it occurred. Here, the evidence is compelling that the shift in voting intentions toward the Yes side took place along the economic dimension, rather than being driven by an increase in Quebecers' sense of national identification.

One team of political scientists analyzed two comparable Léger &

Léger polls, one taken in June 1995 and the second during the last week of the campaign (Blais, Nadeau, and Martin). In the first, 52 percent of Francophones were intending to vote Yes; in the second, 62 percent. Over this period, there was a slight increase in the reported propensity of respondents to think of themselves as "Quebecers only" or "Quebecers first," but this difference was not statistically significant. On the other hand, economic expectations about sovereignty became much more positive (as did expectations about the situation of the French language in Quebec). In a regression equation that included as variables the sense of identification, economic and linguistic expectations, age, and domestic situation, the strongest predictor of voting intentions was the economic variable.[5] Further experimentation showed that the rise in *Québécois* identification accounted for a one percent increase in Yes support, as did views about linguistic security. The shift in economic expectations, however, produced an increase of about 6 percent in the Yes vote. So the rise in sovereignty support took place along the economic dimension. Substantively, when asked about the short-term economic consequences of sovereignty and the long-term effects, most respondents anticipated only minor short-term deterioration, and the majority envisaged long-term economic improvement. It would seem that the sovereigntists' arguments about the smooth transition to sovereignty and the benefits of the partnership were effective in lifting the Yes side to its near-victory.

Further evidence about the significance of economic arguments is provided by Lachapelle, who shows that even in April 1995 the option of sovereignty – including an economic association with Canada – would attract almost 60 percent of the electorate (though this was still less popular than the notion of transferring certain powers from Ottawa to Quebec). More striking, the SOM-Radio-Canada poll done in late September showed that if voters were certain that Canada would negotiate an economic and political partnership, 56% would vote for sovereignty and 34% would vote No; if, however, they were certain that Canada would not negotiate such a partnership, only 30% would vote Yes and 57% would vote No. Finally, it seems that the credibility of the partnership increased throughout the campaign period. A series of three CROP polls asked voters whether they believed that Canada would indeed agree to negotiate after a Yes vote: the proportion answering Yes to this

---

[5] A competing explanation might be that the salience of each factor changed in the interval between the two polls, so that national identification, while shifting little in absolute terms, came to have a greater bearing on the voting decision. But this did not occur: there was no significant interaction between the weight of each factor and the poll.

question rose from 46% in late September to 51% in late October, while those answering No fell from 39% to 29%.

Yet more evidence is provided by Pinard (1997b). In explaining the "Bouchard effect," Pinard stresses the leader's charisma and the confidence and trust he inspired, and presents some necessarily fragmentary evidence that some poll respondents had changed their voting intentions after the *Bloc* leader took center stage in the Yes campaign. Undoubtedly Mr. Bouchard was a charismatic presence, but what message was effective in shifting votes? In Pinard's analysis, it was the economic partnership. Through the course of the campaign, Quebecers' sensitivity to historic grievances and their sense of insecurity seem not to have budged (although there may have been some increase in pride). What clearly did change was the perception that the partnership was probable. Using some unpublished polls, Pinard shows that the proportion of voters believing this increased steadily, from 43 percent in the first week of the campaign to 54 percent in the last week. In this analysis, Mr. Bouchard's impact was to diminish fears about the economic consequences of sovereignty.

> In assuming the role of the chief negotiator of this new partnership, of which he had been the instigator through the virage of April 1995, Lucien Bouchard became for many, thanks to his personality and message, the guarantor that the negotiations would be successful. He brought himself, moreover, to insist on the fact that the rest of Canada could not refuse to negotiate this partnership, that it was inevitable. This was important, because without a preliminary agreement on the partnership, any future accords remained uncertain and this constituted a weakness in the sovereigntist option. (1997b: 288–9, my translation)

This research, like the other studies, shows that the partnership proposal was attractive, that it helped make sovereignty seem realizable, that it weighed substantially on the voting decision, and that it gained credibility during the referendum campaign itself. But this was not the only element of the battle between the federalists and sovereigntists; indeed, it may not have been the decisive one.

Heresthetics

Modern political campaigns are organized around a limited number of dimensions of discourse. On these, the partisan forces adopt positions strategically. The objective is not merely to develop arguments that are persuasive, in the sense that good political rhetoric can draw support, but also to structure voters' perceptions of the situation. In the words of William Riker, who coined the term "heresthetics" to describe the structuring of discourse, people can be led strategically to find themselves on one side or the other "without any persuasion at all" (1986: ix).

The arguments deployed along these dimensions are crucial. While they are filtered by the media, and while many voters may put little effort into understanding them, as one experienced strategist has written, "in a close race it comes down to the 3 to 7 percent available undecided, and you'd better be there with your best at the exact moment they're making up their minds. If you're not, you might as well not even start." (James Carville, in Matalin and Carville: 19). Strategic discourse involves choosing dimensions and positions on them according to several considerations. One is winnability. The set of positions must have majority appeal, reaffirming the core supporters' reasons for their choice while also reaching voters who may occupy a rather different position. Second is constancy: the positions must be consistently maintained over time, in order to drive the message home and to maintain credibility (Page: 108–51). As well, the dimensions chosen and the positions taken on them must be logically coherent. This means that contradictory positions cannot be adopted about one theme; more important, taking certain positions on one dimension will preclude the adoption of some contradictory positions on another relevant dimension. Finally, the campaign discourse should be tailored in anticipation of the opponents' positions and arguments. Campaigns are competitive, and counterarguments must be foreseen, because the requirement of consistency will constrain the responses that can be made to them. If the opponents are making gains, an inability to respond effectively will leave open dangerous areas of vulnerability.

In the Quebec referendum, the critical dimensions were predictable, and the themes of the campaign developed much as some had expected (Young, 1995a: 178–84). The major difference is that the Yes forces did not propose a clear, straightforward question on sovereignty; instead, after Mr. Bouchard's *virage*, they fought on the twin proposals of sovereignty and the economic and political partnership. This rendered the argumentative strategy more complex for both sides, because the three main dimensions – national identification, the economic consequences of a Yes victory, and the existing constitutional system – became tightly interrelated. As well, the sovereigntists opened up a new, unanticipated dimension of discourse: democracy. This one became the crucial underlying element in the campaign. It was because the No side was incapable of taking a position on this dimension that the sovereigntists were able to make such headway with their arguments about the economy and the partnership, and almost to win the referendum.[6]

The constitution

On the constitutional dimension, the No forces stood at zero – the status quo. This was consistent with the position that had helped Prime Minister Chrétien win the 1993 election, when he argued that the economy and jobs were the only matters of real concern to Canadians and Quebecers. After the sovereigntists opened the dimension by calling the referendum, the federalists continued to argue that the existing constitutional framework was adequate, and flexible enough to accommodate, in a cooperative fashion, any genuine demands from Quebec or other regions and groups. As Mr. Chrétien put it during the referendum campaign, "The best way for Quebecers to assure positive change is to vote No. A No vote will allow Quebecers and other Canadians to work together to respond to new challenges." (19.10) Of course this position made the Quebec wing of the No side increasingly uncomfortable, but it was maintained until the sudden shift during the final week of the campaign. The federalists argued consistently that the onus was on the sovereigntists to prove why their constitutional option – "separation" – was necessary for Quebecers.

This was not an easy task for the Yes side. On the simple issue of political independence, the sovereigntists could not point to great advantages in having a seat in the United Nations, representation in the Olympics, and so on, and when sovereignty *tout court* was on the table they were often reduced to stating that sovereignty is "normal" for distinct peoples. But the shift to advocating a political and economic partnership brought the Yes side to focus on constitutional relationships with Canada itself. A Yes victory would bring about a new *"rapport de forces"* between the partners, as Mr. Bouchard so often put it. Sovereigntists could also argue that "separation" would not actually occur. "Will we be separate?" one of their leaders asked: "The answer is No." Instead, the system would resemble the European Union. "We look after our affairs without asking permission from others but without being separated; we are united on things where we have a common interest. This is the inverse of separation." (*London Free Press*, 5.10) Obviously, the partnership proposal allowed the Yes side to emphasize a range of positions along the constitutional dimension. In fact, as the campaign began, sovereigntists saw

---

[6] This possibility was also forseeable after the *virage*: see Young, 1995b.

some advantages in emphasizing the differences among the Yes leaders, hoping they could convince hesitant voters that Mr. Bouchard and his allies could rein in the harder-line PQ under Mr. Parizeau (8.9). But the Quebec premier was always clear: "If some people want to vote Yes to change Quebec's bargaining power and join the ranks, all the better. But let it be clear for everyone that by voting Yes they are voting for Quebec sovereignty." (13.10) And, especially on the political dimension of the partnership, Lucien Bouchard was also insistent: "I want it clearly understood that the question is on sovereignty and partnership after, but they aren't dependent. There is no hyphen between the two. The first will be achieved for all time, the second will come after as we think it will, but there's no guarantee it will come. There's no link of cause and effect. I have always been extremely clear: sovereignty per se, on its own, as a solution." (*Montreal Gazette*, 20.10)

The constitutional dimension was associated with two others. First, on the economic dimension, the federalists could, and did, argue that political separation would necessarily entail a costly long-term reduction in economic integration. On the other side, the Yes position favoring political association had some cost, because it weakened the economic argument that sovereignty would eliminate a lot of waste, overlap, and duplication in the federation. It was logically hard to argue on the economic front that Quebec had "*un gouvernement de trop*" ("one government too many") when the constitutional position advocated a new set of common institutions. Here the sovereigntists were vulnerable.

More complex was the linkage with the national-identification dimension. One sovereigntist position was that a No vote would hurt Quebecers. As Mr. Bouchard declared when the campaign was going poorly, "It's not true that Quebecers are weak, that Quebec will say No to itself. They will say Yes because the consequences of saying No would be too serious." (25.9) This could not be pressed too hard, however, because it was the sovereigntists themselves who had chosen to hold the referendum, so creating the very possibility of a damaging No vote. But they did argue that a No would expose Quebecers to Ottawa's centralizing tendencies, and to the spending cuts favored by the Reform Party and several other provincial governments. A much stronger positive effect was achieved by the partnership proposal, which, while allowing for a continued association with Canada, would finally provide for negotiations and policies to be decided on the basis of equality – "*égal-à'-égal*," as it was constantly phrased. This theme had a strong nationalistic appeal, and when he assumed the leadership of the Yes campaign, Mr. Bouchard consistently stressed it, while emphasizing the solidarity that would result from a collective choice for change: "A Yes vote will lead to unity of all Quebecers. We will all be sovereigntists, so much so that people will no longer refer to us as sovereigntists but simply as Quebecers." (9.10) Again, typically: "The people of Quebec must take their place in the empty chair facing English Canada to make the changes that we both need. . . . We will no longer have to ask anyone to recognize us as being specific or as an asymmetrical society or anything else. We don't want labels. . . . We just want one word – Québécois." (11.10)

The link between the constitutional issue and the national-identification dimension was problematic for the federalist side. While the No leaders could point to some evidence of flexible federalism, they were not prepared at the outset to promise the symbolic recognition as a "distinct society" that many Quebecers desired. Further, despite strenuous efforts, they could not entirely silence leaders in the rest of Canada who argued that all provinces must be constitutionally equal. For example, one provincial premier summarily rejected any notion of a partnership as "totally inconsistent with everything Canadians across the country have been saying for the last ten years." (14.10) Because such outright rejection of Quebecers' constitutional demands could be portrayed as insulting and demeaning, Mr. Chrétien preferred that federalists in the rest of the country either stay out of the campaign or send messages of affection. As he told a Vancouver audience, "You all have said, 'We want you to stay in Canada.' You didn't provoke them. Some were hoping for that. It's easy to get mad." (*London Free Press*, 11.10)

Nevertheless, in his first major campaign speech, Mr. Chrétien did predict that the partnership could not work: "The proposal for a political partnership flies in the face of the most elementary good sense. . . . It would be rejected because it would impose another level of government in Canada, with equal representation, even though Canada is three times the size of Quebec, and a right of veto that would totally paralyze both those broken countries." (7.10) Later, he pointed out some practical difficulties: "Canada with Quebec forms a country. Nobody knows what would remain of Canada without Quebec. Who has a mandate to speak for the so-called rest of Canada?" (*London Free Press*, 19.10) Similarly, Mr. Johnson warned, "Will Canada reach out to seven million Quebecers and say: 'You just broke up our country, but here's your passport?' It's unthinkable." (13.10) And the prime minister declared at an early campaign rally that a victory for the Yes side would bring independence, not a new partnership: "In that case, there will be no more Quebecers in the House of Commons, no more Quebecers running the government. Quebecers won't be Canadian citizens or hold Canadian passports." (*London Free Press*, 7.10) But this theme was very much muted in the federalist discourse on the constitutional dimension. Generally the No side stuck to the initial position that the existing constitution was flexible, and that whatever the question formally posed in the referendum, the real issue was "separation," a prospect that offered unknowable consequences and incalculable risks.

National identification

On this dimension the two sides lavished a great deal of discourse during the campaign, and the empirical studies suggest that the result was a standoff. Here, the federalists simply aimed to hold their ground. They stressed that Canada is a wonderful country, the envy of the world. Within it, Quebecers had a proud and honorable history, and a great deal of political influence. Separation would end all of that. It would bring an end to the country to which many Quebecers felt attached. The No side pressed this theme very hard at the end of the campaign. In his televised address to the nation, Mr. Chrétien posed a long series of questions about Canada, concluding with the following: "Have you found one reason, one good reason, to destroy Canada? Do you really think it is worth abandoning the country we have built, and which our ancestors have left us? Do you really think it makes any sense – any sense at all – to break up Canada?" (26.10) As well, the federalist side emphasized that there was no contradiction between being a Canadian and being a Quebecer. In what became a mantra toward the end of the campaign, they repeated that Canada is their country ("*pays*") while Quebec is their homeland ("*patrie*").

This dimension offered much scope to the sovereigntists, who devoted a lot of emotionally charged discourse to it. Their core position was that Quebecers constitute a people, distinct from those in the rest of Canada. So sovereignty would represent a logical stage in Quebec's evolution. By contrast, a No vote, in Mr. Parizeau's words, "would mean breaking away from what we are and what we have always wanted to become." (12.9) Part of the Yes position involved reciting the long series of humiliations and oppressions to which the Quebec people had been subjected, beginning with their conquest by the English, through conscription in the wars, and peaking with the "imposition" of the 1982 constitution; as well, the failure of the Meech Lake accord was characterized as a rejection of Quebec by Canada. Always the emphasis was on unity and solidarity, and on the need of Quebecers to put the endless squabblings of Canadian federalism behind them. In a much-misquoted remark, Mr. Bouchard held out this vision: "A Yes has something magical about it. With a wave of a wand, it transforms the whole situation. It produces within us solidarity and unity."[7] Finally, said the sovereigntists, a Yes result would end the historic doubts, the hesitation of Quebecers to declare themselves a people. At the last rally of the campaign, Mr. Bouchard beseeched the voters, arguing that now was their best chance: "We have no right to let it pass. God knows when it will present itself again. We have it before us. Seize it and vote Yes. Say Yes to ourselves. Say Yes to the people of Quebec." (*Montreal Gazette*, 30.10) This was powerful stuff. But however much the two sides contested on the national-identification dimension, it was not the crucial one.

The economy

On this dimension, the sovereigntist position was that secession would entail no economic losses, and that it would be economically advantageous in the long run. The discourse on the latter point was far less intense than on the former one, but the Yes side did speak about how sovereignty would end wasteful federal-provincial duplication, allow taxes to be frozen if not reduced, and permit the formation of autonomous policies suited to the Quebec economy. As well, sometimes with rather muddy appeals to endogenous growth theory, the Yes side referred to the advantages possessed in the global economy by small, relatively homogeneous, and solidaristic polities.

But the critical message concerned the prospect of economic disruption and loss in the transition period. Here is where the economic crunch would come, in the view of most experts, as investment was staunched by the uncertainty following a Yes vote, trade flows contracted, tax revenues shrank, deficits grew, talent emigrated, and so on (McCallum and Green). A sovereign Quebec would be a viable economic unit, most agreed, but the problem lay in the transition to sovereignty, which could involve a serious recession, damaging to Quebec and Canada both. Yet the sovereigntists dismissed every dire prediction as a threat or a bluff. It was rational, they argued, for the federalists to make such predictions in the hope of dissuading Quebecers from voting Yes. But after an actual Yes it would be irrational for Canada to retaliate economically, because this would impose losses on its own citizens. Indeed, economic rationality would lead Canada, inevitably, into a partnership, so as to manage the common economic space and avoid losses. The sovereigntists, in short, equated rationality with cooperation (Young, 1994).

This position meshed well with some traditional stereotypes – that

---

[7] *Globe and Mail*, 19 October 1995. The federalists derided this as implying that the "magic wand" would solve all of Quebec's problems, not just that of internal division.

English Canada is dominated by business interests (and business would not countenance disruption), and that its citizens are cold and canny (and hence willing to cut their losses and support cooperation with Quebec after a Yes). As one Anglophone commentator put it, "The separatists portray 'les anglais' as dessicated calculating machines, ready to cut deals the day after the destruction of their country." (Webster) As well, some aspects of the formal campaign were designed to provide reassurance about items particularly worrisome to the public; hence the provisions in Bill 1 about use of the Canadian dollar, accession to treaties, and other areas of economic concern. But on the economic dimension the sovereigntists pushed relentlessly to argue that none of the predictions of economic loss constituted a credible threat: the No side was bluffing, and cooperation was inevitable.

Early in the campaign, for example, Mr. Bouchard said, "All these stories we are being told that business people in Ontario, for example, will not want to do business with Quebec, we all know . . . it doesn't make any sense." After a Yes vote, he went on, the typical Toronto businessman "will go to his office and sit at his desk, and he will examine his sales figures. And he will see that he conducts 25 percent of his business in Quebec. Sure he'll be in a bad mood, but you know what he'll do. He will pick up his phone and call his biggest buyer in Quebec. And you know what he will say to him. He'll say, 'let's not mix politics with business.' " (28.8) Mr. Bouchard was equally dismissive of threats that governments would not cooperate after a Yes result: "English Canada would run after Mr. Parizeau to ask him, to beg him, to sit down and discuss the national debt." (*Maclean's*, 9.10) Again and again the sovereigntists hammered home their argument about where the self-interest of Canada lay. English Canadians, argued one PQ minister, "need our help to pay their debt, and they need our market if they want to continue selling us wheat, beef, Western gas, cars and financial services from Ontario. . . . To put up a border and customs would compromise these jobs, and the first victim would be Ontario." (*London Free Press*, 18.10) Sensing momentum after mid-October, Mr. Parizeau put in a nutshell the logic of the Yes argument about the economy and the partnership: "For heaven's sake, it's perfectly understandable that before the 30th all of these guys in Ottawa will say no, no, no, no. Well, after the 30th, they might say Yes to a few things." (*Montreal Gazette*, 21.10)

Obviously, this position helped fortify the pride and confidence to which the Yes side appealed on the national-identification dimension. Mr. Bouchard's discourse often combined equality and the economy. He said, for example, that sovereignty "is a powerful springboard to go and get a partnership which will impose itself after an assessment of each other's interests." (20.10) Again, toward the end of the campaign: "Those two peoples will talk to each other about their mutual interest and about what they want to deal with in common. The talk will be of commercial exchanges that are to be maintained and increased, of jobs to protect and to create." (26.10) Mr. Parizeau even referred jokingly to the effect a Yes would have. Noting that some provincial legislatures were passing motions favorable to Quebec just after two polls had found the Yes ahead, he crowed, "Imaginez, avec un Oui, à quel point ces gens vont devenir des partenaires volontaires du Québec!"[8] And summing up at the end of the campaign, Mr. Bouchard reflected: "My worries are about the fact that Quebecers have too often been impressed by the attempts to raise a scare in their minds.... But I trust, as we have been seeing in this campaign, that fear has been overcome by confidence. I'm happy to see Quebecers no longer take scare tactics seriously." (*Montreal Gazette*, 27.10)

As for the federalists, on this dimension they had little to say about Quebec's long-term prospects, except to point out generally that it would be a smaller, more vulnerable economic unit. Quebec would not benefit, for example, from Canada's weight in trade negotiations or membership in the G-7. On the whole, however, the No side preferred to couch such matters in more positive terms, referring to the strength and prosperity of a united Canada.

In fact, the basic federalist position on this dimension was to make no concrete predictions about the economic effects of a Yes vote. Federalist leaders consistently dismissed the entire issue as purely hypothetical: it would not happen, and there was no point in speculating about it. When pressed, the No forces emphasized the huge risk and uncertainty that "separation" would involve. Rather than say, for example, that Quebecers' geographic mobility would be restricted under sovereignty, they simply insisted that people's economic prospects after a Yes vote were quite unknown. The concrete promises of the sovereigntists certainly were not to be believed, for they could guarantee nothing about the future, which would become radically uncertain after a Yes vote. It was this uncertainty, with its consequent risk of severe economic disruption and loss, that the federalists believed would dissuade Quebecers from supporting sovereignty. This position was exemplified by the prime minister: "What is immediately guaranteed after a No vote is that we will still have a sovereign country. A country that guarantees us Canadian citizenship, Canadian passports, and the Canadian dollar. . . . On the one

---

[8] *La Presse*, 28 October 1995. ("Imagine, after a Yes, the extent to which these people will become voluntary partners with Quebec!")

hand stands separation, which would hurtle us all into the unknown, with all the risks it would involve. It is an invitation to an adventure from which no one, including those who believe in it, would emerge a winner. On the other hand stands an economically and politically strong Quebec, continuing its tremendous development in Canada." (*Montreal Gazette*, 20.10)

At times the federalists went a bit further. Mr. Johnson in particular stressed economic issues, arguing, for example, that "voting Yes is a risky adventure that will bring economic upheaval, affect the value of the dollar, mortgage rates, and raise interest rates on other things we buy." (*London Free Press*, 11.9) He also produced a sovereignty budget that showed a very large deficit and consequent tax increases, and he made precise predictions about job losses based on extant studies. But these predictions were derided as blackmail and bluff by the sovereigntists, especially after Mr. Martin's comments about 1,000,000 jobs being at risk. When Mr. Johnson stated that a Quebec dollar would be worth 63 cents, he had to defend himself against accusations of fear-mongering, and showed the strain of trying to make headway against the Yes side's position: "I am utterly and personally convinced that separation means economic dire consequences for all Quebecers and I certainly am not going to shut up before the referendum date just because I'm being accused of being a fearmonger. I'm a realitymonger. I'm a truthmonger." (*Montreal Gazette*, 20.10)

The No side also pointed out that many economic matters covered by the partnership proposal were strictly within the power of Canada to determine. At their annual meeting, for example, the provincial premiers indicated that interprovincial trade agreements could not be taken for granted by a sovereign Quebec.[9] Federalists also referred to Canada's control of the currency, milk quotas, labor mobility, equalization payments and other transfers, and even the deployment of the military forces and the jobs they created. But, consistent with their basic position that a sovereigntist victory would produce enormous uncertainty, they did not state what would actually happen after a Yes vote. With few exceptions, it was never clearly predicted that labor mobility would end, milk quotas would be reallocated, military bases would close, and so on. The core position was to maintain uncertainty about the behavior of the rest of Canada, in the expectation that this would induce a No vote by risk-averse Quebecers.

There were strategic weaknesses in each side's position. The sover-

---

[9] This was dismissed by Mr. Parizeau as evidence of a conspiracy to frighten Quebecers: see the *Globe and Mail*, 24 and 26 August 1995.

eigntist argument that a Yes result would bring no economic disruption was open to the counterargument that this demonstrated the acceptability of the status quo. If a partnership was necessary, what then was the purpose of sovereignty? As Mr. Johnson said at the outset of the campaign, "I'm still waiting for the government to tell us why we should vote Yes. It's voting Yes to Quebec's departure from Canada with no guarantees – we close all the doors." (*London Free Press*, 11.9) But the federalists were much more vulnerable. Making no precise statements about what a Yes would bring economically, including Canada's response about those matters covered by the partnership proposal, they aimed to sustain uncertainty. But this strategic position left a gap into which the sovereigntists could spin their web of arguments about post-secession cooperation. In the absence of declarations about what would happen on the economic front, the Yes side advanced with its arguments that the rest of Canada would need to negotiate out of its own self-interest, that the secession would be tranquil, and that economic links would not be severed.

There are several reasons why the federalists did not close off this line of argument by spelling out the economic effects of a Yes vote. At the outset of the campaign, the No side was confident, and it probably appeared that stressing uncertainty alone would suffice to deter marginal voters from choosing sovereignty. To have been more definite would also have meant moving toward positions taken by the Reform Party, which was unattractive for partisan reasons. More important, there is no evidence that federalist leaders and their advisors had spent much time or effort in thinking about what a Yes actually would bring, and so it would be difficult, honestly, to make concrete predictions. Further, it was not evident who in the No camp had the legitimacy to lay out the terms of separation, on matters like the currency, trade arrangements, agricultural policy, and the division of the debt. Had any federalist leader taken a strong, clear position on these matters, the unity of the No side could have been gravely weakened. Moreover, such statements could have been portrayed by the Yes side as initial bargaining positions rather than a credible bottom line. Were such predictions or positions rather harsh toward Quebec's interests, this also would have contradicted the No side's stance on the national-identification dimension, where the consistent theme was Canada's civility, tolerance, and openness to Quebecers, as well as a long-standing sense of shared citizenship and community. These are all good reasons. But another one has to do with how economic positions were linked with those taken on the final dimension of the campaign.

Democracy

Compared to the preceding dimensions, democracy was the subject of much less explicit discourse and commentary during the referendum campaign, but it was nevertheless the most strategically significant one. The sovereigntists opened it, and it provided them with an important degree of freedom. William Riker showed how opening dimensions of discourse is an heresthetic device that can structure debate and produce different outcomes, but he also argued that constraining dimensions, or "fixing dimensionality," can deter counterattacks (1986: 66–77). In the Quebec referendum campaign, the federalists did not – or could not – take a position on the democracy dimension. Consequently, they were strategically incapable of shutting down the Yes side's economic arguments, and so nearly lost the referendum.

The sovereigntists always insisted on the legitimacy of their *démarche*. They assumed from the outset that Quebecers had the right to determine their collective future. The process of deciding whether Quebec should become sovereign, they said, was a highly democratic one. It involved a major exercise in public consultation – regional commission hearings in early 1995, at which, despite a boycott by the QLP, thousands of people had appeared. It also involved a legitimate referendum process. The question put to the citizenry had been debated in the National Assembly, according to the referendum law. That law was itself highly democratic, in the sense that it provided a framework for organizing two sides around the issue, and imposed strict spending limits on each while providing public funding for the competing organizations. Finally, and crucially, since Quebec was a highly advanced and democratic society, all those involved would accept the outcome of the vote. In a parliamentary system, of course, referenda cannot be binding, but the sovereigntists had accepted the No verdict of Quebecers in 1980. Similarly, the 1995 result would be accepted by all. These themes were fundamental to the whole approach of the Yes side to the referendum.

On this dimension, the No side simply refused to take a position. A Yes was hypothetical, so its possible consequences were not worth discussing. The federalist leaders condemned the process leading to the referendum as manipulative, and they consistently attacked the question as ambiguous, but they were carefully noncommital about the implications of any result other than a No vote. As one journalist put it, for the federalist side "separation is not so much an evil as a non sequitur." (Wells: 17) Consistently, the federalists refused any engagement to accept a Yes result as valid. Their discourse on this dimension of the debate was minimal – far less than on those of national identification or the economy or the constitution – but their strategic choice here was highly significant. The No forces insisted that separation was an economically uncertain and costly adventure; yet the choice to be noncommital about the legitimacy of a Yes result left the No side vulnerable to the economic counterarguments of the sovereigntists.

The federalist ambiguity on the democracy dimension was shown well before the referendum campaign began. In late 1994, Prime Minister Chrétien suggested that Ottawa would not be compelled to negotiate sovereignty after a Yes vote: "It's not in the constitution. . . . If you want to talk legality and constitutionality, there's nobody who will argue that it is legal and constitutional." (*London Free Press*, 20.12.1994) Treading lightly, however, an aide to Mr. Chrétien immediately said that this position should not be regarded as a threat or a refusal to accept a Yes result: "He's just pointing out that the separatists have tried to gloss over a lot of tough questions."

Undoubtedly the federalists' frustration with their heresthetical situation grew when the sovereigntists adopted the partnership proposal, and launched a campaign on a question that the federalists regarded as deceptive and ambiguous. But Mr. Chrétien remained noncommittal about what a Yes vote would entail, dismissing all discussion of the matter as speculative. In his first public comments during the campaign, which set the tone for all subsequent remarks, the prime minister refused to say whether he would accept a Yes victory: "You're asking a hypothetical question. We have a referendum and they are proposing separation. We're going to tell Quebecers that, and Quebecers will vote for Canada." (12.9)

This position was briefly shaken when the same question was put to the federal minister formally in charge of the referendum, Mme. Robillard. She replied, "We have always said that Quebecers have the right to express themselves about the future of Quebec in Canada, inside or outside Canada. We are in a democratic country, so we'll respect the vote." (13.9) Pressed immediately on this matter in Quebec, Mr. Johnson took a similar line. "The people of Quebec will abide by the results – end of story." He continued: "We want a democratic vote – it is. The referendum process is acceptable; the law is clear for everyone – the campaign, financing, timing. It's *vox populi*." (13.9) But all this was reversed after Mme. Robillard consulted with colleagues and advisors to the prime minister. She amended her remarks to the effect that the government would respect "the democratic process," rather than any particular outcome. In a damage-control news conference, Mr. Chrétien reaffirmed his noncommital position: "There is a vote and, of course, we'll receive the result of the vote, but you're asking me a hypothetical question. I'm standing here telling you we're going to win." (13.9) After the matter was the subject of heated questions in the House of Commons, Mr. Johnson also reversed his field, saying, "How can you break up a country on a judicial recount? It has to be clear either way if you want to go on to other things." (20.9)

That Commons exchange revealed how steadfast were the federalists in taking no position on the democracy dimension, despite the conflicting pressures on them to do so. First, the *Bloc québécois* demanded that Mr. Chrétien make a commitment to accept the result, and he refused to do so. One reason was that the sovereigntist leaders had indicated they might call yet another referendum should they lose in 1995; hence, the Yes side was refusing to be bound by the results. More important, the question was ambiguous:

> I have always said they had the right to have a referendum in Quebec. Quebecers can be consulted and can explain their point of view. However, we on this side of the House are convinced that Quebecers, if they are asked an honest question about the separation of Quebec from Canada, not a trick question, no clever twists and turns but an honest question: Do you want to separate from Canada? If the leader of the Leader of the Opposition, Mr. Parizeau, was truly intellectually honest, he would have asked Quebecers: Do you want to separate? And Quebecers would have answered: No, never. (*Debates*, 18.9: 14528)

Through more than a dozen questions over two days about whether the federal government would recognize a Yes vote, the prime minister remained noncommital, accusing the sovereigntists of posing a deceptively ambiguous question, arguing that Quebecers wanted to put the constitution aside and enjoy economic growth and good government, and predicting that the voters would never choose to separate.

But there was also pressure on this dimension from the Reform Party, whose leaders argued that clarity was crucial. Mr. Manning asked, "[W]ill the Prime Minister make clear that a yes vote means Quebec is on its way out, that a no vote means Quebec is in the federation for the long haul, and that 50 percent plus one is the dividing line between those two positions?" Mr. Chrétien would not do so. "I have been asking them for a long time in this House of Commons to give us a real question, an honest, clear question on separation. They have clouded the issue talking about divorce and remarriage at the same time. They want me on behalf of all Canadians to say that with a clouded question like that with one vote I will help them to destroy Canada. You might, I will not, Mr.

Manning." (*Debates*, 18.9: 14530) But the Reform Party continued to press. In their view, if a Yes vote might not actually produce separation, then it was less risky to cast one. As Mr. Manning put it, "They think they can vote for separation and still enjoy the benefits of federalism. That is why we asked the Prime Minister to make clear that yes means separation and only no means federalism. I will again ask the Prime Minister sincerely, as we are not playing games here, why he is so reluctant to make that distinction crystal clear." Mr. Chrétien responded:

> In a country like ours to recognize that at one time a rule of majority plus one could break up the country would be irresponsible on my part. Even in the Reform Party, as a journalist wrote this morning, in order to change its constitution one has to ask for two-thirds of its membership. Therefore I will not break up the country with one vote. It is not real democracy. Real democracy is to convince the people they can express themselves clearly, which is what we are doing. This is why we are telling Quebecers these people want to separate but they will not succeed because it is our collective duty to tell all Quebecers the scheme they have, the virage, the mirage and so on will not work. They will not succeed in fooling the people of Quebec because the people of Quebec will know when they vote thirty-nine days from now that they will not separate. They will stay in Canada because it is their destiny, their future and their desire. (*Debates*, 19.9: 14608)

But the issue did not go away. During the campaign, Mr. Bouchard regularly spoke of the great democratic exercise in which Quebecers were engaged, and in the final days before the referendum the democracy dimension reemerged strongly. In his reply to the prime minister's televised address to the nation, Mr. Bouchard stated that "Quebecers will make a decision on Monday, a decision that they will have carefully reflected upon through a democratic process, the fairness of which does not afford any challenge." He continued:

> One supreme and fundamental issue that Quebec and Canada share and cherish is democracy. . . . With respect to the decision that will be taken by the majority of Quebecers next Monday, I expect this common value of democracy to prevail. I am reassured by the citizens of Canada that I have met who are saying that Quebecers can decide their own future and that such a decision should be accepted by the rest of Canada. The voices of these people have been heard by political leaders, and I call upon all leaders and their sense of democracy to show the same respect for the will of the people of Quebec. (26.10)

Similarly, he argued, the result would be accepted in Quebec, "because we live in a democracy. We sovereigntists proved it in 1980 when we accepted the verdict." (*Montreal Gazette*, 27.10) And on the last day of the campaign, he predicted that Canadians would peacefully accept a Yes result. "There must be surprise because they have been put to sleep by Mr. Chrétien who told them all the time that there was no problem." However, he continued, "I fully expect the rest of Canada, as all Quebecers, whatever happens, to accept the verdict of democracy." (30.10) Mr. Parizeau, with victory in sight but Ottawa's intentions unclear, insisted not only that the transition would be calm, but also that all Quebecers would have to show solidarity in accepting the result of the vote, and he singled out his main provincial opponent: "The example comes from the top. Without misgiving, I say that the leader of the Quebec Liberal Party, Mr. Daniel Johnson, fought fiercely, but always was a democrat." (25.10)

Mr. Chrétien, however, never said he would accept a Yes result. He was noncommital to the end. In a television interview, while striking the federalist chords of constitutional flexibility, patriotism, and the economic uncertainty that a Yes would bring, he refused to agree that a 51 percent sovereigntist victory would be decisive: "Non, je n'ai pas reconnu rien. Vous ne savez pas le résultat et moi non plus. Les gens auront exprimé leur point de vue. Les méchanismes, après, c'est très nébuleux."[10]

In the end, those *"méchanismes"* were never tested. But the federalist decision not to take a position on the democratic dimension was both risky and costly. The strategy was risky because it precluded the federalists from making a convincing reply to the sovereigntists' position on the economic dimension. There, the Yes side was arguing that cooperation between Canada and a sovereign Quebec would be inevitable because of the self-interest of each side in minimizing economic disruption. Moreover, they advanced the partnership idea, and this had a strong appeal because it promised a framework for economic management that would minimize losses in the transition to sovereignty. This is where the sovereigntists made their gains in the summer and autumn of 1995.

To shut down the progress of the Yes side on the economic dimension, the federalists had to state clearly that the partnership would never materialize. They would have had to declare that constitutional amendments would excise Quebec from Canada, that economic integration would drop sharply, that there would be border-posts around Quebec, that agriculture would contract, that social entitlements and labor mobil-

---

[10] *La Presse*, 27 October 1995 ("No, I haven't recognized anything. You don't know the result and neither do I. People would have expressed their point of view. After that, the mechanics are very nebulous.") See also *Le Devoir* and the *Globe and Mail*, 27 October 1995.

ity would end, and so on. All these outcomes would have been unattractive to the undecided, soft-nationalist voters. The No side did raise questions throughout the campaign about how a Yes vote would affect these substantive matters, but federalists never presented a coherent position about the economic consequences of a Yes vote. Some reasons for this have been suggested already – complacency, the difficulty of integrating the No forces, and the unattractive air of harshness that such statements might have conveyed – but a deeper one was the linkage between the economic and democratic dimensions. On the economic dimension, the sovereigntists pressed the vision of the partnership that would protect Quebecers from losses, while the federalists mainly predicted only economic uncertainty and risk. For the No side to be more precise about the negative economic implications of a Yes result, its leaders had to be more than noncommital on the democratic dimension. The federalists would have had to accept in principle that a Yes vote in the October referendum meant that Quebec would become a sovereign country. Only then could the sovereigntists' economic arguments – and their sanguine predictions of cooperation and partnership – be countered effectively.

But this the federalists did not do. There are undoubtedly many reasons for this decision. Apart from those mentioned already is another, more speculative one. This is that the key strategists on the federalist side, most of whom had deep roots in Montreal, literally could not contemplate a Canada without Quebec.[11] The intensity of their discourse on the national-identification dimension is testimony to this (just as Mr. Bouchard's insistence on referring to Quebecers as "*nous*" attests to the ethnic nationalism that the cosmopolitan federalists abhorred). For example, federalist leaders commonly spoke about Quebec as the "heart" or "soul" of Canada. At the Montreal pro-Canada rally, Mr. Chrétien shouted, "We say No to those who would strip us of our Canada." (*Montreal Gazette*, 28.10) And at the final No rally of the campaign, in Hull, the prime minister expressed his sentiments clearly: "For all of us, Canada without Quebec is unthinkable just as Quebec without Canada is unthinkable." (*Montreal Gazette*, 30.10) Because of this deep attachment, the key strategists on the No side were not able to concede – even in principle, and even to win a contest with enormous stakes for all Canadians – that Quebec could become a sovereign state. As a consequence, they almost lost.

---

[11] See Guy Laforest, "L'establishment du nationalisme canadien," *Le Devoir*, 5 May 1995, and Jane Taber, "Ministers come and go, but kitchen cabinet stays," *Ottawa Citizen*, 28 January 1996.

Conclusion

The effects of ambiguity on the democratic dimension were profound. The sovereigntists continued to advance in the polls as the disincentives to voting Yes diminished because of their winning economic arguments. The No side could not bring itself to move on the democracy dimension and block those arguments. Since there was a standoff on the identification dimension, there was only one possible axis along which the federalists could shift. They moved on the constitution. At the Verdun rally on October 24, and in the televised speech to the country the next day, Mr. Chrétien committed the federalists to formal constitutional change – recognizing Quebec as a distinct society, decentralizing powers, and restoring Quebec's constitutional veto. This major shift followed profound disagreement in the No campaign, and was reported to be very much against the prime minister's own instincts. (23.10) But it did allow the No forces to portray themselves as agents of the change most Quebecers wanted, within the Canada they enjoyed, and with no risk of economic loss. Given the fundamental refusal to countenance a Yes, this was all the federalists could do, and it may have produced the narrow No victory on October 30. But there was a cost. This strategic move ensured that the question of Quebec's constitutional status has not been laid to rest. The competition continues.

References

Blais, André, Richard Nadeau, and Pierre Martin (1996), "Pourquoi le Oui à-t-il fait des gains pendant la campagne référendaire?", in Trent, Young, and Lachapelle, 71–80.

Bernier, Robert (1997), "Les motivations, les perceptions et les attitudes des Québécois francophones à l'automne de 1994", in Pinard, Bernier, and Lemieux, 135–213.

Canada, House of Commons, *Debates*, vol. 133, 1st Session, 35th Parliament.

Cloutier, Édouard, Jean H. Guay, and Daniel Latouche (1992), *Le virage: L'évolution de l'opinion publique au Québec depuis 1960* (Montreal: Québec/Amérique).

Lachapelle, Guy, "La souveraineté partenariat: donnée essentielle du résultat référendaire et de l'avenir des relations Québec-Canada", in Trent, Young, and Lachapelle, 41–63.

Lemieux, Vincent (1996), "Le référendum de 1995: quelques pistes d'explication", in Trent, Young, and Lachapelle, 65–69.

McCallum, John, and Chris Green (1991), *Parting as Friends: The Economic Consequences for Quebec* (Toronto: C.D. Howe Institute).

Matalin, Mary and James Carville (1994), *All's Fair: Love, War, and Running for President* (New York: Random House).

Page, Benjamin (1978), *Choices and Echoes in Presidential Elections* (Chicago: University of Chicago Press).

Pinard, Maurice (1997a), "Le cheminement de l'opinion publique," in Pinard, Bernier, and Lemieux, 261–276.

Pinard, Maurice (1997b), "Le contexte politique et les dimensions sociodémographiques," in Pinard, Bernier, and Lemieux, 277–315.

Pinard, Maurice, Robert Bernier, and Vincent Lemieux (1997), *Un Combat Inachevé* (Sainte Foy, Québec: Presses de l'Université du Québec).

Quebec (1995), National Assembly, 1st Session, 35th Legislature, Bill 1 – An Act Respecting the Future of Quebec (Quebec: Québec Official Publisher).

Riker, William (1986), *The Art of Political Manipulation* (New Haven: Yale University Press).

Simpson, Jeffrey (1995), "Bouchard electrifies Yes voters, fulfilling an old and powerful dream," *Globe and Mail*, 12 October.

Trent, John, Robert Young, and Guy Lachapelle, eds. (1996), *Québec-Canada: What Is the Path Ahead?* (Ottawa: University of Ottawa Press).

Webster, Norman (1995), "C'mon Canada, it's time to do something. NOW," *Montreal Gazette*, 21 October.

Wells, Paul (1995), "Be vewy, vewy quiet," *Saturday Night*, September: 17–21.

Young, Robert (1994), "The Political Economy of Secession: The Case of Quebec," *Constitutional Political Economy*, 5:2: 221–245.

Young, Robert (1995a), *The Secession of Quebec and the Future of Canada* (Montreal: McGill-Queen's University Press).

Young, Robert (1995b), "'Maybe Yes, Maybe No': The Rest of Canada and a Quebec 'Oui'," in Douglas Brown and Jonathan Rose, eds., *Canada: The State of the Federation 1995* (Kingston: Institute of Intergovernmental Relations), 47–62.

Young, Robert (1998), *The Secession of Quebec and the Future of Canada*, 2nd ed. rev. (Montreal: McGill-Queen's University Press).

PART V

Governments and the market

CHAPTER 14

Public subsidies for private firms in a federalist democracy

Dennis C. Mueller

A normative theory of democracy sees the government as created by the citizens to advance their collective interests (Buchanan and Tullock, 1962, Chapter 1; Mueller, 1996). Given the now almost-universal recognition of the role private markets play in advancing individual interests, any democratic constitution written today would certainly establish institutions that encourage and protect market competition.

The movement of firms from one location to another, and their occasional disappearance through bankruptcy, are normal occurrences in a market economy. In general, such firm movements and disappearances can be expected to improve the long-run efficiency of the economy by locating capital where it is most productive and eliminating inefficient producers. Governments that seek to promote economic efficiency should welcome capital mobility and tolerate, if not celebrate, the disappearance of weak competitors.

Occasionally, however, the impending departure or demise of a company induces public concern, calls for public assistance, and then some form of subsidy or other government action to keep the firm from moving or dying. Such government interventions advance the interests of *all* citizens only in the presence of some sort of "market failure" that makes the survival of the company a form of "public good." Alternatively, such subsidies and other forms of protection may be examples of "rent-seeking" interventions that harm one group to benefit another. Subsidies, for example, might well be harmful, not only to the citizens who pay taxes to fund them, but also to competitors of the subsidized companies, and thus to the competitive process itself. Considerations such as these have led the European Union (EU) to adopt a policy of opposing subsidies by member countries to their domestic firms, which in turn has led to clashes between the EU Commission and individual national governments, as in 1994 over France's subsidies to its troubled national airline, Air France, and again in 1996 over Saxony's subsidies to Volkswagen. Since the EU itself engages in various forms of subsidies and other sorts of protection for individual firms as a part of its industrial and agricultural policy programs, clashes such as these raise questions over both when subsidies should be allowed and what level of government should provide them.

In this chapter we explore conditions under which subsidies can produce a Pareto-optimal allocation of resources in the context of a federalist governmental structure (section II), and in cases where subsidies to private firms are justified whether they should be made by the central government or a lower level government. This latter question is part of the general "assignment problem," with which Albert Breton and Anthony Scott (1978) were concerned in their pioneering study of federalism. In section III we examine whether communities may enter into a form of destructive competition for businesses that leads to Pareto-inferior outcomes. We then consider the impact of public subsidies on the competitive process (section IV), and the proper policy to apply to public subsidies to protect consumer welfare (section V). The public choice of the origin and effects of public subsidies is discussed in section VI. In section VII we contrast the implications of our analysis with current EU policies. Conclusions are drawn in section VIII. We begin by briefly examining the issue of the optimal taxation of capital in a federalist system.

I   The optimal taxation of capital under federalism

Let us assume that the citizens of a nation have sorted themselves into communities with identical tastes to consume optimal bundles of local public goods (Tiebout, 1956; McGuire, 1974). Each member of a particular community has the identical utility function, $U(x, s, g, H)$, where x is a private good imported into the community, s are services supplied by other members of the community, g is local governmental services, and H is the stock of housing owned by an individual citizen. For simplicity, we begin by assuming that H is a function of past investments, and does not depreciate. Thus, the representative individual must choose x, s, and g so as to maximize U, subject to the budget constraint, $y = P_x x + P_s s + T$, where T is her local tax payments. With n members of the community, $T = P_g g / n$. From the first order conditions it is easy to derive the usual optimality relationships for private and public goods

$$\frac{\partial U/\partial x}{\partial U/\partial s} = \frac{P_x}{P_s}, \quad n\frac{\partial U/\partial g}{\partial U/\partial x} = \frac{P_g}{P_x} \tag{1}$$

Ideally, T would be raised as a lump-sum tax on all citizens. Taxing either x or s would result in the usual deadweight losses, as would a tax on y if the individual could trade off leisure for income. With H fixed, it becomes an alternative to a head tax as an ideal basis for taxation.

Suppose that the only source of outside income for the community is a single firm that employs m members of the community. It has a capital stock K, and the owners of this capital reside outside of the community. Assume further that the parameters of a community member's utility function are such that $y/3 = P_x x = P_s s = T$. Each employee of the firm spends a third of her income on local private services and a third on local public services. Thus, every three employees of the firm directly support one service worker in the private sector and one in the public sector. Each of these divides his income of y in the same way as an employee of the firm, however, so that taking into account multiplier effects, the community has n members, $n = 3m$, divided equally across the three sources of employment.

The existence of the firm in the community provides another possible source of tax revenue. Indeed, if K is totally sunk, i.e., does not depreciate, then the community can effectively export its taxes by taxing K up to the value of K itself. This potential is reduced, however, to the extent that the capital of the firm depreciates.

Let δ be the depreciation rate on K, and r_c the gross of depreciation return on capital in the community. If other communities do not tax capital, then the suppliers of capital will demand $r_o - \delta$ as a net return in this community, where r_o is the gross return on capital in other communities. If the community's tax rate on capital is t_k, then r_c must satisfy the following relationship:

$$r_c - \delta - t_k = r_o - \delta \tag{2}$$

under the assumption that δ is the same in all communities. The unexpected introduction of a tax on K by the community will therefore cause the owners of the firm to reduce the capital employed in it until r_c rises enough to satisfy equation (2). If the elasticity of capital with respect to return were one, a new tax on capital of 10 percent would result in a 10 percent reduction in the firm's capital stock, and with a fixed coefficient production function an eventual 10 percent fall in employment. Since, given the multiplier effect, each employee of the firm supports two other members of the community, a 10 percent tax on the capital of the firm will reduce employment and income in the community by 10 percent.

A community that set a given percentage tax on the value of capital employed in the firm could look forward to a steady state in which the firm continued to operate in the community, but at a lower level of activity, assuming that the return on capital invested in the community rose fast enough as capital was reduced to fully offset the effect of the tax on the net returns on capital. If the return on K in the community was constant and equaled r_o, the community could not raise *any* revenue by taxing K, as *all* of the capital would earn a lower return than elsewhere and would be withdrawn.

Now consider what happens if a community tries to raise a fixed amount of revenue, say mT, through a tax of t_k on capital. Two possibilities exist. If the present value of the tax (mT/r_o) exceeds the value of the firm's capital, K, the firm exits immediately. If $mT/r_o < K$, the firm will choose to stay in the community, but to reduce the value of its capital stock. To raise a constant amount of revenue, the community must continually *raise* t_k, as the firm's owners adjust the capital stock downward. At some point the present value of the firm's taxes exceeds the value of its capital, and it exits the community.

Even when the firm does not exit, there are costs to its reducing its capital stock, *unless* other firms move into the community to replace it. The loss in income caused by the contraction of the firm must either be shared by all of the community through some employment insurance program, or fall entirely on the subset directly affected. If these persons leave the community, then they lose the consumption benefits associated with their fixed housing stocks, and/or suffer a capital loss as the price of these assets falls due to the reduction in demand for them. The Tiebout literature argues that individuals group themselves into local communities with homogeneous tastes. Someone leaving the community because of the contraction of the firm might therefore be forced to enter a community with different tastes for local public goods than his own, and thus will experience a utility loss from the move. Nevertheless, if the depreciation rate on the firm's capital is low, some of the community's members may benefit enough from taxing the firm's capital rather than themselves to bring about this policy.

We conclude that the attractiveness of taxing externally owned capital declines with its mobility. If local public goods are not inputs into a local firm's production process, then its capital goes untaxed if it is perfectly mobile (Gordon, 1986). If local public goods are inputs into local production, then the local community adopts benefit tax formulas such that the marginal local tax paid by capital just equals the marginal benefits it receives from local public goods and services (Oates and Schwab, 1988, 1991). With capital perfectly mobile, capital will not be able to exploit local communities, nor will local communities be able to exploit capital.

II   The private firm as a public good

In the previous section we have seen that a community will wish to raise all of its revenue by taxing externally held capital when it is completely immobile, and none of its revenue from such a tax when this capital is completely mobile. Since, by definition, complete or perfect mobility is the upper bound of mobility, it would seem that a zero tax on capital must be the lower bound for this tax. How then can one explain *negative* taxes on externally owned capital; how can one rationalize subsidies?

We have also seen in the previous section that some, perhaps all, members of a local community may be hurt by a withdrawal of capital from it. Any unexpected event that causes the firm to incur losses, not just a tax increase, may induce the firm's owners to withdraw some or all of their capital from the community. Two polar cases are of interest: a one-time loss of L, and an annual flow of losses f.

If the unexpected, one-time loss of L is less than the value of the firm's capital stock K, the firm's owners will simply absorb the loss and continue operating as before, since once the loss is covered the firm's capital is again worth K. If $L > K$, however, it is in the owners' interest to walk away from the firm, declare bankruptcy, and cap their losses at K. In the extreme case that no new external source of employment comes to fill the departing firm's place, the loss of L causes those employed by the firm to exit and eventually destroys the community, taking with it all of its fixed capital, nH, and any additional benefits associated with membership in this particular community. Even ignoring the latter, members of the community are obviously better off preserving the firm and with it the community, if $nH > L$.

When the loss is a constant flow, f, the same logic applies as when the community tries to raise a fixed amount of tax revenue over time. If the present value of the loss exceeds K, the firm exits immediately; if not, it continually reduces its assets until $f/r_o > K$, and then it exits.

Some unexpected shocks, for example, a permanent downward shift in demand, are better treated as shifting the demand for the firm's capital, resulting in, say, a constant percentage reduction in the return on its capital, λ. The firm then reduces its output and capital stock until

$$r_c - \delta - \lambda = r_o - \delta \tag{3}$$

holds. This action reduces employment and income in the community and, if it results in the emigration of α fraction of the community, wipes out privately held assets with a value of αnH. If the community's discount rate is i, it will gain by imposing an annual tax on itself of λK and subsidizing the firm to offset this loss, if $\alpha n H > \lambda K/i$.

The attractiveness to a community of taxing externally owned capital depends on the capital's mobility. The attractiveness of *subsidizing* externally owned capital depends on the mobility of both capital and the members of community. If the departure of one firm would be immediately offset by the arrival of another, the community would not tax itself to retain a particular company. If residents possessed no fixed assets or other benefits specific to this particular community, they would not tax themselves to remain there. But if *members of the community are immobile* – because they own immobile assets, because they have personal attachments to other members of the community, because they cannot obtain as attractive a bundle of local public goods for the same taxes elsewhere – then taxes on community residents to subsidize externally held capital may be optimal.

III   Tax and subsidy competition across communities

It is sometimes argued that when communities compete for businesses by offering tax breaks, a "race to the bottom" occurs in which the communities themselves are harmed through the erosion of their tax bases and the consequent reduction in their local public goods supply.[1] Such a race to the bottom could presumably lead to negative taxes, and thus this critique applies to local subsidies for firms as well. As noted in section I, however, with perfect capital mobility local communities will level zero taxes on capital or, if they provide capital public goods benefits, will merely charge for these benefits. No community would rationally make itself worse off through a tax to subsidize a particular firm, if another firm would enter the community without such a subsidy. For the race-to-the-bottom argument to have merit with respect to taxes and subsidies for firms, capital must not be available to communities in infinitely elastic supply.

To see what is involved, let us consider an example where there is a perfectly inelastic supply of capital. Assume first that there are N communities, each containing one firm with capital stock K, and employing m workers. The technology is such that neither a larger nor a smaller firm is viable. Each community has a population of $n = 3m$, as in the earlier example, and each resident of community c owns fixed, nondepreciating housing capital of H_c, $c = 1, N$. The values of housing capital are assumed

---

[1] Although the fear of a "race to the bottom" is often expressed, there is scant empirical evidence to support such fears (Levinson, 1996). Wilson (1996) also questions the logical foundations for such fears.

to be identical within a community, but possibly different across them. We assume that the initial equilibrium arose at a time when both individuals and capital were perfectly mobile, so that firms are untaxed, and all local public goods are financed through benefit taxes on their residents. Capital is perfectly inelastic to the nation, but perfectly mobile within it.

Now assume that an external shock destroys one firm, say that of community d. No new capital can flow in from outside of the nation to replace community d's firm, but firms can move from other communities into d. If community d must disband, its residents lose capital with a value of nH_d. It is prepared to offer up to this amount to attract a firm with capital K from another community. Any other community c will offer nH_c to retain its firm, however, so that a bidding war ensues with the community with the lowest value capital stock, nH_l, being the ultimate loser. Every other community must match the loser's bid to keep its firm, so that the shortage of capital results in a massive transfer of $(N-1)nH_l$ from residents of the $(N-1)$ communities to the owners of the $(N-1)$ surviving companies. Nevertheless, each winning community is better off from bidding by the difference in value between its housing stock and that of the losing bidder. The bidding process is efficient in that the limited available capital is allocated to the communities that have the most to gain from it.

A more realistic assumption would be that capital is in relatively inelastic supply in the short run, but in elastic supply in the long run. The unexpected and sudden departure of a major source of employment in an isolated rural community might lead it to offer generous subsidies to firms willing to enter the community. But in the long run the general mobility of capital should eliminate these subsidies, and bring about the zero-tax-and-subsidies outcomes predicted with perfect capital mobility.

Thus, there is no reason to expect competition for capital across communities to result in a misallocation of resources. Communities will not bid for capital that is in infinitely elastic supply; bidding for inelastically supplied capital will allocate it to the communities having the most to gain from it.

IV   Protecting competition or competitors

A   Subsidies and competition policy

A second and independent objection against local subsidies for private firms is that they harm other *firms* rather than other communities. That public subsidies to private firms might harm competitors by allowing the subsidized firms to underprice unsubsidized firms is obvious. But it is equally obvious that consumers benefit from the lower prices brought about by the subsidies. If consumers are better off, and taxpayers are better off (or they would not have taxed themselves to pay for the subsidies), why worry about other firms?

One reason to worry about other firms is that their survival may be necessary to maintain the health of the competitive process. Whether this is so at all, or if so under what conditions, has been much debated throughout the more than 100-year history of the U.S. antitrust laws (Neale and Goyder, 1980, pp. 439–44). Most American economists today would probably agree with Robert Bork (1978, Chapters 2, 3) that the antitrust laws *should be* used exclusively to protect and improve consumer welfare. Sections 85 and 86 of the Treaty of Rome recall the language of the U.S. Sherman Antitrust Act, and so one can argue that this is also the major goal of the European Union's competition policy. Other language in the EU's treaties calls this interpretation into question, however. For now, I shall assume that the exclusive goal of competition policy is to improve consumer welfare, and judge the competitive effects of subsidies by this criterion. The goals and consequences of EU competition policies are taken up in section VII.

We have seen that the only rational reason a community would have for subsidizing a firm would be to preserve valuable community capital dependent on this firm. Suppose, however, that these subsidies allow the firm to survive by underpricing other firms in its industry. If other firms must cut their prices to survive, they too may have to obtain subsidies from their communities. They shall succeed in obtaining these subsidies only if the value of community capital protected exceeds the value of subsidies paid. The situation is no different from the one discussed in the race-to-the-bottom example except that the consumers of the product are better off at the local taxpayers' expense, as well as at that of the capital owners.

Suppose, on the other hand, capital were sufficiently mobile so that the communities of the subsidized firm's competitors did *not* respond by subsidizing their firms. They let them go out of business and allowed other, more profitable firms to enter in their place. Our original subsidized firm becomes a monopoly, and then raises its price to earn monopoly rents. We now have an argument – indeed, the only legitimate argument – against public subsidies on consumer welfare grounds. Public subsidies for private firms can injure competition when they are part of a strategy to create a monopoly, which will eventually raise prices and impose welfare losses on consumers. The proper competition policy to apply to public subsidies for private firms is thus an antipredation, anti-monopoly policy.

B   *Antipredation policies and public subsidies*

A variety of proposals to deal with predatory practices have been put forward. We shall not review and analyze all of them, but rather confine ourselves to three proposals that seem particularly relevant and feasible for dealing with public subsidies.

1. Price less than short-run marginal cost: Areeda and Turner (1975) reason that any transaction at a price greater than marginal cost provides consumer benefits greater than the costs of producing them, and thus improves economic efficiency. They thus propose that any price equal to or greater than short-run marginal cost should be presumed to be nonpredatory.

A lump-sum subsidy to help a firm survive some presumably short-run difficulty would not affect its short-run marginal costs and thus would not figure in the application of the Areeda-Turner criterion to public subsidies. In the unlikely event that the subsidy were per unit of output, one would have to decide whether short-run marginal costs would be calculated net or gross of this subsidy. If firms were allowed to calculate short-run marginal costs after deducting any per-unit subsidies, then the Areeda-Turner criterion would in general allow firms to survive through public subsidies.

The Areeda-Turner criterion allows firms to set prices below long-run average total costs so long as they are above short-run marginal costs. It thus allows short-run transfers from the capital owners of a firm to the buyers of its product, if the firm could have charged a price that covered its full costs.[2] If firms are allowed to calculate short-run marginal costs net of any wage concessions by employees, then the Areeda-Turner rule would allow transfers from both capital owners and workers to consumers. If firms are allowed to calculate marginal costs net of per unit subsidies, then the rule would also allow transfers from the community of the subsidized firm to consumers. If the logic of the Areeda-Turner rule is accepted, that is, that the welfare of consumers in the short run is to dominate all other considerations, and transfers from capital and labor suppliers are construed as improving social welfare, then transfers from

---

[2] Such transfers may of course be in the long-run interests of the capital owners if they allow the firm to prey successfully on its rivals.

the firm's community should also be construed as doing so. All would seem to be on an equal footing.

2. Sustainable price: The Areeda-Turner rule abstracts entirely from the intertemporal aspects of predation. If a predator succeeds in driving its rivals out of business and then raises prices to monopoly levels, it is allowed to keep the rents it earns, so long as it did not set prices below short-run marginal costs in so doing.[3] Baumol's (1979) rule avoids this problem. It allows a dominant firm to set any price during the period of rivalry, but requires that this price be maintained in the period after rivals have been driven from the field. Baumol's rule forces the potential predator to choose a long-run sustainable price, that is, one equal to or greater than long-run average costs. Thus, if a company succeeds in driving its rivals out, it does so only if it has lower long-run average costs than they do. Moreover, consumers are allowed to benefit from the dominant firm's efficiency through the requirement that prices be kept low after the rivals depart.[4]

The Baumol rule requires no examination of company costs. Thus, its application would implicitly allow public subsidies. It would, however, raise the potential costs of these subsidies by requiring that the price, and thus perhaps the subsidy, be sustained in the long run. If this feature of the rule did not discourage the subsidies, however, application of the rule would not either.

3. Sustainable monopoly: Joskow and Klevorick (1979) treat predation as a question of sustainable monopoly. Because no firm can survive indefinitely at a price less than long-run average costs, they recognize that such prices must be inherently short-run in nature, and inevitably followed by either higher prices or reduced costs. Prices less than long-run average costs pose a potential threat to competition, however, only when a firm possesses sufficient market power to be able to raise its prices in the future – for example, when it is a dominant firm (market share at least 50 percent) in a market with high entry barriers.

If one suspected that a community was subsidizing its "local champion" with the intent of becoming a monopolist and charging monopoly prices, then one would calculate long-run average costs *before* deducting

---

[3] Areeda and Turner actually soften the criterion further by allowing a defense if price is at least equal to short-run average costs on the grounds that short-run marginal costs are difficult to measure. Since the cost data must be supplied by the firms, this either/or provision allows the firm to choose that cost criterion that is easier for it to meet.

[4] As a practical matter, a limit would have to be placed on the length of the post-departure period of constant prices.

local subsidies. If the firm's price were below unsubsidized long-run average costs, one would know either that price would later rise or that the community would have to go on indefinitely subsidizing the firm. If the firm is already dominant in an industry with high entry barriers, one might suspect the former motive and disallow the subsidies on the grounds that they are an attempt to create a monopoly. If the market structure conditions are not satisfied, the firm will not be able to raise prices in the future, and the subsidies pose no threat to consumer welfare. In this situation, the local community should be allowed to subsidize the firm as long as it chooses.

4. Discussion: Some observers believe that predation seldom, if ever, occurs.[5] To succeed, a predator must incur large immediate losses. The gain if he succeeds is the uncertain, discounted future profits. Under reasonable assumptions, the former typically exceed the latter. By this logic, predation that is harmful to consumers seems likely to be so rare that public subsidies to private firms as predation strategies could safely be ignored.

The predation-is-irrational logic figured heavily in the U.S. Supreme Court's decision *not* to hear the case brought by U.S. television manufacturers Zenith and National Union Electric against Matsushita and several other Japanese television manufacturers.[6] The court reasoned that it would not have been consistent with rational profit-maximizing decision making for the Japanese companies to charge such low prices and incur such large losses to obtain the possible future profits of monopoly. But what if the Japanese companies were not maximizing profits? What if they were rational growth maximizers àla Robin Marris (1964), and were willing to accept low returns on investment to achieve a substantial fraction of the U.S. television market?[7] While such an explanation refutes the logic of the court's decision, it does not lead to the conclusion that the outcome of the Japanese firms's actions harmed U.S. competition. If Japanese television manufacturers are willing to accept low returns on investment to supply U.S. consumers televisions at low prices, why should U.S. competition policy prevent them?

Similar arguments can be made with respect to public subsidies.

---

[5] See McGee (1958, 1980), Koller (1971), and Easterbrook (1981). For counterarguments and further debate, see Adams, Brock, and Obst (1996a,b), Elzinga and Mills (1996), and Rosenbaum (1996).

[6] For accounts of this case from both protagonists' sides, see Elzinga (1994) and Schwartzman (1994).

[7] Hiroyuki Odagiri (1981, 1992) has argued that Japanese managers are Marris growth maximizers.

Indeed, the public-choice literature implies an even higher probability that collective decisions by a community are "irrational." But, as argued at greater length in section VI.D, even if one doubts that a community's subsidy to one of its firms will provide net benefits to its citizens, this does not justify the actions of a higher level of government in preventing it from offering the subsidy. If there appears to be no danger that the subsidy will lead to a monopoly and subsequent consumers' surplus losses, there is no reason to prevent it.

The market conditions that are necessary for predation to succeed, as discussed by Joskow and Klevorick, are not the ones usually present for publicly subsidized firms. These companies are typically tottering on the brink of bankruptcy. If predation is occurring, it is more likely that the subsidized firms are its targets than that they are its perpetrators. We conclude that local public subsidies for private firms are unlikely to pose a threat to competition, and when they do, the appropriate policy response is not to prohibit them outright, but to challenge them under prevailing competition policy.

V   European Union policy and local community taxes and subsidies

A   Taxes

We noted in section I that local communities will find it attractive to tax externally held capital if it is immobile. When capital is mobile, however, a community's freedom to export its taxes is limited by the opportunities capital owners have to invest in other communities. Should some communities not tax capital at all, pressure is brought on the other communities not to tax capital.

Much discussion and some progress has been made in the European Union in the direction of "tax harmonization." The Ruding committee proposed, for example, a uniform 30 percent withholding tax on dividends across Union member countries, and a range of from 30 to 40 percent for taxes on corporate profits (European Community Commission, 1992). Although the latter is below some countries' corporate profits' tax rates – for example, that of Germany – it is considerably above that of others, for example, Ireland's 15 percent rate. The proposed withholding tax on dividends is also higher than those in several countries. The unanimity rule requirement for passing proposals in the EU Council prevented the adoption of a minimum 15 percent withholding tax on dividends in 1989 (Genser and Haufler, 1996, p. 74). But the pressure to raise or maintain taxes brought about by the EMU criteria, combined with the reluctance of Union member governments to cut expenditures, can be expected to produce additional efforts for the harmonization of taxes on capital within the European Union.

The implementation of the EMU will increase capital mobility within Europe, and make it even more difficult for individual countries to export their tax burdens by taxing externally held capital. If there were significant barriers to capital's movement out of the Union, "harmonized" taxes on capital within the Union could be defended if they substituted for more elastic sources of revenue, like the value-added tax or taxes on labor income. At the same time, however, such tax harmonization can be expected to reduce the pressure on individual national governments to match benefits from expenditures to the taxes that pay for them.[8]

B   *Subsidies*

An unexpected drop in a company's profits falls first of all on the owners of its capital. Assuming that the firm is able to survive the loss, and no other measures are taken, the loss is borne entirely by capital. In this case, capital can be said to have subsidized the firm to help it stay in business. Current EU policies do not prohibit capital owners from subsidizing their companies in this way.

If the present value of the unexpected loss, L, exceeds the value of the capital invested in the firm, K, the firm's owners will walk away from it. If the firm's workers expect that no other firm will replace the company, and that they will have to leave the community, they will be willing to offer wage concessions with a present value of up to mH, the value of the fixed assets that they own, to keep the firm operating. If $mH + K > L$, it will be possible to keep the firm alive through some combination of reduction in wages and payments to capital owners, that is, through effective subsidies from capital and labor to the company. Other suppliers of factor inputs will accept lower prices to keep the firm alive, if they do not expect to replace its lost business, and if they possess assets that will be lost as a consequence.

Such "subsidies" to distressed companies are regarded as normal parts of the competitive process, and do not run afoul of EU strictures against subsidies, nor of any of its competition policies. But workers, capital owners, and other input suppliers will accept reductions in their incomes only if they own fixed assets that stand to be lost in the event of the firm's

---

[8] For further discussion of the pros and cons of tax harmonization, see Cnossen (1990), Keen (1993), Genser and Haufler (1996), and Haufler (1996).

demise. Public infrastructure is also one of the inputs to a firm's production. The "price" of this input is the firm's local taxes. Thus local tax reductions and subsidies are both reductions in the prices a firm pays for some of its inputs, as are cuts in dividends and wages. A collective decision to cut company taxes or provide subsidies forces either a reduction in expenditures or an increase in other taxes, and thus, ceteris paribus, lowers community welfare. The community will make such a move only if it fears a greater harm from the company's departure than from the other fiscal moves. As with other inputs' suppliers, a local community suffers from a firm's departure only if capital is not mobile, so that the firm will not be quickly replaced, *and* the community is not perfectly mobile, in the sense that it possesses assets that will be lost along with the departing firm.

There is nothing to distinguish between the four subsidy options in terms of their Paretian properties. Workers will not accept a reduction in wages unless they collectively think that they will be better off, nor will capital owners, nor will other inputs' suppliers, *nor* will the citizens of the local community. The main differences among the four ways of keeping the firm alive are in the distributions of their costs. These costs will fall on one of the factor owner groups or on a subset of the community, such as the employees of the company, or they will be spread over all members of the community. Equity considerations would seem to favor spreading the costs across the entire community. Thus, a justification for disallowing this alternative by forbidding subsidies must rest on efficiency considerations, and these must go beyond the company and the community in which it is located to consider, for example, the impact of the subsidies on competition in the firm's industry.

But, since there are possible efficiency gains from preserving the assets of the local community, improvements in efficiency cannot be guaranteed by an outright ban on local subsidies. The proper kind of policy to apply when considering the possible inefficiencies caused by local subsidies is, as discussed in the previous section, a competition policy against predation.

VI   The public choice of public subsidies

A   *Redistribution within the community*

We have until now assumed that the preferences and incomes of all members of a community are identical. Thus, all Pareto-improving collective decisions could be made using the unanimity rule. Most communities are not made up of individuals with identical tastes, of course, and none that I know of uses the unanimity rule. If the community makes decisions with the simple majority rule, a coalition of the firm's owners, employees, and those who have close economic connections to it might succeed in passing a tax-subsidy proposal over the rest of the community's objections, even when the losses of the firm were not large enough to threaten its existence. Indeed, if they can form a majority coalition, they can achieve such a transfer even when the firm is incurring no losses whatsoever. The subsidy would in part be a redistribution from one part of the community to the other.

All collective decisions made with the less-than-unanimous support of the community are likely to involve *some* redistribution, however. A park built in the southern part of the community, whose funding is opposed by residents in the north, redistributes income from north to south. Public schools redistribute from families without children to those with children, and across generations. We have seen that there can be circumstances under which a tax on a community to subsidize a major employer would benefit all, and thus would meet the definition of a pure public good, just as parks and schools can satisfy this definition. There is no obvious difference among these sorts of issues in this respect. There is no obvious reason, therefore, for allowing the central government to "trump" a community's collective choice in one case and not the other.[9] The only reason to allow the central government a veto over local government collective decisions is when they have significant negative external effects on other communities. As discussed previously, there is no reason to presume that subsidies to firms are likely to have this effect.

If one wants to eliminate redistribution within local communities, one should choose a voting rule different from simple majority rule. Although only the unanimity rule ensures that *no* redistribution takes place, higher qualified majorities reduce the amount of redistribution from that which occurs under the simple majority rule (Buchanan and Tullock, 1962, pp. 131–210; Mueller, 1989, pp. 58–63). Redistribution *within* local communities does not produce direct negative external effects on other communities, however. There is no reason to grant the central government authority to forbid such redistribution, therefore, regardless of the form it takes. The decision regarding the proper amount of intracommunity redistribution to allow, and how to achieve it, is essentially a constitutional question that is best resolved by the citizens

---

[9] The issue of who should be able to trump whom in a federalist system is discussed by Gillette (1997). See also Mueller (1997).

directly involved in the collective decision process, that is, by members of the local community.

B   *Redistribution across communities*

Often when a community experiences an unexpected decline in the demand for its main employer's product, it chooses not to levy a tax upon itself to subsidize the local firm, but rather to appeal for a subsidy to the higher level polity of which it is a part. If there are other local communities also seeking subsidies, and the larger polity uses the simple majority rule to decide subsidy issues, then a coalition of local communities may succeed in inducing the larger polity to subsidize the local ones. If the winning coalition is of minimum size, a local community's share of the tax burden is roughly half the value of the assets saved. This situation resembles Gordon Tullock's (1959) famous overinvestment-logrolling example. Unlike the situation in Tullock's example, however, the tax-subsidy package *might* achieve a Pareto improvement. For example, a one-time lump-sum tax would produce a Pareto improvement if it were used to preserve some real assets, no matter how small the value of the assets. The one-time lump-sum nature of the tax would ensure that it introduced no distortions or inefficiencies into the larger community. Any real assets saved by the transfer would constitute a Pareto improvement. Even if the redistributional component of the tax-subsidy package were dominant, it would be Pareto-improving because of its one-time lump-sum nature.

Nondistortionary taxes are rare, however, and one-time subsidies have a way of turning into second- and third-time subsidies, and eventually into constant flows. The redistributional component of broad-based taxes to subsidize particular firms and industries on a continual basis can lead to an overinvestment in declining firms and industries, as predicted by Tullock's logrolling model. If a community benefiting from a firm's survival has to pay the full costs of these benefits, it lets the firm die. But if the larger jurisdiction picks up most of these costs, the community happily accepts the transfer. Inefficient firms and industries survive, and a nation's capital is trapped in the technologies of the past. Such inefficiencies would never arise if the potential beneficiaries from private subsidies bore the full burden of the taxes to pay for them.

Subsidies for private firms are not unique in bringing about inefficient logrolling, of course. Federal financing for urban transit redistributes from the rest of the nation to the largest cities. Farm subsidies redistribute from city to countryside. Subsidies to private firms are neither unique nor necessarily the most egregious forms of geographic redistribution that can occur under the simple majority rule. In addition to raising the required majority in the higher jurisdiction's Parliament, inefficient geographic redistribution could be reduced or eliminated by a procedural rule that prohibited bills of only local interest from coming before the central Parliament (Mueller, 1996, Chapter 6). Such a rule would force the subsidizing of private firms back onto the communities that are the prime potential beneficiaries of such subsidies.

C   Redistribution from consumers to producers

Very often, companies in trouble (and some that are not in trouble) seek help from the state in the form of tariff protection, restraints on the entry of firms into their industries, price supports, exemptions from cartel prohibitions, and the like. Here the redistribution sought is from consumers to producers, and thus differs fundamentally from the other sorts of redistribution just described, in the sense that there are definite losers as well as winners as a result of the government action.

Competition policy has, or at least should have, as one of its primary objectives the advancement of consumer welfare.[10] Prohibitions against cartels are central elements in any effective competition. To allow a cartel in one industry to benefit its constituents for whatever reason contradicts the logic of competition policy, and violates the laws upon which it rests. Restrictions on entry, price supports, and even tariffs, to the extent that they are instigated at the behest of producers, fall into the same category. These policies, unlike public subsidies, are likely to result in consumers' paying higher prices for the products of the firms helped, not lower prices. The institution of a competition policy is a collective decision to place consumer interests above producer interests insofar as interference with the market process is concerned. Consistent with this revealed preference for consumer welfare, communities should refuse to suspend competition policy when asked to do so by individual firms or industries. One way to accomplish this would be to authorize the agency charged with enforcing competition policy to challenge actions by other parts of the government, be they federal or local, that violate this policy. A more powerful approach would make free trade and competition part of the federal constitution to deter if not prohibit both federal and local governments from interfering with the market in ways that lower social welfare, such as price floors and government-sponsored cartels (Mueller, 1996, Chapter 15).

---

[10] Robert Bork (1978) has forcefully argued that it should be the *sole* objective of competition policy.

D   *Governmental inefficiency*

Many arguments have been put forward to explain why governmental institutions produce inefficient outcomes. Oates and Schwab (1988), for example, after demonstrating the optimality of local provision of public goods and taxation when capital is fully mobile, show that a Pareto-inferior outcome arises if local governments are run by budget-maximizing bureaucrats as first modeled by Niskanen (1971). Such an argument can be used to justify constraining local bureaucrats and governments vis-à-vis the market, say, by requiring larger than simple majorities for these *and other* collective decisions. It cannot be used, however, to justify locating authority for subsidizing private firms at the highest level of a federalist government. The relevant comparison in a federalist context is not the outcome when local governments are run by budget maximizers against the first-best outcome. The relevant comparison is the outcome when local budget-maximizing governments have authority to subsidize local firms against the outcome when a budget-maximizing central government has this authority. One expects governments at both levels to expand beyond the socially optimal size. In the case of local governments, however, citizens can resort to Tieboutian migration to avoid excessive taxes. This option is more limited at the highest level of government, since it requires citizens to migrate to another country, or in the case of the European Union to leave the Union. Thus, one expects that bureaucrats in the central government have if anything *more* discretion to pursue their interests than do bureaucrats in local governments, and consequently that greater inefficiencies will result when only central governments are allowed to subsidize private firms, as opposed to when these subsidies are restricted to the communities that pay for them.

A second concern about the efficiency of government actions stems from the belief that individuals act less rationally when they participate in the democratic process than when they make private decisions (Buchanan, 1954; Brennan and Buchanan, 1985). These arguments are equally valid against *all* collective decisions, however, and thus again cannot justify singling out public subsidies for private firms. Nor can they be used to defend placing the authority for making public subsidies with the highest level of government. An important justification for the claim that citizens make less rational choices when they vote is that they have poorer incentives to gather information about collective decisions than about their own private decisions. A citizen of Denmark is much more likely to be informed about the possible benefits and costs to her of the Danish government's subsidizing a Danish firm than about those of the European Union's subsidizing a Spanish firm. Arguments against government intervention that stress citizens' lack of information buttress the case for placing authority for subsidizing private firms with local governments.

VII   Implications for EU policy

The competition policy of the EU has been designed to complement the "free trade" goals that first led to the Union's formation. Hay and Morris (1991, p. 617) have gone so far as to claim that "the promotion of effective competition is the *sole* focus of this policy" (emphasis added). Many provisions of the Treaty of Rome and subsequent refinements support this claim. Articles 85 and 86 of the treaty, for example, are sufficiently close to the language of the U.S. Sherman Act that one might reasonably assume that their intended beneficiaries are only consumers.

Other dimensions of EU competition policy and other EU policies raise some doubts, however. In its ninth Report on Competition Policy (1980, p. 9 ff.), the Commission explicitly set "fairness" as one of this policy's goals, and stated that this goal would be pursued by preserving equal chances for persons and companies engaged in business. Equal chances in turn would be promoted by preventing member states from aiding their domestic firms and thereby harming companies in other member states.[11] EU industrial and agricultural policies allow cross-national subsidies and interference with market processes to benefit certain firms and industries.[12] Thus, current EU policies with respect to subsides prohibit member states from engaging in the kinds of subsidies that are most likely to be efficiency enhancing, those where there is a large overlap between possible beneficiaries and possible losers. At the same time, EU policy allows the Commission to implement the kinds of cross-community tax/subsidy programs that are most likely to be driven by rent-seeking considerations. Ironically, given the reference to fairness in the ninth Report on Competition Policy, current EU policy allows capital owners, workers, and other factor input suppliers to subsidize a company in trouble, but does not allow the fairest sharing of this cost, namely, its distribution across the entire community that benefits from the subsidy.

A set of policies that was both fair and consistently sought to promote economic efficiency and consumer welfare would: (1) allow member

---

[11] See discussion in Schmidt and Binder (1996, pp. 92–4).

[12] For critical discussions of EU industrial policies from the perspective of optimal competition policy, see Möschel (1992), Hamm (1993), Streit (1993), and Oberender and Okruch (1994).

states and regional governments to subsidize their own firms out of their own tax revenues, (2) apply the Union's competition policies to these subsidies, (3) severely constrain or eliminate cross-national subsidies, and (4) severely constrain or eliminate all other Commission programs that interfere with market processes, where no obvious externalities or other market failures are present.

VIII   Conclusions

The central goal of competition policy should be to protect consumers, not competitors. The only situation in which public subsidies for private firms are clearly inconsistent with this goal is when they are part of a predatory strategy to create a monopoly. As such, they should be subject to the laws and regulations that define competition policy. The typical firm seeking public subsidies is not on the verge of monopolizing an industry, however. The typical beneficiary of subsidies is on the brink of exit rather than in the process of driving rivals out of business. Public subsidies to such companies cannot harm competition.

In a world of perfect competition and perfect mobility, public subsidies would neither pose any threat to competition nor benefit the community providing them. Perfectly mobile capital owners would not accept a reduction in the value of their capital assets; perfectly mobile workers would not accept lower wages; and community members who could either costlessly exit, or could costlessly find a replacement for a departing firm, would not tax themselves to subsidize a firm in danger of leaving or closing. If the main employer in a community cannot survive competition in a world in which competition and mobility are not perfect, its workers and capital suppliers must bear the transaction costs of exiting to other firms. If their departure brings an end to the community, its residents must bear the transaction costs of departing to other communities. If one of these groups offers to accept a financial sacrifice to keep the firm alive, it implies that these transaction costs exceed the magnitude of the offer.

If the death of a firm results in the death of a community, it wipes out all tangible and intangible (friendships, for example) assets that the community's residents might own, and imposes the transaction costs of dislocation upon it. Citizens would not agree to tax-subsidy schemes to keep a major employer in their community going, if they did not think that they would be better off bearing the costs of the subsidies than bearing the costs of the firm's departure.

In each of these cases a group – bondholders, workers, or citizens of a community – accepts a reduction in its income to keep a firm alive, because it believes it is in its best interests to do so, given its current mobility and the prospects of the company.[13] In each case a redistribution occurs from a group making a sacrifice to all other groups that would be harmed by the firm's death, including its customers. Each voluntary decision by a group to sacrifice income to keep the firm alive may constitute a Pareto move. There is no reason consistent with the Pareto criterion to favor one group's sacrifice over any other's.

In the United States, in which state and local communities have independent taxation authority, numerous examples of interventions by local communities to save local firms can be cited. For example, TWA's probable demise was prevented by joint action by the city of St. Louis and the state of Missouri. Several cities and states have provided subsidies to professional sports teams to prevent their departures. Here the fixed assets at stake are probably a form of "intangible capital" consisting of community pride, the loyalty of fans, and the like. Similar forms of intangible capital are presumably associated with national efforts to save flagship airlines in Europe.

A particularly striking example of community effort to save a local firm occurred in the early 1950s, when people in and around the tiny city of Green Bay, Wisconsin, prevented the departure of their financially troubled football team by purchasing shares in the team, shares that promised zero financial return. These purchases were voluntary contributions to the provision of a public good. In this instance, the voluntary contributions sufficed to keep the team alive and in Green Bay; but the danger of free-riding makes this method of preserving community assets inferior to a local tax/subsidy package. Changes in National Football League policies have made a similar rescue effort impossible today, just as European Union policy opposes such solutions to local economic crises.

The integration of the East German and West German economies made much of East Germany's industrial sector economically nonviable. East Germans faced two options: abandon their homes and communities and migrate to the West to find jobs, or attract industry into their region. Given the low productivity levels and poor infrastructure in East Germany, this latter option could be pursued only with the help of subsidies for private firms. The subsidies to Volkswagen to locate a plant in

[13] Note that it may be in a community's interest to share some of the costs of keeping the firm alive even if it could impose all of them on capital. In the long run, capital is the most mobile of the three groups involved. By showing a willingness to bear some of the costs of keeping the firm alive, the community lowers the price of attracting new capital to the community in the future. The action may save the community by inducing another firm to enter, even if the subsidized firm eventually dies.

Saxony appear to be the kind of community-asset-preserving policy that can produce Pareto improvements.[14] They do not seem likely to lead to Volkswagen's monopolization of the automobile industry. They should not be of concern to the rest of the European Union.

In the typical subsidy case, one of two scenarios ensues: either the difficulty of the firm is temporary, it returns to profitability, and the subsidies cease; or alternatively, the difficulty of the firm is chronic and the subsidies must persist indefinitely. In this latter case, residence in the community is less attractive ceteris paribus than residence in other communities, since taxes are higher per unit of public benefits *not including the survival of the firm*. In the earlier example, we assumed that all citizens owned identical housing stocks, and that these did not depreciate. But real housing stocks differ in value and do depreciate. A scenario similar to that for the local firm can be predicted for the local community, if the former must be subsidized indefinitely. Citizens with small stocks of housing or long time horizons exit; immigration into the community does not offset emigration to other communities. The tax base erodes, and the firm and the community die anyway. But even in this case, one cannot claim that the initial decision to allow the subsidies is necessarily wrong. If assets are to some degree fixed, a gradual run down can be superior to wiping them out all at once. If the community votes for subsidies, it must be assumed that it believes at the time that they are the optimal policy.

References

Adams, Walter, Brock, James W., and Obst, Norman P., "Is Predation Rational? Is it Profitable?", *Review of Industrial Organization*, 11(6), December 1996a, pp. 753–58.

Adams, Walter, Brock, James W., and Obst, Norman P., "Is Predation Rational? Is it Profitable? – A Reply," *Review of Industrial Organization*, 11(6), December 1996b, pp. 767–70.

Areeda, Philip, and Turner, Donald F., "Predatory Pricing and Related Practices Under Section 2 of the Sherman Act," *Harvard Law Review*, 88, 1975, pp. 697–733.

Baumol, William J., "Quasi-Permanence of Price Reductions: A Policy for Prevention of Predatory Pricing," *Yale Law Journal*, 89, November 1979, pp. 1–26.

Bork, Robert H., *The Antitrust Paradox*, New York: Basic Books, 1978.

---

[14] In contrast, the "bail-out" of U.S. automaker Chrysler by the federal government resulted in a poor match between potential beneficiaries and taxpayers. Because the assistance offered Chrysler took the form of federal loan guarantees, however, and Chrysler recovered, U.S. taxpayers actually bore no costs from this rescue effort.

Brennan, Geoffrey, Buchanan, James M., *The Power to Tax*, Cambridge: Cambridge University Press, 1980.

Breton, Albert, and Scott, Anthony, *The Economic Constitution of Federal States*, Toronto: University of Toronto Press, 1978.

Buchanan, James M., "Individual Choice in Voting and the Market," *Journal of Political Economy*, 62, August 1954, pp. 334–43.

Buchanan, James M., and Tullock, Gordon, *The Calculus of Consent*, Ann Arbor: University of Michigan Press, 1962.

Cnossen, Sijbren, "The Case for Tax Diversity in the European Community," *European Economic Review*, 34, 1990, 471–79.

Cnossen, Sijbren, and Shoup, C. S., "Coordination of Value-Added Taxes," in S. Cnossen, ed., *Tax Coordination in the European Community*, Deventer: Kluwer, pp. 59–84.

Devereux, M., "The Ruding Committee Report: An Economic Assessment," *Fiscal Studies*, 13(2), 1992.

Easterbrook, Frank, "Predatory Strategies and Counter-strategies," *University of Chicago Law Review*, 48, Spring 1981, pp. 263–337.

Edwards, J., and Keen, Michael, "Tax Competition and Leviathan," *European Economic Review*, 40, January 1996, pp. 113–34.

Eichengreen, Barry, "European Monetary Unification," *Journal of Economic Literature*, 31, September 1993, pp. 1321–57.

Elzinga, Kenneth G., "Collusive Predation: *Matsushita v. Zenith* (1986)," in Kwoka, John E., Jr., and White, Lawrence J., *The Antitrust Revolution*, 2nd ed., New York: Harper Collins, 1993, pp. 238–59.

Elzinga, Kenneth G., and Mills, David E., "Is Predation Rational? An Answer to Adams, Brock and Obst," *Review of Industrial Organization*, 11(6), December 1996, pp. 759–64.

European Communities-Commission (Ruding Report), "Report of the Committee of Independent Experts on Company Taxation," Brussels, 1992.

Genser, Bernd, and Haufler, Andreas, "Tax Competition, Tax Coordination and Tax Harmonization: The Effects of the EMU," *Empirica*, 23(1), 1996, pp. 59–89.

Gillette, Clayton P., "The Exercise of Trumps by Decentralized Governments," *Virginia Law Review*, 83(7), October 1997, pp. 1347–1417.

Gordon, Roger, "Taxation of Investment and Savings in a World Economy," *American Economic Review*, 76, December 1986, pp. 1086–102.

Hamm, Walter, "Die europäische Wirtschaftsunion – eine Gefahr für die Marktwirtschaft?" *Ordo*, 44, 1993, pp. 3–14.

Haufler, Andreas, "Tax Coordination with Different Preferences for Public Goods: Conflict or Harmony of Interest?" *International Tax and Public Finance*, 3, January 1996, pp. 5–28.

Hay, Donald A., and Morris, Derek J., *Industrial Economics and Organization*, 2nd ed., Oxford: Oxford University Press, 1991.

Joskow, Paul L., and Klevorick, Alvin K., "A Framework for Analyzing Predatory Pricing Policy," *Yale Law Journal*, 89, December 1979, pp. 213–69.

Kanbur, Ravi, and Keen, Michael, "Jeux sans Frontières: Tax Competition and Tax Coordination when Countries Differ in Size," *American Economic Review*, 83, September 1993, pp. 877–92.

Keen, Michael, "The Welfare Economics of Tax Coordination in the European Community: A Survey," *Fiscal Studies*, 14(2), 1993, pp. 15–36.

Knieps, Günter, "Wettbewerbspolitik," Discussion Paper 19, Albert-Ludwigs-Universität Freiburg, February 1995.

Koller, Roland H., "The Myth of Predatory Pricing: An Empirical Study," *Antitrust Law and Economic Review*, 4, Summer 1971, pp. 105–23.

Levinson, A., "Environmental Regulations and Industry Location: International and Domestic Evidence," in J. N. Bhagwati and R. E. Hudec, eds., *Fair Trade and Harmonization*, vol. 1, Cambridge, MA: MIT Press, 1996.

Marris, Robin, *The Economic Theory of "Managerial Capitalism"*, New York: Free Press, 1964.

McGee, John S., "Predatory Price Cutting: The Standard Oil (N.J.) Case," *Journal of Law and Economics*, 1, October 1958, pp. 137–69.

McGee, John S., "Predatory Pricing Revisited," *Journal of Law and Economics*, 23, October 1980, pp. 289–330.

McGuire, Martin, "Group Segregation and Optimal Jurisdictions," *Journal of Political Economy*, 82, January/February 1974, pp. 112–32.

Mintz, J., and Tulkens, H., "Commodity Tax Competition Between Member States of a Federation: Equilibrium and Efficiency," *Journal of Public Economics*, 29, 1986, pp. 133–72.

Möschel, Wernhard, "EG-Industriepolitik nach Maastricht," *Ordo*, 43, 1992, pp. 415–21.

Mueller, Dennis C., *Public Choice II*, Cambridge: Cambridge University Press, 1989.

Mueller, Dennis C., *Constitutional Democracy*, Oxford: Oxford University Press, 1996.

Mueller, Dennis C., "Federalist Governments and Trumps," *Virginia Law Review*, 83(7), October 1997, pp. 1419–32.

Neale, A. D., and Goyder, A. G., *The Antitrust Laws of the U.S.A.*, 3rd ed., Cambridge: Cambridge University Press, 1980.

Niskanen, William A., Jr., *Bureaucracy and Representative Government*, Chicago: Aldine-Atherton, 1971.

Oates, Wallace E., and Schwab, Robert M., "Economic Competition among Jurisdictions: Efficiency Enhancing or Distortion Inducing?", *Journal of Public Economics*, 35, April 1988, pp. 333–54.

Oates, Wallace E., and Schwab, Robert M., "The Allocative and Distributive Implications of Local Fiscal Competition," in Daphne Kenyon and John Kincaid, eds., *Competition among State and Local Governments*, Washington: Urban Institute Press, pp. 127–45.

Oberender, Peter, and Okruch, Stefan, "Gegenwärtige Probleme und zukünftige Perspektiven der europäischen Wettbewerbspolitik," *Wirtschaft und Wettbewerb*, 44, 1994, pp. 507–20.

Odagiri, Hiroyuki, *The Theory of Growth in a Corporate Economy: An Inquiry into Management Preference, R&D and Economic Growth*, Cambridge: Cambridge University Press, 1981.

Odagiri, Hiroyuki, *Growth through Competition, Competition through Growth: Strategic Management and the Economy in Japan*, Oxford: Oxford University Press, 1992.

Rosenbaum, David I., "Comment to Adams, Brock and Obst: 'Is Predation Rational? Is it Profitable?'", *Review of Industrial Organization*, 11(6), December 1996, pp. 765–66.

Schmidt, Ingo, and Binder, Steffen, *Wettbewerbspolitik im Internationalen Vergleich*, Heidelberg: Recht und Wirtschaft, 1996.

Schwartzman, David, "*Matsushita v. Zenith*: An Economic Analysis," *Review of Industrial Organization*, 9, February 1994, pp. 1–23.

Streit, Manfred E., "European Industrial Policy: An Economic and Constitutional Challenge," *Staatswissenschaften und Staatspraxis*, 4, 1993, pp. 338–416.

Tiebout, Charles M., "A Pure Theory of Local Expenditures," *Journal of Political Economy*, 64, October 1956, pp. 416–24.

Tullock, Gordon, "Some Problems of Majority Voting," *Journal of Political Economy*, 67, December 1959, pp. 571–9, reprinted in Arrow, K. J., and Scitovsky, T., eds., *Readings in Welfare Economics*, Homewood, IL.: Richard D. Irwin, 1969, pp. 169–78.

Wilson, J. D., "Capital Mobility and Environmental Standards: Is There a Theoretical Basis for a Race to the Bottom?", in J. N. Bhagwati and R. E. Hudec, eds., *Fair Trade and Harmonization*, vol. 1, Cambridge, MA: MIT Press, 1996.

CHAPTER 15

Economic constitutions, protectionism, and competition among jurisdictions

Viktor Vanberg

1   Introduction

For the past few centuries nation-states have been the predominant political entities exercising the power of defining economic constitutions, that is, the frameworks of rules and institutions that constrain economic activities carried out within their jurisdictions. The twentieth century, in particular, has witnessed a significant increase in the role that the nation-state has played in this regard, with the socialist experiments probably marking the culmination of such a role. As this century comes to a close, the power of the nation-state to determine its economic constitution appears, however, to be challenged by developments that are summarily called "globalization,"[1] developments that increasingly subject national governments and national constitutions to competitive constraints.[2]

Nation-states, in their efforts at shaping the economic constitutions within their jurisdictions, have always been subject to constraints that international trade and the mobility of productive resources impose on their discretion in matters of constitutional choice. Yet, such constraints have recently grown stronger, due to the forces of "globalization." Political and institutional changes as well as advances in communication and transportation technologies have contributed to making economic opportunities outside of domestic jurisdictions more easily accessible, creating increasingly global markets for goods, services, and productive resources.

In Western welfare states, particularly in Europe, these developments have triggered heated debates about how politics ought to respond to

[1]   See, e.g., Nunnenkamp, Gundlach, and Agarwal (1994).
[2]   "Competition among governments" is one of the themes to which A. Breton has made significant contributions. See Breton (1965, 1987), Breton and Scott (1978), and, most recently, Breton (1996).

364

the challenges of globalization that appear to pose a threat to central elements of established economic constitutions, notably those elements that can be broadly defined as "social" regulations. The principal conflict in these debates is between, on the one side, those who essentially call for protectionist strategies in order to defend – against the presumably destructive forces of global competition – what they consider to be important constitutional achievements of the modern welfare state, and, on the other side, those who regard global competition as an essentially beneficial force that helps to shape up economies that have become sluggish from institutional sclerosis.

The purpose of this chapter is to examine, from a constitutional economics perspective, some of the basic issues that are raised by the debate on the appropriate policy response to globalization. I shall discuss, in particular, some of the implications that globalization may have for the power of national governments to choose and to maintain economic constitutions that reflect the common preferences of their constituencies.

2   Economic constitutions and constitutional interests

Nation-states are, of course, not the only political entities that define the rules of economic constitutions. There are subnational as well as supranational jurisdictions that take part in shaping the inclusive framework of rules and institutions under which economic agents operate. Subnational units, such as states within federations or local communities, may also be authorized to legislate some of the relevant rules of the game, as may be supranational units, such as the EU or the WTO. The discussion in this chapter will, however, largely neglect the complications introduced by the role that such sub- and supranational units play in the inclusive shaping of economic constitutions, and will instead concentrate on the role of the nation-state, a simplification that does not affect the principal arguments to be developed here. These arguments can, appropriately modified but without substantial change, be applied to a world of multilayered jurisdictions, including subnational as well as supranational levels of constitutional choice.

As noted, the term *economic constitution* refers to the entire framework of rules which are binding for all members or *citizens* of a jurisdiction, and which are of relevance with regard to their economic activities and transactions.[3] It is the differences between the internally

---

[3] The concept of the economic constitution is central to the theoretical approach to economic policy developed by the so-called Freiburg School (Vanberg 1998).

enforced economic constitution and the rules in force (or *not* in force, respectively) outside the jurisdiction that separate a jurisdiction from its socioeconomic environment. Using F. A. Hayek's distinction between the *order of rules* and the *order of actions* (Hayek 1969), one can contrast a jurisdiction's economic constitution (the order of rules) with the patterns of economic activities (the order of actions) that result from the advantage-seeking behavior of economic agents within the constraints imposed on them by the rules of the game. Hayek's distinction parallels the distinction drawn in constitutional economics[4] between the *constitutional level* of rule choice and the *subconstitutional level* of strategy choice within rules, or – in short – between the *rules of the game* and the *moves within the game*. And it is similar to the distinction drawn by Ludwig Lachmann (1963) between *internal* and *external* institutions, a contrast that is meant to distinguish the framework of rules and institutions that constitutes a market (property rights, contract law, liability rules, patent law, etc.) from the rules of behavior and institutional arrangements that emerge within the framework, as a result of the mutual adjustments between market participants (private ordering). All of these distinctions are based on the idea that, in the study of socioeconomic systems, we can look at economic constitutions as frameworks of constraints that help to explain the patterns of economic activities that emerge within the respective jurisdictions.[5]

Constitutional arrangements are the product of human efforts to adapt the socioeconomic environment to *human needs*. Humans tend not to simply accept their environment as given, but to strive to mold it according to their own preferences. This is true for both the social and the natural environments. To the extent that the shaping of an economic constitution can be considered not only a matter of blind evolutionary forces but also an act of deliberate political choice, it can be viewed as an attempt to create a *constitutional niche* that provides for its inhabitants in some respects a more hospitable environment than would otherwise exist. As noted before, such efforts at creating hospitable constitutional environments need not be limited to one particular level of constitutional choice, but can, simultaneously, occur at several levels.

---

[4] Compare, for example, Buchanan (1990).
[5] Where there are several levels of jurisdictions (local communities, states, federation, supranational organizations, etc.) the above distinctions are, of course, to be understood in a relative sense: What must be attributed to the outer institutions at one level of analysis (for example, in studying the impact of a community's zoning rules or tax regulations on local business activities) can be viewed as an inner (public) institution in relation to a higher level of jurisdiction (e.g., local regulations viz-à-viz state or national legal frameworks).

Constituents of nation-states, for instance, are not limited to the option of adapting their national jurisdictional niche to a given environment, but may, instead, seek to implement, together with other national constituencies, constitutional rules that provide, on a more inclusive jurisdictional level, a more desirable environment for all parties involved. Stated more generally, one can look at constitutional choice as a process occurring on several levels. At each level, opportunities exist for more and more inclusive constituencies to create more hospitable socioeconomic environments for themselves, by jointly adopting certain constitutional constraints that, at each level, serve to secure mutual gains for the respective groups of citizens.

The rules of an *economic constitution*, or in Lachmann's terminology the *outer institutions*, define important characteristics of a jurisdiction as a "constitutional niche." They are the rules of the game to which all members of the jurisdiction are subject. The *inner institutions* comprise standardized practices or rules of behavior, which evolve within a given constitutional niche from the behavioral adaptations among economic agents within the jurisdiction, be it as an unintended result of their spontaneous mutual adjustments or as a result of their deliberate collective choices. The principal objective of constitutional choices is the desired impact that they are predicted to have on the emerging pattern of activities at the subconstitutional level. In other words, rules are not chosen for their own sake, but because of the *consequences* expected from adopting them, and their principal consequences are their effects on the emerging subconstitutional order of actions. Accordingly, rules are typically judged to be desirable because of the desirability of the order of actions that they generate.

If we look at nation-states as constitutional niches in the above sense,[6] what are, then, the appropriate criteria against which the desirability of their economic constitutions can be judged? It is presumed here that for democratic polities, as associations of citizens, the appropriate criterion is *mutual benefit* to all citizens as the principals of the polity. In their factual historical evolution economic constitutions are, of course, shaped by a multitude of factors that interact in complex ways. They are explicitly chosen and modified, however, through political decision-making processes that, in a democratic polity, are to be measured against the standard of how well they serve to advance the common interests of the jurisdiction's citizens, the polity's ultimate sovereigns or principals. Accordingly, the desirability of economic constitutions should be judged

---

[6] Again, nation-states may, of course, include subnational "constitutional niches," and they may themselves be embedded in supranational "constitutional niches."

in terms of the interests of the relevant constituency, where the issue at hand decides what is considered the *relevant* constituency or, in other words, what is the appropriate jurisdictional level at which the desirability of constitutional rules should be examined.[7]

In what follows, I shall speak of *constitutional interests* or *constitutional preferences* when I specifically refer to citizens' interests with regard to the framework of rules under which they prefer to live, compared to feasible alternatives. In light of what has been said here about the relation between rules and emergent outcomes, we can conjecture that citizens' constitutional preferences will be informed by their "*outcome interests*," that is, by their preferences regarding the outcome patterns that they expect to result from particular rules. This means, of course, that persons' constitutional preferences will be informed by their *fallible* theories about the working properties of alternative rules, that is, by their (implicit or explicit) conjectures about the outcome patterns that potential alternative rule regimes are likely to generate. Persons' constitutional preferences may, therefore, be *ill-informed* in the sense that they are based on mistaken expectations about the kind of outcome patterns that alternative rules will tend to produce. This, again, implies that persons' constitutional preferences may be inconsistent with their outcome preferences.[8]

Regardless of the level at which efforts at constitutional design occur, they are inevitably always subject to the constraints imposed upon them by their respective environments, and efforts at changing these constraints themselves by constitutional design are necessarily limited to those aspects that can, indeed, be altered by such means. This implies, among other things, that not all constitutional preferences that constituents at various jurisdictional levels may harbor, need to be viable in the sense that the respective economic constitutions can be sustained in the environment in which they exist. Prudence in constitutional choice requires, therefore, that constitutional preferences be subjected to a viability test.

3   Globalization and competition among economic constitutions

Jurisdictions with their economic constitutions always exist in an environment, and they must, in one way or another, adapt to the ever-

---

[7] For instance, where externalities are involved, a national constitutional provision that is desirable from the perspective of a single national constituency may be undesirable when judged from the perspective of a more inclusive multinational constituency.

[8] To this issue, and its relevance with regard to different methods of "constitutional choice," I will return later in this chapter.

changing conditions in their environment. The viability of economic constitutions depends on just how successful they are in enabling their respective constituencies to cope with the constant changes that occur not only internally but also in a jurisdiction's environment. This problem has existed throughout the ages for all constitutional niches. It has, however, without doubt, become especially topical because of the increasing interdependence and accelerated economic integration of the world economy in recent decades.[9]

The ways in which jurisdictions adapt to changes in their environments depend critically on the nature of their economic constitutions. Their respective frameworks of outer institutions channel the actions and interactions of economic agents within the jurisdiction as well as their transactions with agents outside. External influences affect a constitutional niche always through their impact on the behavior of members of a given jurisdiction, and what we describe as adaptation to the environment is, in the final instance, the result of reactions of individuals, principals and/or agents, to changes in the environment – whether these reactions occur by way of separate individual responses, or through deliberately coordinated, organized activities, including reforms of the economic constitution itself.

What is called "globalization" is, ultimately, nothing but the fact that economic opportunities outside of domestic jurisdictions have increasingly become available, or more accessible, due to institutional as well as technological changes that have dramatically decreased transaction costs for economic activities cutting across jurisdictional boundaries. These developments mean not only that firms are facing increasingly worldwide competition. They also mean that national economic constitutions are coming under more intense competition, in the sense that their comparative working properties, relative to each other, more speedily translate into visible economic effects within their respective jurisdictions (Vanberg and Kerber 1994).

There are two interrelated ways in which national economic constitutions can be said to compete in a global economy. They compete, first and more indirectly, via their effects on the competitiveness of domestic producers. To the extent that the "rules of the game" under which domestic producers have to operate affect their production costs, national economic constitutions can further or hinder their ability to compete with

---

[9] Killick (1995a: 2): "There is thus an ever-present need to respond to – and take advantage of – such changes in the economic environment. The imperative to do so has been intensified in recent decades as economic interdependence among nations has increased, with the rise of trade and international capital movements relative to domestic economic activities."

foreign producers, and they can, thereby, positively or negatively affect the creation of wealth within the jurisdiction. Secondly, and more directly, national economic constitutions compete via their impact on the respective jurisdictions' attractiveness for mobile productive resources, investment capital as well as human capital. To the extent that the productivity of immobile, or less mobile, domestic resources is enhanced by their combination with mobile resources, the ability of a jurisdiction to attract such mobile resources is a critical factor in its potential to create wealth. And to the extent that its economic constitution affects a jurisdiction's attractiveness, it is a significant ingredient in that potential.

Quite obviously, as globalization leads to intensified competition among national economic constitutions it imposes constraints on the power of governments to sustain existing constitutional provisions, or to legislate constitutional reforms, in response to domestic demands. This raises the issue of how national governments *can* respond, and how national constituencies *may want* their governments to respond, to the challenges of globalization. In particular, the question arises as to whether protectionist responses can be a desirable and viable way for constituencies to implement their constitutional preferences in the face of these challenges.

4   The classical free-trade argument as constitutional advice

Considering what Adam Smith had to say about the division of labor and the extent of markets, it would seem that globalization ought generally to be welcome. It means a widening of markets and, thus, growing opportunities for specialization, which in turn should lead to general increases in wealth. The advantages of living in a jurisdiction that is, internally and externally, open to competition have been almost unanimously stressed by economists since Smith. The arguments that they have made can be seen as advice regarding constitutional choice. They inform citizens of the reasons why it is in their best interest to opt for an open economic order and to share in the benefits that extended, competitive markets have to offer.

In a completely open economic system, intrajurisdictional economic activities are, of necessity, always adapted to the alternative options available in the extrajurisdictional economic environment. Under conditions of completely open access to potentially more advantageous external options, only those cooperative arrangements and exchange relations will survive inside the jurisdiction that are at least as attractive to all parties involved as their most advantageous alternative opportunities outside. Internal economic activities would have constantly to adapt to ever-changing external options, and the structure of economic activities inside the system would always develop toward the pattern that corresponds to the relative advantage of internal and external transactions. In other words, a completely open economic system would, in consequence, be perfectly adapted to its economic environment.

The unshakeable confidence of most economists in the free-trade argument cannot eradicate the fact that people have always been voicing discontent with certain consequences of competitive openness. The principal source of such discontent appears to be the constant pressure to adapt to changing circumstances to which people are exposed in open, competitive systems where their earning prospects may be challenged at any time by domestic or foreign competitors, and where they may be forced by such competition to seek alternative employment opportunities for their respective resources. Whereas the classical economic argument sees the constant inducement for productive resources to search for their most profitable employment as the particular advantage of an open economic system, economic actors may well experience such competitive pressure as an unwelcome burden imposed upon them. Indeed, there are probably not too many individuals who enjoy seeing their earning prospects constantly exposed to the challenges of competition. They may wish to escape from such competitive pressures, and it is not difficult to understand why demands for protection from such pressures are voiced in the political arena.

It does not come as a surprise, then, that in public discourse one often encounters arguments that, in one way or another, put forward the diagnosis that a completely competitive and open economic constitution is not congenial to human needs and that it cannot be claimed to constitute a generally desirable social ecology.[10] In this context, human needs for social integration, stability, and security are mentioned, all of which are allegedly in conflict with the flexibility, the risks, and the restlessness of open competitive systems. Many provisions of the modern welfare state were clearly motivated by intentions to create constitutional

---

[10] Jones (1995) refers to this issue when he asks, "[w]hether a world of completely open markets would be hospitable" (ibid.: 96), and when he remarks, "Whereas a stagnant society will miss some advantages, a society in a perpetual state of rapid factor mobility runs a risk of trading-off stability for the sake of febrile adaptability. The 'optimality band' within which it may be desirable to operate has scarcely been located, but the political disinclination to open all borders to all goods, services and factors of production seems more than the result of compounding sectional interests. It is the understandable reaction of people who are being urged to hurry towards a goal the posts of which are always moving" (ibid.: 97). What alternatives people in fact have in this regard, and how these alternatives are to be assessed in light of their constitutional interests, is the problem at issue in the present context.

frameworks that might offer a more hospitable niche to the entirety of human needs than does a system of open competition.[11] In recent socio-philosophical discourse it is, in particular, the advocates of *communitarianism* who accuse the liberal market order of disregarding such aspects of human needs.

The issues raised here are about matters of constitutional choice, and, as noted, the relevant standard in questions of constitutional choice is the *common constitutional interests* of the relevant constituency. The political economist can provide information that may assist citizens in making better-informed constitutional choices. He can help citizens to realize their constitutional interests more successfully. Yet he cannot tell citizens which constitutional interests they should pursue, except in the sense of pointing out to them that their constitutional preferences may be ill informed, may be based on mistaken conjectures, or may lead to consequences that they dislike. Because citizens may evaluate alternative economic constitutions in terms of other criteria than those considered by the advising economist, his arguments about the preferability of competitive orders are no more than conjectures about the kind of order that people find preferable, if they have a clear understanding of the relevant constitutional alternatives. The ultimate test of which economic constitution is, indeed, desirable to them must always be reserved to their own constitutional choices.[12]

5   Flexibility versus commitment

An important aspect of the kinds of interests that are potentially in conflict with competitive openness seems to concern advantages that persons can realize only through mutually binding agreements or commitments, that is, through a *renunciation of flexibility*. Openness to the environment means access to alternatives, and to enhance competition means to provide for easier access to alternatives. There are occasions, however, in which persons may wish to commit to mutual constraints, that is, to bind themselves if others do likewise. By entering contractual

---

[11] Neuber (1995: 120) points to the national differences with regard to how much concern is given to "security needs": "[O]ne could argue that the US economy is more flexible ... than, say, that of Germany. The state presence in the economy is lower, regulation is less pervasive, and contracts are more flexible, particularly in the labor market. The inherent flexibility is bought at the cost of more uncertainty (less welfare state, more open competition, fewer institutional safeguards)."

[12] This raises, of course, the question as to which "acts of choice" can be said to provide the most reliable indicators of the constitutional preferences of citizens. I shall return to this issue in a later section.

agreements people always limit, to a certain extent, their leeway in deci-sion making and thus their access to alternatives, and they do so because they hope for advantages through the reciprocal renunciation of the full range of flexibility.[13]

In markets we can find innumerable instances in which actors are willing to enter mutually binding agreements or commitments (such as long-term sales contracts, employment contracts, partnership agree-ments, etc.) that limit, for example, the parties' freedom to change their counterparts in trade relations or cooperative ventures as new opportu-nities arise. Such instances of mutual self-binding in markets prove that persons may voluntarily choose to sacrifice to some extent their freedom of choice in exchange for advantages to be gained from commitment. The market is the paradigm arena, in which voluntary contracts are the principal instrument of social coordination, and in which economic rela-tions are constantly subject to revision in response to the emergence of more attractive alternative options. Yet, at the same time, it is an arena of action where actors have the option to bind themselves mutually in a voluntary manner. The market principle of voluntary coordination includes the option for actors to enter into voluntarily *constitutional* agreements the very purpose of which is the renunciation of certain kinds of subconstitutional freedom of choice. Transactions and activities at the subconstitutional level that are not directly based on voluntary agreement (e.g., the giving and obeying of commands as a means of coor-dination within a firm) are indirectly legitimized by the parties' volun-tary consent to the constitutional arrangement.[14] With contractual arrangements of mutual self-binding, those involved have to weigh the advantages and disadvantages resulting from the limitations of freedom of choice imposed on all parties to the contract, including themselves. The different kinds of contracts to be found in markets reflect these tradeoffs.[15]

---

[13] It is the central notion of constitutional political economy that mutual (as well as uni-lateral) commitments may bring advantages that could not be realized otherwise.

[14] This raises a number of issues that, while they cannot be discussed here in any detail, should at least be mentioned. For example, how can one measure how voluntary the consent to a contractual arrangement is? What is relevant, the voluntary consent at the time of the original contract-making only, or, instead, the ongoing voluntary consent to the continuation of the arrangement? If the latter is the case, what can count as a reliable indicator of voluntariness at that level? On this issue, see Vanberg (1994: 224–227).

[15] Again, it is a question of constitutional choice, which kinds of contracts should be con-sidered legitimate, or should be enforced by the apparatus of the state. The question of whether the directly concerned parties agree voluntarily to a contract at the subconsti-tutional level, must therefore be distinguished from the question of whether the citizens

The role that the voluntary consent of the parties involved plays as the criterion of legitimacy can easily be misunderstood if the distinction between the constitutional and the subconstitutional decision levels is not carefully considered. Market and free-trade regimes are not self-legitimizing in the sense that the voluntariness of the transactions performed within their frameworks would legitimize not only these transactions, but also the regimes themselves. With their voluntary consent to *transactions within* a market framework persons express their agreement to these transactions, not their agreement to the constitutional framework within which they take place. Whether or not they would like to live under a competitive market or free-trade regime, as opposed to some alternative constitutional arrangement, is a question of their *constitutional* preferences, preferences they do not express through the decisions they make under the auspices of such a regime. It would be by no means inconsistent for someone to advocate a protectionist regime, but at the same time, under free-trade conditions, to prefer to purchase foreign goods over domestic products. The latter is a question of subconstitutional interests, and the first a question of constitutional interests.

If actors in markets, through their voluntary consent to mutual constraints, reveal that they do not in all regards prefer the advantages of complete flexibility and freedom of choice to advantages that are attainable through binding commitments, one cannot rule out, in principle, the possibility that similar considerations apply to matters of constitutional choice at the level of political communities or jurisdictions. Therefore, one cannot rule out a priori as a possible explanation for protectionist provisions that the members of a jurisdiction find it to be in their best interest to enter mutually binding agreements which, on the one hand, limit their own flexibility to respond to economic opportunities emerging outside of their jurisdiction, but which, on the other hand, as a result of the same obligations on the part of their fellow citizens,

of a jurisdiction may want to decide, at a constitutional level, that certain contracts be considered invalid, irrespective of whether the parties to these contracts agree to them voluntarily. Thus, while it is certainly conceivable that contracts of enslavement could come into existence in a completely voluntary fashion, there may nevertheless be good reasons for citizens to come to the conclusion, at the constitutional level, that such contracts should be invalid, notwithstanding their potentially voluntary genesis. The decisive question at the constitutional level is how the nature of the demarcation between admissible and inadmissible contracts impacts on the functional characteristics of a given economic order. Which limitations of the freedom to make contracts are desirable to the members of a jurisdiction, is in the final consideration a question of their *constitutional interests*, i.e., of their interests regarding the kind of constitutional regime in which they desire to live.

shelter them from extrajurisdictional competition. Economists may well suspect that such preferences for a protectionist "insurance arrangement" can be based only on misperceptions of the true costs of such arrangements. Yet, they cannot rule out the possibility that the citizens of a jurisdiction may still consider a regime of this sort to be in their constitutional interest, even after they have diligently weighed all relevant costs and benefits.

Again, the political economist can only advance conjectures about what kinds of constitutional regimes are presumably in citizens' common constitutional interest, but these conjectures cannot find their ultimate test in anything other than the citizens' own judgments. This leads us, however, to the question of what can be considered a reliable indicator of citizens' informed constitutional interests. We need to explore the issue of what kind of decision-making processes could be expected to express adequately citizens' informed assessment of their own constitutional interests.

6   Protectionist interests: Interests in privileges or common constitutional interests?

In the previous section it has been argued that, notwithstanding the economist's arguments on the benefits of free trade, it cannot be ruled out a priori that the citizens of a jurisdiction may voluntarily agree to protectionist restrictions. If they were indeed, after careful consideration of the alternatives and in full knowledge of the consequences, in agreement in preferring a protectionist over a competitive regime, there would be no ground on which the economist could object to such constitutional choice. Yet, what is the proper test to decide whether demands for protection reflect such agreement or whether they reflect no more than the desire to gain differential advantages at others' expense, to enjoy the benefits of protectionist *privileges* for which others, consumers or taxpayers, are made to pay?

Obviously, we need to draw a distinction between two forms in which protectionist interests may appear, namely, on one side, as *partial* interests in protectionist *privileges* and, on the other side, as *common* interests in *nondiscriminatory, general* protectionist provisions. In their first variety, protectionist interests are directed at protectionist privileges that are granted, in a discriminatory fashion, to particular persons or particular groups in a jurisdiction, but not to others. Though one can expect their beneficiaries to have a preference for such privileges, it is difficult to think of reasons why the nonprivileged – in full knowledge of the relevant facts – should consent to such discriminatory regimes.[16] In their second form, protectionist interests are directed at protectionist provisions that apply equally to all citizens, provisions in which all share a common interest. Whether such common protectionist interests do in fact exist, and how one can, in practice, distinguish them from interests in protectionist privileges, is the crucial issue.

The issue of protectionism can, from a constitutional economics perspective, be discussed in terms of a conflict between our constitutional interests as consumers and our interests as producers. The argument that Adam Smith and many subsequent economists have made on this issue is essentially that, first, it is only as producers that we are interested in protection, while as consumers our interests are best served by a competitive, free-trade regime, and that, second, we should give our consumer interests precedence over our protectionist producer interests, since it is, after all, in order to consume that we produce.[17] A constitutional economist can refine this argument by putting the issue as a matter of constitutional choice. The question to ask is: What kind of economic constitution, a protectionist or a free-trade regime, might citizens agree on who take into account that they are typically on both sides of the issue, as producers – in their roles as investors, employees, and so forth – as well as consumers. Looked at in this manner, the classical free-trade argument can be restated as the conjecture that as consumers (respectively as producers on the *demand* side of the market) citizens clearly share a *common constitutional interest*, namely an interest in a competitive, free-trade regime, while with regard to the protectionist interests that they hold as producers (on the *supply* side) they are typically divided, as these interests aim at *protectionist privileges* rather than at general constitutional provisions equally applicable to all producers.

The economist's general suspicion is that calls for protection voiced in the political process typically reflect producer interests, aimed at protectionist privileges. Special-interest groups seek to attain protection for themselves. They do not lobby for protectionist measures to be extended without distinction to all branches of the economy. With their arguments

---

[16] It is, to be sure, conceivable for protectionist privileges that are granted exclusively to particular groups to be, nevertheless, in the common constitutional interest of all citizens of the respective jurisdiction. Yet, it is not easy to think of examples that can be plausibly assumed to fall into that category. In any case, this possibility is disregarded here.

[17] The well-known passage in Smith (1981: 600) reads: "Consumption is the sole end and purpose of all production; and the interest of the producer ought to be attended to only so far as it may be necessary for promoting that of the consumer. The maxim is so perfectly self-evident, that it would be absurd to attempt to prove it."

on the benefits of free trade, neither Adam Smith nor other economists have overlooked the fact that protectionist regulations that are restricted to particular persons or groups can be advantageous to them, and that the prospective beneficiaries can therefore be expected to seek to secure protection for themselves. They do not want to dispute the obvious fact that privileges can be in the constitutional interests of the privileged. Their claim is that protectionist regimes cannot be in the *common* constitutional interest of all parties involved. While a nondiscriminating, completely protectionist regime (i.e., a perfectly closed economy) is unlikely to be in anybody's interest, a selectively protectionist regime is not in the constitutional interest of the nonprivileged.

If one looks at the issue of protectionism in this sense only as a matter of consumer interests versus producer interests, it might seem as if protectionist interests can only be interests in protectionist privileges. Accordingly, one might be inclined to conclude that there are no protectionist provisions that could be claimed to be in citizens' common constitutional interest, and, hence, that there are no protectionist interests that citizens could be expected to share. This conclusion would, however, overlook the possibility that citizens' special interests as producers may not be the only source of protectionist inclinations, but that citizens *in their capacity as citizens* may share an interest in maintaining certain characteristics of their jurisdiction that they see threatened under a competitive, free-trade regime, and that they may wish to defend by protectionist provisions. In order to distinguish potential interests of this sort from producer interests in protectionist privileges one can think of them as *citizenship-interests*.[18]

7   Protectionism and rent seeking

When confronted with the necessity to adapt to changes in external economic conditions, there are basically two alternatives available to the members of a jurisdiction. One alternative consists in leaving it to the respective actors directly concerned to adapt to these changes either by accepting a loss in income, by reestablishing their competitiveness through reducing costs or improving the quality of their products, or by finding alternative employment for their resources. The second alternative consists in attempts to spare those persons who are directly affected the necessity to adapt by shielding them, for example, through protectionist measures from external competition, or by subsidizing them in

---

[18] I have adopted this term from J. Kincaid's (1992) discussion of what he calls a conflict between "consumership and citizenship." On this issue see also Vanberg (1997).

order to compensate for the economic consequences of such competition. Whichever alternative is chosen, the necessity for adaptation to the changed environmental conditions cannot be eliminated. Choosing the second alternative means essentially that the burdens of adaptation are being diffused and made anonymous by being shifted to large groups of consumers and taxpayers. It is apparent that the latter alternative may seem enticing to those directly affected in particular instances. The relevant question is, however, which method of adaptation is more advantageous for all citizens in the longer run. Or, in other words, the issue is which of the two alternative constitutional regimes is more desirable overall, for all members of a jurisdiction as a whole when considering the working properties of the respective arrangements.

Protectionist regulations always result in the use of the coercive apparatus of the state for transferring income from some to others favored by the regulation. In contrast to income derived from production and voluntary exchange in the market, protection income relies on forcible transfers. Subsidies involve forcible transfers from taxpayers to the recipients; tariffs and other trade restrictions involve forcibly hindering or completely denying actors access to extrajurisdictional economic opportunities to the benefit of the "protected." Juxtaposed to the protectionist privileges of one group, therefore, always stands the "exploitation" of others who, through state coercion, are denied otherwise accessible advantages. The better the chances are of attaining protection privileges through the political process, the stronger the incentives will be for actors in the jurisdiction to shift their efforts away from the realization of income through market performance and into the attainment of such privileges (or into warding off measures that provide privileges for others). The fatal consequences this process has for potential wealth-creation within the respective jurisdictions is the theme of the theory of "rent seeking."[19]

The theory of rent seeking complements and reinforces the classical free-trade arguments by focusing on the dynamics of the political process in a jurisdiction in which protectionist privileges can be attained. The theory points to the fact that even if there were protectionist provisions that might be in the common constitutional interest of all the members of a jurisdiction, citizens might still be ill-advised to allow protectionist provisions to be attained through the political process, as long as that process could not be trusted to be sufficiently reliable in sorting out protectionist provisions that reflected their common citizenship-interest

---

[19] Buchanan, Tollison, and Tullock (1980).

from those that bring advantages only for some and disadvantages for others, or possibly even disadvantages for everybody involved. The critical issue is therefore, how – by what procedure – it is to be decided which demands for protectionist measures are actually in the common interest, and how – by what procedure – citizens can protect themselves against measures that discriminate against them to the benefit of others, or that are detrimental to all of them. If there is no practical procedure available that sufficiently guards against these risks, the interests of all members may well be better served by not allowing any kind of protection. Even if this means forgoing potential benefits of common-interest protection, such a regime may generate an overall more desirable pattern of outcomes than one that allows for adopting possibly desirable protectionist provisions, but that entails a considerable risk of ending up with a bundle of measures that in the sum of its impact is undesirable for everybody.

The desire of single groups to gain protection from competition for themselves, but at the same time to enjoy the advantages of an open economic system, is, as noted before, not hard to understand. This explains why efforts to attain such privileges are a widespread phenomenon in all modern welfare states. As the theory of rent seeking shows, the members of a jurisdiction in which the political process permits protectionist privileges are caught in a kind of prisoner-dilemma: For each single group the striving for such privileges is the dominant strategy, but the pursuit of this strategy, while rational at the level of separate individual choice, puts the constituency as a whole into a situation that is desirable for no one. If citizens had to decide between the resulting system of widespread protection and a regime generally open to competition, they would have good reasons to choose the latter. But as participants in the political process they are not faced with a choice of this kind. Here they are confronted with the choice of whether to seek to secure protection privileges for themselves or to abstain from such rent seeking. Whether they choose one option or the other will typically not be the decisive factor in determining which kind of regime they find themselves living in. Even if they are convinced of the merits of a generally open, competitive regime, by their own abstention from rent seeking they cannot bring about or secure such a regime. As a result of the rent-seeking dilemma, the dynamics of the political process will result in a drift toward a state of pervasive protectionism, which is not even desirable to the "beneficiaries" of the protectionist regulations when compared to the conditions that would prevail in a generally open, competitive system.

8   Globalization and constitutional choice

When it comes to the question of what possible procedure may serve to discern the common constitutional interests of the members of a jurisdiction, and to separate them from interests in protectionist privileges, in constitutional economics usually the conceptual model of rule choice behind a veil of ignorance (Rawls 1971), or a veil of uncertainty (Buchanan and Tullock 1962), is invoked. Behind such a veil, where an individual does not know (or is uncertain about) what *specific* effects alternative rules may produce for him *personally*, he is induced to assess the working properties of such rules from an impartial perspective. That is, under such conditions of constitutional choice one can expect common constitutional interests to prevail. Efforts at a practical political utilization of the desirable characteristics of this conceptual model would seek to design the process of rule choice in a fashion that would increase uncertainty with regard to the personal impact.

There is another, alternative theoretical model, which has similar implications to the model of rule choice behind a veil of uncertainty. Imagine a world – like the one described in R. Nozick's (1974: 297–334) "Framework for Utopia" – in which actors can choose freely and without any impediment between alternative jurisdictions or constitutional regimes, much as a person may choose the condominium she would like to live in from a range of available alternatives.[20] If one assumes that in such a world one can choose among various types of economic constitutions, ranging from regimes totally open to competition, through various kinds and combinations of protectionist privileges, to completely protectionist regimes, then one should expect a sorting process to work, driven by trial and error, that results in the depopulation of discriminating regimes in favor of arrangements that correspond to the common constitutional interests of the inhabitants.[21] Even if the actors in this world are able to see clearly how they would be personally affected by alternative eco-

---

[20] Note that the model of free choice among alternative constitutional regimes is not the same as a free-trade regime. The focus of the free-trade regime is on the freedom of choice between transaction partners internal or external to the jurisdiction, where this choice can be made separately for each single transaction. The model of free choice among constitutional orders centers around the choice of membership in alternative jurisdictions, where this choice can only be between alternative *packages* or *bundles* of regulations.

[21] Not only would, in such a world of voluntary choice among constitutional orders, the discriminating orders suffer from a loss of members, but the nondiscriminating but inefficient orders would also lose members to the degree to which information about the relative efficiency of alternative regimes becomes available.

nomic constitutions, and even if their interests in being privileged might initially attract them to constitutions that discriminate in their favor, they would, in the end, come to opt for nondiscriminating constitutions. The reason is, of course, that they would be bound to learn from experience that jurisdictions in which they are privileged are desirable not even for them, for under the assumed conditions of free choice among regimes they would soon find themselves deserted by the nonprivileged fellow citizens who would have to fund their privileges. Whereas in the model of rule choice "behind a veil" the preference for a common-interest constitution is driven by the uncertainty about personal impact, it is the need for willing cooperation that achieves the same in the model of free regime choice.[22] In a world in which one has to rely on the voluntary cooperation of others, privileges are hard to obtain and impossible to maintain in the longer run.

The practical political relevance of the discouragement of privilege interests predicted by the model of free choice among economic constitutions lies in its implications for provisions or circumstances that increase the factual possibilities for individuals to choose between alternative jurisdictions. It is these implications that lead us back to the issue of globalization. Since, as noted earlier, "globalization" is a summary term for various kinds of developments that all contribute to increased mobility of resources across jurisdictions, it can be said to move the real world in the direction of the conceptual world described by the model of free choice among constitutional regimes.

The easier it is for resources to move between jurisdictions, the lower will be the level of willingness of their owners to accept less advantageous conditions in one jurisdiction compared to those in the jurisdiction next-door.[23] This, again, induces, as noted earlier, competition among

---

[22] The model of rule choice behind a veil of ignorance/uncertainty and the model of free regime choice are asymmetrical in the sense that the former presupposes that the persons involved have perfect knowledge of the general working properties of rules, but are ignorant/uncertain about their own particular situation, while the latter model assumes that they know perfectly well "who they are," but does not require them to possess any general constitutional knowledge.

[23] Jones (1995: 100–101) emphasizes the importance that historically competition among jurisdictions has had for Europe, and he stresses the parallel to today's globalization of competition: "Europe's mosaic of little polities, its emergent system of nation-states, was immensely interconnected and competitive. . . . The polities of Europe were separately ruled but leaky: capital, entrepreneurship, technology and labour circulated among them. These productive factors did not, however, need to shift *en masse*. Shifts at the margin were all that were required to nudge most rulers away from damaging acts of expropriation. . . . There was in effect a single market for information. . . . When a policy was deemed ineffective or worse, it could be avoided. When it was thought good, it would

economic constitutions as mobile resources seek out jurisdictions that offer them more hospitable constitutional environments than others. The critical issue in the present context is whether such competition can be expected to select against protectionist privileges only, in which case it could be said to help citizens realize their common constitutional interests, or whether it will also tend to work against constitutional provisions that all citizens would benefit from, a claim that is sometimes made in the current debate on the prospective effects of competition among jurisdictions (Sinn 1997).

As globalization facilitates mobility of resources across jurisdictions, one should expect the sorting process mentioned previously to select against protectionist privileges,[24] without prohibiting those provisions that are advantageous for all members of a jurisdiction in the sense that they make the jurisdiction a more hospitable niche for all of them. If such generally advantageous protectionist rules indeed exist, there is no reason why they might not be implemented and maintained in a world of free choice among jurisdictions. The relevant test of whether protectionist measures are not just serving the privileges of some while being disadvantageous to others, but instead actually do contribute to making a jurisdiction a more desirable "social niche" for all citizens, lies, ultimately, not in whether such provisions are being called for, and sought after, in the political process. The relevant test lies in the overall attractiveness of the respective jurisdiction as a constitutional regime.

Communitarian or other critics of the liberal market order who claim that open, competitive regimes leave important constitutional interests of their citizens uncovered would have to prove their case, in the final instance, under the conditions of competition between jurisdictions, that is, in terms of the actual choices that persons make in the "market" for alternative orders. To be sure, feelings of uneasiness with living conditions in modern, open societies are often expressed, but such complaints

---

be copied. The ebb and flow of factors around the European-cum-Atlantic world had some of the consequences loved or loathed in the globalized market of today: international rivalry to retain or attract them, tamed governments, curbed their taxing power, and infringed their sovereignty, although they scarcely knew it and had to pretend otherwise." Jones (ibid.: 101) adds the interesting remark: "How Europe's governments reasserted a considerable part of their sovereignty during the nineteenth century is another story. They went on straining to create nationhood out of the ethnic and linguistic fragments."

[24] Streit (1995: 374) points out the limitations that the competition of jurisdictions for mobile resources imposes on national policies and remarks that the forces of globalization make it increasingly difficult for national governments to favor particular group interests through regulation.

are, in and by themselves, not convincing proof that the persons who express them are prepared to pay the price that life in a "communitarian order" (however specified) would call for. The relevant test would be, indeed, the willingness to opt for communitarian regimes over alternative options. In the final instance, the only reliable indicator of the constitutional interests that people truly do have in common, would seem to be their voluntary participation in regimes that implement them, in the presence of available alternatives.

9   Conclusion

Jurisdictions with their economic constitutions co-evolve with the environment in which they are placed. It is simply not possible for jurisdictions as constitutional niches to exempt themselves from the necessity to adapt to continuously changing conditions. More than ever before, this is true under conditions of increasing globalization of markets.

That jurisdictions cannot evade the necessity to adapt in an evolving world does not mean, however, that their constituencies cannot seek to shape the manner in which such adaptation occurs according to their preferences. They can do this by choosing appropriate constitutional frameworks at the level of their particular jurisdictions as well as at the more inclusive levels where constitutional agreements between jurisdictions may be implemented. Attempts to channel, by adopting adequate rules of the game, the competition inevitable in a world of scarce resources into desirable and socially productive directions, can be applied on various, more or less inclusive jurisdictional levels, keeping in mind that all such attempts to create more hospitable constitutional niches remain subject to the constraints that an ever-changing environment imposes on them (Vanberg 1995).

If economic constitutions in democratic polities are there to serve citizens' common constitutional interests, the central problem that globalization poses can be stated in terms of the following questions:

How can citizens create and maintain an economic constitution that reflects their *common constitutional interests*, interests that may include shared protectionist preferences in maintaining certain attributes of their jurisdiction?

How can they prevent interests in protectionist privileges to cause a drift toward a constitutional regime that is desirable for nobody?

How can they guard against the error of adopting, or seeking to maintain, constitutional provisions that may appear to be in their common interest, but that cannot – or only at excessive costs – be sustained in the world as it is?[25]

It has been the purpose of this chapter to discuss some of the arguments that ought to be considered in approaching these questions.

References

Breton, Albert (1965), "A Theory of Government Grants," *Canadian Journal of Economics and Political Science*, Vol. 26, 175–187.

Breton, Albert (1987), "Towards a Theory of Competitive Federalism," *European Journal of Political Economy*, Vol. 3, 263–329.

Breton, Albert (1996), *Competitive Governments – An Economic Theory of Politics and Public Finance*, Cambridge: Cambridge University Press.

Breton, A. and A. Scott (1978), *The Economic Constitution of Federal States*, Canberra: Australian National University Press.

Buchanan, James M. (1990), "The Domain of Constitutional Economics," *Constitutional Political Economy*, Vol. 1, 1–18.

Buchanan, J. M. and G. Tullock (1962), *The Calculus of Consent: Logical Foundations of Constitutional Democracy*, Ann Arbor: University of Michigan Press.

Buchanan, J. M., R. D. Tollison and G. Tullock (eds.) (1980), *Towards a Theory of the Rent-Seeking Society*, College Station: Texas A&M University Press.

Hayek, F. A. (1969), "Rechtsordnung und Handelnsordnung," in *Freiburger Studien – Gesammelte Aufsätze*, Tübingen: J.C.B. Mohr (Paul Siebeck), 161–198.

Jones, E. L. (1995), "Economic Adaptability in the Long Term," in T. Killick (ed.), 70–110.

Killick, Tony (ed.) (1995), *The Flexible Economy – Causes and Consequences of the Adaptability of National Economies*, London and New York: Routledge.

Killick, Tony (1995a), "Relevance, Meaning and Determinants of Flexibility," in T. Killick (ed.), 1–33.

Kincaid, John (1992), "Consumership versus Citizenship: Is There Wiggle Room for Local Regulation in the Global Economy?", in B. Hocking (ed.), *Foreign Relations and Federal States*, London and New York: Leicester University Press, 27–47.

Lachmann, Ludwig M. (1963), "Wirtschaftsordnung und wirtschaftliche Institutionen," *Ordo*, Vol. 14, 63–77.

Neuber, Alexander (1995), "Adapting the Economies of Eastern Europe: Behavioral and Institutional Aspects of Flexibility," in T. Killick (ed.), 111–153.

Nozick, Robert (1974), *Anarchy, State, and Utopia*, New York: Basic Books.

---

[25] Pelikan (1995: 189) speaks of the "*wisdom condition*" that requires constitutional frameworks to "be able to induce the members of the society to choose objectives that do not destroy the basis on which their continuing existence of the institutions depends." As Pelikan (ibid.: 200) notes: "Much as medicine has found that the preference for longevity is incompatible with the preference for smoking, the social sciences should be able to find that the preference for civilization and welfare (in the broadest meaning of these terms) is incompatible with the preference for certain types of institutions."

Nunnenkamp, P., E. Gundlach and J. P. Agarwal (1994), *Globalization of Production and Markets* (Kieler Studien, 262), Tübingen: J.C.B. Mohr (Paul Siebeck).

Pelikan, Pavel (1995), "Competition of Socio-Economic Institutions: In Search of the Winners," in L. Gerken (ed.), *Competition among Institutions*, London: Macmillan, 177–205.

Rawls, John (1971), *A Theory of Justice*, Cambridge, Mass.: Harvard University Press.

Smith, Adam (1981), *An Inquiry into the Nature and Causes of the Wealth of Nations*, two volumes, Indianapolis: Liberty Classics.

Sinn, Hans-Werner (1997), "The Selection Principle and Market Failure in Systems Competition," *Journal of Public Economics*, Vol. 66, 247–274.

Streit, Manfred E. (1995), *Freiburger Beiträge zur Ordnungsökonomik*, Tübingen: J.C.B. Mohr (Paul Siebeck).

Vanberg, Viktor (1994), *Rules and Choice in Economics*, London and New York: Routledge.

Vanberg, Viktor (1995), "Ordnungspolitik und die Unvermeidbarkeit des Wettbewerbs," in H. H. Francke (ed.), *Ökonomischer Individualismus und freiheitliche Verfassung*, Freiburg: Rombach, 187–211.

Vanberg, Viktor (1997), "Subsidiarity, Responsive Government and Individual Liberty," in K. W. Nörr and Th. Oppermann (eds.), *Subsidiarität: Idee und Wirklichkeit – Zur Reichweite eines Prinzips in Deutschland und Europa*, Tübingen: J.B.C. Mohr (Paul Siebeck), 253–269.

Vanberg, Viktor (1998), "Freiburg School of Law and Economics," in P. Newman (ed.), *The New Palgrave Dictionary of Economics and the Law*, vol. 2, London: MacMillan, 172–179.

Vanberg, Viktor und Wolfgang Kerber (1994), "Institutional Competition Among Jurisdictions," *Constitutional Political Economy*, Vol. 5, 193–219.

CHAPTER 16

A cautious view of international harmonization: Implications from Breton's theory of competitive governments

Michael Trebilcock and Robert Howse

I Introduction

It is a commonplace in international trade law and practice to note that with the very substantial success of the GATT over the postwar years in dramatically reducing the level of tariffs worldwide (from an average of over 40% on manufactured products in the late 1940s to about 3% after the Uruguay Round tariff cuts are fully implemented) and in reducing the scale of other border measures such as quotas, temptations arise for countries to substitute other forms of protectionism.

A somewhat parallel, although from a trade policy perspective substantially more ambiguous, trend has been the dramatic expansion over the past three decades or so of domestic regulations pertaining to health, safety, consumer protection, the environment, and labor markets. In many respects, these regulatory trends can be viewed as part of the elaboration of the modern welfare state in much of the industrialized world, reflecting in part the proposition that greater safety, a cleaner environment, and so forth, can be thought of as normal economic goods, the demand for which rises as income levels rise, so that greater prosperity (in significant part engendered by trade liberalization) has been accompanied by increased demands for these kinds of domestic policies. However, as trade liberalization, at least with respect to border measures, has continued to advance, these "within the border" regulatory measures are increasingly seen by many liberal trade proponents as the most prominent and arguably the most costly form of nontariff barriers to trade (NTBs), requiring new disciplines under international trade rules,

This chapter is adapted from a longer paper, "Trade Liberalization and Regulatory Diversity: Reconciling Competitive Markets with Competitive Politics," (1998) *European Journal of Law and Economics* 6, 5–37.

particularly in a globalizing economy which, it is argued, has a low tolerance for "system frictions."[1]

The relatively recent focus on these forms of domestic regulation as potential NTBs has substantially heightened both domestic and international political conflicts, as trade policy linkages have increasingly been drawn with broad sweeps of domestic policy domains previously thought to lie largely outside the arena of trade policy.

These conflicts over NTBs have drawn new domestic political constituencies into debates over trade policies, such as consumer and environmental groups and other nongovernmental organizations (NGOs) that seek to resist the imposition of constraints on domestic political sovereignty by international trade agreements. A further and at least as potentially divisive political fault line relating to many of these issues has emerged between developed and developing countries. Many interests in developed countries see the much laxer environmental and labor standards that often prevail in developing countries as threatening their more stringent standards by precipitating a race to the bottom. On the other hand, many interests in developing countries see the insistence by interests in developed countries on developing countries adherence to the same environmental or labor policies, for example, that prevail in many developed countries (a race to the top) as a frontal assault on essential features of their international comparative advantage.

In responding to these diverse pressures, Alan Sykes (among others) notes that a wide array of remedial options is available.[2] At one end of the continuum lies complete deference to national sovereigns. At the other end of the continuum lies total harmonization. Between the extremes lie many alternatives that impose greater or fewer constraints on national sovereigns while still affording some opportunity for variation across nations. Many of these alternatives involve "policed decentralization," whereby national authorities are largely free to pursue their own policy objectives but must do so subject to a set of broadly applicable legal constraints. The options here include nondiscrimination principles, the sham principle, transparency requirements, generality requirements, presumptive deference to negotiated international stan-

---

[1] See Sylvia Ostry, "Beyond the Border: The New International Policy Arena," in E. Kantzenbach, H. Sharrer, and L. Waverman (eds.), *Competition Policy in an Interdependent World Economy* (Nomos, Baden-Baden, 1993) at 261.

[2] Alan O. Sykes, *Product Standards for Internationally Integrated Goods Markets* (Washington, D.C.: The Brookings Institution, 1995) at 117; see also Sykes, "The (Limited) Role of Regulatory Harmonization in the International System" (unpublished manuscript, University. of Chicago Law School, 1997).

dards with specified procedures for deviation, mutual recognition, and benefit/burden balancing tests.

In this chapter, we will argue for a relatively conservative view of the case for domestic policy harmonization or convergence. This general orientation is influenced by at least four basic premises.

First, as Sykes also notes, the analysis of regulatory barriers to trade is complicated by both theoretical and empirical uncertainty in many cases about their effects on social welfare (given the wide array of values and concerns that domestic policies are designed to serve), and in this respect regulatory barriers stand in sharp contrast to traditional impediments to trade, such as tariffs and quotas, which can be shown both theoretically and empirically to be welfare-reducing in almost all cases, from both a global and a domestic perspective.[3] Thus, it is emphatically not the case that international harmonization of domestic policies will always increase both domestic and global welfare – indeed, often, depending upon how harmonization is induced, it may have the opposite effect.[4]

Leebron has insightfully reviewed the wide range of normative claims that are often made for harmonization of domestic regulation.[5] These include: (1) jurisdictional interface costs such as different railway gauges, telecommunications protocols, or aircraft navigation systems that inhibit mutually beneficial cross-border transactions; (2) externalities ensuing from different regulatory standards, such as transborder pollution; (c) leakage and the nonefficacy of unilateral rules, for example, the undermining of domestic intellectual property protection by the importation of infringing goods; (4) fair competition, for example, lesser regulatory burdens in one jurisdiction that give producers in that jurisdiction an unfair advantage over foreign producers in international trade; (5) economies of scale, such as different technical requirements in various jurisdictions that may prevent manufacturers based in any one jurisdiction from achieving economies of scale from servicing more than one jurisdictional market; (6) political economies of scale, for example, reg-

---

[3] See Sykes, *op. cit.* at 5; see, more generally, Douglas Irwin, *Against the Tide: An Intellectual History of Free Trade* (Princeton: Princeton University Press, 1996).

[4] For insightful discussions of the welfare effects of harmonization, see Jagdish Bhagwati, "The Demands to Reduce Domestic Diversity among Trading Nations," in Jagdish Bhagwati and Robert Hudec (eds.), *Fair Trade and Harmonization: Pre-requisites for Free Trade?* (Cambridge, Mass.: MIT Press, 1996), vol. 1, Chapter 1; Bhagwati, "Fair Trade, Reciprocity and Harmonization: The Novel Challenge to the Theory and Policy of Free Trade," in Dominick Salvatore (ed.), *Protectionism and World Welfare* (Cambridge University Press, 1993), Chapter 2; David Leebron, "Lying Down with Procrustes: An Analysis of Harmonization," in Bhagwati and Hudec, *op. cit.*, Chapter 2; Alan O. Sykes, "The (Limited) Role of Regulatory Harmonization in the International System" (unpublished manuscript, University of Chicago Law School, 1997).

[5] Leebron, *ibid.*

ulatory requirements that entail marshalling of specialized resources that are beyond the capacity of any single jurisdiction; (7) transparency, that is, preventing the adoption of laws or regulations that appear to address legitimate public policy concerns but are in fact disguised restrictions on foreign competition.

However, Leebron also points out that differences between nations may also have value, and that harmonization can be achieved only at the cost of eliminating or reducing differences. He argues that nations can be said to differ in five attributes that affect the laws and policies they adopt: endowments, technologies, preferences, institutions, and coalition formation. If preferences, endowments, and technologies were the only differences between nations, one could perhaps assume that differences in governmental regulation and policy were legitimate determinants of comparative advantage. In cases where differences in policies or legal regimes reflect differences in preferences, harmonization will entail a potential welfare loss for citizens in at least one of the jurisdictions. However, according to Leebron, once differences in institutions and coalition formation are taken into account, the presumptive legitimacy of differences in regulatory choices is less clear.

Second, we believe that proponents of more sweeping or extreme forms of international harmonization in domestic policies in the interest of creating more open and competitive international markets in goods and services severely discount the importance of what our colleague at the University of Toronto, Albert Breton, whose illustrious career this volume celebrates, calls in a recent and important book "competitive governments."[6] In contrast to a view of government as a monolith or monopoly, whose policies are typically viewed by Public Choice theorists as the product of rent-seeking behavior by special-interest groups that have captured Leviathan, Breton argues that governments in most democracies are intensely competitive in a wide variety of dimensions: opposing parties compete for political office (competition for the market in Demsetz's terms);[7] agencies within government compete with each other over policy priorities and claims on resources; lower houses compete with upper houses, and both compete with constitutional courts; central governments compete with subnational levels of government and with nonprofit organizations; subnational levels of government compete among themselves; and national governments compete with other national governments. In Breton's thesis, these competitive features of government serve a crucial demand revelation function, and yield a more benign view of public or collective provision of goods,

---

[6] Albert Breton, *Competitive Governments* (Cambridge University Press, 1996).
[7] Harold Demsetz, "Why Regulate Utilities?" (1968) 11 *J. of L. & Economics*.

services, and public policies than that taken by Public Choice theorists by establishing linkages between revenue and expenditure decisions of the kind that economists like Wicksell and Lindahl earlier in this century viewed as a precondition to efficient public policies.[8] While polit- ical markets are unlikely to function perfectly competitively, rendering governments vulnerable on occasion to rent-seeking behavior (political market failure), one should not assume (as many public-choice theorists tend to) that *all* government policies are explicable in these terms.[9]

Breton argues explicitly that while the European Union is quite stable, that stability has been acquired by the virtual suppression of intercoun- try competition through excessive policy harmonization.[10] While the prin- ciple of subsidiarity seems intended to address these concerns,[11] it has often proven difficult to give it clear operational content. According to Breton, "policy harmonization reduces competition by neutralizing and, at the limit, by extinguishing the Salmon and Tiebout mechanisms. Mini- mizing competition in this way ensures stability but at the cost of forego- ing the benefits that go with competition."[12] Compounding this problem is the so-called "democratic deficit" that supranational European (and indeed other international) institutions typically exhibit, rendering them highly imperfect mechanisms for preference revelation. Thus, from this perspective it would be a major and unfortunate irony if the price of adopting rules that are designed to remove constraints on and enhance competition in international goods and services markets is the adoption of rules or institutions that have the effect of monopolizing or cartelizing government policy making, that is, enhanced competition in economic markets at the price of reduced competition in political markets.

A third premise that motivates the relatively conservative view we take of trade-policy-driven harmonization is the distinction that we draw between unilateralism and consensus-based approaches. In our view, the basic ground rules adopted in international trade treaties and the like pertaining to domestic policies as potential NTBs should minimize the

---

[8] See also Donald Wittman, *The Myth of Democratic Failure: Why Political Institutions Are Efficient* (Chicago: University of Chicago Press, 1995), Chapter 3.

[9] One of us has been guilty of this tendency in the past: see Michael Trebilcock, Douglas Hartle, Robert Prichard, and Donald Dewees, *The Choice of Governing Instrument* (Ottawa: Economic Council of Canada, 1982); Michael Trebilcock and Douglas Hartle, "The Choice of Governing Instrument," (1982) 2 *International Review of Law and Economics* 29; but see Trebilcock, *The Limits of Freedom of Contract* (Cambridge, Mass.: Harvard University Press, 1993), 261–268.

[10] Breton, *op. cit.* at 275.

[11] See Willem Molle, *The Economics of European Integration* (Dartmouth, 2nd ed., 1994) at 18–23.

[12] Breton, *op. cit.* at 276.

extent to which harmonization can be induced by judicial fiat, on the one hand, or by threats of unilateral sanctions, on the other, thus attenuating the "threat points" of nation-states in interactions with each other, and conversely increasing the scope for mutually beneficial agreements on policy convergence. However, if the multilateral system is not to degenerate into a thicket of discriminatory managed-trade arrangements, additional ground rules need to be agreed on regarding the form that such agreements may take, for example, the application of the Most Favored Nation principle, so that international forms of discrimination among trading partners are constrained.[13]

A final premise that motivates our relatively conservative orientation to the trade-policy-based case for international harmonization is that whatever view one takes of the European experience, the crucial shift that occurred in Europe with the enactment of the Single European Act of 1986 from an emphasis on negative integration (rules proscribing what domestic policy measures countries may *not* adopt) to positive integration (supranational regulations and directives prescribing what domestic policies member states *must* adopt) is simply not feasible in most other institutional contexts. As we have argued elsewhere,[14] deep economic integration among nation-states is typically predicated on either the existence of a hegemonic power with the ability to impress its will on other smaller and weaker states (the U.S. in the immediate postwar years), or willingness among member states to cede substantial aspects of their domestic political sovereignty to supranational political institutions – a willingness that for the most part is likely to be conditional on a reasonably egalitarian distribution of political influence and a common interest in overarching political objectives (in the case of Europe, the mitigation of conflicts that had devastated the continent militarily and economically over the first half of the twentieth century). Neither of these conditions is likely to apply in the foreseeable future outside of the European context, either with respect to other regional trading blocs or with respect to the multilateral system at large. For example, under NAFTA, it is inconceivable that Canada and Mexico would be prepared to cede to the U.S. a major hegemonic role in imposing its own domestic macroeconomic and microeconomic policies on them. Conversely, it is equally inconceivable that the U.S. would accept the creation of supranational political institutions with substantial legislative authority

---

[13] See K. Nicolaides, "Mutual Recognition of Regulatory Regimes: Some Lessons and Prospects" in O.E.C.D., *Regulatory Reform and International Market Openness* (Paris: O.E.C.D., 1996).

[14] See Michael Trebilcock and Robert Howse, *The Regulation of International Trade* (London, New York: Routledge, 1999 2nd ed.), pp. 129–134.

over major aspects of macro- and microeconomic policies in the three countries, on the basis of a relatively egalitarian sharing of political influence in these institutions. Such impediments to deep economic integration are likely to be compounded several times over at the multilateral level.

This suggests to us that in these other institutional contexts the focus of attention on domestic policies that may constitute nontariff barriers to trade should relate principally to two objectives: first, elaborating on the principles of negative integration that have historically characterized the approach of the GATT to these issues, that is, the application of the national treatment principle in Article III of the GATT to domestic policy measures of member states (requiring that products of foreign countries receive no less favorable treatment than that accorded to like products of national origin), and elaborating the criteria presently contained in Article XX of the GATT that justify exceptions to this basic obligation of nondiscrimination and the constraints thereon, in particular constraints on disguised or unjustified forms of discrimination (the sham principle and the least trade-restrictive means or proportionality principle); and second, structuring the ground rules pursuant to which mutually beneficial agreements between member states can be reached over policy harmonization or convergence that are both noncoercive and nondiscriminatory vis-à-vis other trading partners (i.e., respect for the Most Favored Nation principle). In short, we would be in much less haste than other commentators[15] to abandon well-established principles of nondiscrimination in international trade law as the primary analytical framework for addressing the consequences for international trade of domestic regulatory diversity, in favor of governing principles of harmonization, mutual recognition, or managed trade.

With these observations as backdrop, we now briefly explore a number of issues of policy harmonization or convergence that have arisen, in order to illustrate our general themes or premises. We have divided this review, first, into an examination of domestic policies of countries of origin in trading relationships with others where countries of destination make claims that the domestic policies of the country of origin of the goods and services in question are unacceptable to them; and, second, an examination of various aspects of domestic policies of countries of destination where countries of origin claim that the policies of countries of destination are unacceptable to them.

---

[15] See, e.g., Kalypso Nicolaides, "Comments," in Sykes (1995) *op. cit.* at 140–143.

II   Objections to domestic policies of countries of origin

A   *Antidumping duties*

In the current preoccupation with domestic regulatory policy divergences as potential nontariff barriers to trade, it is often overlooked that there are other long-standing areas of international trade policy where claims of policy convergence have been made, often under threat of unilateral sanctions. Perhaps the most obvious, and in our view most egregious, example is antidumping laws, authorized under Article VI of the GATT and the Anti-dumping Agreement negotiated during the Uruguay Round, and reflected in domestic legislation in an increasingly large number of members of the GATT/WTO. The essence of complaints against foreign exporters dumping goods into import markets is that they are charging lower prices in the country of destination than they charge in their country of origin. The unilateral imposition of antidumping duties by the country of destination is designed to neutralize these price differences. Thus, only prices that are the same in both countries are thought to be fair. Is there any case for this insistence on price equivalence?

As we and many other authors have repeatedly argued,[16] there is absolutely no case for insisting on price equivalence from the perspective of the country of destination: after all, consumers in this country derive the benefits of the lower prices, and it would seem a perverse form of egalitarianism to insist that they must share equally in the pain of the higher prices borne by consumers in the country of origin. While producers in the country of destination lose market share to the dumped imports, increases in consumer welfare more than offset losses in producer welfare – consumers who previously paid higher domestic prices obtain imports at cheaper prices, and consumers who were previously priced out of the market can now enter the market, thus eliminating the deadweight loss associated with the previously higher domestic prices. The fact that the dumping firm may have some form of protected domestic monopoly in its country of origin provides no justification for replicating monopoly prices in countries of destination. Only cases of predatory dumping legitimately engage welfare concerns in the country of destination, in the sense that if international predation is successful in banishing all domestic and foreign rivals from the country of destina-

---

[16] See, e.g., Michael Trebilcock and Robert Howse, *The Regulation of International Trade* (London: Routledge, 1999, 2nd ed.), Chapter 7.

tion's market and thereafter raising the prices to supra-competitive levels without attracting new entry, long-run consumer and total welfare in the country of destination is reduced. However, antidumping laws are not framed to focus exclusively on international predation, and empirical studies undertaken of dumping cases suggest that only in a tiny percentage of them are predation concerns legitimately engaged.[17] Thus, antidumping laws present an important case in which insisting on policy equivalence as a precondition to international trade *reduces* international trade, reduces net welfare in the country of destination, and reduces welfare in the country of origin. Its only explanation is protectionism dressed up in a crude and incoherent form of egalitarianism or level-playing-field discourse.

B   *Competition/antitrust laws: Export cartels*

In curious juxtaposition to antidumping laws, antitrust laws in many jurisdictions, including Canada, the U.S., Europe, and Japan, provide an explicit exemption from general prohibitions on cartels in the case of export cartels, even though the effect of this dispensation is to enable domestic firms in countries of origin to charge higher prices (not lower prices, as in the case of dumping) to consumers in countries of destination.[18] This is the most overt form of discrimination and simply permits rent extraction from foreigners for the benefit of domestic producers in countries of origin. This is a case where international trade rules should insist on the *same* treatment of domestic and export cartels and domestic and foreign consumers under an expanded principle of national treatment, but instead has countenanced differential treatment.

C   *Subsidies and countervailing duties*

Countervailing duties are also authorized under Article VI of the GATT, the Subsidies Code initially negotiated during the Tokyo Round, and the substantially revised Subsidies Agreement negotiated during the Uruguay Round, and are provided for in domestic legislation in many member states of the GATT, although the U.S. is the only significant user of countervailing duty laws in the world.[19] The argument here is that it

---

[17] See Susan Hutton and Michael Trebilcock, "An Empirical Study of the Application of Canadian Anti-Dumping Laws: A Search for Normative Rationales," (1990) 24 *J. of World Trade* 123; OECD Anti-dumping Study (Robert Willig, 1995).

[18] See Report of the American Bar Association, Special Committee on International Anti-trust (1991), Chapter 3.

[19] See Trebilcock and Howse, *The Regulation of International Trade*, Chapter 8.

is unfair for domestic producers in countries of destination to have to compete not only with foreign producers but with foreign fiscs who are subsidizing the activities of firms in countries of origin whose products are then exported at artificially low prices to customers in countries of destination, and that countervailing duties are justified to neutralize the effect of the subsidies. Again, however, why should it be of any concern to governments in countries of destination that subsidy policies in countries of origin are different from those prevailing in countries of destination? As Professor Sykes has convincingly demonstrated, in almost every conceivable scenario both consumer welfare and total welfare in countries of destination are increased as a result of foreign subsidies.[20] Instead of penalizing foreign firms that benefit from government subsidies in countries of origin, governments in countries of destination should send governments in countries of origin thank-you notes for unsolicited foreign aid, expressing only their regret that the subsidies are not larger and permanent. In short, with the possible exception of a parallel qualification to that noted above for antidumping laws, that is, predatory subsidization, countries of destination should have no right to insist on equivalence of subsidy policies. To condition international trade on the existence of policy equivalence in this respect is to reduce welfare at least in the country of destination and has an indeterminate impact on welfare in the country of origin, depending on the view one takes of the appropriateness of the subsidy policy; but this is surely an issue for political authorities and the citizens to whom they are accountable in the country of origin to resolve.

D Environmental policies

Drawing to some extent on the level-playing-field discourse that is often invoked to support the case for countervailing duties, domestic producer interests in countries of destination often argue that lax environmental policies in countries of origin constitute an implicit and unfair subsidy to foreign producers that should be neutralized, for example, by countervailing duties or by insistence that foreign countries adopt environmental policies similar to those that obtain in countries of destination.[21]

---

[20] See Alan O. Sykes, "Countervailing Duty Law: An Economic Perspective," (1989) *Columbia L.R.* 199.

[21] See Vogel, *op. cit.*; Kym Anderson, "Environmental Standards and International Trade," in M. Bruno and B. Pleskovic (eds.), *Annual World Bank Conference on Development Economics 1996* (Washington, D.C.: World Bank, 1997), 317; Trebilcock and Howse, *The Regulation of International Trade*, Chapter 15.

This insistence on equivalence of environmental policies is, in many contexts, incoherent. First, countries differ widely in environmental and climatic conditions, meaning that even if citizens in various countries shared similar environmental preferences, policies would differ significantly. Second, in fact preferences of citizens in different countries with respect to the priority they accord to environmental concerns relative to other concerns are likely to differ systematically depending on stages of development, levels of income, alternative economic opportunities, and the like. Thus, where the impacts of the environmental policies chosen by a country of origin are purely local in their environmental impact, governments in countries of destination have no normative basis for insisting on policy equivalence. This proposition is subject to significant qualifications in cases where the activities of firms in countries of origin either generate cross-border spillovers or threaten the global environmental commons (which a sympathetic reading of U.S. regulatory policies in the highly controversial GATT panel decisions in the two *Tuna-Dolphin* cases might fairly be viewed as addressing),[22] in both of which cases countries affected by these externalities have a legitimate case for objecting to these activities (although not necessarily through unilateral invocation of trade sanctions).[23] Even in these cases, it is not obvious that legitimate concerns over externalities lead necessarily to a case for policy equivalence, as opposed to some form of supranational regulation or agreement designed to constrain the costs of these externalities.

The externality argument sometimes takes a different form – that is, if countries of origin are permitted to maintain lax environmental policies this will place pressure on governments in countries of destination to relax their policies in order to maintain the competitiveness of their own producers. In other words, lax policies in one country generate political externalities in another. In response to this argument (effectively a

---

[22] United States – Restrictions on Imports of Tuna 30, I.L.M. 1594 (1991); United States – Restrictions on Imports of Tuna DS 29/R. June, 1994. In these cases, GATT panels held that at a U.S. embargo on tuna imports from countries adopting less dolphin-friendly fishing techniques than those which U.S. fishermen were required to adopt violated Article 11 of the GATT and was not saved by Article 20 (b) or (g), holding in the first panel decision that the latter could only be invoked with respect to environmental threats within the importing country's *own* territorial jurisdiction and in the second panel decision that the exceptions could not be invoked where the efficacy of the measures was predicated on changing another country's domestic polices: See further Robert Howse and Michael Trebilcock, "The Fair Trade-Free Trade Debate: Trade, Labour and the Environment" (1996) 16 *International Review of Law and Economics* 61.

[23] See Howse and Trebilcock, *ibid.*

race to the bottom argument), it is worth noting, first, that the empirical evidence does not support this claim. In a wide-ranging review of the evidence, Vogel concludes that international trade liberalization and international trade agreements have generally exhibited the opposite (although not inevitable) tendency, that is, a race to the top (or what he calls the California Effect rather than the Delaware Effect).[24] Second, whatever the empirical evidence shows, to deny to countries of origin the political ability to set their own environmental policies, in the absence of technological externalities, is to flatly contradict the view of governments, persuasively developed by Breton, as competitive organizations that in the process of competing among each other enhance the accuracy of demand revelation for public goods and policies. To reemphasize, we (like Breton) are as much concerned about competition in the provision of public goods and policies as we are about international competition in private markets for the sale of goods and services. Moreover, the theory of comparative advantage is centrally predicated on nations' exploiting their differences (not similarities) in international trade. Few international trade theorists believe any longer that comparative advantage is exclusively exogenously determined; rather, it is significantly shaped by endogenous government polices (e.g., collective investments in infrastructure, education, law and order, health care, research and development). Exploiting differences in government policies is no less legitimate than exploiting differences in natural endowments.[25]

E   *Labor standards*

Paralleling the intense domestic and international political controversies that have recently surrounded the relationship between trade and environmental policy, a similar series of debates have erupted over the relationship between international trade and domestic labor standards.[26] Here, given a conjunction of persistently high levels of unemployment, especially long-term unemployment, in Europe, a dramatic decline in real wages for unskilled workers in the U.S., an increasing share of world manufacturing employment accounted for by LDCs, and increasing shares of imports into developed countries similarly accounted for

---

[24] See Vogel, *op. cit.*
[25] See Trebilcock and Howse, *The Regulation of International Trade*, 6–7.
[26] For a review, see Alan B. Krueger, "International Labor Standards and Trade," in M. Bruno and B. Pleskovic (eds.), *Annual World Bank Conference on Development Economics 1996* (Washington, D.C.: World Bank, 1997), 281.

by LDCs,[27] arguments are increasingly made by interests in countries of destination for convergence in domestic labor policies between countries of origin and countries of destination. Lax labor standards in countries of origin can be analogized to lax environmental standards, which in turn can be analogized to implicit subsidies that, when rendered explicit, have historically attracted countervailing duties.

These concerns are no more convincing in the case of labor standards than in the case of environmental standards or foreign subsidies. A central feature of the comparative advantage of many developing countries is relatively low labor costs, often with respect to unskilled or semiskilled labor but also in some cases (e.g., India) with respect to highly skilled labor. Relatively low labor costs may constitute the central form of comparative advantage for some developing countries.

However, again as in the case of environmental standards, important qualifications to this position need to be noted. In some cases, labor practices can be viewed as violations of universal or international human rights, as reflected for example in International Labour Organization (ILO) conventions, to which many countries throughout the world are signatories. Thus, freedom of association and the right to engage in collective bargaining; prohibitions on forced labor; some restrictions on child labor; and nondiscrimination on racial or gender grounds may appropriately be thought to fall within the ambit of a conception of universal human rights, in which event enforcement of these norms through international trade sanctions cannot be rejected out of hand.[28] A recent important study by the OECD, *Trade, Employment and Labour Standards*,[29] finds that recognition of these core workers' rights is likely to have a minimal impact on international trade and investment flows, and hence issues relating to their vindication can largely be separated from international trade and investment effects.[30]

However, designing international institutional arrangements that can credibly determine whether in fact such norms exist, whether they have been violated in particular cases, whether economic sanctions are

---

[27] See Richard Freeman, "Are Your Wages Set in Beijing?" (1995) 9 *J. of Economic Perspectives* 15; J. David Richardson, "Income Inequality and Trade: How to Think, What to Conclude?" (1995) 9 *J. of Economic Perspectives* 33; Adrian Wood, "How Trade Hurt Unskilled Workers," (1995) *J. of Economic Perspectives* 57.

[28] See International Labour Office, "The ILO, Standard Setting and Globalization" (Geneva: ILO, 1997).

[29] OECD, *Trade, Employment and Labour Standards: A Study of Core Workers' Rights and International Trade* (Paris: OECD, 1996).

[30] See Brian Langille, "Eight Ways to Think About International Labour Standards," (1997) 31 *J. of World Trade* 27.

appropriate in the event of violation, and whether targeted or selective unilateral attempts to impose such sanctions are motivated indeed by altruistic concerns over violations of human rights and are not disguised efforts at protectionism (i.e., bootleggers masquerading as Baptists),[31] is a challenge that the international trade policy regime has barely begun to take up (but needs urgently to address). Nevertheless, the point needs to be emphasized that however these legitimate concerns are resolved they should not lead to any legitimation of the claim for across-the-board equivalence in labor standards (e.g., common minimum wage laws) between countries in trading relationships with each other.

III   Objections to domestic policies of countries of destination

A   Domestic subsidies

Suppose a country of destination chooses to subsidize a set of activities that differentially benefit domestic producers relative to foreign exporters who do not qualify for the subsidy and who do not receive a similar subsidy from the government in their country of origin. Should firms or governments in countries of origin be entitled to complain of such subsidies on the grounds that they differentially disadvantage imports (as they now can do under the Uruguay Round Subsidies Agreement if they are specific subsidies that do not fall within tightly defined exceptions relating to depressed regions, support for R&D, and support for environmental investments)? We are not convinced that they should be. Governments all over the world, simply by virtue of the fact that they are governments, subsidize to a greater or lesser extent all manner of activities through direct and indirect and general or specific forms of assistance, which one way or another shape the comparative advantage of firms who benefit from these activities. The distinction between specific and general subsidies that is a central feature of the Subsidies Agreement (and of U.S. countervailing duty law) has never seemed to us to capture any distinction of normative relevance, and moreover has proven arbitrary and mechanical (even metaphysical) in its application, as demonstrated in the acrimonious dispute between Canada and the U.S. over alleged subsidies to the Canadian softwood lumber industry through the stumpage rates charged by Canadian governments to lumber firms.[32]

---

[31] See Vogel, *op. cit.*, Chapter 6.
[32] See FTA binational panel decision in the Canada-U.S. *Softwood Lumber Case*, May 6, 1993, and subsequent extraordinary challenge committee decision therein.

However, this presumption warrants some qualifications. At a minimum, in a case where the two countries have previously negotiated tariff bindings, one might view such a subsidy as violating the reasonable expectations of firms in countries of origin surrounding the effects of the tariff concessions and might on that account justifiably support a claim for nonviolation nullification and impairment, as a GATT panel found in the controversial *Oil Seeds* case.[33] One might go further and apply the national treatment principle to such a subsidy with a view to establishing whether it is discriminatory. Here a refined test of discrimination is required, because clearly almost all domestic subsidies have a differential impact on domestic relative to foreign firms, so that a disparate impact in itself would not, for our purposes, constitute objectionable discrimination, any more than when a country chooses to maintain distinctive language or driving laws. Under Article 11 of the Tokyo Round Subsidies Code (which we prefer in this respect to the Uruguay Round Subsidies Agreement), a wide range of policy objectives for domestic subsidies were recognized as legitimate, although member countries were urged to be sensitive to the effects that subsidies might have on international trade. One could formalize this approach somewhat and apply a least-restrictive means test to domestic subsidies (as in other contexts explored later) and ask whether the subsidy addresses a legitimate public purpose (beyond trade) and does so in a way that is least distortive of trade relative to alternative subsidy or policy instruments that are available for vindicating these policy objectives. If a less trade-restrictive instrument is available, one could view the subsidy as either a sham or a gratuitous and unjustified form of discrimination against foreign exporters. At the limit, if pressed, we might be prepared to apply a similar test to export subsidies, discussed in the previous section, although the welfare effects in the country of destination in the case of export subsidies are so unambiguously positive that it is not clear that such discrimination as might be thought to be entailed in an export subsidy causes any cognizable form of harm in the country of destination. By contrast, in the case of domestic subsidies that frustrate access to a country of destination's market by firms in a country of origin, such discrimination might be thought to be entailed because it clearly has unambiguously negative net welfare effects in the country of origin.

At the same time, developing rules that prevent or terminate beggarthy-neighbor subsidies wars is entirely consistent with the overall approach of this chapter. The Uruguay Round Agreement on Agricul-

---

[33] European Community: Payment and Subsidies on Oilseeds and Animal-Feed Protein," BISD, 37th supp. (1989) 86.

ture exemplifies the kind of framework required to deal with such beggar-thy-neighbor policies, including important methodological issues in converting different forms of domestic support to a common metric, transitional measures, and the need to distinguish trade-impacting, potentially beggar-thy-neighbor subsidies from those intended for some specific domestic policy purpose (e.g., environmental protection, research and development, labor adjustment). This simply demonstrates the ineffectiveness of general or generic trade rules in dealing effectively with those instances where global and domestic welfare most clearly suffers from the use of subsidization.

B   *Competition/antitrust policy*[34]

In general, we take the position that foreign firms trading into another country's markets should take the latter's competition/antitrust laws as they find them and comply with them, even if they substantially diverge from competition/antitrust laws in a firm's country of origin.[35] That is to say, there is no normatively robust basis here for a claim of policy equivalence. For example, foreign producers trading into the U.S. market who collude to fix prices in the U.S. market should not be permitted to complain of the relatively stringent U.S. price-fixing laws (per se illegality; treble damages) on the grounds that in their home jurisdictions price-fixing laws are lax or nonexistent. Thus, we see no objection to the United States asserting jurisdiction in such cases, as the majority of the U.S. Supreme Court held in *Hartford Fire Insurance Co. v. California*.[36]

Conversely, U.S. producers trading into or investing in jurisdictions with lax or nonexistent anticollusion laws (that, e.g., may affect the price or supply of inputs) equally have no basis for complaint, provided that these policies are applied in a nondiscriminatory manner. This observation would extend to permissive provisions on joint research and production ventures, research consortia, and other forms of strategic alliances, provided again that the provisions are not framed or applied in a discriminatory manner. Equally, U.S. or other producers trading into or operating in the European market have no basis for complaint because the abuse of dominant position provisions of Article 86 of the

---

[34] For essays covering many of the issues noted here, see Leonard Waverman, William S. Comanor, and Akira Goto (eds.), *Competition Policy in the Global Economy: Modalities for Cooperation* (London: Routledge, 1997).

[35] See Michael Trebilcock, "Competition Policy and Trade Policy: Mediating the Interface," (1996) 30 *J. of World Trade* 71.

[36] (1993) 1621 ATRR 30.

Treaty of Rome are applied somewhat more stringently than the monopolization provisions in Section 2 of the Sherman Act. Similarly, if the European Union should choose to take account of industrial policy considerations, and not only consumer welfare considerations, in the administration of its merger law, or conversely some other country should apply its merger law in a more populist fashion designed to prevent concentrations of economic power, foreign firms operating in these markets, notwithstanding sharp differences from competition laws obtaining in their home markets, should accept the local rules of the game (whether perceived to be well-conceived or not), *provided* that these rules are applied in a nondiscriminatory fashion to both domestic and foreign firms. Again, if one country chooses to create or maintain state-owned or sanctioned monopolies in some sectors, foreign producers should have no right of complaint about being excluded from these markets, given that other domestic producers face similar exclusion, although discrimination by such monopolies in sales or purchasing decisions against foreign firms would be objectionable (as both the GATT and NAFTA presently provide).[37]

Other cases are admittedly more difficult. One controversial case relates to the relatively quiescent state of Japanese competition law as it applies to both vertical and horizontal *keiretsu*. Vertical production and distribution *keiretsu* and other exclusive dealing arrangements are alleged to prevent foreign firms from gaining ready access to Japanese manufacturing, retail, and distribution networks. Horizontal *keiretsu*, because of the prominent role played by lead banks and because of cross-shareholding, are alleged to prevent foreign investors from readily acquiring Japanese firms as a means of lower cost and more efficient entry into the Japanese market than greenfield entry. It is true, of course, that as framed Japanese competition laws on these matters are facially neutral as between the ability of domestic and foreign firms to challenge these arrangements, although one should not be so naive as to terminate the analysis there. If the evidence were to disclose discrimination in the application and enforcement of these laws, depending on whether the complainant was a domestic firm or a foreign firm, this would constitute a form of discrimination for our purposes. Moreover, even if the laws were both framed and enforced in a neutral fashion, one would still want to ask (as many GATT decisions under Article III (national treatment) and Article XX (exceptions to GATT obligations) have done, whether

---

[37] See Neil Campbell, William Rowley, and Michael Trebilcock, "The Role of Monopoly Law in the International Trading System," (1995) 1 *International Trade Law and Regulation* 167.

these laws are a disguised form of protectionism or discrimination. This question is not always easily answered, because it may be the case that Japanese competition laws do have a disparate impact on foreign exporters or investors relative to domestic producers. However, this is equally true of differing language laws, driving laws, and so forth, so that mere demonstration of disparate impact is not sufficient unless disparate impact is also indicative of a disguised or unnecessary form of discrimination. In the case of the Japanese *keiretsu*, given the central role that they have traditionally played in corporate governance and organizational structures in Japan,[38] it is difficult to believe that the primary purpose of their adoption has been to differentially disadvantage foreign producers, even though that may be a consequence.

C   *Intellectual property*

A highly contentious feature of the Uruguay Round multilateral trade negotiations related to negotiations over a TRIPS Agreement, which for the first time in GATT history requires member states essentially to harmonize an important aspect of domestic regulatory policy to a common set of substantive and procedural standards. Here, developed countries of origin, principally the United States but also the EU and Japan, argued that their exports to other countries were being reduced by virtue of these countries maintaining lax intellectual property laws that permitted imitation and local production of similar products (setting aside cases of counterfeit goods, which entail obvious forms of fraud and consumer deception in both countries of origin and countries of destination).

The strength of the general claim for policy equivalence in this area is not straightforward.[39] The overall trade-offs between innovation and imitation may well differ from country to country. A country where innovation is not a major source of economic activity and growth is likely to choose, on balance, a less stringent intellectual property regime than would a country whose economy is highly dependent on innovation. From this perspective, there is nothing suspect or unreasonable about the preference of many developing countries for a relatively lax system of intellectual property rights, provided this regime applies equally to

---

[38] See Michael Gerlach, *The Keiretsu: A Primer* (New York: The Japan Society, 1992); Gerlach, *Alliance Capitalism: The Social Organization of Japanese Business* (Berheley: University of California Press, 1992); Ronald Gilson and Mark Roe, "Understanding the Japanese Keiretsu: Overlaps Between Corporate Governance and Industrial Organization," Columbia University Law School, Working Paper No. 83, September 14, 1992.

[39] See Trebilcock and Howse, *The Regulation of International Trade*, 307–312.

domestic and foreign firms. These countries have much to gain, in terms of consumer welfare, from countenancing cheap domestic imitations of innovations made elsewhere, and perhaps little to lose if they are not at a stage of development that makes domestic research and development an important ingredient in domestic welfare. From the point of view of at least some developing countries, then, an agreement on TRIPs that raised intellectual property protection to developed country levels could rightly be seen as a welfare-reducing or Pareto-inferior bargain.

However, several arguments have been advanced to show that such a bargain could be in the long-term self-interest of developing countries. The first is that these countries, like all others, benefit from innovation that occurs outside their own borders, and that the increased incentives to inventors due to increased global revenues from innovations will yield higher levels of innovation, and therefore new benefits in which developing countries will share. However, often industry estimates of "foregone" revenues from substandard intellectual property protection in developing countries assume that if proper protection were afforded, a quantity of original products would be consumed equal to that of the imitations now being purchased. This, as is widely noted in more recent economic literature, may be quite misleading – since original products (e.g., patent as opposed to generic drugs) would likely be much more expensive, one could expect a considerable decline in demand (depending on elasticities). Deardorff questions whether the marginal benefit of extra protection, in terms of products that would not have been invented but for the additional incentive from higher monopoly rents in developing countries, is likely to outweigh the reduction in consumer welfare in these countries due to higher prices.[40] Another line of argument is that developing countries will attract greater amounts of foreign investment and technology transfers if foreigners believe that products, processes, and trade secrets will be adequately protected. Empirical evidence that this is the case is, however, sketchy and anecdotal. In addition, the appropriate response might be to negotiate specific guarantees with investors, rather than to increase intellectual property protection across the board.

Apparently, many developing countries were eventually induced to accede to the TRIPS Agreement by a combination of threats of unilateral sanctions and concessions by developed countries in other areas of trade policy (e.g., the Multifiber Arrangement, Safeguards, Agriculture). However, as a stand-alone measure, the TRIPS Agreement seems likely to reduce welfare in many developing countries.

---

[40] See Alan Deardorff, "Should Patent Protection Be Extended to All Developing Countries?", (1990) 13 *World Economy* 497.

D   *Health, safety, environmental and conservation measures*

Divergent health, safety, environmental conservation, and related regulatory standards between countries of origin and countries of destination, principally in cases where these standards are more stringent in countries of destination, provide a fertile source of allegations by countries of origin that they are subject to discrimination in countries of destination in violation either of Article XI of the GATT, which prohibits quantitative restrictions or prohibitions on imports, or of Article III, which enshrines the national treatment principle, and that the differential treatment cannot be justified under any of the exceptions enumerated in Article XX of the GATT but rather represents disguised or gratuitous forms of discrimination. Clearly, such regulations can be devised solely for this purpose and cannot be justified as "necessary to protect human, animal or plant life or health" under Article XX(b) of the GATT. These cases might, in Sykes's terms,[41] be viewed as falling within the sham exception to the ability of national governments to adopt whatever health and safety regulations they regard as appropriate for the protection of their citizenry. However, outside cases of relatively transparent shams, other cases present more difficulties because the measures to which countries of origin have taken exception can plausibly be related to and viewed as advancing to some degree some legitimate health or safety objective, but they nevertheless have a disparate impact on foreign trade.

Early in the jurisprudence of the European Union, the scope of the Treaty of Rome was extended beyond measures that discriminated on their face against nondomestic products to those that merely had a disparate impact. Thus, in its 1979 *Cassis de Dijon* decision,[42] the European Court of Justice held that a German law that prohibited the sale of the liqueur Cassis with less than 25 percent alcohol content violated Article 30 of the treaty. The law had prevented the import of French Cassis which had an alcohol content below 20 percent. However, the court suggested that where measures are not facially discriminatory but have a disparate impact, they may be saved if they are necessary in order to satisfy mandatory requirements related in particular to the effectiveness of fiscal supervision, the protection of public health, the fairness of commercial transactions, and the defense of the consumer. The test of necessity involves consideration of whether alternative measures less restrictive of intra-Union trade might adequately satisfy the mandatory requirements at

[41] Sykes, *op. cit.* (1995) at 67, 68.
[42] *Cassis de Dijon* E.C.J. 120/78.

issue.[43] Hence, if the goal was to ensure that consumers were not misled by an assumption about the domestic product into thinking that the foreign product contained an equivalent amount of alcohol, labeling requirements would suffice. Similarly, in its 1987 *German Beer Standards* decision,[44] the court impugned a German law that required any product sold with the label "beer" in Germany to meet Germany purity standards. The court reasoned that consumers could be informed of the difference between beers through the use of appropriate labeling requirements. Where health risks are claimed as a basis for content requirements that affect trade, and where less stringent requirements are in place elsewhere in the Union, the court places some burden on the defendant member state to produce empirical evidence of the risks in question.

Reflecting to a significant extent doctrinal evolution in the EU case law, the Uruguay Round Technical Barriers to Trade Agreement (TBT Agreement) provides that

> 2.1 Members shall ensure that in respect of technical regulations, products imported from the territory of any Member shall be accorded treatment no less favourable than that accorded to like products of national origin and to like products originating in any other country.

> 2.2 Members shall ensure that technical regulations are not prepared, adopted or applied with a view to or with the effect of creating unnecessary obstacles to international trade. For this purpose, technical regulations shall not be more trade-restrictive than necessary to fulfil a legitimate objective, taking account of the risks non-fulfilment would create. Such legitimate objectives are, *inter alia*: national security requirements; the prevention of deceptive practices; protection of human health or safety, animal or plant life or health, or the environment. In assessing such risks, relevant elements of consideration are, *inter alia*; available scientific and technical information, related processing technology or intended end-uses of products.

> 2.4 Where technical regulations are required and relevant international standards exist or their completion is imminent, Members shall use them, or the relevant parts of them, as a basis for their technical regulations except where such international standards or relevant parts would be an ineffective or inappropriate means for the fulfilment of the legitimate objectives pursued, for instance because of fundamental climatic or geographical factors or fundamental technological problems.

[43] This proportionality principle is similar to that adopted in the GATT panel decision in relation to U.S. intellectual property laws disproportionately affecting imports: United States – Section 337 of the Tariff Act of 1930, op. cit.

[44] Case 178/84 (1988) 1 CMLR 780.

2.5 A Member preparing, adopting or applying a technical regulation which may have a significant effect on trade of other Members shall, upon the request of another Member, explain the justification for that technical regulation in terms of the provisions of paragraphs 2 to 4. Whenever a technical regulation is prepared, adopted or applied for one of the legitimate objectives explicitly mentioned in paragraph 2, and is in accordance with relevant international standards, it shall be rebuttably presumed not to create an unnecessary obstacle to international trade.

2.6 With a view to harmonizing technical regulations on as wide a basis as possible, Members shall play a full part, within the limits of their resources, in the preparation by appropriate international standardizing bodies of international standards for products for which they either have adopted, or expect to adopt, technical regulations.

2.7 Members shall give positive consideration to accepting as equivalent technical regulations of other Members, even if these regulations differ from their own, provided they are satisfied that these regulations adequately fulfil the objectives of their own regulations.

2.8 Wherever appropriate, Members shall specify technical regulations based on product requirements in terms of performance rather than design or descriptive characteristics.

Whenever a relevant international standard does not exist or the technical content of the proposed regulation is not in accordance with the relevant international standard, and if the technical regulation may have a significant effect on trade of other members, members are obligated to publish a notice in a publication at an early stage so as to enable interested parties and other members to become acquainted with it and to provide opportunities for other members to make comments in writing on the proposed regulation. Members must also allow a reasonable interval between the publication of technical regulations and their entry into force in order to allow time for producers in exporting countries to adapt their products or methods of production to the requirements of the importing members.

A separate Uruguay Round Agreement on Sanitary and Phytosanitary Measures (SPM Agreement) adopts in most respects the basic structure of obligations contained in the TBT Agreement. Article 2.2 provides that "members shall ensure that any sanitary or phytosanitary mesure is applied only to the extent necessary to protect human, animal or plant life or health, is based on scientific principles and is not maintained without sufficient scientific evidence . . ." This is subject to Article 5.7, which allows members to take provisional measures "on the basis of available pertinent information" where "scientific evidence is insufficient." Where a member acts on the basis of Article 5.7, it is required to seek a more objective evaluation based on fuller evidence within a reasonable period of time. Article 2.3 requires that "members shall ensure that their sanitary and phytosanitary measures do not arbitrarily or unjustifiably discriminate" between members where identical or similar conditions prevail, including between their own territory and that of other members. Further, "sanitary and phytosanitary measures shall not be applied in a manner which would constitute a disguised restriction on international trade." Other provisions of the SPM Agreement amplify the obligations in Articles 2.2 and 2.3. Article 3 requires that, to facilitate harmonization, members base their sanitary and phytosanitary standards on "international standards, guidelines or recommendations" wherever possible. Significantly, Article 3.3 makes it clear that a higher level of protection requires scientific justification to be GATT-consistent, whereas any other kind of difference from international standards (i.e., inferior protection) shall be deemed to be GATT-consistent. Article 5 requires that all sanitary and phytosanitary measures be based upon risk assessments that take into account "risk assessment techniques developed by the relevant international organizations" (Article 5.1). Finally, the Agreement provides for the establishment of a Committee on Sanitary and Phytosanitary Measures to act as a forum for consultations on the implementation of the Agreement, and also to monitor progress with respect to the evaluation of harmonized international standards with respect to sanitary and phytosanitary measures (Article 12).[45]

The first decision by a WTO panel on the SPS agreement addressed the long-standing dispute between the U.S. and the EU in the *Beef Hormones* case.[46] In this case, the United States initially filed a complaint against the EU under the GATT Tokyo Round Standards Code, alleging that a 1988 EC Directive banning the sale of hormone-fed beef in the EC had no basis in scientific evidence of a health danger from human consumption of the hormones. The EC viewed the ban as a legitimate response to public concerns about use of hormones as growth stimulants, while admitting that there was little scientific support for these concerns. The more technical legal disagreement surrounded whether the Code applied to standards that were not product standards in the strict sense but involved the "process or production method" (PPM) by which a product was produced (clearly, the ban on hormone-fed beef went to the method of production of the beef). The EC claimed that the

---

[45] Similar provisions to those contained in the Uruguay Round TBT and SPM agreements appear in NAFTA, Chapters 7 and 9.

[46] See A. Dick, "The EC Hormone Ban Dispute and the Application of the Dispute Settlement Provisions of the Standards Code," (1989) 10 *Michigan J. of International Law* 872; Vogel, *op. cit.*, 154–171.

Code did not apply to PPMs. The United States, however, invoked a provision of the Code that suggested PPMs would be covered in circumstances where their effect was to circumvent the primary obligation of the Code not to create "unnecessary obstacles to trade." In the event, a technical panel under the Code was never established to decide the matter, since the EC refused to accept its jurisdiction, arguing that the Code did not apply at all to the kind of measure at issue. The EC was prepared to have a special panel of legal experts address the threshold issue of the Code's jurisdiction over the dispute, but this was unacceptable to the United States.

The United States subsequently revived the complaint under the new SPM Agreement. A WTO Panel upheld its complaint in an important decision in September 1997.[47] The Panel held that for five of the six growth hormones in dispute, international (Codex) standards existed, which the EC ban did not conform to, casting the burden of proof on the EC to demonstrate that its more stringent standards were based on a scientific risk assessment, which it failed to do. In the case of the sixth hormone, for which an international standard did not exist, the Panel similarly held that the EC ban was not based on a scientific risk assessment. Given that a much smaller percentage of EC-produced beef had in the past been treated with growth hormones as compared to U.S. beef, the Panel found that the EC measures were an arbitrary and unjustifiable differentiation in treatment, resulting in discrimination or a disguised restriction on international trade. The Panel's decision was largely upheld by the WTO Appellate Body on appeal.

Several important features of the TBT and SPM Agreements are worth noting. First, they both adopt the sham principle by prohibiting disguised forms of discrimination. Second, in one form or another they adopt a least-trade-restrictive means or proportionality test that places some burden of justification on a country adopting standards that are not in conformity with international standards or lack independent scientific justification and thus can be viewed as an "unjustifiable" restriction on trade. Third, while the GATT/WTO lacks supranational institutions with legislative authority comparable to those of the EU to impact directly on any process of positive integration, it places a significant premium on adherence to international standards, albeit international standards typically formulated by nonlegislative bodies such as ISO (International Organization for Standardization), the Codex Alimentarius of the U.N. Food and Agriculture Organization, and other similar international standard-setting bodies which hitherto have operated

---

[47] WTO panel decision, September 1997.

in relative public obscurity, typically generating voluntary standards through industry negotiations that national and international industry associations may choose to adopt or national or subnational levels of government may choose to impose. Even the mere presumption that adoption of the standards of these bodies constitutes conformity with the TBT and SPM Agreements and that more stringent standards require some burden of justification is likely to change dramatically the politics and public scrutiny of these bodies. But at least they possess the kind of expertise and institutional culture suited to transnational dialogue about regulation and its enforcement. However, to go further and vest supranational regulatory powers in these institutions would entail a very significant democratic deficit – almost certainly more severe than that widely claimed to exist in the case of supranational EU institutions.

A more general characterization of the TBT and SPS code provisions is that they provide a more sophisticated formulation of the principle of nondiscrimination contained in Article III of the GATT and a more elaborated set of justifications that must be offered in cases of disparate impact presently dealt with in the exceptions contained in Article XX of the GATT/WTO. While these rules clearly constrain the ability of countries of destination to adopt regulations that have a disparate impact on imports from other countries, they nevertheless leave substantial room for the exercise of national political sovereignty and policy autonomy both in choosing policy objectives (as long as these are not a sham) and policy instruments (as long as these are not disproportionate to the objective, given their effect on trade).[48] In short, if countries generally feel committed to adopting more stringent health, safety, consumer protection, environmental, or conservation standards for legitimate (non-trade-related) reasons, they remain largely free to do so, subject to demonstrating that there is some rational scientific basis for their actions beyond the impact on international trade, and that such measures do not gratuitously encumber international trade when other less restrictive policy instruments are available to achieve the same objectives.

IV   Conclusions

In this chapter, we have argued the case for substantial national political autonomy in formulating domestic regulatory and related policies, even though such policies will often have significant impacts on result-

---

[48] For an argument in favor of these approaches, see A. O. Sykes, "The Economics of Regulatory Protectionism and Its Implications for Trade Regulation: The WTO and Other Systems," unpublished manuscript, University of Chicago Law School, 1997.

ing trade flows. Provided that countries respect the principle of nondiscrimination by avoiding the adoption of policies or practices that violate the national treatment principle understood as guaranteeing effective equality of competitive opportunities (not outcomes) and do not engage in disguised or unjustifiable forms of discrimination, they should have broad latitude to determine their own (but not other countries') domestic policies. That remaining policy divergences will have an impact on trade cannot be gainsaid. However, requiring policy convergence or equivalence in some cases reduces trade (e.g., antidumping policies, countervailing duty laws, environmental and labor policies). In other cases, it may expand trade by reducing multiple compliance costs, permitting the realization of economies of scale in production and distribution and the attainment of network efficiencies, avoiding the costs of regulatory duplication and permitting the realization of regulatory economies of scale and specialization. In our view, the costs that are associated with these policy divergences may in many cases be worth incurring as the price of maintaining competitive governments. An indiscriminate attack on so-called system frictions[49] subordinates the value of competitive politics entirely to the value of competitive markets.

Having said this, we do not want to be understood as being opposed to consensual forms of harmonization where mutual benefits are to be derived from policy convergence by reducing these costs of divergence.[50]

Much regulatory harmonization is likely to occur as a result of private initiatives at either the firm or industry level. Firms have private incentives in many contexts to minimize product incompatibilities if they wish to maximize access to export markets. Private or public-private standardizing organizations, national and international, can often promote standards that avoid pointless incompatibilities. However, in some cases, incompatibilities are an unavoidable, indeed desirable, by-product of product innovation and differentiation. In other cases, both firms and national governments may face incentives to promote strategic standard-setting, for example, technical interfaces in network industries, in order to realize first-mover advantages and possibly monopoly profits; in such cases international standardizing bodies are likely to encounter difficulties in achieving voluntary consensus on appropriate standards.[51]

---

[49] See Ostry, *op. cit.*

[50] An excellent overview of the issues and approaches of importance in consensual harmonization is to be found in O.E.C.D., *Regulatory Co-operation for an Interdependent World* (Paris: OECD Public Management Service, 1994).

[51] Sykes (1995) *op. cit.* at 110–117.

However, even intergovernmental harmonization efforts, outside the context of the EU, must necessarily be consensual in nature. Evidence from the early history of the EU and elsewhere suggests that such state-to-state negotiations will often be slow and limited, at least when they occur between countries with roughly symmetric bargaining power. Nevertheless, it is important to recall that it was the concept of reciprocity – carrots, not sticks – that facilitated tariff reductions (the GATT's greatest achievement) by changing the domestic political dynamics surrounding trade protectionism and more closely aligning them with the economics of trade liberalization by enlisting a new political constituency in favor of trade liberalization (exporters).[52] Tariff reductions were not achieved, by and large, by legal fiat or by threats of unilateral trade sanctions but by providing acceptable quid pro quos for other countries' tariff concessions. In the NTB context, countries may well be prepared to make similar concessions to reduce the costs to them of policy divergences, increase competition and innovation in their domestic markets, and increase access to foreign markets, even if these gains require some compromise of legitimate policy objectives previously served by the policy measures being modified. Within the EU, this bargaining has been facilitated through EU supranational institutions and the adoption of qualified majority rules that mitigate the strategic holdout problem while still respecting reasonable equality of influence among member states. Outside the EU, in the absence of supranational institutions with paramount legislative authority, a more purely consensual approach is likely to dominate, although to the extent that greater reliance is placed on standards generated by international standard-setting bodies like ISO and the Codex Commission, the decision-making processes of these institutions, which often do not involve direct government-to-government negotiations, will attract greater scrutiny in the future in terms of the relative influence of various stakeholders, public transparency, and democratic legitimacy.

Where negotiations over alleged NTBs occur between countries with asymmetric bargaining power, as arguably exemplified by the Strategic Impediments Initiative between the United States and Japan, they carry the serious risk of gross overreaching into the domestic policy affairs of one country by another (e.g., domestic savings rates, public investment policy, land costs), and moreover are likely to result in managed trade arrangements that are antithetical to a nondiscriminatory multilateral trading system. Out of frustration with the prospects for achieving extensive harmonization, some commentators (principally so-called American

---

[52] *Ibid.*, Chapter 1.

revisionists) argue for "black boxing" domestic systems by relying on managed trade (results-oriented or "crowbar"-based trade policy) to achieve more balanced economic relations, even at the risk of some international disintegration.[53] However, this both flatly denies fundamental elements of the theory of comparative advantage and often constitutes a gross interference in the domestic affairs of countries who are parties to such arrangements and whose governments are required to orchestrate domestic economic activities in extraordinary detail in order to meet these targets, while at the same time typically discriminating against other member states (as exemplified by the Semi-Conductor Agreement between Japan and the United States). On the other hand, liberal traders who find themselves unattracted by the concept of managed trade and who feel frustrated at the likely pace of international policy harmonization and who propose instead that a central role be assigned to a relatively unqualified principle of mutual recognition[54] (at least where not complemented by negotiated harmonization of minimum standards) fail to acknowledge that such a principle would confer major forms of extraterritorial jurisdiction on countries of origin in exporting goods or services (and their policies with them) to other countries that may well have legitimate reasons for maintaining distinctive policies of their own, provided that these meet basic principles of nondiscrimination.[55]

Thus, at the end of the day we believe that trade regimes and institutions should largely confine themselves to a more fully elaborated principle of nondiscrimination with well-defined exceptions thereto – that is, a concept of negative rather than positive integration.[56] The principle of effective equality of opportunity (not of outcome) lies at the heart of the national treatment principle, and exceptions to it should require a demonstration that policy measures that have a substantial disparate impact on foreign trade (a) genuinely serve some legitimate (non-trade-related) domestic policy objective and are not merely a disguised form of discrimination (the sham principle) and (b) are not an unjustified means of attaining those objectives (the least trade-restrictive or proportionality principle). Thus, the policy objective should be genuine and the means of attaining it proportionate. These principles have the additional virtue of

[53] Kahler, *op. cit.* at 301.
[54] See Kalypso Nicolaides, "Comments," in Sykes, *op. cit.* (1995), 139–153.
[55] See Kalypso Nicolaidis, "Mutual Recognition of Regulatory Regimes: Some Lessons and Prospects," in OECD proceedings, *Regulatory Reform and International Market Openness* (Paris: OECD, 1996), 181.
[56] For a similar perspective, see Frieder Roessler, "Increasing Market Access under Regulatory Heterogeneity: The Strategies of the World Trade Organization," OECD, *ibid.*, Chapter 10.

enjoying wide familiarity in many domestic constitutional contexts and in EU constitutional law with respect to the protection of human and other constitutional rights from state encroachment.

In designing institutional processes in an international context in which these concepts can be rendered justiciable and operational, more attention needs to be given than hitherto to relative burdens of proof. As a tentative proposition, we would argue that a complainant should bear the burden of proving that a domestic policy measure of another country has a disparate and substantial impact on international trade. If this can be proven, it seems to us that the burden of proof should then shift to the respondent country to demonstrate that notwithstanding this, the policy measure genuinely engages a legitimate policy objective – the sham principle (and here we would contemplate a much longer list of legitimate policy objectives than is presently embodied in Article XX of the GATT, reflecting in part, for example, the legitimate policy objectives regarding domestic subsidies formerly contained in Article 11 of the Tokyo Round Subsidies Code) – and that no less trade-restrictive policy instrument is reasonably available for vindicating these policy objectives as effectively – the least trade-restrictive means or proportionality principle ("effectively" being understood here to mean both the extent of attainment of the objective in question and the cost to the country in question of achieving it through one instrument rather than another).

As to what constitutes adequate discharge of the burden of proof on these latter issues, there is an important consequential issue of the standard of judicial or panel review to be applied. This has been a bitterly contentious issue in a somewhat analogous context with respect to FTA and NAFTA binational panel reviews of ITA and ITC determinations in the U.S. in antidumping and countervailing duty cases.[57] One view (reflecting a "correctness" standard) would require that the respondent country bear the burden of adducing substantial evidence on the record that the challenged policy is necessary for the attainment of a legitimate policy objective and that no less trade-restrictive means is available to achieve this purpose (arguably a difficult negative to prove). An alternative view (reflecting a "patently unreasonable" standard) would be substantially more deferential to the country whose domestic policies are under challenge and would simply require that the evidence adduced be sufficient to suggest that the policy choice is not patently unreasonable or a grossly disproportionate adaptation of means to ends, or put otherwise is a plausible means of attempting to achieve the legitimate policy

---

[57] See the Canada-U.S. *Softwood Lumber* case, *op. cit.*

objective in question, even if the reviewing body could itself imagine superior instruments. We favor something close to the latter approach (perhaps a "clearly unreasonable" standard) because it seems to us more respectful of domestic political sovereignty and policy autonomy than the former view, which invites supranational panels to second-guess the domestic policy choices of democratically elected, accountable, and competitive governments by applying a strict de novo cost-benefit analysis of their own. Moreover, by substantially limiting the ability of one country to challenge the domestic policy choices of another in quasi-judicial supranational forums, the "threat point" of the former in political negotiations with the latter over possible policy convergence is sharply reduced, thus also reducing the risk of coerced forms of harmonization reflecting asymmetric bargaining power or, worse, coerced forms of discriminatory managed-trade arrangements.

Name index

417

Subject index

accidental natural monopoly, and favoritism, 287–96, 301
accountability, 143; in federal finance, 136
administrative decentralization, 134, 135, 140
Africa, 130, 284; ethnic groups, 305–6
agency problem, 6, 67–8, 83–4, 136, 139
Alberta, 163, 164, 169n30, 191n32; and environmental programs, 183n18, 188, 194
allocative effects, 74, 79–80, 135; information on, 77–8
altruistic bonds, 285
anarchy, 40
"Anonymous Iamblichus, The," 27
antidumping duties, 393–4, 395
antipredation policies, and public subsidies, 347–50
antitrust policy, 394, 401–3, 411
art and culture (AC) goods: assignment of powers regarding, 9; and fiscal federalism, 220–38; levels of government, 228, 233–5; lumpiness of benefits of, 229–30; as matter of public intervention, 223–4, 225–9, 232; preferences in, 222–3; supply/demand, 227–8; undersupply, 229–30
assignment of fiscal powers: Australian federation, 157–8t; economic analysis of, 150–1; equilibrium, 170
assignment of powers, 4, 8, 177, 340; over Canadian environment, 174–219; through competition, 199, 209; competitive theory of, 203, 214–15; spillovers, 176; vertical competition in, 186–7
assignment of public functions/services: art and culture goods, 9, 224–7; preferences in, 222–3

Australia, 8, 225n10; central government powers, 182; environmental federalism, 209; ethnic groups, 287n1; federation, 133; fiscal history, 152, 159, 169; Loan Council, 158n14; Supreme Court, 156; reassignment and balance of fiscal powers in, 154–9

Beef Hormones case, 408–9
Belgium, 54, 116, 133, 242
Bill of Rights, U.S., 107, 114, 115, 123
Bloc québécois, 310, 316, 331
"Bouchard effect," 316, 318
branches of government: competition among, 2; in constitutions, 106
breaching trust, 62–3, 64
British North America Act, 154, 159–60
budget maximization, in business firms, 53, 54
bureaucracy(ies), 3–4, 6, 243–4, 259, 297; analyzing, 5, 53–5; and art and culture goods, 221; biases in information produced by, 79–83; breach and repudiation of trust in, 53–64; competition within and between, 2, 3; control of, 76, 79; corporation as, 5, 48–9, 52, 53, 64; economic theory of, 67–8, 83–4; efficiency of production of information, 81–3; environmental, 184–5, 186; ethnic groups in, 291–2, 296; parallel, 302

Canada, 8, 54, 136, 143n26, 145–6; amendments to constitution, 119n17; antitrust laws, 394; assignment of powers over environment, 174–219; centralized decentralization, 137; Charter of Rights and Freedoms, 115n13, 190n29; constitution, 154; constitutional reform,

423